Economic Thinking in a Canadian Context
Volume 2 Macroeconomics

Gordon F. Boreham
Professor of Economics
University of Ottawa

Richard H. Leftwich
Professor of Economics
Oklahoma State University

Holt, Rinehart and Winston of Canada, Limited
Toronto : Montreal

Preface

About a century and a half ago, Thomas Robert Malthus, a distinguished member of the classical school in economics remarked that:

> "Political economy is perhaps the only science of which it may be said that the ignorance of it is not merely a deprivation of good, but produces great positive evil."

I need hardly labour the point that modern economists share this same belief. However, what to teach beginning students in economics and how to teach it are perennial and unsolved problems.

Although this Canadian version of *An Introduction to Economic Thinking* (1969) by Richard Leftwich represents a major revision and rewriting of the U.S. edition, there has been no change in the approach to the problems of "what" and "how" to teach newcomers to economics. I fully subscribe to Professor Leftwich's view that we cannot cover the whole broad scope of the discipline of economics in depth in the principles course. But it appears that this is what our profession has been trying to do in recent years and, correspondingly, principles of economics books are becoming basic economic encyclopedias. To attempt to teach in depth all that is typically included is to invite frustration and disappointment on the part of both students and teachers. For most beginning students I suspect that extended discussions of methodology and of sophisticated analytical models are simply irrelevant and boring. In my judgment a thorough grasp of a limited number of elementary principles, together with the economist's way of thinking about things, will do much more toward building economic literacy in the land.

This, then, is not a complex book and there are indeed omissions of a number of topics that are currently fashionable in principles textbooks. Yet I believe it is complete enough to provide the fundamental background for a reasonably correct analysis of both our current and our recurring economic problems. Moreover, it is so organized as to present the material in an order designed to arouse the interest of the student in the subject matter. Needless to say, the book has been conceived and written with the Canadian student of economics in mind. I believe, too, that if the principles contained herein are mastered those desiring to do so will have little difficulty in moving into more advanced, complex, and sophisticated realms of analysis.

It is a pleasure to pay tribute to those who have helped me with this book. Unquestionably I owe most of all to Professor Richard Leftwich who has read the entire manuscript and provided numerous helpful suggestions, and for allowing me full freedom to adapt the U.S. original for Canadian use. Others whose comments on parts of the book are greatly appreciated include Miss Catherine Starrs, Economic Council of Canada (chapter 13); Mr. I. F. Furniss, Canada Department of Agriculture (chapter 14); Dr. Eugene Forsey, formerly of the Canadian Labour Congress (chapter 19); Dr. J. A . Galbraith and Miss A. L. Guthrie, The Royal Bank of Canada (chapters 21, 22 and 23); and Mr. Maurice Strong, Mr. Peter M. Kilburn and Mr. P. Slyfield of the Canadian International Development Agency (chapter 34). Nor can I easily forget the help received from my research assistant, Mr. Stephen Wiseman. Thanks are also due to Mr. Brian Carter, another graduate student, for his help in preparing the index. Finally, I owe an overwhelming debt to my wife and family for their patience and understanding while this work was in progress. None of the persons mentioned above are, of course, in any way responsible for the shortcomings of this book.

Gordon F. Boreham
Professor of Economics
University of Ottawa

August 1970

Richard H. Leftwich
Professor of Economics
Oklahoma State University

Preface

Like most academic disciplines, economics can be classified in several ways. Classified by content of economic activity, there are two broad types: microeconomics and macroeconomics. Microeconomics is concerned with the behaviour of individual economic units such as the household, the firm, the industry, or single commodities. Macroeconomics deals with the broad aggregates of economic activity. It is concerned with the economy as a whole. Prior to the Second World War, economics dealt mainly with microeconomics. Since then, however, an increasing emphasis has been placed on macroeconomics. Today we study both aspects of economic analysis.

With a view towards flexibility, *Economic Thinking in a Canadian Context* has been divided into two volumes. The order in which these two volumes are used is not crucial; each volume is an integrated unit. Thus they can be used interchangeably to meet the preference of instructors who teach macroeconomics first, as well as those who cover microeconomics first.

The focus of the present text is on macroeconomics. It provides the student with the tools for analysing the level of economic activity, which includes *total* amounts, such as aggregate employment, or total output, and with *average* amounts such as the average level of prices.

G.F.B.
Ottawa, Canada
June, 1971.

Contents

Contents

Part 1

An Overview of Economic Activity and Analysis

There are many facets to the study of economics. In order to achieve a depth of understanding, we shall examine each one in turn as we proceed through this book. But we shall find out that the analysis of any one area is not independent of the others, and that our grasp of each is enhanced by some knowledge of the others. Chapters 1–3 provide an overview of economic activity and analysis. Hopefully, they will give us a place to hang our hats—a place to which we can return time and again to make the apparently different aspects of economics fall into proper place within an overall framework of knowledge.

1

What Economics is About

You discovered long ago that what you have to spend is not sufficient to obtain as much as you would like to have of the many goods and services available. Your diet is probably varied but it is unlikely that you can afford champagne and gourmet food day in and day out. Your wardrobe is somewhat less than perfect for the kind of life you want to lead, and the room in which you live is not exactly a palace.

In short, you are confronted with the fundamental principle upon which economic activity rests – the wants of mankind are unlimited while the means available for satisfying those wants are not. Individuals and societies must determine how they are going to use the relatively scarce means available to them. They must determine which of their many desires they will apply their means to attain and the extent to which the chosen desires will be fulfilled. Steel used in making automobiles is not available for construction purposes and land used for growing wheat cannot at the same time produce corn.

Accordingly, Lionel Robbins' famous definition of economics as "the science which studies human behaviour as a relationship between ends and scarce means which have alternative uses"[1] is a good generalization of what economics is about. Or, to put the same point another way, economics is essentially a study of the logic whereby we choose among

[1]*Lionel Robbins*, An Essay on the Nature and Significance of Economic Science. *London: Macmillan Co., 1935, p. 16.*

alternative possible economic objectives. It is this decision making process that is the core of economics.

In this introductory chapter we shall consider the nature of economic activity, and we shall take a brief look at some of the economic problems that confront us from day to day. We shall then differentiate between the analysis of economic activity and the policies aimed at solving economic problems. Finally, we shall point out the relationship between economics and the other social disciplines.

Economic Activity

We devote much of our time to different kinds of economic activity. We earn our incomes by engaging in the production of the goods and services that society wants and in turn we use what we have earned to satisfy our own wants as fully as we can. In a society in which there are millions of people, almost as many different goods and services desired, and a great many different means of contributing to the processes of production, patterns of economic activity develop as an integral part of the social fabric. These patterns become exceedingly complex, frequently obscuring cause and effect relationships. Think of our task, then, as one of sorting out these relationships in order to understand how our economic system works, to determine its shortcomings, and to devise means of improving the operation of the system. The first step is to examine systematically the elements involved in economic activity. These are (1) human wants, (2) resources, and (3) techniques of production.

Human Wants

We have mentioned already that there are no limits to the range of goods and services that people want. We hear from time to time that we in Canada are surfeited with material things, but this is not so in any sort of absolute sense. Why do people want higher wages and salaries? Why do we have so many slums? Why is "a more concerted and purposeful attack on poverty urgently required now."[2] Not many people are so affluent that additional quantities of goods and services would add nothing to their satisfactions.

[2]*Economic Council of Canada, "The Challenge of Growth and Change"*, Fifth Annual Review. *Ottawa: Queen's Printer, 1968, p. 130.*

Human wants arise from several sources. Those of a biological nature are always in the foreground. We require certain minimum amounts of food and protection from the elements – shelter and clothing – in order to stay alive and to function. But a full stomach does not end our desires for food, nor does an eight-room house fully satisfy our wants for housing. Once our basic needs are met we want more variety and more elegance in the goods and services used to meet these needs. Consider the desire for variety in entertainment. Among university coeds, too, although there will be some degree of conformity in types of clothing worn, within those types every effort will be made to avoid duplications in patterns and colour schemes. Social pressure, too, generates wants. For example, the purchase of a colour television set by a neighbour makes us feel that we should have one too. Additionally, as we engage in the activities necessary to satisfy a given desire, new wants are born. Who wants to move into a new house without buying at least a few new pieces of furniture? Does the pursuit of a bachelor's degree create wants that would otherwise never have come into being for an individual?

These unlimited human wants are the mainsprings of economic activity. All economic activity is carried on for the purpose of fulfilling people's desires. It is directed toward satisfying as fully as possible the wants of individuals, of groups, and of the entire society.

Resources

The extent to which wants in any society can be fulfilled is determined largely by the availability of the ingredients that can be put into processes of production. What do you have that can contribute toward the production of goods and services desired by the society in which you live? You certainly are able to do physical labour and, given the opportunity, you may be able to put a little mental effort into the economic machine. You may also own a piece of land or other property that you can rent out to others. Or perhaps you own a few shares of stock, making you part owner of the assets of some corporation, and you let the corporation use your part of these assets to produce its products.

Resource Classifications

We call the ingredients that go into the production of goods and services *resources,* and for convenience we classify them into two broad categories: (1) *labour* and (2) *capital.* Each category contains a great many subcategories which may differ widely: corporation executives and garbage collectors, for example, both fall within the labour classification. While the classification is useful for many purposes, undue importance should not be attached to it. It is primarily a device to help us keep our thinking orderly when we consider resources.

Labour consists of all the muscular and mental effort that mankind can put into the productive processes. It includes what common labourers are able to do, but it is also made up of the capabilities of actors, musicians, artists, university professors, lawyers, accountants, railroad engineers, and so on. Labour, then, represents all productive efforts rendered directly by human beings.

Nonhuman resources are called *capital*. We include as capital all kinds of tools such as pencils, notebooks, hammers, pliers, and nails; machinery; and buildings. We shall place so-called natural resources in the capital category also, although some economists prefer to set these up in a third category called *land*. Natural resources consist of farm land, space for residential and industrial sites, mineral deposits, water, fish and wildlife, forests, and other such items. Inventories of goods comprise still another type of capital resource. For example, grocery inventories are a part of the capital resources of a supermarket and stocks of iron ore make up a portion of the capital resources of a steel mill.

A substantial part of the capital resources of the economy consists of *intermediate goods*—goods produced to be further used in production processes rather than directly by consumers. Steel, for example, is not consumed directly but is fabricated into any number of products that are then used by consumers. Thus resources may be used to produce other resources that are in turn employed to produce resources that are then used in the production of consumer goods and services. Pyramiding of this kind is common in the productive process.

Scarcity of Resources

We know from everyday experience that the quantities of resources available for producing goods and services are inadequate for fulfilling our unlimited wants. If resources were not scarce relative to wants they would not command a price; that is, they would be free like the air we breathe. That consumers and, in turn, producers are willing to pay to put resources into the productive process is evidence that they are scarce and are not to be had simply for the taking.

It is easy to see that there is an upper limit to the size of the labour force. The total population of an economy, if nothing else, would be the ultimate limiting factor. But there are a number of factors that restrict the labour force to something like one third of the total population. These include the age distribution of the population, its state of health, attitudes toward employment of women and children, whether or not aristocrats and would-be aristocrats are willing to get their hands dirty, and other factors of a similar nature.

The quantity of capital that an economy has available to place in production is also limited, but by a somewhat different set of factors. An economy may experience a paucity of natural resources—for example, many of the areas of North Africa and the Middle East. But scarcity of machines, buildings, tools, and other intermediate goods is even more significant. We might ask ourselves how an economy accumulates a stock of capital goods to put into productive processes. Generally, in order to do this, an economy must use existing resources that could have been used for the production of consumer goods to produce intermediate or capital goods instead. The production of intermediate goods thus involves a sacrifice of some quantities of consumer goods, unless unemployment of resources exists in the economy and these unemployed resources can be put to work. As consumers, we may not be willing to tighten our belts sufficiently to release the quantities of resources needed to bring about large relative increases in the economy's stock of capital. The poorer a country, the more difficult capital accumulation becomes.

Techniques of Production

The amounts of goods and services that can be produced with given quantities of labour and capital depend, of course, on how well those resources are used. Two students with the same degree of intelligence, the same books, and in the same surroundings may perform at different levels on an examination. The difference may well be in the techniques of study used by each. Similarly, with given quantities of resources one shoemaker may turn out a larger quantity of shoes than another because he employs superior techniques. In the same way, the general level of technological know-how varies among countries. The economies of Asia, Africa, South America, and the Middle East are behind those of western Europe and the United States and Canada in this respect.

By production techniques we mean the methods, knowledge, and means available for converting resources into want-satisfying goods. Engineering is generally thought of as the discipline most directly concerned with this process, which includes the development of new energy sources, improvements in construction methods, more efficient plant design and layout, development of new products, and anything else that increases the want satisfaction attainable from available resources. But we are also concerned with techniques of production in economics. Since resources are scarce relative to wants, we concern ourselves with whether or not the "best" techniques are used. The best techniques are those that enable given quantities of resources to yield the highest outputs of goods and services, or, to put it the other way around, those that permit given quantities of goods and services to be produced with the least expenditure of resources. We shall come back to these points again and again in a variety of contexts.

Goals of Economic Activity

The primary economic goal of most societies is to achieve a standard of living as high as its resources and its techniques of production will allow. Having made this statement, we must qualify it immediately. No society is likely to focus single mindedly on maximizing average living standards. There are other values to be achieved in "the good life," and the fulfillment of some of these objectives may require backing away from the achievement of the highest possible living standards. Preservation of a free as opposed to a totalitarian society, for example, may require that some resources be diverted from the production of want-satisfying consumer goods and services toward the production of armaments. Too, Canada has supported income-redistribution measures—the farm price-support program, progressive taxation, minimum wage legislation—which many people believe have held the total output of the economy below what it would be in their absence, in order to secure a greater measure of economic justice. But most modern societies most of the time are interested in continually raising the levels of want satisfaction they can achieve. Through newspapers, television programs, conversations, and other contacts with the rest of society we are reminded that the economic system operates imperfectly. Problems arise, the solutions to which make up a set of subgoals toward which economic activity is directed. What are some of a country's major economic problems? *Unemployment* is surely an important one. Another is *economic instability*. A third is *low levels of growth and development,* particularly in the poorer countries of the world. A fourth is presumed *injustices in income distribution*—in the way the economic system treats certain individuals and groups in the society as compared with others. A fifth problem centers around what *type of economic system* will best promote the goals toward which society wants to work. Let us examine the subgoals in greater detail in order to grasp more securely the dimensions of the problems that systematic economic analysis must attack.

Full Employment

The economy of Canada has experienced some difficulty in keeping its labour force and its productive capacity fully employed. During the depression of the 1930's, unemployment did not fall below 9.1 percent of the labour force. In the worst year, 1933, 19.3 percent of the labour force was unemployed. From 1957 to 1964, the unemployment rate was more than 4.5 percent. As individuals and as a society, we are concerned; unemployment implies hardship for ourselves and for fellow human beings. It also means that the economy is turning out smaller quantities of goods and services than it is capable of producing and that our standard of living is lower than it need be.

What are the causes of unemployment? What can be done to decrease it? Economists are not entirely in accord on either point, but they do agree that identification of the causes is a prerequisite to taking intelligent action to mitigate the problem. Unless we can diagnose the disease, we are not likely to get far in curing it.

Economic Stability

Economic instability, characterized by periods of recession and periods of inflation, is cause for much uneasiness in a society. A *recession* refers to a reduction in economic activity in which unemployment will increase, and it presents the possibility of becoming a serious depression such as that of the 1930's. *Inflation*, on the other hand, is characterized by rising prices and is ordinarily, but not necessarily, associated with high levels of economic activity. Both recessionary and inflationary periods have occurred in Canada since 1940, but none has been as severe as those of the 1870's, the 1890's or the 1930's.

Economists believe they have learned much in recent years about economic instability and how to control it. In fact, many feel that our present state of economic knowledge is such that there will never be another depression of the magnitude of the Great Depression. Other economists, however, are more cautious and maintain that although we may know how to prevent future depressions, the political climate may impede or even prevent the application of this knowledge. Nevertheless, we continue to have periods of inflation and of recession. At the very least, we must be able to prevent them from getting out of hand; hopefully we can make them less and less damaging. We must learn all we can about the causes and consequences of recession and inflation in order to decrease their adverse effects on living standards.

Economic Growth and Development

We expect modern economic systems to provide rising standards of living over time. We want growth and development to take place particularly in the poorer countries of Latin America, Africa, and Asia, but most of us anticipate that living standards in Europe and North America will rise as well. What are the forces that produce economic growth? What annual growth rate can reasonably be expected in Canada and in other countries? Why are growth rates so low in the underdeveloped nations? What, if anything, can be done to accelerate growth rates in the latter? Is economic aid from the advanced to the less advanced countries in order, and if so, how and in what quantities should it be provided?

There is much to be learned about the processes of economic growth and the obstacles that lie in its path. Growth processes as such should be amenable to economic analysis, but many of the factors that hinder economic development are outside the province of economics proper, lying rather in the fields of political science, sociology, psychology, and cultural anthropology.

Economic Justice and Economic Security

As individuals and as a society we are concerned with the twin problems of economic justice and economic security even though we are seldom clear as to what we mean by these terms. In a very broad sense, *justice*, or lack of it, is inferred from the treatment received by one person in economic affairs as compared with that received by others. *Security* refers to a guarantee of some minimum level of consumption. Some measure of security is ordinarily thought to be necessary for the individual in the interests of economic justice.

A great many questions arise with respect to what is just and what is not. Should people share equally in the economy's output or should they share in proportion to their contribution to the productive processes? If they are to share equally, what incentive does an individual have to make his maximum contribution? If they are to share in proportion to their contribution, security for many goes out the window. Many people do not own sufficient quantities of resources to earn a large enough share of the economy's output to keep them alive. Consider those who are permanently disabled and who own no capital. Problems of economic security and of economic justice cannot be solved with economic theory alone, although theory is an important ingredient in arriving at satisfactory solutions.

Ideas of what constitutes security and what constitutes justice depend upon the value judgments of individuals and groups in society, that is, upon their particular view of how things should be. We have not been able to reach a consensus in these areas and, consequently, in Canada we have a broad range of governmental and private arrangements designed to achieve some measure of security and justice. Among these are social security laws, the system of graduated income taxes, minimum wage laws, and laws providing for free public education. In the private sector we have insurance of many types. One of our main tasks from the point of view of economics is to subject such arrangements to thorough examination in order to determine whether or not they accomplish their objective. In addition, we need to assess their impact on the over-all level of economic activity.

Economic Systems

What type of economic system is most conducive to "the good life" as envisaged by people all over the world? Obviously people and societies hold widely differing opinions on this subject—indeed the Cold War has largely turned on this issue. Which will lead to the highest living standards, the socialistic system of the Soviet Union and Red China, the free enterprise system as represented by Canada and the United States, or some combination of the two? Which will come closest to fulfilling society's complex of economic and noneconomic goals?

Although we shall not define the terms "socialism" and "free enterprise" with precision at this point, let us consider the characteristics of each of these economic systems. In the *socialistic system* the economy is state directed, that is, the means of production are owned and controlled by the state. In the *free enterprise system* the means of production are owned privately. Economic activity is carried on through the volition of and under the direction of private individuals and groups. Neither the socialistic system of the Soviet Union nor the free enterprise system of Canada is pure in form. For example, recent evidence indicates that the U.S.S.R. is making increasing use of private ownership of some resources, while in Canada we find that some industries are socialized—the postal services and many provincial and municipal utility companies are cases in point. Further, half the railway system and more than half the airline system and the broadcasting system are government owned. Final choices of the type of economic system that will predominate have not been made in either sphere of influence and likely will never be made. But societies are continually making choices that move them in one direction or the other, and these choices should be made as intelligently as possible.

Economic Analysis and Economic Policy

Legislative bodies as well as groups of private individuals are constantly engaging in activities designed to remedy defects in the operation of the economic system. Some of these measures accomplish their objectives, but some produce results and by-products that are unexpected and unwanted. For example, for many years Parliament has been concerned with the problem of low average incomes in the agricultural sector of the economy, and thus a farm program built around price supports for key storable farm products has been built up in order to increase farm incomes relative to other incomes in the economy. The general public, as well as a number of members of Parliament, have expressed surprise that surpluses of a number of farm products have accumulated, and in addition, many are also surprised to learn that the wealthier farmers on the large farms receive the bulk of price support payments while smaller, poorer operators receive very little. The problem illustrated here is that those who attempt to remedy the economy's defects do not always understand how the economic system operates and thus the ramifications of their actions. For this reason we must distinguish clearly between economic analysis and economic policy. We need to understand both and to ground the latter on the former.

Economic Analysis

Economic analysis is the process of making sense out of economic relationships. Economists examine and record economic behaviour and economic events in order to establish causal relations among the data and activities they have observed. Some of their conclusions are reached through reasoning deductively from more general to more specific events. As an illustration, the Cold War requires military preparedness, which in turn requires the use of steel. Thus, economists reason, an increase in military activities will increase demand for steel. Other causal relationships are established inductively, with analysts inferring from a series of events that certain relationships must exist. Suppose that over a number of years it is observed that increases in prices and increases in the total money available for spending in the economy always occur simultaneously. Economists might then reason that these conditions are causally related, or perhaps that they have common causes.

Tentative statements of causal relationships are called *hypotheses*. Such statements need to be tested again and again in order to determine whether or not they are valid. They can be weighed for logical consistency and they can be tested empirically in the world of facts. As a consequence of testing they may be verified, modified, or rejected.

Hypotheses that have withstood repeated testing and that seem to be able to explain or to predict economic activity with a fair degree of accuracy become known as *principles*. It must be emphasized, however, that principles are not necessarily absolute truths but rather should be thought of as subject to correction and refinement.

The general body of economic analysis is made up of principles designed to explain causal relationships among what are believed to be the more important economic variables. All possible variables surrounding all possible economic events obviously cannot be taken into account because of the limitations of the human mind. Principles are essentially simplifications of complex relationships and are intended to indicate what will happen most of the time in most cases, but almost any principle is subject to exceptions.

Economic analysis serves three main purposes. First, by explaining relationships among various economic variables it is a valuable aid in understanding the operation of an economy. Second, it aids in predicting the consequences of changes in economic variables. Finally, economic analysis serves as the fundamental framework for economic policy-making—indeed, if wise policy-making is to occur, it must be based on correct economic analysis.

Economic Policy

Economic policy refers to conscious intervention in the economic processes by government or by private groups in order to affect the results of economic activity. Associations of employers may agree not to "pirate" each other's labour, that is, not to try to hire each other's employees, in order to prevent wages from rising; labour organizations may use coercion to raise the wage levels of their members; Parliament enacts laws that influence the behaviour of businesses, employees, and consumers. Such legislation includes antimonopoly laws, social welfare laws, farm legislation, tax laws, and many others.

Whereas economic policies of private groups in the economy are generally pursued with the intent of furthering the interest of those groups, we have every right to expect that government policies will be in the interests of the general public. To put it another way, we anticipate that government policies will increase economic efficiency. Although greater efficiency may result from a number of such measures, a healthy skepticism is in order, too. Individual members of Parliament often have different ideas of how the economy should operate—and so do their advisers and the witnesses at their hearings. In addition, their economic analysis is not infallible. This is not to say that governmental policy-making usually goes off on the wrong track but rather that the more sound the economic analysis underlying governmental policy-making, the more effective that policy-making is likely to be. Yet there will always be conflict in this area.

Economics and the Other Social Sciences

Social science is the broad field of study which includes all the disciplines that deal with man in his social or group relations. Economics centres its investigation of social relationships "on the activities and arrangements by which people provide services to create products, and are thereby entitled to other products". More simply, economics is concerned with those aspects of social organization and social behaviour involving trade—exchange of service for service, exchange of commodity for service, exchange of commodity for commodity, or exchange of financial instrument (such as money) for service or commodity.[3]

Quite obviously, economics overlaps with and is closely related to the other social sciences. It overlaps with sociology which studies the structure and functioning of social groups, from the family to the tribe, to local communities, to nations and international units. Since man reacts to other motives besides pecuniary ones, economics is closely related to psychology, especially social psychology which deals with the behaviour

[3]*For a more detailed discussion of economics as a social science, see Melvin A. Eggers and A. Dale Tussing,* The Composition of Economic Activity. *New York: Holt, Rinehart and Winston Inc., 1965, pp. 1-4.*

of the individual as it affects, and is affected by the behaviour of others. Since laws relating to taxation, to regulation of commerce and business behaviour, to commercial treaties and agreements with other countries, are the result of political and governmental decisions, it is also clear that economics overlaps with political science. Because each society has its distinctive habits, ideas, and attitudes, economics impinges on cultural anthropology which studies and compares both prehistoric and extinct cultures (archaeology) and living cultures of mankind (ethnology). Since economics deals with human acts, it is also related to philosophy, and in particular to ethics, a branch of philosophy that deals with morality of human acts.

Other important fields of study which should be mentioned are: (i) history, which describes and to some extent explains the past development of human societies; (ii) human geography, which places man in his physical setting and studies his relations with that environment. Economics also draws heavily on the studies of statistics and mathematics and on logic, the science of exact thinking.

Clearly, anyone who expects to acquire much depth of economic understanding must have some broad knowledge of the other aspects of man's social life.

Summary

This chapter introduces the study of economics. Economic activity stems from the unlimited range of man's wants and the comparative scarcity of means available for fulfilling them. Wants arise from many sources, including biological necessity, desires for variety, social pressures, and want-satisfying activity itself. The means available for fulfilling wants comprise the resources of the economy and its technology. Resources are the ingredients that go into the processes of production and can be classified into a labour category and a capital category. Labour includes all human efforts that contribute to production while capital consists of resources that are nonhuman in character. By technology we mean the know-how and the means available to a society for converting resources into want-satisfying goods and services. The level of want satisfaction, or the average standard of living, that a society can attain depends upon the quantities and qualities of its available resources as well as the level of its technology.

The ultimate economic goal of a society is ordinarily the achievement of a standard of living as high as its resources and production techniques will permit. A number of subgoals related to problems that arise in the operation of the economic system can be identified. These include full employment of resources, economic stability, economic growth and development, economic justice and security, and determination of the type of economic system that best serves the purposes of the society.

The relation between economic analysis and economic policy must be clearly understood. Economic analysis is concerned with the establishment of causal relations among economic events. Its purposes are to help us understand how the economy operates, to enable us to predict what the consequences of changes in economic variables will be, and to serve as the basis for economic policy-making. Economic policy refers to the conscious attempts of private groups and governmental units to make the economy operate differently than it would in the absence of those attempts. Wise economic policy must rest on sound economic analysis.

Since economics is primarily concerned with human behaviour in a group context, it is classed as one of the social sciences. And inasmuch as many of the vital factors which contribute to material well-being are social, cultural, psychological and political in character, economics overlaps with and is closely related to the other social sciences.

Exercises and Questions for Discussion

1. During the course of a day make a list of the things you would like or would like more of, but cannot afford. Why is your income (or your family's income) inadequate to make these purchases?
2. Per capita income, or average income per person, in India is less than $100 per year. What explanations can you offer for this relatively low standard of living?
3. Look through a current issue of your favourite news periodical, noting the articles pertaining to economic issues. Classify these articles under the five problem areas discussed in the chapter.
4. What do you think were the main causes of the relatively high rate of unemployment (over 5 percent of the labour force) between 1958 and 1963?
5. Which of the following are examples of socialism and why: (a) a municipally owned power plant; (b) Polymer Corporation Limited; (c) Bell Telephone Company of Canada; (d) the federal government's farm price-support program; (e) public medical care programs.
6. Evaluate this statement: "That may be all right in theory but not in fact."

Selected Readings

Boulding, Kenneth E., *Economic Analysis*, 4th ed., Vol. 1. New York: Harper & Row, Publishers, Inc., 1966, Chap. 1.

Heilbroner, Robert L., *The Making of Economic Society*. Englewood Cliffs, N.J.: Prentice-Hall, Inc., 1962, Chap. 1.

Lewis, B. S., "Economic Understanding: Why and What", *American Economic Review*, Papers and Proceedings, May 1957, pp. 653–670.

Daly, F. St. L., "The Scope and Method of Economics", *The Canadian Journal of Economics and Political Science*, May 1945, pp. 165–76.

Taylor, K. W., "Economic Scholarship in Canada", *The Canadian Journal of Economics and Political Science*, February 1960, pp. 6–16.

2

How an Economic System Works

Consider your morning coffee break. It had its origins some time ago with investment in a piece of land in Brazil, Colombia, or some other tropical country. Labour and machinery cleared the land and brought it under cultivation. Coffee trees were planted and cultivated, bearing fruit after some five years. The berries were picked and pulped, leaving only the seeds or beans. These were hulled, peeled, sorted, sacked, shipped to Canada, cleaned, blended, roasted, and ground. The student union purchased the ground product and made it into the brew you drink. In addition to the resources used in the direct production process sketched above, still others were needed for the containers, railway cars, trucks, and ships in which the coffee product was transported through its different stages of manufacture. Still other resources were needed to construct the machinery and the buildings that were used at every point in the production of the coffee you drink.

A modern economic system is enormously complex. Thousands of economic operations are required to produce almost any product, and all of these processes must be efficiently coordinated. We attempt in this chapter to strip away the complexities and get down to the bare essentials of economic activity so that we may begin to understand how an economic system works. We shall consider first the functions that every economic system must perform and we then shall take a brief, preliminary look at how different types of systems perform them. Third, we shall construct a simple model of a free enterprise system.

The Functions of an Economic System

Most economists list three basic functions that every economic system must perform. First, the system must determine what goods and services are to be produced as well as their order of importance. Second, it must organize productive effort so that the goods and services selected are produced in the proper quantities. Finally, it must determine how the finished output is to be shared among the members of the society. All societies are confronted with these same central functions, but the methods used to achieve them can differ widely.

Determining What is to be Produced

The fundamental economic problem of unlimited wants and scarce means of satisfying them makes it necessary for an economic system to have some method of determining not only what goods and services are to be produced but also their order of importance. We find two basic methods of performing this function in use in the world today. In the first instance the function is performed by the private action of the individuals making up the society and in the second by the state, that is, by the government or its agencies.

In a society that depends upon private action, consumers themselves determine the comparative values of goods and services through the price system. Individuals spend their available purchasing power however they wish, and each dollar spent is a vote on what is to be produced. The more urgently consumers want specific items, the higher will be the prices of these items relative to those of other items. Less urgently desired items command relatively lower prices. The more abundant the quantity available of any one product, the lower its price will be. Changes in consumers' preferences bring about changes in the prices of goods. For example, if the desires of housewives for television sets rise relative to their desires for dishwashers, they will channel their spending away from the latter toward the former and prices of television sets will rise while those of dishwashers will fall. The array of prices established for goods and services reflects the relative per unit values of the quantities currently available to consumers as a group.

In economies in which the state determines what is to be produced much detailed planning is necessary. In making estimates of future production needs, difficult questions arise concerning whether larger quantities of some products are in order. For example, a decision to step up automobile production is also a decision to increase the quantities of sheet metal, rubber tires, copper wire, batteries, and other items used in their manufacture. Since the resources of the economy are limited, additional quantities of these items can be had only if the quantities of other products are reduced. But by how much must they be reduced? Even with high-speed computers the task confronting the planners is a difficult one.

Government planning of what is to be produced may be based on (1) consumer desires, (2) governmental decisions as to what is best for the public, or (3) government aims and objectives apart from what the public wants. When governments attempt to plan in accordance with consumer desires, they may make use of a price system to register those desires, although it is not essential that they do so. Where government planning is based on governmental decisions as to what is best for the public, arbitrary decisions are made as to what is to be produced, and production quotas are established for each item in a vast array of goods and services. There is likely to be a move toward narrowing the types, models, and styles available in order to simplify planning—for example, a consumer may not be able to obtain the red necktie he desires. When government objectives are given priority, conflicts between these objectives and the desires of consumers are sure to occur. The government may find military strength essential to maintain itself in power when the public would prefer that more consumer goods be produced instead. Or the government, looking toward the future, may want to divert resources away from consumer goods and services at the present time in order to accumulate capital and increase future productive capacity while consumers want more goods and services now.

Actually, we see combinations of the two methods of determining what is to be produced in use throughout the world. In Canada consumer choice is the predominant method, but it is tempered by governmental decisions in a number of areas. For example, there are legal prohibitions against the sale of certain drugs; governmental units make decisions with regard to road building; and a number of other examples could be cited. In the Soviet Union government planning is the predominant method of allocating resources, yet even here consumer choice plays at least a limited role.

Organizing Production

Every economic system must have some means of mobilizing productive effort in order to turn out in appropriate quantities the goods and services desired. The organization of production has two main aspects.

One is the process of moving resources away from the production of goods where they contribute less to consumer desires and into the production of goods where they contribute more. The other is the attainment of the greatest possible efficiency by individual production units or business enterprises in the economy. Again we can think in terms of two alternatives. Private individuals can be left to organize production on their own or the state can undertake the task.

Can we avoid chaos if individuals are left to their own devices—to work wherever they desire and to place the capital they own in employments of their own choosing? Even if chaos can be avoided, the task of getting the right resources to the right place at the right time seems highly remote. But we have omitted the price system from our thinking. The price system and the profit motive, maligned as they are, perform the task of organizing production in an unobtrusive, automatic way. It is evident that businesses can make higher profits by producing goods that consumers want most rather than those that consumers want least. Further, the most profitable businesses pay the highest prices for labour and capital resources while the least profitable businesses are those that resource owners prefer to avoid. We, as resource owners, move our labour and capital away from the lower-paying areas toward the higher-paying ones. As production of what consumers want most is expanded and of what they want least is contracted, prices and profits fall in the former and increase in the latter, diminishing the incentive of resource owners to make further transfers.

The profit motive also provides the prime incentive to private businesses to operate efficiently. The greater the value of output that can be obtained from a given value of resources, the more efficient the production process. Or, what amounts to the same thing, the smaller the value of resource inputs necessary to produce a given value of product output, the more efficient the process. It follows that the more efficient an enterprise is in its operations, the more profit it will make; hence the quest for profit spurs a drive for efficiency.

Organization of production by the state will be neither automatic nor unobtrusive. The magnitude of the planning task is almost overwhelming simply by virtue of the millions of decisions that must be made. Suppose that the state planning agencies have determined what goods and services are to be produced and have established production quotas for each that are within the capabilities of the economy, given its resources and its level of technology. How can one get workers who prefer the seaside to work in the mines? How can one decide on the degree of mechanization to use in road building as compared with that to use in agriculture? How far should one go in producing intermediate goods, and what kinds of intermediate goods should be produced? What if someone makes a mistake with respect to the amount of natural rubber that can be imported and an insufficient number of tires are available for the automobiles that are being produced? Of course, these problems also arise under a price system, but the price system corrects them before they become critical.

What are the incentives for efficiency in the operation of individual production units in the state-planned economy? Bonus incentives and promotion possibilities for managers and workers can be and are used to some extent. It is also common for the state to establish production quotas and for penalties to be assessed if these quotas are not met. But individual units may not be free to obtain resources in the kinds and quantities that will contribute most to efficient operation. They are usually obliged to accept whatever they can get, that is, whatever is allocated to them.

In the organization of production most economies will use some combination of the two alternatives discussed above, although it is apparent that some rely more heavily on one than on the other. The economy of Canada is largely price directed, but at a number of points governmental decisions are superimposed on, or substituted for, the price mechanism. The Soviet Union illustrates the opposite emphasis.

Distributing the Product

Every economic system must provide a method of determining how its citizens are to share in the economy's output. This function too can either be performed by private enterprise or by the state.

Here too the private approach utilizes the price system as the controlling device. How does it work? You know that the part of the economy's total yearly output that you can claim depends on the yearly income that you earn. Your income, in turn, depends upon how much labour and how much capital you put into the production process and the prices (wage rates, interest, dividends, rents, and so on) you receive for them. Most of us believe that we are not paid enough for our resources, but by and large we receive for them about what they contribute to the value of the economy's output. If one employer is not willing to pay that much for them it will be profitable for another to do so. But a fuller explanation of this point must wait.

The distribution of the economy's output thus depends on the distribution of income. In turn, the distribution of income depends on the distribution of resource ownership and the prices individuals receive for placing their resources in production. People well endowed with capital and labour resources and who place these where they contribute much to the value of the economy's output will have large incomes relative to others and will receive large shares. The Rockefellers and the Fords are cases in point. People with few resources that they utilize poorly receive low incomes and small shares.

In the state-planned approach income distribution can be whatever the state wills it to be. As a first approximation it might think in terms of rationing equal quantities of each product to each member of the society, but this would not be a satisfactory arrangement. People differ in their preferences and in their consumption patterns for a variety of reasons—different ages and residence in different parts of the country are two important ones. Indeed, if all were to share equally in the economy's output, how could workers be induced to move from employments where they want to be into employments where they are needed?

Economies such as Canada that rely mainly on the private approach make considerable use of state-planned distribution measures. Similarly, state-planned economies such as the Soviet Union make some use of the private approach. In Canada the government redistributes income in a number of ways—through progressive taxation, free public education, farm subsidies, and others. In the Soviet Union equal sharing in distribution is not followed in practice. Distribution is partly fixed as the state determines what is to be produced—what parts of total output are to be military hardware, heavy industrial goods, consumer goods, and so on. Wages and prices are rather rigidly controlled, but there are differentials between skilled and unskilled workers. Sometimes certain managerial positions or certain professions carry bonuses in order to attract more persons into them. These differences in income make it possible for some people to obtain greater shares of what is produced than others.

Types of Economic Systems

The private approach to the three functions of an economic system is provided by a *free enterprise* type of economic system while the state-planned approach is typical of *socialistic* economies. Although a detailed discussion of these alternative types of systems is out of order at this point, we should have some grasp of the fundamental characteristics of each. The economic system that evolves in any particular society is not the consequence of decision-making on economic grounds alone. In fact, political and philosophical issues are likely to predominate—witness the Russian Revolution in 1918; and in some cases, such as Nazi Germany and Facist Italy of the pre-World War II days, personal aggrandizement on the part of an individual may be the molding force. But our concern here is with the economic aspects of the different systems.

The Free Enterprise System

The right of private persons and private organizations to own things is the foundation of a free enterprise economic system. We call this the *institution of private property*. Generally, legal guarantees are given to private individuals, partnerships, corporations, and other associations to own capital resources and consumer goods of almost all kinds. Individuals also own their own labour power, although this would not be so if slavery were permitted.

The fundamental methods by which such an economy operates are voluntary exchange and cooperation by private individuals and organizations. Why do people work 40 hours a week, week in and week out? They do so primarily because the time and effort they give up are worth less to them than the money they receive for working. The same proposition holds for the willingness of people to exchange capital resources for income. Producers who pay for the services of labour and capital must also feel that those services are worth more to them than what they pay out to resource owners. Unless both parties gain, the exchanges would never occur. Why do you give up purchasing power you have in exchange for goods and services? Again because the items you purchase must be worth more to you than the purchasing power you give up, otherwise you would not make the trade. The seller too must believe that the money he receives will be of greater benefit to him than the goods and services he gives up. Exchange occurs whenever and wherever two or more parties believe that they can benefit from the transaction.

Individuals or groups cooperate with each other whenever they believe they can gain more from working together than from working individually. You help your neighbour move his refrigerator; in turn he helps you haul a dead tree out of your yard. People in a society join their labour and their capital in more extensive productive efforts—in the manufacture of automobiles, houses, airplanes, and almost everything else that is needed.

In the exercise of voluntary exchange and cooperation there are three areas in which people are free to act either as individuals or in groups. First, as consumers people are free to purchase whatever goods and services they want within the limits of their income. Second, as resource owners they are free to sell or hire out their resources for income wherever they can find takers. Third, they are free to establish business enterprises for the production and sale of any desired product or service, and they can terminate those enterprises whenever they see fit to do so.

Largely because of its emphasis on individual freedom and voluntary exchange, many people conclude that the free enterprise system operates in a highly disorganized way. This, however, is not the case. As noted in the preceding section, prices and profits provide the guiding mechanism: the things that consumers value most highly are also those that it is most profitable to produce, and those valued least are produced at losses. The termination of enterprises and the contraction of productive capacity occurs in the latter while new enterprises and expansion of productive capacity occurs in the former. The profitable enterprises attract resources away from those incurring losses by paying more to resource owners. The mechanism is automatic, and although it is not perfect in its operation, neither is it chaotic.

The free enterprise system places a high premium on individual freedom of choice and action. Individuals are thought to be the best judges of the economic objectives of the society. Economic activity, guided and directed by prices, is motivated by the pursuit of self-interest. Each consumer attempts to spend his income in such a way as to maximize his individual well-being, and each business firm attempts to maximize its profits. Individuals as resource owners seek to maximize their incomes. Pursuit of individual self-interest in these ways is thought to lead to the greatest common economic welfare of the society as a whole.

The Socialistic System

Government ownership or control of the economy's resources underlies the socialistic type of economic system. The government owns such capital resources as land, buildings, and machinery, but since ownership of labour power is hard to separate from the individual who furnishes it, control of labour resources rather than outright government ownership is the usual case.

In the socialistic system government planning is used to organize economic activity. The government plans what is to be produced and it operates enterprises in different lines of production accordingly. Business enterprises can be established, labour resources can be directed, and capital resources can be allocated in whatever way government officials believe they will make their maximum contribution to the economic objectives specified by the state. Distribution of the product, too, will be in accordance with government's over-all economic plan.

The socialistic system is based on the philosophy that individual self-interest should be subordinated to the interests of the society as a whole. The government is thought to be the best judge of what constitutes the best interests of the society and, therefore, of its economic objectives. As a consequence, important restrictions may be placed on individual freedom. Consumers may find that their choices of some products, along with the quantities available for purchase, are curtailed when state objectives and consumer objectives are in conflict. The government may give planes higher priority than cooking utensils and may divert aluminum from the production of the latter into the construction of the former. Individuals may not be free to go into the occupations of their choice. Potential nuclear physicists may be diverted toward medicine or some other profession depending upon the number of physicists the government decides should be trained. Workers may not be able to move to the geographic area they desire because the state needs people with their qualifications elsewhere. On the face of it, there appears to be more compulsion by the state and less voluntary action on the part of individuals in the socialistic economy than in the free enterprise system.

Mixed Systems

In practice we find neither the free enterprise nor the socialistic economic system in its pure form. Canada leans heavily towards the free enterprise type of economy, but government regulation, control, and even ownership of production facilities are common. On the other hand, the Soviet Union, while predominantly socialistic, uses the market mechanism to accomplish some of its economic tasks.

In Canada governmental units influence in some way almost one third of the economy's output. Since some government action has the effect of redistributing income, patterns of consumer demand are affected. In addition, regulatory and control activities affect what many industries are able to produce and the prices they can charge. Regulation of railway, commercial air and merchant marine services by the Canadian Transport Commission, and of energy resources by the National Energy Board are examples. Furthermore, the government, having reduced consumer demand through taxes, spends those tax receipts to build roads, buildings, and dams and to provide services such as police protection and national defence, items that individuals might not purchase if they were free to spend the tax dollars directly.

In the Soviet Union almost all production facilities are state owned and operated. Workers are paid wages, however, and differentials have been established between professional and manual workers as well as between the skilled and the unskilled in order to provide incentives for developing labour potential. These measures, however, are supplementary to others taken in order to ensure that supplies of different kinds of labour are developed as the state desires. Goods are sold in state-owned stores at set prices, but the prices are controlled by the state and so do not perform the function of reflecting how consumers value different goods and services relatively. It has recently been proposed in the Soviet Union, notably by an economist by the name of Liberman, that production units should be given some form of profit motive in order to stimulate efficiency.[1]

A Model of a Free Enterprise System

In this section we shall develop a highly simplified model of a free enterprise system. Its purpose is to identify the main operating units of such an economic system and to explain how they interact. Hopefully it serves as an introduction to economic analysis. However, the model presented here is not intended to provide a complete explanation of how the economy works. Indeed, it does not take into account an important factor in the operation of a free enterprise system—the government—but rather embraces the private sector of the economy only.

Classification of Economic Units

There are two groups of economic units that interact or engage in economic activity. These are households on the one hand and business enterprises on the other. Both are familiar concepts. *Households* consist either of family units or of unattached individuals who do not live with families. *Business enterprises* include individual proprietorships, partnerships, corporations and cooperatives.

Since everyone in the economy belongs to some household unit, households play two roles in economic activity: (1) they are the consumers of the economy's output—its food, automobiles, houses, barbers' services, and books; and (2) they are the owners of the economy's resources—its labour and its capital. Much of the economy's capital is owned by corporations, but these are in turn owned by households, so that the entire available supply of capital is owned either directly or indirectly by households.

[1] *See* Time, *Vol. 85, February 12, 1965, pp. 23-29.*

Business enterprises are the units that carry on the production of goods and services at all levels and stages. They include the family farm, the supermarket, and companies turning out sophisticated computers or electronic devices. The production processes carried on by business enterprises consist of the processing or conversion of resources either into final usable form or into states closer to that form. The economic activity of this group of units includes buying or hiring resources, processing or combining them, and selling the resulting goods and services.

Not all of the economy's population is embraced in the business enterprise group of economic units. Many resource owners prefer not to operate firms but instead to sell or hire out what they own to those who do. Sometimes a household unit is also a business enterprise. A neighbour-

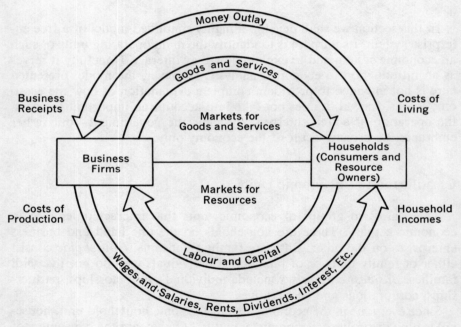

Figure 2-1
The circular flow.

hood grocery store and a family farm are cases in point. But these firms present no analytical difficulties. We simply view their activities as households in the same light as we look at other household units and we analyze their behaviour as business firms in the same way as we analyze other business firms.

Interaction of Economic Units

The well-known circular flow diagram of Figure 2–1 brings the two groups of economic units together and provides a convenient means for exploring the interaction that takes place between them. Consumer groups are represented by the box on the right and business firms by the one on the left. Resources or resource services flow from households to business firms and are converted into consumer goods and services.[2] Goods and services then flow to households in their role as consumers. As consumers pay for the goods and services purchased, a money flow is established in the opposite direction—toward business firms. The money flow continues around the circle from business firms to households as the former pay for the resources they use in the production of goods and services. Thus a physical flow of resources, goods, and services moves around the circle in one direction while a money flow moves around it the other way.

The money flow takes on different but closely related aspects at different points in the circle. As it is paid out by consumers for goods and services it is *costs of living*. As it reaches business firms the same flow becomes *business receipts*. Business receipts are paid to resource owners for the use of labour and capital in production. After materials, labour, and other operating costs are met, whatever is left of business receipts goes to the owners of enterprises in payment for the use of their physical plant and equipment. The money flow as it is paid out by business firms represents *costs of production*. When households receive it the same flow becomes *household incomes*, or what consumers have available to spend.

The Two Sets of Markets

Households and business enterprises interact in markets or places of exchange. These can be separated into two categories: (1) markets for goods and services, represented by the upper half of Figure 2–1, and (2) market for resources, represented by the lower half.

In the consumer goods market the physical flow of goods and services is linked to the opposite flow of money by prices. Prices of goods depend on the amounts that consumers are willing to spend for the goods and the quantities available for purchase. Suppose that 1000 identical auto-

---

[2]*In the interests of simplicity we shall ignore the possibility that some resources may be used to produce net additions to the economy's stock capital. In technical language we are working with a* stationary economy *in which productive capacity neither increases nor decreases.*

mobiles are sold and that a total of $3 million is spent for the entire lot. The average price per automobile obviously must be $3000. If more were spent—say, $4 million—the average price would be $4000. If only $2 million were spent, the average price would be $2000.

If we extend the analysis to cover all goods and services sold and all purchasing power spent for them, several simple but important propositions emerge. The total value of goods and services flowing from business firms to households must equal the money flow going in the opposite direction. If the money flow rises, that is, if households increase their rates of spending, but the physical volume of goods and services sold does not, then prices must rise. A decrease in household spending with no change in the physical volume of sales means that prices must fall. On the other hand, if the money flow is constant while the physical volume of goods and services declines, prices must rise, whereas if the volume of goods and services increases, prices must fall.

The same relations hold in resource markets. The flow of resources and their services to business firms is linked to the reverse flow of money by resource prices, although we seldom talk in terms of the "price" of resources. Generally we refer to the price of labour as *wages*. *Dividends* are prices paid to corporation stockholders for the complex of resources that they permit the corporation to use. *Interest* is the price paid for borrowing funds used by businesses to invest in capital equipment. In many instances when a firm uses resources that it does not purchase, for example, land and buildings, the prices for their use are called *rents*. But whatever name we give to the prices of different resources, a change in the spending of business firms on given quantities of resources will cause price changes to occur in the same direction as the change in spending. Given the total spending of business firms on resources, decreases in the quantities of resources made available will increase their prices while increases in the quantities will decrease their prices.

An Application of the Model

There are many uses to which the foregoing model can be put. Let us apply it to the problem of economic instability. As a starting point, suppose that the money flow around the circle is constant—that consumer outlays or cost of living are equal to consumer incomes and that business outlays or costs of production are equal to business receipts. Suppose also that initially the flow of goods and services from firms to households and the flow of resources and resource services from households to firms are constant. These conditions mean that average price levels are constant also.

What happens if the public develops a depression psychosis? Fear of depression induces people to save money for anticipated hard times ahead. In addition, if people believe that prices are going to fall in the near future, they will spend as little as possible at present prices, postponing purchases to the anticipated future period of lower prices. The reduction in household spending is a reduction in the money flow from households to business firms. Firms find their sales volumes lagging and inventories of goods building up. They reduce prices in order to limit the reductions in volume and the inventory build ups. Thus far, then, we find that a fear of depression reduces total household spending, which in turn reduces the volume of goods sold and the prices received for these goods.

When we turn to business firms we discover that since sales volume and business receipts have fallen, businesses desire to contract production. Since the promise of profits has faded and the funds available for obtaining resources have declined, firms want smaller quantities of resources.

Households now find that some of the resources they own are unemployed, so they reduce asking prices in order to limit the magnitude of unemployment. Some unemployment, coupled with lower resource prices, means that consumer incomes are decreased. Consumer spending is likely to be further reduced, and the decline in economic activity may become progressively worse.

The downward movement may eventually be halted and reversed, however. Suppose that the public, and particularly business enterprises, begin to feel more optimistic about the future of the economy. Businesses may then decide to expand production of goods and services. Since expansion requires higher levels of resource use, there may be some slight increase in resource prices as firms attempt to attract larger quantities of resources. However, if unemployment is serious, employment opportunities alone may be sufficient to put larger quantities back in production. In any case, the increased expenditures of firms generate higher consumer incomes, thus providing incentives for households as consumers to increase their spending on goods and services. Prices tend to rise, as does the volume of goods purchased. Greater spending by consumers means larger receipts for businesses, which in turn spark expansion of production and increased business expenditures on resources. Progressive expansion of economic activity occurs in much the same way as progressive contraction.

A special situation may develop in which increases in spending are reflected solely in price increases with no expansion in resource employment or in the output of goods and services. Suppose, for example, that

economic activity has expanded to the point at which all available resources are employed. Further increases in consumer spending on goods
and services can serve only to raise prices, since it is not possible to increase the quantities of goods available. Similarly, since further increases
in business spending cannot increase the quanties of resources available,
the prices of resources are driven higher.

Micro- and Macroeconomics

The circular flow model is useful in distinguishing between the two
main branches of economic theory: (1) *microeconomics*, or price and allocation theory, and (2) *macroeconomics*, or national income analysis. Both
are used extensively in the areas of study into which economics has traditionally been divided—money and banking, public finance, international
trade, economic development, industrial organization, manpower economics—the precise division depending upon who is doing the dividing.

Microeconomics, as the name implies, is concerned with parts of the
economy rather than with the economy as a whole. It is the economics of
individual units, households and business firms, as they carry on their
activities in the two sets of markets. The pricing and output of the goods
and services that make up the flow from firms to households are also the
concern of microeconomics, as are the pricing and employment of each
of the many resources that constitute the flow from households to firms.

Macroeconomics, on the other hand, examines the economic system
as a whole rather than in terms of individual economic units or specific
products, resources, and prices. As such, it is the aggregate flows in
Figure 2–1 that are important rather than the items that make up each
flow. Macroeconomics is particularly concerned with problems of
economic stability—with the causes and control of depression and
inflation—and is relevant to the aggregate level of employment. It is
concerned also with problems of economic growth and development.

Summary

All economies must perform three basic functions: (1) determine what
goods and services are to be produced and their priority; (2) organize
production; and (3) distribute the goods and services through some sort
of sharing arrangement. In the world today two methods are used to

perform these functions. One is the private approach while the other is the state-planned approach.

The private approach utilizes the price system and the profit motive to guide economic activity. The system works automatically, though not perfectly, as individual economic units engage in economic activity, trying to make the most of what they have. The Canadian and U.S. economies best illustrate the use of the private approach.

The state-planned approach is based on governmental decision-making. The system does not work automatically but requires detailed planning and coordination by a great many individuals and groups throughout the economy. A price system may be used to some extent to assist in the planning and organizing process. The Soviet Union and the socialist countries of Eastern Europe provide examples of the state-planned approach.

The private approach is that of a free enterprise type of economic system. Such a system rests on the institution of private property and accomplishes its ends through voluntary exchange and cooperation. It places a high value on individual freedom and employs self-interest as its primary motivating force.

The state-planned approach is that of a socialistic economy. In this system the government owns the capital resources of the economy, controls labour, and owns and operates its business enterprises. Rather than individual self-interest, the interests of society as a whole as the government conceives them are paramount.

In a simple circular flow model of a free enterprise economy, leaving the government out of account, economic units can be classified into two groups, households and business firms. A flow of resources and their services moves from households as resource owners to business firms. At this point resources are made into goods and services that then flow from firms to households as consumers. A flow of money moves in the opposite direction. The two flows are linked together by prices as households and business firms interact in markets for goods and services and in markets for resources. The model can be used to present a highly simplified analysis of economic instability and is also helpful in distinguishing between micro- and macroeconomics, the two main facets of economic theory.

Exercises and Questions for Discussion

1. What are some industries in Canada in which the government determines prices and organizes production?
2. Explain how the Canadian government redistributes income through progressive taxation, free primary and secondary education, the Agricultural Stabilization Act, and the Medical Care Act.

3. Classify each of the following situations as a micro- or a macroeconomic problem. explaining your answer in each case.
   a. The Ford dealer in your city sets a price on a Galaxie 500.
   b. The ABC Canning Company decides to lay off 1200 men during the winter slowdown in business.
   c. Uncle Harry debates whether or not to install a modern meat counter in his corner grocery store.
   d. The Bank of Canada decides to tighten credit.
4. How would a surtax of 10 percent on personal incomes affect the circular flow?
5. Who runs a free enterprise type of economic system?

Selected Readings

Boulding, Kenneth E., *Economic Analysis*, Vol. 1, *Microeconomics*. New York: Harper & Row, Publishers, Inc., 1966, Chap. 2.

Heilbroner, Robert L., *The Worldly Philosophers*, rev. ed. New York: Simon and Schuster, 1961, Chap. 2.

Lange, Oskar, and Fred M. Taylor, *On the Economic Theory of Socialism*, B. E. Lippincott, (ed.). Minneapolis: University of Minnesota Press, 1938.

Smith, Adam, *An Inquiry into the Nature and Causes of the Wealth of Nations*. New York: Random House, Inc., Modern Library edition. Book 1, Chap. 2.

Turgeon, Lynn, *The Contrasting Economics*, 2d ed. Boston: Allyn and Bacon, Inc., 1969.

3

Business Firms

Since business firms play a major role in the economic activity of a free enterprise economy, we must at this point examine the nature and functions of these institutions. What part do business firms play in overall patterns of economic activity? What is their organizational structure? What is the current business firm population in Canada? What is the general health of business firms in Canada as measured by the rate of failure? What are the broad underlying causes of business failure? What role do publicly-owned corporations play in the Canadian economy? What is the extent to which Canadian corporations are externally controlled? These are the questions considered in this chapter.

Economic Activity of Business Firms

In the preceding chapter we introduced business firms as the production units of the economy. But what does this mean? What constitutes production? The primary objective of economic activity is to satisfy man's wants as fully as possible from the limited means available—from the resources of the economy and from its usable technology. Production refers to any activity that moves or transforms resources from their current places or forms to places or forms that are either closer to the satisfying of wants or that make them more useful in accomplishing this objective. Schematically, production is often thought of in terms of using technology to transform resources into finished goods. With some refinements this conceptualization is essentially correct. When we think of an individual business firm we are usually considering only one link in a long chain of production processes, each of which brings raw and semi-finished materials closer to their ultimate users. But production for the economy as a whole is not complete until what is being produced is actually in the hands of its ultimate user. We call the outputs of processes farther removed from the ultimate consumer *lower-order goods and services* and those that are closer *higher-order goods and services*.

The extractive activities in the economy provide examples of firms producing lower-order outputs. Firms engaged in mining crude oil, iron and copper ore, lead, and zinc are typical, as are those engaged in agricultural pursuits. Most such outputs require further processing before they are ready to be consumed.

At the other extreme, retail stores produce higher-order outputs. Some people have difficulty thinking of a retail store as engaging in production at all, but its activity is fundamentally the same as that of a manufacturing firm. The resources it uses are items not yet accessible to the final user, and these include inventories in the hands of wholesalers and manufacturers, labour, and buildings and equipment. These resources are utilized to put products where they are accessible to consumers; that is, to complete the production process.

Between these extremes are firms operating at many different levels of production. Basic steel firms use iron ore and other resources to make steel ingots, which may be sold to processing firms and steel frabricators to be converted into forms useful in making many different products. Milling companies turn wheat into flour, cereal, feed for livestock, and other items that are further processed before being sold to consumers. The outputs of a great many firms are the resource inputs of a number of other firms as lower-order goods go through the many production processes necessary to make them useful to consumers.

Profit expectations provide the primary incentive for establishing and expanding business firms. Firms are born and flourish in areas where revenues from the sale of goods and services exceed the costs of all resources used in producing them. Where losses occur, that is, where revenues are less than the costs of all resources used, firms contract and die. The profit incentive may be tempered or supplemented by other incentives—the safety of diversification into several product fields, the desire to obtain a large sales volume, the prestige of ownership of a business, and others—but firms will not remain in areas where losses persist over long periods of time.

Forms of Business Firms

With respect to legal organization, there are four major types of profit-seeking firms in Canada: (1) the sole proprietorship, (2) the partnership, (3) the corporation, and (4) the co-operative. There are, of course, non-profit-seeking organizations that use resources to provide goods and services. These include religious, charitable, philanthropic, scientific, and educational institutions. This chapter focuses on the former, but it should be kept in mind that the latter exist also, frequently in the same four legal forms.

The Sole Proprietorship

Sole proprietorships are individually owned business firms. Many grocery stores, restaurants, gas stations, barber shops, doctors' offices, and farms are in this category. One individual owns most of the capital resources of such a business—its building, equipment, and inventories of goods in process—although lease or rental arrangements may be made for some. Usually the proprietor operates the business as well. As one of four alternative forms of organization, the sole proprietorship has its pros and cons.

The Pros

The most common reason for a businessman to choose the sole proprietorship form of organization is the *ease with which it can be established*. What does it take to establish a farm? Usually all that is required is a decision to do so plus the means of financing the minimum amount of capital resources necessary to get started. For a grocery store no more is required. Some entrepreneurs (e.g., tavern and cabaret owners) must have in addition a license or permit in order to set themselves up in business, although this requirement holds as well if the business is a partnership or corporation.

Proprietors have greater *freedom and flexibility* in making a wide variety of decisions than the managers of other forms of business organizations simply because there is no one other than themselves to whom they are accountable for their actions. The proprietor is free to switch from one line of business to another. He can withdraw money from the business for his personal use or he can invest more money in the business as he desires.

The Cons

The most important restraints placed on a sole proprietor are (1) his limited access to funds for investing in the business and carrying on its operations and (2) his inability to separate his business assets from his personal assets for liability purposes. A sole proprietor about to get a good thing going may find that he has *difficulties in securing funds* to convert his dreams into reality. To set up a business in the first place he must have money available to purchase the minimum amounts of capital resources —land, buildings, and equipment—necessary to operate. If he wants to expand the business, still more money is needed, both to increase his productive capacity and to pay the additional costs of operating at higher levels of output. He has access to two types of financing: (1) equity financing and (2) debt financing.

Equity financing refers to the financing of a business through the acquisition of ownership interests in it. The owner uses whatever savings he may have to purchase his plant and equipment and to operate it. Over time, if the business does well, some of the profits, or the excess of receipts over the costs of all resources used in the production process, can be used to finance expansion. The limitation on the equity financing available to the proprietor is set by the extent of his personal assets or his personal fortune.

Debt financing refers to funds that the owner of the business borrows. A single proprietor may go to a commercial bank, to the federal Industrial Development Bank, or to some other type of lending institution, but the amount that he can borrow will depend upon the lending institution's evaluation of him and his business prospects. Most proprietors are not able to obtain money in the way of long-term loans simply because their long-term prospects are uncertain.[1] Thus borrowing by proprietorships is largely in the form of short-term loans to carry on current operations, for example, to finance inventories.

Debt financing of a slightly different sort may be used also in carrying on current business operations. The proprietor of a grocery store may purchase canned goods on credit from a wholesaler, agreeing to make payment in 30, 60, or 90 days, depending upon the terms of the agreement. Short-term credit of this kind can be quite important for sole proprietors, but it may be largely offset by credit that the proprietor in turn extends to his customers.

---

[1] *A sole proprietorship lacks permanence because it ends with the financial, mental, or physical death of the owner. This is a serious defect in obtaining long-term credit as it may be impossible to sell the firm for anything near the amount it was previously worth as a going concern.*

Unlimited liability of the proprietor for debts of the business constitutes the second disadvantage of the sole proprietorship. The proprietor cannot separate claims by creditors upon his business from their claims on his personal belongings. If the proprietor does not pay his business debts, his creditors can legally attach not only his business property but also such personal property as his house and his automobile up to the extent of their claims. This creditors' weapon is double-barrelled. If the proprietor's wife runs up personal debts for mink coats, jewellery, and the like, her creditors can attach the business property. All provinces provide some relief for the debtor, however, by specifying a minimum value of property that is not subject to attachment.

The Partnership

As defined by the Partnership Act, a statute originally passed in 1890 by the British Parliament and subsequently adopted in all the provinces of Canada except Quebec, a partnership is "The relation which subsists between persons carrying on business in common, with a view to profit". Carrying on business in common means that the assets of the business are owned by the partners as a group rather than by the individual partners; one partner cannot pick out which specific assets are his and which belong to the other(s). Similarly, business liabilities are group liabilities. Operation of the business for profit means that this is the objective of the group, even though losses may in fact be incurred. Though somewhat more complex, the characteristics of the partnership are similar to those of the sole proprietorship.

The Pros

The partnership is also born easily, since its existence does not require approval by any governmental unit. Only an agreement among the partners is necessary. This may be written or oral; in fact, it may even be inferred from the activities of persons carrying on some business activity jointly. A written agreement drawn up by a lawyer is ordinarily used, since it provides some measure of protection to each partner from the others. Among other things, it spells out what each partner is to put into the business in the form of money, managerial effort, or capital goods, and it usually specifies the ratio in which profits or losses are to be shared as well as the distribution of business assets in the event of dissolution. If the agreement has been properly drawn up and one or more partners fail to live up to their specified obligations, the others can sue. Apart from such agreement, provincial and territorial laws require that partnerships must be registered with the appropriate authorities. Registration consists in filing a declaration containing the names of the partners, the firm name and the time during which the partnership has subsisted, and stating that the persons therein named are the only members of the partnership.

Another advantage of the partnership is that *it lends itself more to specialization of talents* than does the sole proprietorship. Partnerships are often formed to take advantage of complementary skills. A medical partnership may be formed by an obstetrician and a pediatrician; a legal partnership may include a skilled trial lawyer and one whose specialty is contracts and negotiable instruments; an accounting partnership may be formed by an accountant who directs the office work and a non-accountant with good public contacts. A partnership, taking advantage of complementary fields of specialization, may prosper where any one of the partners working alone would fare badly.

Compared with the single ownership, the partnership *permits enlarging the scale of operations* because it is able to draw on the financial resources of more than one person.[2]

The Cons

One of the most serious drawbacks to the partnership is *unlimited liability* of each partner for the debts of the firm. If a partner cannot meet his share of the obligations of the business, the remaining partner(s) are personally liable for the business debts. As in the case of the sole proprietorship, the personal property of any one co-owner can be attached by creditors to satisfy their claims against the business. Partners that are obliged to meet partnership debts from their personal assets have a right to recover from those members who have not borne their agreed share of the liability, but this in no way diminishes their individual responsibilities to creditors.[3]

---

[2]*It is worth noting here that four provinces limit the number of partners that a firm can admit. In Newfoundland, no unincorporated enterprise may have more than 10 members or partners. In Alberta, British Columbia and Saskatchewan, a firm must be incorporated if it consists of more than 20 persons in business for profit.*

[3]*Most provinces provide for "limited partnerships" which protect one or more of the partners from the unlimited liability feature of general partnership. A limited partnership is composed of one or more general partners who manage the business and have unlimited liability, and one or more persons, called special or limited partners, who contribute an amount in actual cash for the duration of the partnership, who take no part in the management or control of the business, and who are liable to the firm or to its creditors only to the extent of the capital they have agreed to contribute.*

Closely related to the unlimited liability principle is the *agency rule* of partnerships. In the general type of partnership arrangement, any one of the partners may act in the name of the firm, committing the firm to those actions. The firm is bound even though the partner acts without the consent of the others and even though the action is outside the area assigned to him by the partnership agreement. This statement should be qualified. If it has been agreed by the partners that certain restrictions shall be placed on the authority of any one or more of them to commit the firm, no act done in breach of the agreement is legally binding on the partnership with respect to persons having notice of the agreement.

Another weakness of the partnership form of organization is the fact that if a partner dies or wishes to withdraw from the firm, the remaining partners must either find someone else to take his place or purchase his share. Many times the death or retirement of a partner will seriously disrupt the affairs of an enterprise, especially if it is growing rapidly and is in need of all the capital and managing ability it can muster.

Partnerships encounter much the same kinds of *financing limitations* as sole proprietorships, although the partnership has an advantage in equity financing in that there are more co-owners to provide it. Debt financing, too, may be easier, since creditors know that they will have recourse to more than one individual should the firm default on its payments. Nevertheless, limits are set by the personal assets of the partners and by the fact that a dissolution of the partnership could occur at any time. An understandable reluctance to grow by taking in more partners arises in the business from the unlimited liability principle and from the doctrine of mutual agency.

The Corporation

Most large business enterprises are organized as corporations. A corporation can be thought of as an entity separate and apart from the individuals who own it. From a legal point of view in many ways it functtions like a person. It can contract debts or extend credit in its own name; it can hold title to property; it can be taxed; and it can sue and be sued. Since a corporation is a collective entity, not a single individual, it enjoys certain immunities that individuals do not. It cannot commit murder or treason. (As Pope Innocent IV explained, a corporation cannot be excommunicated because it lacks a soul.) It can act only through its members or through the directors and officers who manage its affairs. Let us now consider what makes this organizational form so attractive for large enterprises.

The Pros

One advantage of the corporation is that *ownership of the business can be transferred* among individuals independently of the life and operation of the business. When ownership of a sole proprietorship or any part of a partnership changes hands, the old business ceases to exist and a new one is established. Frequently the death of an owner will result in the liquidation of the assets of the firm. On the other hand, if one buys a share of Algoma Steel Corporation stock he becomes a part owner of the firm. The purchase of the share does not affect business operations and neither does its sale. Every stock market transaction is a transfer of ownership, and to a large extent the impact on business operations of the firms involved is either negligible or slight, since the stock purchased or sold is a small proportion of the total amount outstanding for any one firm. Stockholders do, however, elect boards of directors, and these in turn appoint the corporate officers. Obviously, the transfer of a large enough block of stock of a corporation can change the composition of management and the course of business operations, but the continuity of the firm's business —its legal obligations to others and their obligations to it—is unaffected.

Another attractive feature of the corporate form of business is the *limited liability* of owners for business debts. If the corporation's gross income is not sufficient to meet its expenses and its debt obligations, the most that a stockholder can lose is what he has invested in his stock. Business creditors have no claim on the personal assets of any owner. They can force the firm into bankruptcy and divide the proceeds from the sale of its assets, but this is as far as they can go. The corporate structure is an effective device for insulating any one owner from the actions of other owners or of management.

Corporations also possess a greater *capacity for obtaining financial backing* than do proprietorships and partnerships. Equity financing is accomplished partly through the sale of stock. Debt financing can come from loans to the corporation, credit extended to it, or the sale of the corporation's bonds. The ease with which shares of stock can be transferred and the limited liability of stockholders makes incorporation an attractive way of bringing together equity funds to start a business or to expand it. The firm can have a very large number of stockholders—Bell Telephone of Canada has over two hundred thousand—and the holdings of each can be almost as large or as small as the individual desires. It is not at all difficult for a successful company to issue and sell additional shares of stock to obtain money for expansion.

Corporations frequently use retained earnings to finance expansion; this too is a form of equity financing. After a firm has paid all of its expenses—costs of resources hired or purchased from others—whatever remains from its total receipts belongs to its owners. A corporation may pay all of these net earnings to stockholders as dividends, or it may elect to pay out a part of them only, holding the rest as retained earnings. If it follows the latter course, retained earnings may be used to finance expansion of the firm. Since these earnings really belong to the stockholders, their use for this purpose can legitimately be thought of as equity financing.

The corporation can also use debt financing to a greater extent than either proprietorship or the partnership. It has special capacities for obtaining loans from financial institutions and issuing and selling bonds. The greater stability of the corporation, arising out of its ownership structures and its equity-financing capabilities, makes it a better risk on the average and enables it to borrow more easily from banks or other institutions.

Bond sales provide an important source of borrowing for corporations. A *bond* is a promise to pay to its purchaser at the end of a stated period of time a certain sum of money, with interest to be paid on the sum at regular intervals. The purchaser of the bond is in effect making a long-term loan to the corporation. When the bond reaches its maturity date and is paid off, the debt of the corporation is, of course, cancelled.

The Cons

The corporation is *more difficult to set up* than the proprietorship or the partnership, but this frequently cited disadvantage should not be over-emphasized. Governmental approval is required, but it is ordinarily automatic if the proper organizational steps have been completed. In Canada there are 11 general Companies Acts, one for incorporation under federal law and one each for incorporation under provincial law.[4] It may be generally stated that federal charter is usually preferable for a company intending to operate in more than one province. In practice, most corporations come into existence under provincial authority. In such cases the procedure is relatively straightforward. An application for a charter is made to the Provincial Secretary or the Registrar of Companies of the appropriate province by a minimum of three persons intending to incorporate. Among other things, the application contains the name of the corporation, the purposes for which the company is formed, the location of its head office, the amount of stock it is authorized to issue, and the class

[4]*Certain types of companies are created by special Act of the Federal Parliament or of the legislature of any one of the provinces. The formation of a public company by special Act is restricted mainly to banks, insurance companies, trust and loan companies, and railways.*

and number of shares to be taken by each applicant and the amount to be paid therefor. Upon approval by the appropriate provincial agency, the application becomes the corporation charter. Stock is issued and the first meeting of the stockholders is held. By-laws for the operation of the corporation are adopted and a board of directors is elected. The directors appoint the corporation officers and the corporation is ready to engage in the economic activities for which it was established. Since the provisions of the charter and of the by-laws can be amended easily, no great handicap is placed on the corporate form of business by legal organizational requirements; the process of organization is just more cumbersome than that for the other forms of businesses.

A more significant disadvantage of the corporation is the *treatment accorded it by tax laws*, both federal and provincial. Corporations pay corporate income taxes on their net earnings. When net earnings are distributed as dividends to stockholders, the latter pay personal income taxes on all dividends received except for a small exemption.[5] The owners of the corporation thus find two tax bites taken out of the income of their business. Proprietorships and partnerships pay no business income tax on their net earnings; rather, net earnings are taxed only as personal income of the owners.[6]

Another alleged disadvantage of the corporation is that *corporate management and corporate ownership are distinct from one another*. The managers may be owners or stockholders, but they typically hold a small minority of total shares outstanding. Thus, if they so desire, the managers can pursue courses of action contrary to that desired by stockholders. To whom is the possibility of separation of ownership and control a disadvantage? It probably plays little part in the initial decision of whether to organize a business as a corporation or as a proprietorship or partnership. In a large enterprise managers may take actions such as paying themselves large bonuses that benefit them at the expense of the stockholders, but by and large both groups are interested in making the firm a profitable enterprise. Much controversy surrounds the issue of ownership versus control, but not much in the way of definitive conclusions have been reached.

---

[5]*Under present Canadian law taxpayers are permitted a credit against personal tax due of 20 percent of dividends received from "taxable Canadian corporations".*

[6]*Much can be said on both sides about the "fairness" or "justice" of so-called double taxation of corporate net income. Most arguments for double taxation maintain that the privileges or advantages of doing business as a corporation justify it. Arguments against it are to the effect that all forms of business enterprise should be accorded the same tax treatment.*

Co-operatives

Legally, the co-operative is organized as a corporation to do business under a corporate name, but it has certain partnership characteristics that differentiate it from an ordinary business corporation.[7] The principal characteristics of a co-operative enterprise are as follows:

1. **Common law voting.** Each shareholder, or member, has but one vote, regardless of the number of shares he holds in the co-operative. Since every stockholder has an equal voice in determining policy, control is more democratic than in the ordinary business corporation.
2. **Limited return on share capital.** Each member receives a fixed rate of return on his monetary investment—perhaps 5 percent. The member who put in $50 will receive $2.50 a year on his investment and no more. This means that profits are not distributed to members on the basis of how much each invested in shares.
3. **Distribution of net earnings by patronage dividends.** In a co-op, profits are distributed to members on the basis of how much business each member transacts with the organization. If the directors elect to pay a 10 percent patronage dividend, member A who did $100 worth of business would be paid $10, whereas member B, whose purchases or sales amounted to $1,000, would get $100. Thus, those who contribute to the success of the concern by their patronage profit in proportion to their contribution.

To this list of principles many co-ops concerned with selling at the retail level add cash trading (because it is more economical) and trading at prevailing prices (in order to avoid a price war with other retailers).

Co-operatives may be classified into two main types on the basis of the kind of business they do. Those organized to sell something *to* their members are called consumers' co-operatives; those which sell something *for* their members are called producers' or marketing co-operatives. In Canada, consumers' co-operatives sell farm supplies (feed, fertilizers, spray materials, gas and oil, machinery, equipment and building materials) and also food products, auto accessories, hardware, clothing and home furnishings and many other consumer goods. Other consumers' associations provide fire, life, automobile, hail, general casualty, fidelity and medical insurance, electricity, housing and other services including water, transportation, telephone, cold storage and seed cleaning. Credit unions and

[7]*Nearly all Canadian co-operatives are organized under provincial law. There is not yet any general federal legislation for incorporation of co-operatives. However, a few co-operative concerns that operate in more than one province have been formed under the Canada Corporations Act, or special Act of Parliament.*

caisses populaires are a special class of consumers' co-operatives. Such associations enable groups of individuals with a common alliance (the parish, the place of employment, etc.) to combine their savings and thereby provide loan funds to members of the organization for good purposes at relatively low interest rates. Today credit unions and *caisses populaires* have more members and more assets than all other types of co-operatives added together. At the end of 1968, there were 4,663 credit unions and *caisses populaires*, with 3,953,200 members and total assets of $3.7 billion. It is also interesting to note that one out of every four Canadians is a member of a credit union or *caisse populaire*, and more than 10 percent of all consumer credit flows through such co-operative societies.

Producers' co-operatives are usually organized for the purpose of marketing primary products. In Canada co-ops are extensively used in the marketing of grains and seeds, dairy products, livestock and products, poultry and eggs, fruits and vegetables and fish. About one-third of all agricultural products sold commercially in Canada are sold through co-operative marketing associations. In dollar volume of business, the western grain elevator companies greatly exceed all other Canadian marketing co-operatives. Also deserving of mention is the fact that sometimes these marketing associations play a dual role and serve the needs of their members not only as producers but likewise as consumers. Farm supplies generally account for the greater part of Canadian co-operative purchases.

The Pros

Advocates of co-operatives maintain that wherever there are private concerns making monopoly profits the co-operative form of business organization *can obtain more favourable prices* for its members, whether they are producers or consumers. Also, this type of organization *permits large-scale operation* while preserving democratic control. A further advantage is that earnings paid out to members in the form of *patronage dividends are not subject to the corporation income tax.*

The Cons

The greatest weakness of the co-operative concern is the *difficulty it faces in raising large amounts of capital* in formation and in expansion. It cannot attract financial investors as an ordinary business corporation can. As a consequence, the co-op must rely on retained earnings the sale of shares to new members, and on loans from other co-operative ventures.

A potential drawback of this form of organization is that *management may not have sufficient control* to assure the success of the enterprise as a commercial business. Since the organizers of co-operatives frequently include people who are more interested in social reform than in financial gain, this makes it hard to follow policies which economic efficiency demands.

Importance of Business Forms

Having described the four major types of business organizations, let us now compare them with respect to their impact upon employment provided and business transacted. The census figures for 1961, shown in Table 3–1, reveal that in that year slightly more than one-half of all manufacturing establishments were organized as corporations. As for the other half, 34.4 percent were proprietorships, and 9.4 percent used the partnership. Other forms were but little used. What is more significant is that corporations employed 94.4 percent of all the production workers and produced 96 percent of the total value of products in the manufacturing industry.

TABLE 3–1
Relative Importance of Organizational Forms, 1961 Manufacturing Establishments

	Establishments		Employees		Sales (Millions of Dollars)	
	Number	Percent	Number	Percent	Amount	Percent
Proprietorships	11,160	34.4	38,210	2.9	425	1.7
Partnerships	3,058	9.4	20,195	1.6	231	1.0
Corporations	17,439	54.0	1,225,535	94.4	23,221	96.0
Co-operatives	758	2.2	13,862	1.1	366	1.3
Other forms*	—	—	—	—		
Total	32,415	100.0	1,297,802	100.0	24,243	100.0

Refers to charitable, religious, philanthropic, scientific and educational institutions.
Source; Based on Canada Census data for 1961.

In merchandising, the corporation also dominates the wholesale field, as shown in Table 3–2. While 52.3 percent of the number of wholesale establishments in 1961 were corporations, they enjoyed 77.7 percent of the total sales and accounted for 84.2 percent of the employees.

In the retail field, the sole proprietorship is the most important form of business organization insofar as the number of units is concerned with 72.4 percent of the total, but corporation units show the greatest volume

TABLE 3–2
Wholesale Establishments

	Establishments		Employees		Sales (Millions of Dollars)	
	Number	Percent	Number	Percent	Amount	Percent
Proprietorships	11,642	37.7	21,373	8.9	2,079	10.7
Partnerships	1,942	6.3	6,609	2.6	652	3.3
Corporations	16,136	52.3	201,909	84.2	15,117	77.7
Co-operatives	1,105	3.6	8,803	3.7	791	4.1
Other forms	30	0.1	1,339	0.6	814	4.2
Total	30,855	100.0	240,033	100.0	19,453	100.0

of sales and number of employees, as Table 3–3 reveals. Only 18.1 percent of retail establishments were incorporated, but they hired 67.8 percent of the employees and accounted for 58.5 percent of the total business volume.

TABLE 3–3
Retail Establishments

	Establishments		Employees		Sales (Millions of Dollars)	
	Number	Percent	Number	Percent	Amount	Percent
Proprietorship	110,642	72.4	148,735	25.3	4,964	30.9
Partnership	12,209	8.0	27,897	4.7	995	6.1
Corporations	27,262	18.1	398,010	67.8	9,391	58.5
Co-operatives	849	0.6	5,802	1.0	168	1.0
Other forms	1,294	0.9	6,934	1.2	556	3.5
Total	152,256	100.0	587,378	100.0	16,074	100.0

In the field of "service" enterprises, the individual proprietorship is still pre-eminent in terms of numbers, constituting 74.8 percent of the firms. However, in 1961 incorporated companies took in 50.3 percent of the receipts and employed 55.4 percent of the total labour force.

TABLE 3–4
Service Establishments

	Establishments		Employees		Sales (Millions of Dollars)	
	Number	Percent	Number	Percent	Amount	Percent
Proprietorship	63,543	74.8	96,177	31.2	1,066	35.8
Partnership	8,779	10.4	34,344	11.1	365	12.3
Corporations	11,715	13.8	171,009	55.4	1,500	50.3
Co-operatives	199	0.3	1,649	0.6	15	0.5
Other forms	529	0.7	5,286	1.7	33	1.1
Total	84,760	100.0	308,465	100.0	2,979	100.0

Only in agriculture is the corporation overshadowed by the other organization forms. The agricultural census figures for 1966 indicate that in that year there were 430,522 separate farm operating units in Canada, of which 72 percent were owner-operated; 23 percent were partly owned by the operator and party rented; and only 5 percent were operated by a tenant or manager.

To sum up, while the sole proprietorship still dominates the Canadian scene from the point of view of numbers, the corporation accounts for the greatest part of our production and employment. However, it should be pointed out that the relative importance of the corporate form of organization differs widely as between different industries.

Business Concentration

Although there are thousands of corporate enterprises in Canada, a relatively small number do a large fraction of the business transacted. At the end of 1968 Canada's top 100 industrial corporations, with sales of $25.3 billion and combined earnings of $1.6 billion, accounted for two-fifths of all sales in Canada (excluding merchandising and financial firms) and two-thirds of all earnings; in merchandising, the 11 largest firms made about 40 percent of all store sales; and the 25 largest financial companies, with combined assets of $55 billion, controlled 80 percent of assets held by all financial institutions.[8] The following table lists the 10 largest manufacturing, resource and utility companies in Canada in terms of sales. Separate rankings by assets and earnings are also given. The listing does not include government-owned companies.

The *FP* figures for 1968, shown in Table 3–5, reveal that Imperial Oil Ltd. ranks first in sales, Bell Canada in assets, and International Nickel Co. of Canada in earnings. It is worth noting here that Bell Canada's assets are greater than all except the three largest utilities in the United States and its operating revenues are exceeded only by American Telephone and Telegraph (A.T. & T.). Similarly, Canadian Pacific Railway has larger assets than all except three U.S. transportation companies. Significantly, the number of industrial corporations with sales over the half-billion dollar mark grew from 9 to 14 between 1966 and 1968. Before leaving the industrial front, however, it should be pointed out that some large firms are not members of the "Hundred Largest Club" because they do not publish

[8]*Statistics from* Financial Post, Survey of Large Companies, *1968. See also* Financial Post, *August 2, 1969, pp. 1, 9 and 10.*

TABLE 3-5

Canada's 10 Largest Industrial Companies: Ranked by Sales, Assets and Net Profits, Fiscal Year ending nearest to December 31, 1968

(Millions of Dollars)

Rank by Sales	Sales $	Company	Rank by Assets	Assets $	Rank by Net Income	Net income $
1	1,432[1]	Imperial Oil Ltd.	5	1,397	3	100
2	1,292	Ford Motor Co. of Canada	13	732	10	50
3	1,241	Bell Telephone of Canada	1	3,126	2	115
4	1,081	Alcan Aluminium Ltd.	3	1,954	4	71
5	925[2]	Canadian Pacific Railway Co.	2	2,155	6	61
6	917	Massey-Ferguson Ltd.	7	940	17	28
7	823	Int'l Nickel Company of Canada	4	1,497	1	154
8	789	Canada Packers Ltd.	55	164	48	8
9	730	George Weston Ltd.	24	397	20	23
10	622[1]	Shell Canada Ltd.	10	802	8	54

[1]*Excise Taxes excluded.* [2]*Estimate.*
Source: Financial Post, *August 2, 1969, p. 9.*

financial statements and reliable estimates are not available. These firms are mostly wholly owned subsidiaries of U.S. and other foreign companies —such as General Motors of Canada Ltd., Chrysler Canada Ltd., American Motors (Canada) Ltd., Canadian International Paper Co. and Canadian Johns-Manville Co. These five firms would undoubtedly rank among the industrial giants. As partial evidence of this, while Ford Motor Co. of Canada ranked second in sales, as shown in Table 3–5, the largest producer of automobiles in this country is General Motors of Canada. Some other very large corporations are excluded from the 100-largest group because almost all their operations and assets are outside Canada. These include Brascan Ltd. (formerly called Brazilian Light & Power Co.), Mexican Light & Power Co., Canadian International Power Co., and Seven Arts Productions Ltd.

Table 3–6 compares Canada's 10 largest merchandisers according to sales volume. Separate rankings are shown for assets and earnings. The list does not include the vast T. Eaton Co., which, since it is privately owned, does not disclose its financial position. According to the *Financial Post*, its sales in 1968 probably were about $900 million, which would put it in second place in terms of store sales.

It is interesting to note that seven Canadian merchandisers would qualify for the *Fortune* magazine directory of the 50 largest U.S. merchandising corporations.

TABLE 3-6

Canada's 10 Largest Merchandisers: Ranked by Sales, Assets and Net Profits, Fiscal Year ending nearest to December 31, 1968

(Millions of Dollars)

Rank by Sales	Sales $	Company	Rank by Assets	Assets $	Rank by Net Income	Net Income $
1	2,434	Loblaw Cos.[1]	1	571	5	10
2	604	Canada Safeway Ltd.	6	150	4	12
3	603	Dominion Stores Ltd.	7	126	6	9
4	541	Simpsons-Sears Ltd.	2	379	2	14
5	480	Steinberg's Ltd.	5	169	8	8
6	453	Hudson's Bay Co.	4	272	1	15
7	389	M. Loeb Ltd.	10	57	10	2
8	291	Oshawa Wholesale Ltd.	9	90	9	5
9	267	Simpsons Ltd.	3	279	3	14
10	258	Woodward Stores Ltd.	8	113	7	8

[1]*Data consolidates U.S. companies Loblaw-Inc. and National Tea Co.*
Source; Financial Post, August 2, 1969, p. 9.

In the financial field, the chartered banks dominate the area, as Table 3–7 reveals. In 1968, five banks had about 61 percent of the total assets of Canada's 25 largest financial institutions. Or, to put it another way, their combined assets of $33.5 billion were more than double the whole life insurance industry's Canadian assets of $14.5 billion. Another important point is this: any one of the three largest Canadian banks is bigger than 44 trust companies, including the three largest consolidated trust and mortgage loan firms. Furthermore, Canadian financial corporations compare well with their counterparts in the United States. Ranked by assets,

TABLE 3-7

Canada's 10 Largest Financial Institutions Ranked by Assets Fiscal Year ending nearest to December 31, 1968

(Millions of Dollars)

Rank by Assets	Assets $	Company	Net Income $
1	8,743	Royal Bank of Canada	35
2	8,343	Canadian Imperial Bank of Commerce	33
3	6,818	Bank of Montreal	18
4	5,217	Bank of Nova Scotia	15
5	4,378	Toronto-Dominion Bank	14
6	3,370	Sun Life Assurance Co. of Canada	*
7	1,838	Manufacturers Life Insurance Co.	*
8	1,485	London Life Insurance Co.	*
9	1,411	Banque Canadienne Nationale	5
10	1,387	Great-West Life Assurance Co.	*

Insurance companies do not report profit figures as such.
Source: Financial Post, August 2, 1969 p. 10.

six Canadian insurance companies are as large as those of the 28 largest U.S. insurance firms. Five of our banks rate alongside the 15 biggest U.S. banks. In fact, two Canadian banks are among the top 20 in the world. At the end of 1968, the Royal Bank of Canada and The Canadian Imperial Bank of Commerce were the world's twelfth and eighteenth largest banks.

While credit unions and *caisses populaires* do not appear on the list of Canada's top 25 financial companies, their collective importance is evidenced by the assets represented by some of the regional associations. For example, the 1,300 *caisses* which make up La Fédération de Québec des Unions Régionales de Caisses Populaires have assets of $1,750 million. Similarly, the 1,500 credit unions which constitute the Ontario Credit Union League Ltd. have combined assets of $750 million.

Against this background, it is clear that the Canadian economy is well equipped to take advantage of modern large-scale production. However, many Canadians are worried about the implications of big business and business concentration for the operation of a market economy. Does bigness imply, for example, the existence of significant monopoly power? How big must firms in particular industries be in order to be able to produce efficiently? Can we have the efficiency we desire without at the same time generating adverse monopoly power? These are some of the questions for which we will be seeking answers in the chapters that follow.

Foreign Ownership and Control of Canadian Industry

No other characteristic of our economy has stirred as much controversy as the large degree of control exercised by foreign business firms—particularly by United States corporations—over certain key sectors of Canadian industry and commerce. Available information for 1963, presented in Table 3–8, indicates that 54 percent of the capital (long term debt plus shareholders' equity) employed in the Canadian manufacturing industry was owned by non-residents, of which 44 percent was owned in the United States. In the field of petroleum and natural gas, non-resident and U.S. ownership were 64 and 54 percent respectively, while in mining and smelting they were 62 and 54 percent respectively. Turning back to the manufacturing sector, non-resident ownership represented 91 percent of the automobile and parts industry, 87 percent of the rubber industry and 70 percent of the electrical apparatus industry. In each case the whole, or virtually the whole, of foreign ownership was American.

Corresponding figures measuring foreign control of Canadian industry indicate that 60 percent of the manufacturing sector as a whole in 1963 was controlled by non-residents, of which 46 percent was subject to U.S. direction.[9] Non-resident and U.S. control of the petroleum and natural gas industry were 74 and 62 percent respectively, whereas in mining and smelting they rere 59 and 52 percent respectively. Additionally, 97 percent of the total amount of capital invested in rubber and automobiles and parts was subject to foreign control, as was 78 percent in transportation equipment and chemicals and 77 percent in electrical apparatus.

TABLE 3–8
Ownership and Control of Selected Canadian Industries, December 31, 1963

Enterprise classification	Percentage of capital employed owned in				Percentage of capital employed controlled in		
	Canada	U.S.A.	U.K.	other	Canada	U.S.A.	other
Manufacturing							
Beverages	74	23	2	1	83	17	—
Rubber	13	81	6	—	3	90	7
Textiles	80	14	6	—	80	13	7
Pulp and paper	48	44	7	1	53	35	12
Agricultural machinery	51	46	1	2	50	50	—
Automobile and parts	9	91	—	—	3	97	—
Transportation equipment	41	25	34	—	22	33	45
Iron and steel mills	80	8	7	5	86	2	12
Electrical apparatus	30	62	5	3	23	66	11
Chemicals	37	47	13	3	22	54	24
Other	41	47	8	4	30	54	16
Sub totals	46	44	8	2	40	46	14
Petroleum and natural gas	36	54	5	5	26	62	12
Mining and smelting	38	54	4	4	41	52	7
Totals of above industries	41	48	7	4	36	52	12

Source, Dominion Bureau of Statistics. The Canadian Balance of International Payments 1963, 1964 and 1965 and International Investment Position, *August, 1967, p. 128.*

The general nature of the controversy about the international firm is suggested by the following comments:

1. "Many direct investment firms[10] in Canada, it is claimed, are run simply as extensions of the United States market, in contrast with overseas affiliates of the parent. Therefore, the opportunities for Canadians to secure positions among senior management and on boards of directors

[9]*In general a business firm is considered to be foreign controlled if 50 percent or more of its voting shares are known to be held in one country outside of Canada. Foreign controlled enterprises include unincorporated branches of foreign corporations operating in Canada, wholly or partially-owned Canadian subsidiaries of foreign corporations, and Canadian private or public companies which have no parent concern but whose stock ownership is held substantially in a country other than Canada.*

[10]*A direct investment company is either an unincorporated branch owned by non-residents, or a concern incorporated in Canada in which the effective control of voting stock is held, or believed to be held, by non-residents.*

are limited. The consequences of these two points are to limit the development of Canadian managerial resources, to ensure that resident managers from parent companies make decisions in the interests of the international firm, and regardless of the nationality of the managers, to limit greatly the range of decision-making permitted to them.

2. Except for firms established to supply raw materials and partly finished goods to the parent, direct investment companies are often not allowed to export, or can export only to markets where imperial preferences are available ... The result is to prevent exports which are either economically feasible or which could be if the subsidiaries were given the right to seek and develop foreign markets.

3. The development of Canadian production and of service industries is limited (whether within or outside the subsidiary) because of limitations on the sources from which the subsidiary may buy, and particularly because of requirements to buy parts, equipment, and services from the parent and its affiliates abroad or from their foreign suppliers.

4. The centralization of research and development facilities in the parent abroad, and the control over the size and purpose of such facilities in Canada, inhibit the development of this important expenditure in Canada, further restrict the sales potential of the subsidiary, and limit the development of technical and scientific personnel.

5. "The financial policies of such firms, particularly where they are wholly owned by non-residents, may reflect the requirements of parent companies more than those of the subsidiary, may lead to an underdeveloped state for some sectors of the domestic capital market, and may cause serious balance of payments problems."[11]

6. "The fact that a large part of non-resident equity investment in Canadian industry is in the form of wholly-owned subsidiaries and branches means that Canadians are unable to participate financially even through the growth in incomes and the consequent increase in domestic savings will make it increasingly possible for them to so do."[12]

7. Many foreign-owned concerns are relieved of the necessity of public disclosure of their financial situation by virtue of their status as private companies. On the basis of published data, it would appear that approximately 60 percent of foreign firms in Canada are private limited companies. Since the operations of many of Canada's leading corporations are of legitimate interest to several groups of the community, including labour unions, government departments and economic analysts,

[11]*A. E. Safarian*, Foreign Ownership of Canadian Industry. *Toronto: McGraw Hill, 1966, pp. 19-20.*
[12]*Canada, Royal Commission on Canada's Economic Prospects (Gordon Commission)*, Preliminary Report, *Queen's Printer, December, 1956, p. 89.*

and to every individual as a consumer, it is claimed that freedom from publicity enjoyed by large foreign-owned private corporations is not in the public interest.

These and related views pose a conflict of interest between the aspirations of Canada and those of the international firm with its locus of operations in several nations. If these opinions are correct, they indicate what may be significant offsets to the advantages traditionally associated with external direct investment. However, as one might suspect the controversy between those who see direct investment in Canada as a necessary condition for our continued growth and those who identify foreign domination of our country's economy with the extent of foreign ownership and control of Canadian corporations has generated more heat than light. In all probability, the economic factors involved in assessing government policies toward foreign investment in Canada can only be decided in the light of one's judgment about the appropriate rate and nature of growth and development in the Canadian economy. Measures could be devised which might facilitate a larger degree of Canadian stock ownership in foreign-controlled concerns and which might more effectively channel Canadian savings into the resource and manufacturing industries thus far dominated by a relatively few foreign business firms. It would be possible as well to emphasize to non-resident controlled companies the real advantages to be gained by employing qualified Canadians in senior management and technical positions; taking an active and constructive part in community and national affairs; having independent Canadian directors on the board; publishing regular financial statements; fostering a distinct Canadian research effort; developing sources of supply in Canada; processing natural resources in Canada as far as possible; maximizing their market opportunities in other countries as well as in Canada; and by retaining sufficient earnings for growth after paying a fair return to owners. But such steps, however useful, do not go to the heart of the matter. It seems that the basic issues are first, can Canada restrain or reduce the flow of foreign capital investment in this country without undermining the process of economic growth that has been to a large extent based on this outside capital, and second, how high a price are the Canadian people willing to pay in the form of slower growth to secure a greater measure of control over their own destiny.

Government Enterprises

No account of business organization in this country would be complete without mention of the publicly-owned corporation. In Canada, business enterprises have been established by government at the federal, provincial, and municipal levels. Some are run as departments of government, while others are managed by boards or commissions which are responsible in varying degrees to the government concerned. Businesses of this type have been most prominent in the field of public utilities. In most cases they are operated as monopolies.

Abstracting from the propriety of public ownership, two observations are worth stressing. First, some fifty Crown corporations have been established under the Company's Act or by special Act of Parliament, nine of them since 1963. In this connection, it should be mentioned that there are three types of Crown companies—*departmental corporations* are accountable for administrative, supervisory or regulatory services of a governmental character. Examples are the Agricultural Stabilization Board, The Economic Council of Canada, and the Unemployment Insurance Commission. *Agency corporations* are responsible for the management of trading or service operations on a quasi-commercial basis or for the administration of procurement, construction and disposal activities on behalf of federal government departments and agencies, industry, universities and foreign countries. Examples of such agency corporations are Atomic Energy of Canada Ltd., the Canadian Commercial Corporation and the National Capital Commission. *Proprietary corporations* are (1) responsible for the supervision of lending or financial operations, or for the management of commercial or industrial operations involving the supply of goods and services to the general public, and (2) normally required to conduct their affairs without Parliamentary appropriations. Well known examples are the Canadian National Railways, the Canadian Broadcasting Corporation, Air Canada, Central Mortgage and Housing Corporation, Eldorado Mining and Refining Ltd., and Polymer Corporation Ltd. Like an ordinary business corporation, proprietary corporations pay taxes on income earned. Other enterprises owned by the federal government include the Bank of Canada, the Canadian Wheat Board and the Industrial Development Bank. Five prominent provincial proprietary corporations are the Liquor Control Board of Ontario, British Columbia Hydro and Power Authority, Saskatchewan Power Corporation, Alberta Government Telephone Company and the Nova Scotia Electric Power Commission. Examples at the municipal level are the Toronto Transit Commission and the Ottawa Hydro Electric Commission. Clearly some very important businesses are carried on by our three levels of government.

It should also be emphasized that the profit motive is not the only force at work in a publicly-owned corporation. Public concerns are impelled by other motives as well and these other considerations may often exert a perceptible influence over the conduct of their affairs. For instance, many crown corporations have had as their primary purpose the development of a particular product, service, industry, or part of the country. To argue that the public interest is not always served by the pursuit of profit most emphatically does not deny that public enterprises are subject to inefficiency nor does it deny the need to consider other ways of achieving the same ends. To put it differently, it is always proper for the economist to assess whether the public goals are best achieved through public enterprises and agencies or through private enterprises subsidized, if necessary, by the government.

Business Failures

One indicator of the business climate is the number of business failures (defined as concerns that are forced out of business with loss to creditors) per 10,000 firms in operation. Available information presented in Table 3–9, indicates that over the span of years since 1900, there has been an improvement in the general health of Canadian business firms as measured by the rate of failure. During the first three decades of this century, the failure rate exceeded that which has prevailed since then. Yet the failure rate has been generally trending upward since the end of World War II.

To look briefly at the picture for the past several years, Canadian business failures in 1968 decreased, falling to 1,697, the smallest number since 1959. The total dollar liabilities involved in 1968 mortalities fell to a five-year low of $130 million after reaching the all-time peak of $215 million a year earlier. While the average liability per business failure shrank to $76,652, it nevertheless was the second highest figure in history, exceeded only by 1967's record $109,638. Retail trade firms accounted for 42 percent of all business failures in 1968; the construction sector accounted for roughly 20 percent; the manufacturing group accounted for 16 percent; the commercial service group accounted for about 12 percent; and wholesale trade accounted for the rest. By province, the largest number of failures occurred in Quebec (859), Ontario (589), and British Columbia (91). The smallest number occurred in the Maritimes.

The causes of business failure may be divided into two groups—*internal* causes, which can be attributed to management, and *external* causes, over which management has little or no control. Dun & Bradstreet Ltd., the leading supplier of credit information, whose statistics on number and liabilities of business failures have the weight of Holy Writ, reports the cause of failure to lie in management: incompetence, lack of managerial experience, lack of experience in the given line of business, or an un-

TABLE 3–9
Canadian Business Failures 1900-1968

Year	Failure Rate per 10,000 Concerns*	Year	Failure Rate per 10,000 Concerns
1900	140	1934	90
1901	145	1935	78
1902	116	1936	71
1903	101	1937	55
1904	125	1938	58
1905	132	1939	72
1906	113	1940	64
1907	116	1941	49
1908	145	1942	36
1909	123	1943	11
1910	104	1944	6
1911	104	1945	6
1912	99	1946	7
1913	119	1947	15
1914	194	1948	23
1915	110	1949	27
1916	114	1950	32
1917	77	1951	36
1918	62	1952	37
1919	54	1953	44
1920	73	1954	57
1921	159	1955	55
1922	228	1956	53
1923	195	1957	59
1924	148	1958	55
1925	141	1959	57
1926	128	1960	72
1927	125	1961	78
1928	120	1962	82
1929	128	1963	85
1930	152	1964	98
1931	143	1965	103
1932	161	1966	93
1933	138	1967	75
		1968	67

Data includes manufacturers, wholesalers, retailers, building contractors, and certain types of commercial service including public utilities, water carriers, motor carriers and air-lines. It excludes financial enterprises, insurance and real-estate companies, railroads, terminals, amusements, and many small one-man services. Neither the professions nor farmers are included.
Source: Research Division, Dun & Bradstreet of Canada, Ltd., Toronto, 1969.

balanced experience—i.e., strength in some areas, such as sales, but weakness in others, such as finance. More than 95 percent of failures in ordinary years are characteristically laid at the door of management. About two-thirds of these are due to incompetence, less than one-twentieth are attributed to such other factors as neglect, fraud, or disaster.

Table 3–10 indicates in detail the apparent reasons and the underlying causes of Canadian business failures in 1968. Only in the case of ten con-

TABLE 3-10
Classification of Causes of Business Failures in Canada, Year 1968

Number	Per Cent	ALL LINES OF BUSINESS UNDERLYING CAUSES		ALL METHODS OF OPERATION APPARENT CAUSES		
17	1.0	NEGLECT	Due to:	Bad Habits	3	0.2
				Poor Health	9	0.5
				Marital Difficulties	1	0.1
				Other	4	0.2
9	0.5	FRAUD	On the part of the principals, reflected by:	Misleading Name	—	—
				False Financial Statement	1	0.1
				Premeditated Overbuy	2	0.1
				Irregular Disposal of Assets	4	0.2
				Other	2	0.1
157	9.2	LACK OF EXPERIENCE IN THE LINE	Evidenced by inability to avoid conditions which resulted in:	Inadequate Sales	1,044	61.5
137	8.1	LACK OF MANAGERIAL EXPERIENCE		Heavy Operating Expenses	173	10.2
222	13.1	UNBALANCED EXPERIENCE*		Receivables Difficulties	161	9.5
1,132	66.7	INCOMPETENCE		Inventory Difficulties	62	3.7
				Excessive Fixed Assets	53	3.1
				Poor Location	23	1.4
				Competitive Weakness	183	10.8
				Other	21	1.2
13	0.8	DISASTER	Some of these occurrences could have been provided against through insurance.	Fire	7	0.4
				Flood	—	—
				Burglary	1	0.1
				Employees' Fraud	3	0.1
				Strike	1	0.1
				Other	1	0.1
10	0.6	REASON UNKNOWN		Because some failures are attributed to a combination of apparent causes, the totals of these columns exceed the totals of the corresponding columns on the left.		
1,697	100.0	TOTAL				

*Experience not well rounded in sales, finance, purchasing, and production on the part of an individual in case of a proprietorship, or of two or more partners or officers constituting a management unit.

Source: *Research Division, Dun & Bradstreet of Canada Ltd., Toronto, 1969.*

cerns does Dun & Bradstreet state that the cause of failure could not be determined.

Finally, it should be pointed out that more than 50 percent of all new firms fail within the first five years of operation. Among the enterprises that failed in 1968, only 2.7 percent were businesses established during the year. However, firms set up in 1967 accounted for 13.2 percent of all failures, those of 1966 for 16.5 percent, those of 1965 for 12.2 percent and those of 1964 for 8.7 percent. Only 8.6 percent of all the failures in 1968 involved companies established prior to 1950. In short, the first few years is the testing period of the ability, stamina and management instinct of the entrepreneur.

One general remark should be made in concluding this section. Considering the advances in technology and communications that have occurred of late, it is clear that today's businessman requires considerably more factual knowledge and knowhow, as well as a larger initial capital investment, than did his counterpart 20 years ago. This means that the high mortality rate in recent years, even more than in the past, represents a sorting out of the men from the boys, and does not have too dire a meaning for the economy as a whole.

Summary

Business firms are the economic units that engage in production; that is, in activity that moves or transforms resources to a place or form nearer to that in which they are ultimately used. The outputs of production processes further removed from the satisfying of consumer wants are called lower-order goods while those closer to the satisfying of consumer wants are higher-order goods. Business firms produce outputs at all levels, from extraction of raw materials to the placing of goods in the hands of their ultimate consumers. Profits provide the incentive for the creation and operation of business firms.

From a legal point of view there are four forms of business organization: (1) the sole proprietorship, (2) the partnership, (3) the corporation, and (4) the co-operative. Sole proprietorships are business firms owned by one person or one family. Partnerships are firms owned by two or more individuals but which are not incorporated. Corporations are businesses set up as legal entities that can operate as a sort of legal person. Co-operatives are a kind of combination of the partnership and the corporation, in the sense that they have some of the characteristics of each.

The sole proprietorship form has both advantages and disadvantages. Among the advantages are the ease with which it can be established and the freedom and flexibility it offers with respect to decision-making by its owner-manager. The distadvantages of the sole proprietorship are that funds for financing expansion and operation of the business are limited in amount and that the proprietor has unlimited liability for business debts.

We distinguish between equity financing of a business and debt financing. The former means that funds are provided the business by owners or in exchange for ownership interests. Debt financing means that the business obtains funds by borrowing or by going into debt.

Partnerships, like sole proprietorships, are easily formed. They have broader possibilities for specialization of managerial talents and for equity financing than have sole proprietorships. The disadvantages of a partnership are unlimited liability of each partner for partnership debts, the agency rule, under which any one partner can take actions binding the partnership, and limited sources of financing.

The advantages of a corporation are easy transferability of ownership interests, limited liability of owners for business debts, and much broader sources of financing than are available to the other two organizational forms. On the other side of the ledger, corporations are somewhat more complex to establish; their incomes are subjected to more onerous tax treatment than that of proprietorships and partnerships, and there is usually a separation of ownership from control of the corporation.

The co-operative enjoys certain advantages in common with the corporation, but it also possesses others which are more or less unique. Co-ops provide for a large-scale organization while preserving democratic control (one vote for each member). Dividends are based on the purchase or sales of members and not on the amounts of stock held. Management is usually local and in close contact with the members. The chief weakness of the co-operative form of organization is the difficulty in raising capital.

We find that in Canada there are approximately 430,000 farms, and more than 300,000 separate business firms in existence. Four-fifths of these are sole proprietorships, less than one-twentieth are partnerships, and about one-tenth are corporations.

With respect to types of economic activity, the sole proprietorship is predominant in agriculture in terms of number of firms, employment provided and amount of business done. It also outnumbers the other organizational forms in retail trade and in the services; however, corporations predominate in both volume of sales and number of employees. In the manufacturing and merchandising fields, incorporated companies predominate in all categories. The partnership is predominant in none, neither in number of firms nor in sales nor in employment provided.

In recent years there has been much apprehension concerning the high degree of industrial concentration, and the extent to which Canadian business is externally controlled. Perhaps the most basic problem confronting the nation is how to reap the benefits of large-scale production and foreign capital investment without harming the public interest. As yet we have not resolved this dilemma.

In Canada, as in other countries, a substantial proportion of goods and services is produced by publicly-owned business firms. While it has its place, even in a private enterprise economy, government ownership and control of corporations has a number of definite limitations. These follow from the bureaucratic nature of government operations.

In general, it would appear that approximately 50 percent of new businesses fail during the first few years of operation, and that about 95 percent of all failures are due to the shortcomings of management.

Exercises and Questions for Discussion

1. Evaluate the statement: "Separation of ownership and control is common in Canadian corporations because only in very few instances does any one stockholder control 51 percent of the voting stock".
2. Mr. Jones goes into the business of making lamp shades. What kind of business organization is implied by each of the following situations:
   a. He invests $30,000 of his own money and hires Mr. Smith along with 10 other men to work for him.
   b. He invests $30,000 of his money, borrows $20,000 from Mr. Smith, agreeing to pay it back over a five-year period at 6 percent interest, and hires Mr. Smith along with 10 other men to work for him.
   c. He, his wife, Mr. Smith, and Smith's wife apply for a provincial charter for their business. They sell 1000 shares at $50 per share. Mr. Jones manages the business while Mr. Smith and 10 other men work for him.
   d. He invests $30,000 of his money and $30,000 of Smith's, with the agreement that they will share equally in the profits of the business. Jones manages the business, and Smith along with 10 other men work for him.
3. Indicate in each of the following cases whether a business firm is using debt financing or equity financing:
   a. It sells a $10,000 long-term bond.
   b. It sells 1000 shares of stock at $10 a share.
   c. It obtains a loan of $10,000 from a chartered bank.
   d. It obtains a loan of $10,000 from a friend of the manager.
   e. It uses $10,000 out of last year's earnings.
   Explain your answer for each case.
4. Five individuals jointly form a flying club and purchase an airplane. Should they form a partnership or a corporation? Explain your answer in detail.

5. "The day of the small business is past". Do you agree with this statement?
6. What are the two opposing views often advanced in answer to the question, Is big business bad for the economy?
7. Can you give reasons for the public ownership of corporations?
8. Popular opinion has it that when a government and business are interrelated, a less efficient business enterprise generally results. Do you agree? Why?
9. Should Canada take steps to restrain the growth of foreign control over business enterprise in this country? Justify your answer.
10. Can a business be an economic failure and not a financial failure? Can it be a legal failure and not an economic failure? Do you believe the only cause of failure is managerial inaptitude? Give your reasons.

Selected Readings

Ashley, C. A., and Smyth, J. E., *Corporate Finance in Canada*. Toronto: The Macmillan Company of Canada Ltd., 1966.

Berle, A. A., and G. C. Means, *The Modern Corporation and Private Property*. New York: Commerce Clearing House, 1932.

Government of Canada, Department of Industry, Trade and Commerce, *How to Run a Business*. Ottawa: Queen's Printer, 1968.

Guthmann, H. G., and Dougall, H. E., *Corporate Financial Policy*. Englewood Cliffs: Prentice-Hall Inc., 1962.

Rosenbluth, G., "The Relation between Foreign Control and Concentration in Canadian Industry", *The Canadian Journal of Economics*, February, 1970, pp. 14-39.

Safarian, A. E., *Foreign Ownership of Canadian Industry*. Toronto: McGraw-Hill Co. of Canada, 1966.

4

Market, Demand: Supply and Prices

Prices play a stellar role in economic analysis, although this is not always apparent to us as buyers or sellers of goods and services. When we buy textbooks or clothing or entertainment, what is most apparent to us is that we would prefer lower prices. As sellers of used books, labour, services, and well-worn automobiles we seldom receive prices as high as we would like them to be. What causes prices to be what they are?

This chapter focuses on the principles that apply not only to the pricing of consumer goods and services but also to the determination of wage rates, land rents, and the returns on capital goods. The market situation that forms the framework of price determination as it is discussed in this chapter is a simplified one called *pure competition* and its main characteristics will be explained at appropriate points. In a purely competitive market setting the price of any product, service, or resource is determined by the interacting forces of demand and supply. We shall analyze demand and supply in turn and then demonstrate how they interact to determine price. The chapter concludes with an examination of the elasticity of demand.

Markets

Is a market a physical place where buyers and sellers make contact with each other and engage in exchange? It may be, but this is a marked oversimplification. Buyers and sellers need not confront each other physically as they do at an auction or in a grocery store. Many kinds of transactions can be carried out by telephone or by mail. The important point is that a market exists wherever buyers and sellers of a product or service are in touch with one another and can engage in exchange.

The areas embraced by different markets vary widely depending partly upon the nature of what is being exchanged. The markets for some items are local. People seldom travel beyond the neighbourhood, to say nothing of the city itself, to get a haircut. Other markets are regional. For milk and fresh dairy products, the possibility of spoilage precludes shipment across the continent. Some markets are national in scope. Light airplanes from all over the nation are listed in trade publications, and a prospective buyer or seller will go almost anywhere in the country for an advantageous exchange. Still other markets, like that for such well-known securities as Dominion Foundries and Steel stock, operate on an international basis.

The extent of a market will depend, too, on whether we are thinking in terms of a short or a long period of time. Over a short period—say six months—accountants in the Windsor area may not be willing to consider employment in other cities because their homes, their families, and their friends are in Windsor. For this time period the market for accountants would be local. But if business activity in the city should become permanently slack, for example, if Ford and other automobile manufacturers moved elsewhere, better long-term earning possibilities in Hamilton or Toronto might very well entice accountants away from Windsor. The extent of the market is correspondingly broader, but a time period of several years may be required to make it so.

Demand

The behaviour of buyers in the market for a specific good or service is summed up in the term *demand*. We often speak of demand for a product as being some quantity of it that people need, but we shall find that the quantity demanded or needed is not invariate. Rather, it is determined by several factors that will be explored in some detail in this section.

Demand Schedules and Demand Curves

The determinants of demand are best explained in terms of a *demand schedule* or a *demand curve*. Supppose we ask ourselves how much margarine per year will be purchased in a given market. An immediate and important observation comes to mind—the quantity that will be taken depends upon its price. From everyday experience with many goods and services we know that at higher prices less will be taken than at lower prices. This *law of demand* is usually illustrated with a demand schedule or a demand curve showing the quantities that will be purchased at all alternative prices, other things being equal. Such a demand schedule is presented in Table 4–1.

The demand schedule must be read correctly. Note that in the table the quantity column shows the *rates* at which buyers are willing to purchase the product; that is, it shows the quantities per month they are willing to purchase. Unless we specify the time period during which the quantities will be taken, the figures in this column have no real meaning. For example, at a price of 70 cents the schedule states that buyers are willing to take 4000 pounds. If the time period were not specified, we could infer 4000 pounds per month or per year or per day, and the information would be meaningless. However, the quantity column states that the product will be purchased by buyers at a rate of 4000 pounds per month and this is information that makes sense.

TABLE 4–1
Hypothetical Demand Schedule for Margarine

PRICE OF MARGARINE (CENTS PER LB.)	QUANTITY OF MARGARINE (LBS. PER MONTH)
100	1,000
90	2,000
80	3,000
70	4,000
60	5,000
50	6,000
40	7,000
30	8,000
20	9,000
10	10,000

The quantity column shows rates of purchase at *alternative* possible prices. Thus if the price were 70 cents per pound, purchasers would be willing to take only 4000 pounds per month; but if the price were 60 cents per pound, they would be willing to take 5000 pounds per month. Each price–quantity combination must be thought of as a separate and distinct alternative showing the total amount that buyers will take per time period at the indicated price.

A *demand curve* conveys the same information as a demand schedule, but it shows the information graphically instead of arithmetically. The demand schedule of Table 4–1 is plotted as a demand curve in Figure 4–1. Price per pound is measured along the vertical axis and pounds per month that would be purchased are measured along the horizontal axis.

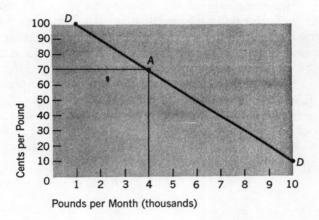

Figure 4–1
A demand curve for margarine.

Any point on the demand curve shows the quantity that would be taken at a particular price, or, alternatively, the price that consumers would be willing to pay for a particular quantity. For example, point *A* shows that at a price of 70 cents per pound, purchasers would be willing to take as much as 4000 pounds per month. It also indicates that for a total of 4000 pounds per month purchasers would be willing to pay as much as 70 cents per pound.

The Law of Demand

The law of demand, which states that more of a product will be purchased at lower prices than at higher prices, is not startlingly new to any of us, but the proposition is an important one in economic analysis. One of its most important implications is that for any given product, price can go high enough to induce purchasers voluntarily to limit their total purchases to the quantity available. This rationing function of price will be discussed in more detail later. Why do purchasers buy less at higher prices than at lower prices? In a way this seems a little like asking why water runs downhill, but our understanding of demand will be more complete if we look at the forces that are operative.

As higher prices of a product are considered by prospective purchasers, a *substitution effect* is at work. The higher the price of steak relative to that of pork chops, the less satisfaction a given expenditure on steak will yield relative to the same expenditure on pork chops—or the more satisfaction the expenditure will yield relatively when spent on pork chops instead of on steak. Thus as the price of steak rises, pork chops are substituted for steak and the total quantity of steak purchased decreases.

Additionally, there is usually an *income effect* at work. An increase in product prices when the dollars that purchasers have to spend is fixed reduces the quantities that can be purchased. A rise in the price of steak reduces the purchasing power of consumers, causing them to buy less steak as well as less of many other goods and services. The income effect ordinarily reinforces the substitution effect, making quantities purchased of any good or service vary inversely with the price.

Changes in Demand

The concept of a demand curve must be sharpened in order to avoid confusion over terminology. Suppose that DD in Figure 4–2 is the demand curve for fluid milk in the Montreal area. Price is initially P_1 and the corresponding quantity purchased by consumers is X_1 gallons. Now suppose that price falls to P_2 and quantity takes increases to X_2. Has demand for fluid milk changed? Alternatively, suppose that a new calcium diet catches on in the area, increasing the intensity of consumer preferences for milk, so that at price P_1 consumers now want X_2 rather than X_1 gallons. Has demand for fluid milk changed?

If we refer to both of the foregoing circumstances as a change in demand, we invite analytical chaos. They are quite different situations. At the outset, then, we shall assign specific terminology to each situation and adhere to it throughout the book. We shall call the first case a *movement along a given demand curve*, or *a change in quantity demanded* because of a price change, and the second case a *change in demand*.

We should think of the term demand as referring to an entire demand curve. It expresses the functional relationship between the price of a product and the quantity of the product that buyers in the market are willing to take, other things being equal or constant. Thus a movement from A to B in Figure 4–2 is not a change in demand according to our terminology.

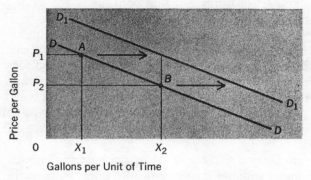

Figure 4–2
A change in demand.

A change in demand means a change in the position or slope of a demand curve. In Figure 4–2 if the demand curve moves from DD to D_1D_1, an *increase in demand* has occurred. This increase may result from such factors as an increase in consumer incomes, anticipation of an imminent increase in the price of the product, an increase in the price of powdered milk, or a decrease in the price of cereals. Conversely, a movement of the demand curve from D_1D_1 to DD represents a *decrease in demand*. The causes of a decrease will be the opposite of those that bring about an increase in demand. It is worth noting that when we define demand for a product, stipulating that "other things" remain constant, we are in no sense leaving the possibility of changes in the "other things" out of consideration. We are setting up an analytical apparatus that permits us to take explicit account of such changes.

"Other Things Being Equal"

We have just noted that the price of a product is not the only factor that affects the quantity of it that consumers in the market are willing to purchase. Several other forces are operative, the most important ones being consumer preferences, consumer incomes, consumer expectations, and the prices of related goods. A change in any one of these will change the quantity of the product that consumers are willing to purchase even if there is no change in the product price. Consequently, to establish how differences in the price alone of a product affect the quantities that consumers will take, we must rule out changes in these "other things." Only if the other things are held constant can we establish a demand curve showing a unique set of quantities that consumers are willing to take at alternative prices.

Consumer preferences refer to the intensities of consumers' desires for products. The preferences of consumers for some items change rather slowly over time. Housing and staple food items are examples. For other items preferences may change rather rapidly, for example, styles of women's clothes. Changes in preference change the demand curve for products. A given demand curve for one product can be established only on the assumption that preferences are constant at the time the curve is established.

Consumer incomes are thought of in demand analysis as the entire amount of money available for the group of consumers in the market to spend per time period. They consist of earnings plus whatever credit sources are available. Obviously, in order to establish a unique set of quantities demanded at alternative prices of a product, the total dollar purchasing power of the group of consumers must not change. If incomes change either up or down, the demand curve itself will move to the right or to the left.

Consumer expectations also affect the quantities of a product that consumers will take at alternative prices. Suppose that consumers develop an expectation that the price of the product in question will rise sharply in the near future. They are likely to increase their rate of purchase at the present price over what it would have been had the change in expectations not occurred; that is, the demand curve shifts to the right. The state of consumer expectations must be assumed constant for a given demand curve to be established for a product.

The effect of changes in the *prices of related goods* on the quantities taken of a given good at alternative prices depends upon the nature of the relationship. Related goods may be complements or substitutes. *Complementary goods* are those that must be consumed together, such as tennis rackets and tennis balls. *Substitute products* are those such as beef and pork that can be consumed in lieu of one another.

Suppose that we are trying to establish a demand curve for tennis balls. We have determined that at a price of 50 cents per ball the market will take 1000 balls per month. But now the price of rackets suddenly doubles. Tennis players cut down on their rates of purchases of rackets and on their tennis activity. The quantity of balls that consumers will take at 50 cents each drops to some figure such as 700 per month. Thus a rise in the price of one of two complementary goods will decrease demand for the other, so in defining the demand curve for one the price of the other must be held at a constant level.

Substitute products affect each other the other way around. A rise in the price of pork will cause people to increase their consumption of beef if beef prices remain unchanged. Consequently, the price of pork must be assumed to remain constant when we establish the demand curve for beef.

Supply

We use the concept of *supply* to analyze the sellers' side of a market, and many of the points developed in demand analysis can be carried over to the supply side. We first examine supply schedules and supply curves and then identify the "other things being equal." Finally, we differentiate between movements along a supply curve and changes in supply.

Supply Schedules and Supply Curves

What determines the quantities of margarine that sellers will place on sale in a given market? Obviously price will be an important determinant, but additional factors are also operative. In order to handle ail of them analytically we define supply of a product as *the quantities that all sellers are willing to place on the market at alternative prices, other things being equal.* A hypothetical supply schedule for margarine is given in Table 4–2 and is plotted as a supply curve in Figure 4–3.

TABLE 4–2
Hypothetical Supply Schedule for Margarine

PRICE OF MARGARINE (CENTS PER LB.)	QUANTITY OF MARGARINE (LBS. PER MONTH)
10	2,000
20	3,000
30	4,000
40	5,000
50	6,000
60	7,000
70	8,000
80	9,000
90	10,000
100	11,000

Whereas demand curves generally slope downward to the right, supply curves ordinarily are upward sloping. The reasons for this are not hard to find. First, at higher prices it becomes more attractive to sellers to place goods on the market rather than to hold them in inventory. Second, at

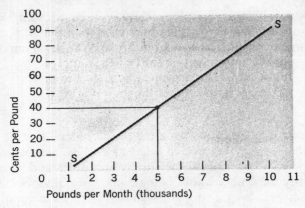

Figure 4–3
A supply curve for margarine.

higher prices the most profitable sales levels for existing producers are ordinarily greater than they are at lower prices. Third, higher profit possibilities attract new sellers into the field, expanding still more the total quantities made available for sale at higher prices.

Changes in Supply

The same considerations apply to supply as apply to demand in differentiating between a movement along a supply curve and a change in supply. We shall use the term supply to mean an entire supply curve. Accordingly, a movement from *C* to *D* in Figure 4–4 is not a change in supply but a change in *quantity supplied* as a result of a change in the product price. The supply curve has not moved.

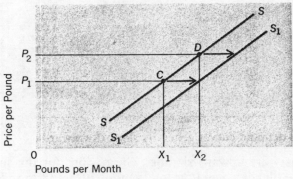

Figure 4–4
A change in supply.

A *change in supply* is represented by a change in the position or shape of the supply curve, such as that from SS to S_1S_1 in Figure 4–4. An *increase in supply* is a movement or shift of the supply curve to the right, while a *decrease in supply* is represented by a shift to the left. These shifts are caused by changes in the "other things."

"Other Things Being Equal"

As with demand, in order to establish a unique functional relationship between the price of a product and the quantity of it that sellers will place on the market, there are "other things" that must be held constant. These are, of course, the factors other than price that influence the quantities that sellers want to sell. The most important are (1) resource prices, (2) the range of production techniques available to producers of the product, and (3) producer expectations. Changes in any or all of these factors will affect the quantities per time period that sellers will place on the market at any given price.

Consider first the effects of different *resource price levels* on supply. Suppose that at current resource prices the sellers of Figure 4–3 are willing to place 5000 pounds of margarine per month on the market at a price of 40 cents per pound. Now suppose that prices of the resources used in making and marketing the product fall by 10 percent. Sellers can now place the 5000 pounds on the market at a lower price, or at the same price they can place a larger quantity on the market. Either alternative should be interpreted as a move off the supply curve SS. Thus in defining a given state of supply or a given supply curve resource prices must be held constant.

Similarly, if *production techniques* become more efficient, production of any particular quantity of a product per month becomes less expensive for producers. This amounts to saying that at any given price such as 40 cents per pound, sellers can place more than 5000 pounds per month on the market. It is clear then that in establishing a specific supply curve the state of production techniques must be held constant.

Changes in *producer expectations* operate in much the same way as do changes in consumer expectations. Suppose again in Figure 4–3 that initially at some such price as 40 cents per pound producers, expecting no price changes, would place 5000 pounds of margarine on the market. Now suppose that a decrease in the price of butter is believed to be just around the corner. Large quantities of margarine will be thrown ón the market at 40 cents and a movement to the right of supply curve SS occurs. In order to stake out a given supply curve, then, producer expectations must remain constant.

Determination of Market Price and Quantity Exchanged

Buyers and sellers interact in markets to determine product prices. Demand curves bring together the forces motivating buyers, while supply curves accomplish the same thing with respect to sellers. In this initial discussion of price determination the market is assumed to be one of pure competition, a market form less complex than others to be discussed later. We shall explain first the concept of pure competition. Next, we shall see how the price and the quantity exchanged of a product are determined under given conditions of demand and supply. Finally, we consider the impacts of changes in demand and supply on market price and quantity exchanged.

Pure Competition

There are three essential conditions that must be met in a market if it is to be one of pure competition: (1) there must be many buyers and many sellers of whatever is being bought and sold in the market; (2) there must be no collusion among buyers or sellers; and (3) there must be no price fixing.

The condition that there be many buyers and many sellers in the market means that there must be enough of each so that any one buyer or any one seller is insignificant relative to the market as a whole. What does insignificance mean in this context? On the buying side it means simply that no single buyer takes enough of the product to influence product price. How important are your purchases of bread at the neighborhood supermarket? Are they important enough for the store to sell to you at a penny less than the posted price rather than to lose you as a bread customer? Similarly, insignificance on the selling side means that an individual seller cannot by himself influence price. Suppose you are a cotton farmer. You can sell only at the going market price—or below. If you try to charge more per bale than the market price, no one will buy from you, since cotton is available from others at the market price.

The absence of collusion is largely a self-evident concept. It means that buyers do not "gang up" on sellers to force them to sell at lower prices and that sellers do not "gang up" on buyers to force them to buy at higher prices.

The absence of price fixing is closely related to the foregoing points. Prices in purely competitive markets are free to move up and down. They are not set by guidelines, minimum wage or price laws, price ceiling laws, or by such private organizations as sellers' associations or labour unions. They are responsive to changes in demand and supply.

Equilibrium Price and Quantity

Suppose we bring the buyers and sellers of margarine together to see how the price and quantity exchanged are determined in a given market. The demand schedule of Table 4–1 appears as columns (1) and (2) of Table 4–3, while the supply schedule of Table 4–2 is shown as columns (2) and (3) of Table 4–3. The meaning of column (4) will become clear shortly.

What will happen if the price of margarine is initially toward the upper end of the range of alternative possible prices—say at 70 cents per pound? The demand schedule shows the reactions of the buyers as a group. They are willing to take only 4000 pounds per month. However, according to the supply schedule, sellers will place 8000 pounds per month on the market at that price, and a surplus of 4000 pounds per mouth, shown in column (4), will come into existence.

Surpluses in the hands of individual sellers set in motion forces that drive the price down. One seller believes that if he lowers his price to slightly less than 70 cents, buyers will favour him and he can unload his surplus. But each of the other sellers thinks the same. In the absence of collusion, they undercut each other. The price drops to 60 cents per pound but surpluses still occur. The undercutting process continues and the price drops to 50 cents per pound. At that price buyers want to buy and sellers want to sell 6000 pounds per month. Because surpluses are no longer being brought into existence, the incentive to undercut no longer exists. Sellers can sell all they want to bring to market at that price.

What happens if the market opens at 30 cents per pound? Buyers want 8000 pounds but sellers are willing to place only 4000 pounds per month on the market. Altogether consumers are 4000 pounds short of what they would like to buy each month at that price. Any individual consumer, unable to get as much as he wants at the going price, will reason that if he offers sellers slightly more than 30 cents per pound they will prefer to sell to him and his personal shortage will be alleviated. Other buyers reason the same way and the price is bid up to 40 cents per pound. The higher price then causes consumers to reappraise their positions and to cut the total amount they are willing to take to 7000 pounds. Sellers, finding the 40 cent price more profitable than the 30 cent price, expand the total monthly amount that they place on the market to 5000 pounds. However, since consumers are still 2000 pounds short of what they would like to have each month, an incentive exists for them to bid the price even higher.

TABLE 4–3
Hypothetical Demand, Supply, and Market Price of Margarine

(1)	(2)	(3)	(4)
			SURPLUS (+) OR SHORTAGE (−)
QUANTITY DEMANDED (LBS. PER MONTH)	PRICE (CENTS PER LB.)	QUANTITY SUPPLIED (LBS. PER MONTH)	(LBS. PER MONTH)
1,000	100	11,000	(+) 10,000
2,000	90	10,000	(+) 8,000
3,000	80	9,000	(+) 6,000
4,000	70	8,000	(+) 4,000
5,000	60	7,000	(+) 2,000
6,000	50	6,000	Neither
7,000	40	5,000	(−) 2,000
8,000	30	4,000	(−) 4,000
9,000	20	3,000	(−) 6,000
10,000	10	2,000	(−) 8,000

At 50 cents per pound, buyers cut the amount they are willing to take per month to 6000 pounds, and sellers expand the quantity they are willing to place on the market to the same amount. The incentive to bid the price higher has been eliminated.

This price and this quantity exchanged—50 cents and 6000 pounds per month—are called, respectively, *the equilibrium price and quantity*. At any other price forces are set in motion that tend to drive the price back to the equilibrium level. This is the level toward which the price will gravitate and settle as long as demand and supply remain as shown by Table 4–3.

This analysis can be presented easily and quickly by means of a demand curve and a supply curve drawn in the same diagram. In Figure 4–5

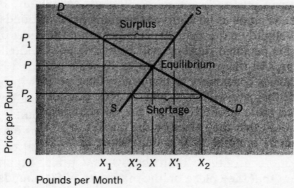

Figure 4–5
Equilibrium price and quantity.

note that at price level P_1, consumers take quantity X_1 per month, while sellers place quantity X'_1 on the market. Thus sellers find themselves accumulating surpluses at a rate of X'_1 minus X_1 per month. This situation induces individual sellers to undercut each other, thus forcing the price down. As the price falls, sellers bring smaller and smaller quantities per month to market while at the same time buyers purchase larger and larger quantities. Finally, when price has fallen to P and quantity exchanged is at X, there is no incentive for buyers or sellers to make further changes in the price and the quantity exchanged.

If the price were initially at P_2 rather than at P_1, buyers would want to buy quantity X_2. Sellers bring to market X'_2, and a shortage of X_2 minus X'_2 per month occurs. This provides an incentive for individual consumers to bid up the price. As the price rises, sellers are induced to place larger quantities per month on the market, whereas buyers are induced to ration themselves to smaller and smaller quantities. When the price level reaches P and the quantity exchanged is at X, the incentives for change no longer exist.

Changes in Demand

In the dynamic world in which we live we do not expect demand for any specific good or service to remain permanently fixed. Consumer preferences change; incomes increase; price changes in some goods cause demand changes for related goods; expectations change; and so on.

Suppose we look at the impact of a change in consumer preferences away from chicken and toward beef. In Figure 4–6(a) the initial demand for and supply of beef are D_bD_b and S_bS_b, so that P_b and B are the equilibrium price and quantity exchanged. The initial demand for and supply of chicken are D_cD_c and S_cS_c in Figure 4–6(b), making P_c and C the equilibrium price and quantity exchanged.

The shift in preferences increases the demand for beef to $D_{b1}D_{b1}$, creating a shortage of BB' at the original price P_b. Consumers bid against each other for the available supply, driving the price up. As the price rises, consumers restrict or ration their purchases more and more while sellers place larger and larger quantities per month on the market. When the price reaches the P_{b1} level, the quantity that buyers want to buy will be the same as the quantity that sellers want to sell. Thus P_{b1} and B_1 are the new equilibrium price and quantity exchanged. We can draw from this analysis the general principle that *an increase in demand ordinarily will increase both the price and the quantity exchanged of a product or service.*

In Figure 4–6(b) the demand for chicken decreases from D_cD_c to $D_{c1}D_{c1}$, resulting in a surplus of $C'C$ pounds per month at the initial price P_c. Sellers undercut each other to get rid of their individual surpluses. As the price falls, consumers increase the quantities they are willing to buy. Sellers curtail their sales levels as the production and sale of chicken becomes less profitable. At the price level P_{c1} and the quantity exchanged C_1 equilibrium under the new demand conditions is established. The

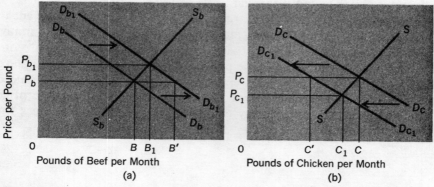

Figure 4–6
(a) Effects of an increase in demand.   (b) Effects of a decrease in demand.

general principle illustrated here is that *a decrease in demand ordinarily will decrease both the price and the quantity exchanged of a product or service.*

Changes in Supply

Changes in the conditions of supply of specific goods and services take place constantly in the economy. New resources are being discovered and existing ones are being improved. New products are developed and resources are diverted from other products toward the production of the new ones. New techniques of production are developed. Resource prices change as conditions of demand for and supply of them change.

We shall look first at an increase in supply. In Figure 4–7, D_rD_r and S_rS_r are the initial demand and supply curves for colour television receivers and P_r and R are the equilibrium price and quantity. Now suppose that as manufacturers become more familiar with production processes, cost-saving technology is developed. The supply curve will shift to the right, to some position such as $S_{r1}S_{r1}$. At the initial price P_r surpluses of

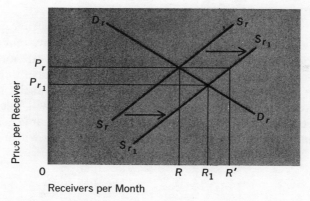

Figure 4-7
Effects of an increase in supply.

RR' per month will accumulate. The surpluses trigger undercutting by sellers and the price falls, increasing the quantities that consumers are willing to buy and decreasing the quantities that sellers will produce and place on the market. At price P_{r1} and quantity R_1, equilibrium is reached. The appropriate principle to draw from the example is that *an increase in supply ordinarily will decrease the price and increase the quantity exchanged of a product or service.*

Turning now to the impact of a decrease in supply, let us suppose that in Figure 4–8 we initially have the demand curve and the supply curve for apple pickers' services at D_aD_a and S_aS_a. The initial equilibrium price or wage rate is P_a and the quantity of labour exchanged is A man hours per week. A significant part of the apple picker supply is assumed to come from outside the country, with the foreign workers being given special work permits during the apple harvest season. Now suppose that legislation is enacted prohibiting the use of foreign apple pickers. This is equivalent to raising the prices that must be paid to domestic apple pickers in order to induce the same quantities of labour as before to seek this kind of employment. Or, from another angle, it decreases the quantities of apple picker labour available at each of the alternative possible wage rates. From either view supply decreases to some position $S_{a1}S_{a1}$, and at the price P_a there will be a shortage. Employers, faced with labour shortages, will bid against each other for the available supply. As wage rates rise more man hours of (domestic) apple picker labour are made available and apple growers want to hire smaller quantities. Wage rates will rise to the new equilibrium level of P_{a1} and quantity exchanged will be A_1. The principle here is that *a decrease in supply ordinarily will raise the price of a product or service and decrease the quantity exchanged.*

Changes in Both Demand and Supply

From the analysis of changes in demand and supply we can easily add four corollaries to the principles already deduced. (1) If both demand and supply increase, the quantity exchanged will increase but the price may increase, decrease, or remain the same. (2) Conversely, if both demand and supply decrease, the quantity exchanged will decrease and again the price may increase, decrease, or remain the same. (3) An increase in demand accompanied by a decrease in supply will increase the

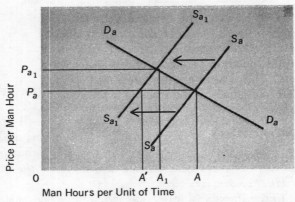

Figure 4–8
Effects of a decrease in supply.

price but the quantity exchanged may increase, decrease, or remain the same. (4) A decrease in demand accompanied by an increase in supply will decrease the price, and again the effects on quantity exchanged depend upon the circumstances of the specific case. It may be useful for the student to draw graphs for these four cases and to experiment with them. The important point to keep in mind is that for any given pair of demand and supply curves there is an equilibrium price and quantity exchanged. A change in demand or supply or both generally leads to a new equilibrium price and quantity combination.

Elasticity

We know that given the demand curve a change in the price of a product usually brings about a change in the quantity demanded even though there is no change in demand. Also we know that given the supply curve a price change usually brings about a change in quantity supplied even though there is no change in supply. But in both cases the door is left open for wide variations in the quantity response to a change in price. To sellers and buyers, as well as to economic analysts, the matter of responsiveness and quantity demanded or quantity supplied to price changes is a significant one. The measure of responsiveness is called *elasticity*. The concept of demand elasticity is more useful in economic analysis than that of supply elasticity, so we shall discuss the former in greater detail.

Elasticity of Demand

An analysis of elasticity of demand falls logically into three parts. First, how is the *responsiveness* of the quantity demanded to changes in the price of a product measured? Second, how do the *effects* of price changes on total spending on a commodity differ for different degrees of responsiveness? Third, what are the *forces that affect the responsiveness of* quantity taken to changes in the price of a product?

Measurement of Elasticity

The degree of responsiveness of quantity demanded to price changes, or the *measure of elasticity of demand*, is found by dividing the percentage change in quantity by the percentage change in price for small price changes. The number resulting from this computation is called the

TABLE 4-4
Elasticity of Demand for Hamburgers

(1) PRICE (CENTS PER HAMBURGER)	(2) QUANTITY (HAMBURGERS PER DAY)	(3) ELASTICITY
100	100	$(-)\ 9$
90	200	$(-)\ 4$
80	300	$(-)\ 2\frac{1}{3}$
70	400	$(-)\ 1\frac{1}{2}$
60	500	$(-)\ 1$
50	600	$(-)\ \frac{2}{3}$
40	700	$(-)\ \frac{3}{7}$
30	800	$(-)\ \frac{1}{4}$
20	900	$(-)\ \frac{1}{9}$
10	1000	

elasticity coefficient, or, more simply, *elasticity of demand*. It can be easily determined given the demand schedule or demand curve for the product being considered. Suppose that the market demand schedule for hamburgers in a small town is that of columns (1) and (2) in Table 4–4. If the price were to fall from 80 cents to 70 cents, the quantity demanded would rise from 300 to 400 per day. The percentage change in quantity is a negative 33⅓ percent, found by dividing the 100-hamburger change by the original quantity of 300. Similarly, the percentage change in price is a positive 12½ percent. Dividing the negative 33⅓ percent by the positive 12½ percent, we find the elasticity coefficient to be a negative 2.67.

All of this is more conveniently done with algebra. Let the Greek letter delta ($\triangle$) mean "the change in." The change in quantity is thus referred to as $\triangle X$. The original quantity is X. The percentage change in quantity is thus $\triangle X/X$. Similarly, if $\triangle P$ is the change in price and P is the original price, the percentage change in price is $\triangle P/P$. If we let the Greek epsilon (ε) represent the elasticity coefficient, then

$$\varepsilon = -\,\frac{\triangle X/X}{\triangle P/P}$$

Why the minus sign? Since the quantity demanded varies inversely with the price, either $\triangle X$ or $\triangle P$ must be negative in sign. They cannot both be positive or both be negative at the same time. Plugging the values of the preceding paragraph into the formula, we find

$$\varepsilon = -\,\frac{100/300}{10/80} = -\,\frac{100}{300} \cdot \frac{80}{10} = -2\tfrac{2}{3}$$

for the decrease in price from 80 to 70 cents.

Suppose the movement of price is from 70 to 80 cents rather than from 80 to 70 cents. The original price is 70 cents and the original quantity is 400 hamburgers. Thus

$$\varepsilon = -\,\frac{100/400}{10/70} = -\,\frac{100}{400} \cdot \frac{70}{10} = -1\tfrac{3}{4}$$

We obtain two different elasticity figures depending upon which way we move between the two price–quantity combinations.

Actually, the discrepancy appears because of the relatively large size of the price change. If the percentage price change had been extremely small, say less than 1 percent, it would have been negligible. Elasticity computations for price changes of 5 percent or larger are subject to considerable error. The smaller the relative price change for which elasticity is computed, the smaller the error will be.

Problems arise, however, in which elasticity must be computed for relative price changes large enough to result in discrepancies like that of the example. In these cases we can find and use an average elasticity coefficient that falls between the two computed above. Economists use two or three different methods of computing such an average, but an easy and convenient one is to use the lower of the two quantities to compute the percentage change in quantity and the lower of the two prices to compute the percentage change in price. In terms of algebra, the elasticity formula becomes

$$\varepsilon = -\frac{\triangle X / X_0}{\triangle P / P_1}$$

in which X_0 is the lower of the two quantities and P_1 is the lower of the two prices.

Using this formula to compute the elasticity of demand for hamburgers, we obtain an elasticity coefficient lying between the negative $2\frac{2}{3}$ and the negative $1\frac{3}{4}$. The percentage change in quantity is $33\frac{1}{3}$, the quotient of 100 hamburgers divided by 300 hamburgers. The percentage change in price is a negative $14\frac{2}{7}$. Thus the elasticity coefficient is a negative $2\frac{1}{3}$, and is more representative of elasticity for the price range of 80 to 70 cents than either of the two previously computed. The elasticities in column (3) of Table 4–4 are all computed in this way.

Turning now to Figure 4–9, we can visualize the formula for elasticity measurement in terms of the demand curve. Starting at an initial price of P_0 and a quantity demanded of X_0, let the price fall to P_1. Quantity demanded increases by $\triangle X$ to X_1. Using the lower of the two quantities as the divisor, we find that the percentage change in quantity is $\triangle X / X_0$. Using the lower of the two prices as the divisor, we find that the percentage change in price is a negative $\triangle P / P_1$. Thus between prices P_0 and P_1.

$$\varepsilon = -\frac{\triangle X / X_0}{\triangle P / P_1}$$

For most demand curves elasticity is high toward the upper end, low toward the lower end, and decreases as price decreases. This situation can be most easily illustrated with a linear or straight line demand curve like that of Figure 4–9. Suppose that for the price change from P_0 to P_1, $\triangle P$ and $\triangle X$ are the same as they are for a price change from P_2 to P_3. When price changes from P_0 to P_1 the percentage change in quantity is great because X_0 is relatively small. The percentage change in price is small because P_1 is relatively large. Consequently, elasticity is relatively high. But for a price change from P_2 to P_3, the percentage change in quantity is much smaller because X_2 is much larger than was X_0. The percentage change in price is much larger because P_3 is much smaller than was P_1. In this second case the percentage change in quantity is smaller, the percentage change in price is larger, and the elasticity coefficient is smaller than in the first case. Obviously, for price changes moving down the demand curve to the right, elasticity will be decreasing.[1] These observations are verified by the elasticity computations in Table 4–4.

Elasticity coefficients can be classified usefully into three groups. When they are numerically greater than one ($\varepsilon > 1$), ignoring the sign, we say that demand is *elastic*. When coefficients are numerically equal to 1 ($\varepsilon = 1$), we say that demand has *unitary elasticity*. And when coefficients are numerically less than 1 ($\varepsilon < 1$), we say that demand is *inelastic*. For example, the demand schedule of Table 4–4 and the demand curve of Figure 4–9 are elastic in the upper regions and inelastic in the lower re-

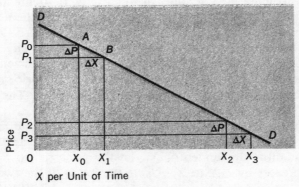

Figure 4–9
Demand elasticity computations.

gions. Between the prices of 60 and 50 cents on the demand schedule, elasticity of demand is unitary. For a linear demand curve such as that of Figure 4–9, unitary elasticity is found at the midpoint; however, this is not necessarily the case for demand curves that are nonlinear.

Effects of Price Changes on Business Receipts

When economists, legislators, sellers, and others consider the market demand for a product they are interested in what will happen to total

[1] *This will be so for demand curves with less curvature than that of a rectangular hyperbola. If the demand curve has the shape of a rectangular hyperbola, for every change in price the percentage change in quantity taken will equal the percentage change in price and the elasticity coefficient will be —1.*

business receipts (equal to total consumer expenditures) for the product when the price is changed. The demand for wheat is a case in point. A most important question for farm policy decisions is what will happen to the total receipts of wheat farmers as a group if a farm program curtailing the supply of wheat is put into effect. Given the demand for the product, the effects of supply changes and the consequent price changes on total receipts of sellers depend upon the elasticity of demand.

Consider the demand schedule for wheat together with the total receipts column in Table 4–5. Note that price decreases for which elasticity is greater than 1 increase total receipts of wheat sellers. Note also that price decreases for which elasticity is less than 1 cause total receipts to decrease. For price increases in both cases the effects on total receipts are just the opposite. When elasticity for a price change is unitary, total receipts will not be affected by a price change.[2]

TABLE 4–5
Demand, Elasticity, and Total Receipts for Wheat

ELASTICITY OF DEMAND	PRICE OF WHEAT ($s PER BU.)	QUANTITY (BU. PER WEEK)	TOTAL RECEIPTS ($s)
$\varepsilon > 1$	1.00	1,000	1,000.00
	.90	2,000	1,800.00
	.80	3,000	2,400.00
	.70	4,000	2,800.00
$\varepsilon = 1$	.60	5,000	3,000.00
	.50	6,000	3,000.00
$\varepsilon < 1$	.40	7,000	2,800.00
	.30	8,000	2,400.00
	.20	9,000	1,800.00
	.10	10,000	1,000.00

Suppose that we look at the same problem with reference to Figure 4–10. The quantity scales of Figure 4–10(a) and (b) are assumed to be identical. The vertical scale of the bottom diagram measures product price while that of the upper diagram measures total receipts of sellers. The curves *TR* and *DD* are, respectively, the total receipts curve for sellers of wheat and the demand curve for wheat. For decreases in price in the region of the demand curve where elasticity is greater than 1 total receipts

[2] *Why is this so? Consider the elasticity formula—the percentage change in quantity divided by the percentage change in price. This means that if demand is elastic, a 1 percent increase (decrease) in price generates a greater than 1 percent decrease (increase) in quantity demanded. The quantity change is thus in the* opposite *direction from and has a greater impact on total receipts than the price change. Can you apply this same line of reasoning to the case in which $\varepsilon < 1$? $\varepsilon = 1$?*

rise. For deceases in price where elasticity is less than 1 total receipts fall.

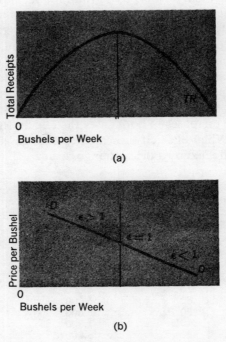

(a)

(b)

Figure 4–10
Price changes, demand elasticity, and total receipts.

If we ask ourselves now what the effects on total receipts of wheat farmers will be of a governmental farm program that decreases the supply of wheat, or if a farm organization withholds supply from the market, we know that the answer turns on the elasticity of demand. In Figure 4–11 suppose that S_1S_1 is the uncontrolled wheat supply curve and that the government succeeds in reducing it to $S'_1S'_1$. Total receipts of wheat farmers will *rise* because the elasticity of demand for the price increase is less than 1. On the other hand, suppose that S_2S_2 is the uncontrolled supply curve and that the government is able to reduce it to $S'_2S'_2$. In this case the receipts of wheat farmers will decrease, since elasticity of demand for the price increase is greater than 1. A farm program designed to increase the total receipts of wheat farmers by reducing the supply of wheat will work only if the elasticity of demand for wheat is less than 1.

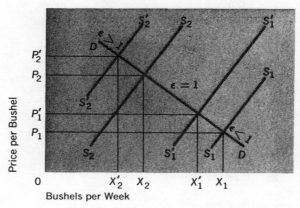

Figure 4-11
Effects of supply decreases under different elasticity conditions.

Determinants of Elasticity

What are the main factors determining whether elasticity of demand for a product is large or small? One of the most important is the *availability of substitutes* for the product to consumers. If several good substitutes for brand X of cigarettes are available, a slight rise in the price of brand X will cause a large switch by consumers to the substitute brands. If the substitute brands are not available, a slight rise in price may cause smokers to smoke somewhat less, but the decrease in quantity taken obviously would be much smaller.

The *importance of a product in consumer budgets* has some influence on elasticity of demand. This factor is most applicable to products occupying positions of insignificance. Pepper provides an example. If the price of pepper were to double, what would happen to the quantity taken off the market? The decrease would not be large because, at double the present price, expenditures for the amount now purchased would still not be large enough for consumers to give it great consideration.

Elasticity of Supply

Not much beyond definition of elasticity of supply is necessary for our purposes. Like the demand elasticity coefficient, that for supply is found by dividing the percentage change in quantity by the percentage change

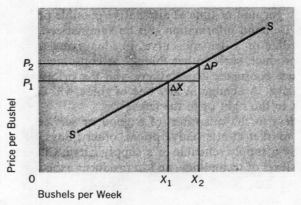

Figure 4–12
Supply elasticity computations.

in price for a small change in price along a given supply curve. In Figure 4–12 supply elasticity for an increase in price from P_1 to P_2 is usually written in the following form:

$$\eta = \frac{\triangle X/X_1}{\triangle P/P_1}$$

The more responsive quantity supplied is to changes in the price of the product, the larger the elasticity coefficient will be. We may note also that the supply elasticity coefficient will be positive in sign for an upward-sloping supply curve, since $\triangle P$ and $\triangle X$ represent changes in the same direction. They are either both positive or both negative, and thus in either case η must be positive.

Summary

This chapter explains the bedrock fundamentals of economic analysis, which include the concept of a market, the nature of demand and supply, the determination of the price of a product or service in purely competitive markets, and the concept of elasticity.

A market for a product or a service exists when buyers and sellers make contact with each other and engage in exchange. The market area varies from local to global, depending upon the nature of what is being exchanged and/or upon the time period under consideration.

Demand for an item refers to the quantities of it that consumers are willing to buy per unit of time at alternative possible prices, other things being equal. Demand information can be summarized in the form of a demand schedule or a demand curve. In identifying a specific demand curve for a product, such "other things" as consumer preferences, consumer incomes, consumer expectations, and the prices of related goods must not change. A change in any one of these will cause the demand curve to shift to the right or to the left.

Supply refers to the quantities of a good or service that sellers will place on the market at alternative prices, other things being equal. It is represented by a supply schedule or a supply curve. Changes in resource prices, in the level of technology, and in producer expectations will cause increases or decreases in supply.

The interaction of buyers and sellers in the market determines the equilibrium price and quantity exchanged of a product in purely competitive conditions. If price is below an equilibrium level, shortages will occur and buyers will bid up the price. If price is above equilibrium, surpluses will cause sellers to undercut each other. Changes in demand or supply or both will cause changes in the equilibrium price and quantity exchanged.

Elasticity of demand refers to the responsiveness of quantity demanded to changes in the price of a product. It is measured by dividing the percentage change in quantity demanded by the percentage change in price for any small price change. Demand may be elastic, of unitary elasticity, or inelastic, and the magnitude of elasticity will determine what happens to total receipts of sellers for price increases or for price decreases. Factors important in determining the elasticity of demand for a product are (1) the availability of substitutes and (2) the importance of a product in consumers' budgets.

Elasticity of supply is a less useful concept than elasticity of demand. It refers to the responsiveness of quantity placed on the market to changes in the price of a product and is measured in the same way as is elasticity of demand.

Exercises and Questions for Discussion

1. Of the following conditions, which would increase a student's demand for hamburgers?
   a. An increase in the price of hot dogs.
   b. An increase in his monthly allowance.
   c. A fall in the price of hamburgers.
   d. A note from the family lawyer that he has inherited $10,000.
   e. A bad piece of pork at a university cafeteria.

   f. A vow to stop smoking.
2. Would you expect the elasticity of demand for the following items to be large or small?
   a. Insulin for diabetics.
   b. Carrots.
   c. Matches.
   d. Automobiles.
   e. Sparkly toothpaste.
   f. Toothpaste.
3. Evaluate the following statements:
   a. If demand for a good decreases and supply remains constant, price will rise and quantity taken will decrease.
   b. If supply decreases and demand remains constant, price will rise and quantity taken will decrease.
   c. If supply decreases and demand decreases, price will fall and quantity demanded will fall.
   d. If demand increases and supply decreases, price will fall but one cannot be sure of the direction of change of quantity.

Selected Readings

Boulding, Kenneth E., *Economic Analysis*, 4th ed., Vol. I. New York: Harper & Row, Publishers, Inc., 1966, Chaps. 7 and 8.

Radford, R. A., "The Economic Organization of a P.O.W. Camp," *Economica*, Vol. XII (November 1945), pp. 189–201.

Smith, Adam, *The Wealth of Nations*, Edwin Cannan, ed. New York: Random House Modern Library edition, 1937, Chaps. VI and VII.

Part 2

The Economy as a Whole

We turn now to the study of the economy as a whole, or, to *macro-economics*. Microeconomic analysis presupposes a given state of affairs from the macroeconomic point of view. It is assumed that unemployment of resources is negligible, and that the economy would, if its resources were correctly allocated, produce almost as much as it is capable of producing. We largely ignore the fact that economic fluctuations occur and that these generate an additional set of problems.

In our study of the economy as a whole we examine the range of issues that surround economic instability. The exposition moves from a simple to a progressively more complex and more complete treatment of the nature of instability, the problems created by it, and its control.

In Chapter 5 we focus on the measurement of economic instability and the effects of instability on economic well-being. In Chapter 6 we introduce a monetary analytical framework that is developed further in Chapters 7 and 8. Chapters 9 and 11 bring government spending and taxation into the picture. These chapters set the stage for the national income analysis of Chapters 11 through 14.

Part 2

The Economy as a Whole

5

Economic Instability

What was your reaction to the recent increase in tuition and fees at your university? What did you think when university housing costs and the food prices at the cafeterias went up? Were you concerned because the money available to you for your education would not go as far after the price increases as it would before? But on the other hand, hasn't your family income risen also? Isn't your family, or at least the average family, able to purchase more goods and services today than it could five years ago? Despite increasing price levels, our levels of living have moved persistently upward because family incomes have been increasing at an even more rapid rate.

We worry about inflation, recession, unemployment, and economic growth without a very clear idea of how or whether these things are related. Our purpose in the next few chapters is to pinpoint the nature of economic fluctuations and their implications for economic well-being and to discuss government policy aimed at controlling them. In this chapter we look specifically at what economic fluctuations are and how they affect us.

Indicators of Economic Performance

We know that the economy does not always run smoothly, but which aspects of its overall performance are of particular importance to us? From the discussion of economic activity in Chapter 1, it is apparent that the *total output* of the economy is of paramount concern. Along with total output, the *level of employment* of resources, particularly labour resources, must rank as a major dimension of economic performance. For less obvious reasons that will be developed as we move through the ensuing chapters, *price level stability* is a third item of crucial importance.[1] In addition, some countries attach much importance to the balance between the nation's foreign receipts and payments.

Total Output

We refer to the value of the economy's total output as *gross national product*, or GNP.[2] Ordinarily the term is used to mean *all* goods and services produced by Canadian residents in final form in a year's time valued at their market prices where they are bought and sold in markets or at the cost of the resources used to produce them where they are not.[3] GNP of Canada since 1926 is presented in **Table 5-1** and is shown graphically in **Figure 5-1** . Note carefully that there are two different kinds of measurements shown on the vertical axis. In reading GNP for different years we interpret the vertical scale as showing millions of dollars. The use of the other kind of measurement, percent, will be explained shortly.

Looking first at column (1) of the table, or at G.N.P. (current dollars)[4] in the graph, we note two things. First, there appears to have been a tremendous growth in G.N.P. over the 42-year period—an increase from $5,146 million to $78,099 million. Second, if we look carefully, we can discern that the growth pattern was not smooth. There was a rapid increase from 1926 to 1929, followed by a sharp decrease to 1933. From 1933 to 1938, a gradual increase occurred, but then as we moved into and

[1]*The term "stability" is used here to mean an absence of large or violent changes and not a complete absence of change.*

[2]*It should be pointed out that Canadian statisticians distinguish between the product of residents of Canada—the* national *product—and the product produced in Canada—the* domestic *product. To determine gross domestic product, it is necessary to add to gross national product, factor incomes paid to nonresidents as a result of production carried on within the geographic boundaries of Canada and to subtract factor incomes paid to Canadian residents as a result of production occurring abroad.*

[3]*National defence is an example of services furnished us that we do not purchase in markets. National income statisticians, as they compute GNP, value it at what it costs.*

[4]*GNP (current dollars) means that for each year the goods and services produced that year are valued at that year's prices—1926 output is valued at 1926 prices; 1927 output is valued at 1927 prices; and so on.*

through World War II, GNP more than doubled in monetary value terms.[5] There was a slight increase from 1945 to 1946 and a small decrease from 1953 to 1954. From 1957 to 1958 and again from 1960 to 1961 the increases were much smaller than the average year-to-year increase. These dips and interruptions in the growth of GNP are indications of what we have come to call *recessions*, and which we shall define more precisely after we have gained more background information.

GNP data alone do not furnish as sensitive or as comprehensive an index of the economy's performance as we might like. They may show a consistent pattern of economic growth and yet tell us nothing about whether or not the economy is producing up to its potential. Further, we sometimes have trouble determining from GNP data alone whether or not a recession or a serious slowdown in economic activity is occurring; the 1957-1958 and 1960-1961 periods are cases in point. We shall return to these matters later.

Employment

Economic fluctuations show up more vividly in the level of unemployment. Indeed, it is here that the impact of depressions and recessions hits hardest. Consumers postpone their purchases of automobiles, homes, refrigerators, and other goods and the dwindling profits induce producers to lay workers off. Imagine, if you can, the situation in 1933 when almost 20 percent of the labour force was unemployed.

Consider for a moment the concepts associated with employment. According to the Dominion Bureau of Statistics, the labour force of the economy consists of all persons 14 years of age or over who are employed, who have a job or business but are temporarily absent when the labour survey is made,[6] who are looking for work, or who are on layoff from a job. The *civilian labour force* consists of these people minus the members of the armed forces. Out of our total population of roughly 21 million, about 8 million comprise the civiliar. labour force. The *employed* at any given time are those who did any work for pay or profit during the reference week or who worked without pay in a family enterprise or who had a job

[5]*As we shall see later, GNP in terms of volume of goods and services did not double. A part of the increase in value terms was due to a rising price level.*

[6]*To provide regular up-to-date information on the labour force in Canada, a monthly labour force survey on an area sample basis is conducted by the Dominion Bureau of Statistics. Interviews are carried out in about 35,000 households in more than 160 different areas of Canada, including 34 cities having a population of 30,000 or over, as well as some smaller urban centres and various rural areas. In the survey, persons are classified on the basis of their activity during the week prior to the survey interview week. This week is called the* reference week.

TABLE 5-1

Gross National Product, Price Levels, and Unemployment Rates in Canada,
1926-1969

Annual Averages	GNP (Millions of Current Dollars)	Implicit Price Deflator (1961 = 100)	GNP (Millions of 1961 Dollars)	Unemployment Rate (Percent of Labour Force)
1926	5,146	50.4	10,203	3.0
1927	5,561	49.8	11,171	1.8
1928	6,050	49.6	12,191	1.7
1929	6,139	50.2	12,237	2.9
1930	5,720	48.8	11,713	9.1
1931	4,693	45.9	10,226	11.6
1932	3,814	41.6	9,166	17.6
1933	3,492	40.8	8,555	19.3
1934	3,969	41.4	9,594	14.5
1935	4,301	41.6	10,343	14.2
1936	4,634	42.9	10,801	12.8
1937	5,241	44.1	11,886	9.1
1938	5,272	44.0	11,984	11.4
1939	5,621	43.7	12,874	11.4
1940	6,713	45.7	14,687	9.2
1941	8,282	49.3	16,800	4.4
1942	10,265	51.5	19,917	3.0
1943	11,053	53.3	20,719	1.7
1944	11,848	55.0	21,539	1.4
1945	11,863	56.3	21,057	1.6
1946	11,885	58.0	20,493	3.4
1947	13,169	63.1	20,861	2.2
1948	15,127	70.8	21,374	2.3
1949	16,300	73.7	22,119	2.9
1950	17,955	75.4	23,809	3.6
1951	21,060	84.2	25,004	2.4
1952	24,042	87.8	27,398	2.9
1953	25,327	87.8	28,862	3.0
1954	25,233	89.2	28,283	4.6
1955	27,895	89.8	31,079	4.4
1956	31,374	92.9	33,780	3.4
1957	32,907	94.8	34,710	4.6
1958	34,094	96.1	35,462	7.0
1959	36,266	98.2	36,929	6.0
1960	37,775	99.4	37,994	7.0
1961	39,080	100.0	39,080	7.1
1962	42,353	101.4	41,778	5.9
1963	45,465	103.3	43,996	5.5
1964	49,783	105.8	47,050	4.7
1965	54,897	109.5	50,149	3.9
1966	61,421	114.5	53,650	3.6
1967	65,608	118.4	55,407	4.1
1968	71,454	123.1	58,041	4.8
1969	78,099	128.3	60,854	4.7

Source: Dominion Bureau of Statistics, National Income and Expenditure Accounts,
1926-1968, August 1969; Bank of Canada, Statistical Summary, *various issues.*

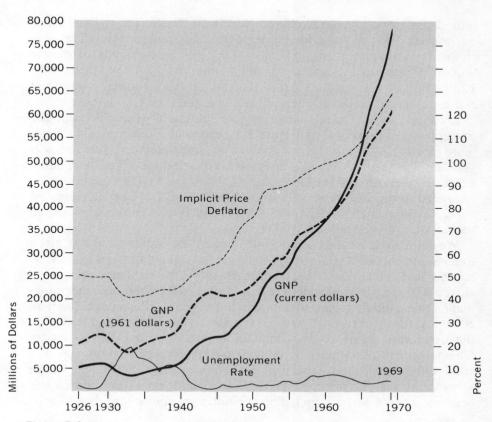

Figure 5-1
GNP, price levels, and unemployment rates in Canada, 1926–1969.

or business, but were not at work, "because of bad weather, illness, industrial dispute or vacation, or because they were taking time off for other reasons" when the survey was made. The *unemployed* are those who "did no work during the reference week and were looking for work (or would have been looking for work except that they were temporarily ill, were on indefinite or prolonged layoff, or believed no suitable work was available in the community)", or "were waiting to be called back to a job from which they had been laid off for less than 30 days". Those *not in the civilian labour force* include the inmates of corrective, penal and mental institutions, T.B. sanatoria, and homes for the aged, infirm and needy (the so-called institutional population); children under 14 years of age; persons over 14 years of age attending school, keeping house (mainly housewives, of course), too old or otherwise unable to work, and voluntarily idle or retired[7]; residents of the Yukon and Northwest Territories; Indians living on reserves (due to their unique economic circumstances). Of a total civilian population, then, of 21,084,000 (there were approximately 96,000 persons in the armed forces) at the end of 1969, there were 12,984,000 (61.5 percent) not in the civilian labour force. Plainly the civilian labour force is considerably less than the total population.

Looking now at the unemployment rate column of Table 5-1 and the unemployment rate curve of Figure 5-1 , economic fluctuations stand out more clearly. In Figure 5-1 , to read off the unemployment rate for each year we use the vertical axis to measure percentages. The very large unemployment rates of the Great Depression of the 1930's were not really alleviated until we were well into World War II. The increases in unemployment in 1953-1954, 1957-1958, and 1960-1961 clearly indicate that all was not well in those periods.

We cannot expect the entire labour force to be employed at any given time. Some part of it is always in the process of moving from one job to another and is therefore listed as unemployed at the time an employment survey is made. Unemployment of this kind is called *frictional unemployment*. Its magnitude is hard to pinpoint, but in general the more affluent an economy, the more time off people can take for job changes and the larger the percentage figure for this kind of unemployment will tend to be. Unemployment of a nonfrictional nature—*involuntary unemployment*—is the difficult and the serious problem that we must face. In general, we seem to think at the present time that an unemployment rate somewhere between 3 and 4 percent, including frictional unemployment, is tolerable.

The Price Level

We are reminded constantly by business columnists in newspapers and periodicals, by television newscasters, by the milkman, and by university professors that the value of the dollar is "going to pot," meaning really that it is decreasing in purchasing power. This latter part of the statement is, of course, correct. The purchasing power of the Canadian dollar in 1969 was about 35 percent of what it was in the mid-1930's. But this does not mean that we are worse off now than we were then; in fact, we know full well that we are much better off.

---

[7]*It may be useful to add that housewives, students and others who worked part-time during the reference week are classified as employed, or if they looked for work as unemployed.*

Price Index Numbers

We measure the changes that occur in the general level of some complex of prices by means of a *price index number*.[8] There are several of these in current use, the most common ones being the consumer price index and the wholesale price index, both compiled by the Dominion Bureau of Statistics. Within each of these broad groups indexes are computed for more narrow classifications of goods and services—for example, for farm products or for consumer durable goods. A broader and more comprehensive price index than either that for consumer goods or that for wholesale goods is the GNP implicit price deflator (generally referred to by D.B.S. as the "implicit price index for gross national expenditures") of Table 5 –1. This is a composite price index intended to measure price level changes for the entire complex of goods and services produced by Canadian residents.

If we construct a simple set of price index numbers for a hypothetical group of goods, we shall understand better what the concept implies. We shall do this in four easy steps. First, from the entire group of goods for which we want to construct the index we choose a representative sample composed of a more limited number. Second, we attach appropriate weightings to each of the representative goods. This is done in order to make commodities count in the price aggregate somewhat in proportion to their economic importance. Third, we make price observations and compute the weighted value of the sample for the years for which we want to construct the index. Fourth, we select a base period—the period with which all other periods are compared—and compute the index.

Consider the first two steps. Suppose that goods X, Y, and Z are representative of the group for which we want to compute the index and that we choose these as our sample. To weight each one we compare their respective sales volumes. Suppose that three units of Y are purchased for every unit of X that is taken and that two units of Z are purchased for every unit of X. We attach a weight of 1 to X, 2 to Z, and 3 to Y. These are listed in the "weight" column of Table 5 –2.

Suppose now that we make the step-three price observations for X, Y, and Z for the years 1966, 1967, and 1968 and that these are duly recorded in the "price" columns of the table. For each of the three years the price of each product is multiplied by the appropriate weight, giving us the weighted values of each good for each of the three years. Now for the year

[8]*An index number is a statistical device used to measure* quantitative *changes in groups of data between one period of time and some other period of time chosen as the yardstick. The object of a price index number then is to combine the prices of a large number of goods and services into a single summary figure which over a period of time will reflect the changes that take place in the group of prices of which it is composed.*

TABLE 5-2

Construction of Price Index Numbers for a Hypothetical Group of Goods
(1967 = 100)

Product	Weight	Price 1966	Price 1967	Price 1968	Weighted Value 1966	Weighted Value 1967	Weighted Value 1968	Price Index 1966	Price Index 1967	Price Index 1968
X	1	$2	$3	$3	$ 2	$ 3	$ 3			
Y	3	4	5	6	12	15	18			
Z	2	6	6	5	12	12	10			
Total					$26	$30	$31	86.7	100	103.3

1966, we sum the weighted values of each good for each of the three years. We do the same thing for 1967 and 1968. These weighted values of the entire sample are recorded at totals of $26, $30, and $31 for the three years, respectively.

The fourth and final step is the computation of the index. In selecting a base year, we should look for a period in which conditions are not unduly disturbed; suppose we select 1967. Now we simply express the weighted value of the entire sample for each year as a percentage of that for the base year, and these percentage numbers are the index numbers. For the 1967 base year, $30 is 100 percent of $30, so the index number for that year is 100. For 1966, $26 is 86.7 percent of $30, so the price index number is 86.7. For 1968, $31 is 103.3 percent of $30, so the price index number is 103.3.

Any one set of price index numbers is intended to reflect the general price movement—both the direction and the magnitude of the movement —of the complex or group of goods for which it is designed. Prices of individual goods making up the complex ordinarily will not all vary in the same proportion. They may even change in different directions over time. In the example of Table 5-2 the movement of the general price level is upward, as is indicated by the set of price index numbers; however, only commodity Y increased in price over all three years. The price of commodity X increased from 1966 to 1967 but remained constant from 1967 to 1968. There was actually a decline in the price of Z from 1967 to 1968.

Changes in the general level of prices of a group of goods, say consumer goods as reflected by a set of price index numbers must always be regarded as approximations. Over time goods change in nature and in quality—an automobile of the mid-1920s was not the same thing as this year's. Weights to be attached to different items in a sample change over time also. A modern consumer price index number sample would attach less relative weight to food prices than one of 40 years ago, since food today occupies a position of less importance relative to other goods than it did at that time.

More faith can be put in an index covering a few years, say five, than in one covering a span of 30 to 40 years, since changes in product quality and patterns of purchase would not be as great during the shorter time span. A price index is no better than the samples and weights selected allow it to be, and these are selected by people who just may on occasion be fallible.

Inflation and Deflation

Changes in the general price level are known as inflation and deflation. *Inflation* is a period in which the general price level is rising and is illustrated by all of the upward movements of the implicit price deflator of Table 5-1 . *Deflation* is a period in which the general price level is falling, or is the opposite of inflation. The best illustration of deflation is the downward movement of the implicit price deflator from 1929 to 1933. Newspaper references to inflation or deflation generally imply a less broadly defined price index, usually the consumer price index.

It should be noted carefully that inflation and deflation refer to price levels in the process of changing. If for a period of three years there were no changes in the price level, there would be neither inflation nor deflation regardless of the absolute level of prices. If prices were then to rise during one year to a higher level, remaining at the new level for three more years, we would say that inflation occurred during the year of rising prices only. During the ensuing three years there is no inflation.

In fact, reference to high or to low prices can be made in relative terms only. What is a high price level? What is a low price level? We can say that prices are high compared with those of some previous time period. Or, alternatively, we can say that prices were low in the previous period as compared with present prices. However, there are no absolute criteria of what is high and what is low.

Economic Fluctuations and the Price Level

Until the 1930's economists concerned with economic fluctuations looked to changes in the general price level as a primary bellweather of economic activity. Recession and depression were expected to be accompanied by—indeed heralded by—falling prices or deflation. Prosperity was expected to be accompanied by either a stable price level or mild inflation. Although these expectations have not been abandoned entirely, they have been considerably modified since the Great Depression.

The trouble with the old theory is that a slowdown in economic activity no longer seems to be accompanied by deflation. Table 5-1 shows the change that seems to have taken place in the relation between economic activity and the price level. The drop in economic activity in the early years of the Great Depression—1929-1933—was accompanied by a decline of some 18 percent in the price level, as the old theory would lead us to expect. As economic activity increased from 1933 to 1937 there was mild inflation. The situation deteriorated in 1938 and the price level fell slightly, as the old theory says it should. Not surprisingly, inflation was the order of the day through World War II, the immediate post-war years (given the enormous backlog of deferred demand for all types of consumer and investment goods, generated by wartime shortages and restrictions), and the Korean War. But from here on the price picture changes. The increase in the unemployment rate of 1954 provides evidence of the decline in economic activity that we call the recession of 1953-1954, *but the price level continued to increase.* The same thing happened in the 1957-1958 recession and again in that of 1960-1961. Either the recessions were not severe or prolonged enough to force prices down or prices have come to be too rigid in a downward direction—that is, not responsive enough to a decrease in demand—for deflation to be a running mate of recession.

Real GNP

Is there any way that we can determine what part of the changes in GNP in current dollars from year to year are actually changes in the output of the economy and what part are merely the result of deflation or inflation? Consider GNP in current dollars for 1956—the $31,374 million is the value of output for that year measured in terms of 1961 prices. If we could "correct" the 1956 GNP for changes in the price level, that is, if we could build the 1956-1961 inflation into it, then a comparison of the "corrected" 1956 GNP and the actual 1961 GNP would be a comparison of actual or *real* outputs. We would have eliminated, or rather, would have taken into account, for comparative purposes, the effects of inflation on GNP from 1956 to 1961.

The set of price index numbers in the form of the implicit price deflators enables us to accomplish what we want to do. Since 1961 serves as the base year, the index of the price level for 1956 means, then, that the 1956 price level was 92.9 percent of that for 1961, or GNP for 1956 in terms of the 1956 price level is 92.9 percent of what it would be in terms of the 1961 price level. Consequently, if we divide $31,374 million by 0.929, the $33,780 million result is 1956 GNP in terms of 1961 prices. The entire GNP (1961 dollars) column is computed in this way. It shows GNP for the entire series of years in terms of 1961 dollars; thus a comparison of the values for different years is a comparison of real outputs and is called *real* GNP.

Potential and Actual GNP

The Economic Council of Canada[9] in recent years has made estimates of the economy's potential GNP, defined as the volume of goods and services that the economy would ordinarily produce under conditions of relatively full and increasingly efficient utilization of resources. These estimates, which reach back only to 1956, are plotted in Figure 5-2 , along with actual GNP for the same series of years. Though the range of years covered is not great and though the estimates of potential GNP are not infallible,[10] the comparison between the two over time provides an excellent base for the study of economic fluctuations.

The difference between potential and actual GNP is called, appropriately, the *GNP gap* or the economic gap. It measures the goods and services lost to the economy because of fluctuations in economic activity.

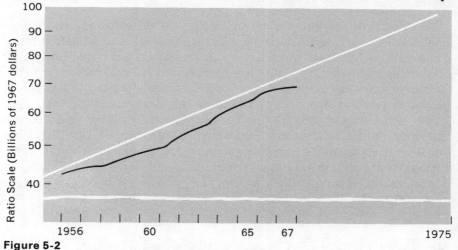

Figure 5-2
Potential and actual GNP, 1956-1975

Source: Economic Council of Canada, Sixth Annual Review, *Ottawa, Queen's Printer, 1969, Chart 2-1, p. 13.*

[9]*The Economic Council of Canada was established by an Act of Parliament in January, 1964, to study and advise upon the medium- and long-term development of the Canadian economy in relation to the attainment of certain basic economic and social goals.*

[10]*In this connection, it should be emphasized that the value of potential GNP depends on both the method of calculation and the assumptions used. Naturally enough, there have been arguments among economists about the possibility of measuring potential output at all. See, for example, Arthur F. Burns,* The Morgan Guaranty Survey, *Morgan Guaranty Trust Company, New York, May, 1961. See also Arthur M. Okun, "Potential GNP: Its Measurement and Significance," Ameri-can Statistical Association: 1962 Proceedings of the Business and Economic Section, American Statistical Association, Washington, D.C., 1962, pp. 98-104.*

The average gap for any one year measures the loss for that year. To make this concept more precise, consider the years 1960 and 1961. As suggested by Figure 5-2 , the GNP gap was quite large at the beginning of the 1960's. According to the Economic Council, actual output in Canada in 1960 and 1961 fell short of its real potential by 6 or 7 percent. (This is not surprising since, by referring back to Table 5-1 , one can see that unemployment for these years hovered about the 7 percent level). Translated into today's levels of production, a GNP gap of this magnitude would represent a loss to the nation approximating $4 billion or $5 billion per year, a loss that would be cumulative for every year in which such a short fall persisted.[11] Clearly over a series of years losses approaching this size add up to a rather staggering total that we could have had—if.

International Balance of Payments

A fundamental disequilibrium in a nation's balance-of-payments position may impede and frustrate its attempts to achieve or maintain other goals such as full employment, high and sustained economic growth or reasonable price stability. Thus the importance of external influences to the Canadian economy necessitates a special concern for the international payments position, the foreign exchange rate and official exchange reserves, and a special need for appropriate reconciliation between internal economic policies and external economic conditions. In short, a viable balance of payments means the maintenance of adequate total international receipts to cover our international payments, a strengthening of our international competitive position, and good access to outside sources of capital.

Nature and Effects of Economic Fluctuations

Why are we so concerned about economic fluctuations? A part of the answer is obvious. When actual GNP is below potential GNP we have fewer goods and services than we could have to consume or to use to add to the productive capacity of the economy. But the answer extends beyond that. In this section we shall dissect and examine fluctuations in order to obtain a more complete picture of how they affect us and to lay the groundwork for analysis in the chapters to some of their causes and how they might be controlled.

[11]*See Economic Council of Canada*, Sixth Annual Review. *Ottawa: Queen's Printer, 1969, pp. 13-14.*

[12]*The subject of international balance of payments is taken up at length in Chapter 16.*

Full-Employment Equilibrium

The circular flow diagram of Figure 2–1 provides a convenient starting point. Suppose that initially actual GNP and potential GNP are equal and that the economic system is in equilibrium. Households are spending all of their incomes and business firms are paying out their entire business receipts to households as resource owners. For all practical purposes there is no involuntary unemployment.

Two additional concepts that will be useful to us are aggregrate demand and aggregate supply. In Figure 5-3 suppose that the total output of the economy is measured along the horizontal axis in some sort of homogeneous physical units—identical baskets of goods. Suppose also that the price level in terms of a set of price index numbers is measured along the vertical axis. *Aggregrate demand* refers to the quantities per time period of all goods and services that will be purchased at alternative price levels. *Aggregate supply* means the quantities per unit of time that will be placed on the market at different price levels.

Figure 5-3 represents the full-employment equilibrium situation described above. The general price level is p and the full-employment output level is X. From Table 5-1 we know that output level X is not fixed for all time. Aggregate supply and aggregate demand ordinarily are moving to the right as the economy's productive capacity expands and as more purchasing power comes into the hands of resource owners. Output X moves to the right and it appears too that the price level tends to rise

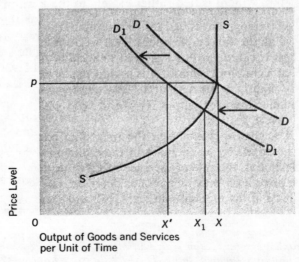

Figure 5-3
Full-employment equilibrium and the effects of a decrease in aggregate demand.

on the average over time. But these dynamic changes are rather complex; we can show what we want to get across at this point with the simple diagram of Figure 5-3 , ignoring for the moment the increases in the full-employment level of GNP over time.

Recession, Depression, and Deflation

Suppose now that total spending in the economy decreases (or fails to increase as fast as it has in the recent past). This can result from any one or a combination of reasons. Political or economic uncertainties may cause people to become more cautious in their spending habits. The government may have taken actions that cause the decline to occur. Or, perhaps, stock market activity generates a wave of pessimism. We shall add to the list of possible causes through the next few chapters.

The change in total spending is reflected in Figure 5-3 by a decrease in aggregate demand (or a failure of aggregate demand to increase as much from year to year as it has in the recent past) to D_1D_1. GNP declines (or fails to increase as much as it has in the recent past), but the amount of the decline depends upon what happens to the price level. If the price level is completely rigid downward at level p—that is, will not decline at all—the volume of goods and services falls off to X'. However, if prices decline as aggregate demand declines, the decrease in real GNP will be smaller—it may decrease to only X_1. (Can you find illustrations of each of these alternatives in the historical data of Table 5-1 ?)

The level of employment is tied rather closely to the level of real GNP. We refer to X as the full-employment level of output for the economy. This is the best it can do with its present quantities of resources and its present level of technology, and for this reason the aggregate supply curve goes only very slightly to the right of X.[13] The employment level for output X' will be smaller than for output X_1—and both will be less than full-employment levels.

We have described a *recession* in the preceding paragraphs. It is ordinarily characterized by an increase in unemployment and by either a substantial decline in the rate of increase of GNP or an absolute decline in GNP. The price level may or may not decrease, but to the extent that it does the effects of the recession on real GNP and employment will tend to be smaller.

The difference between a recession and a depression is one of degree.

[13]*It is possible to have more than a full-employment level of output, temporarily at least, when people for some reason—say patriotism—go to work when they would really prefer not to as a permanent thing. This was illustrated during World War II in 1943, 1944, and 1945.*

Even though every depression starts as a recession, a recession may or may not turn into a full-blown depression.[14] A *depression* is a sharp reduction in economic activity, in GNP and in the employment level, that persists for several years.

Although *deflation* may not occur during a recession, it is almost sure to be present in a depression. The decline into depression from 1929 to 1933 is the latest evidence available on this point; however, the surplus goods and unemployment that would persist over a long depression period would surely exert tremendous downward pressure on the price level. An exception may occur in the case of a country experiencing very rapid inflation. The inflation may engender so much economic uncertainty and loss of confidence that it becomes a proximate cause of depression. This seems to occur rather frequently in the underdeveloped countries of Asia, Africa, and South America.

Economic Effects of Recession, Depression, and Deflation

What are the effects of recession, depression, and deflation on the well-being of the general public? A part of the answer is so obvious that it seems almost silly to ask the question, but some subtle effects are often over-looked. To systematize our thinking, we can divide the effects into two groups: (1) output effects and (2) redistributive effects.

Output Effects

The obvious effects of recession and depression are on the economy's output. In recession the unemployment rate typically rises to some 5–7 percent of the labour force and in depression it rises even more—to approximately 20 percent in the Great Depression of the 1930s. Additionally, capital of different kinds will be underutilized. There will be idle machines and unused plant capacity, more pronounced, of course, in depression than in recession. Actual GNP falls below potential GNP and this means that levels of living are lower than they need be. Although recession does not *necessarily* mean that levels of living decline, depression certainly implies that they do.

Redistributive Effects

As output shrinks during depression and deflation, changes take place

[14]As a matter of fact, most economists believe that we have the knowledge, the techniques, and the necessary sophistication in economic matters on the part of the government to prevent a depression from ever again occurring. We shall develop this line of thought in the next four chapters.

in the distribution of income among families and in the portion of the economy's output that each can claim. The incomes of some families decline more rapidly than those of others; consequently, the former will lose relatively more than the latter from depression. It is even possible that some may gain from depression if the prices they must pay for what they buy decrease in greater proportion than their money incomes. However, there are not likely to be many people in this fortunate position.

One group that loses relatively more from depression than others can be identified immediately. These are the *unemployed*—those who have lost their jobs because of the decline in economic activity.

Another group for whom income declines relatively more when economic activity slows down are *those who furnish resources to durable goods industries and to capital goods industries.*[15] The old car or the old refrigerator can always be replaced later rather than now, so demand for durable goods decreases relatively more than demand for such goods as food. Similarly, business firms can always postpone additions to their plant and equipment, or even replacement of present equipment; consequently, demand for capital goods falls relatively more than demand for most consumer goods. The resource owners hurt most are the owners of the affected businesses and the workers laid off because of the decline in production. Wage rates tend to be quite sticky in a downward direction, especially where unions are strong, and those who remain employed may not be hurt as much, relatively.

During deflation, *salaried employees* frequently find that their incomes decline relatively less than do average incomes. This is particularly the case for the employees of such nonprofit institutions as governments, educational institutions, churches, and those of an eleemosynary nature. They find that as prices move downward the decreases in their incomes are relatively smaller than the decreases in the price level. It is in this group that we find some of those who may gain from depression, although it is by no means certain that any substantial proportion of them will be so affected. Most will simply lose less, relatively, than the average.

Fixed-income receivers stand to gain from deflation. These include persons who receive their incomes in the form of interest, annuity payments, old-age pensions, disability pensions, or other payments of a similar kind. These generally are fixed in terms of dollars per month, so as the price level falls the recipients find that their fixed dollar incomes will buy more and more goods and services.

---

[15]*Durable goods industries are those producing products that are expected to last for several years—automobiles, refrigerators, television sets, and other such items. The capital goods industries produce such goods as basic steel, machines, and tools for industry.*

Debtors are hurt and *creditors gain* from deflation. Suppose that the loans made to a debtor were obtained before deflation occurs and that subsequently the price level declines. When repayment of the loan is made, the number of dollars repaid is equal to the number of dollars borrowed, plus the interest. But since the price level has declined, each dollar repaid will purchase more than each dollar borrowed. So the debtor must repay more purchasing power than he borrowed and the creditor receives back more purchasing power than he loaned out.[16]

Expansion and Inflation

Aggregate demand can increase as well as decrease, leading to an expansion in economic activity or inflation or both. The causes of increases in total spending or in aggregate demand, like the causes of decreases, are varied in nature and will come to light in the next few chapters. For the moment, suppose that both households and business firms have become more optimistic about the future and increase their spending.

What are the effects of the increase in aggregate demand? The effects differ depending upon whether or not the gap between actual and potential GNP is large or small. The size of the gap, together with the rate at which aggregate demand increases, will also determine the amount of inflation that occurs. Again we shall consider in turn (1) the output effects and (2) the redistributive effects.

Output Effects

When the actual GNP of the economy is well below the potential GNP some inflation ordinarily accompanies, and may be a necessary part of, the process of recovery and expansion. Consider, for example, the Canadian economy in 1933 and the years immediately following. Unemployment of labour resources amounted to almost 20 percent of the labour force. There was much unused plant capacity and other capital equipment. In Figure 5-4 , suppose we represent the 1933 state of affairs by an aggregate demand of *DD* and an actual GNP of *X*, well below the full-

---

[16]*As an illustration, suppose that Mr. A obtains a standard bank loan of $120 for one year, with interest at 6 percent paid in advance on the entire principle and with the principle plus interest ($127.20) to be repaid in 12 equal monthly installments of $10.60 each. If the price level falls by 50 percent, the purchasing power represented by each monthly installment is twice what it should have been if deflation had not taken place. To the debtor, the $10.60 monthly installment is twice what it would have been had there been no deflation—that is, it is as though he must repay $21.20 for every $10.60 that he originally owed. To the creditor, the situation is just the reverse—every $10.60 payment he receives will purchase as much for him as $21.20 would have had there been no deflation.*

employment or potential GNP of X_3. An increase in aggregate demand to D_1D_1 now occurs, and at the 1933 output level of goods and services some shortages will arise. These shortages cause prices to rise and business to become somewhat more profitable, providing incentives for expansion in productive activity. Unemployed resources are drawn into production and

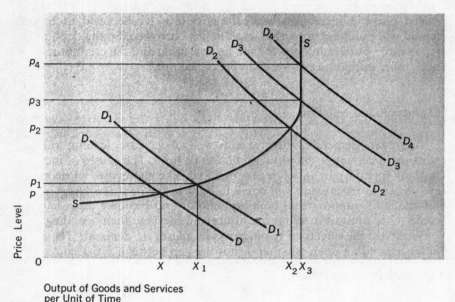

Figure 5-4
The effects of increases in aggregate demand.

the subsequent increase in consumer incomes tends to bring about a further increase in aggregate demand, and the process repeats itself as recovery progresses.

Though the expansion and recovery process is led by inflation, the increases in the price level will tend to be small when the actual-potential GNP gap is large. Note in Table 5-1 the small price level increases from 1933 to 1937. It takes very little in the way of price increases to stimulate business expansion under these circumstances. When large amounts of resources are unemployed, job opportunities rather than higher resource prices are the important factors in the expansion of employment levels, so expansion can take place with only a very small increase in production costs. In Figure 5-4 we represent this situation with a very flat segment of the aggregate supply curve for the increase in aggregate demand from DD to D_1D_1.

The smaller the actual-potential GNP gap becomes, the more effect increases in aggregate demand will have on the price level and the less they will have on output. As aggregate demand increases toward D_2D_2 and then toward D_3D_3 the economy is moving closer and closer to the full-employment level of GNP. But before the full-employment level of *all* resources is reached, full employment will have been reached for *many* resources, particularly those that are most efficient in producing the goods and services most urgently desired. As full-employment levels of the most efficient resources are reached, firms must turn to those that are less and less productive. At the same time, they will bid the prices of the more productive resources higher and higher. When the full-employment level is reached for *all* resources, further increases in aggregate demand can only increase the price level. The economy's output can increase no more.

The distribution of the effects of increases in aggregate demand between the economy's level of output and the price level is illustrated in Figure 5-4 . When unemployment is great and there is a large gap between actual and potential GNP, an increase in aggregate demand is absorbed almost entirely by an increase in output and employment. As unemployment diminishes and the gap becomes smaller, increases in aggregate demand have more and more of an impact on the price level and less and less influence on output. Finally, when full employment is reached, any further increases in aggregate demand must be absorbed entirely by increases in the price level. These effects give the aggregate supply curve its unique curvature.

Redistributive Effects

Economic expansion and inflation, like contraction and deflation, bring about a redistribution of income. When less than full-employment levels of economic activity prevail both redistributive and output effects occur at the same time, but once the economy has reached a full-employment level of output, inflation brings about redistributive effects only. Suppose we consider the redistributive effects, starting from an initial situation in which actual GNP is substantially below potential GNP.

As expansion and inflation occur, the incomes of some groups will increase relatively more than those of others. The most obviously favoured group is made of those whose resources have been unemployed and which are now put back to work. Another group favoured by expansion includes those who furnish resources to durable goods and capital goods industries. While these industries undergo more severe contractions during recession and depression, they also experience more vigorous expansion in prosperity and inflation than do other consumer goods industries.

Debtors gain from inflation while *creditors lose*, relatively. An increase in the price level in the interim between obtaining a loan and repaying it works in the debtor's favour. Because of the rising price level the dollars that he must repay have less purchasing power than those that he borrowed. The creditor, on the other hand, receives back less purchasing power than he loaned out.

Fixed-income receivers lose when inflation occurs. Those whose money incomes consist of fixed amounts of interest, pensions, annuities, and the like find that they can buy less and less as the price level rises. Salaried employees of the government, of educational institutions, and of eleemosynary institutions ordinarily find that their incomes lag behind rising prices. They lose in terms of purchasing power, but to a lesser degree than do those who receive fixed incomes.

Summary

Three major indicators of economic performance have been used in evaluating the seriousness of economic fluctuations. One is the behaviour of GNP, the value of the economy's entire yearly output of goods and services in final form. Another is the movement in the general price level or average level of all prices over time. The third is the unemployment rate or the percentage of the economy's labour force classified as unemployed. The unemployment rate is probably the most sensitive of the three as an indicator of economic fluctuations in a downward direction. The price level tends to be the most sensitive indicator of rapid economic expansion. GNP over time is indicative of the pattern of economic growth.

Movements in the general price level are measured by means of price index numbers, which show percentage deviations in average price levels for specific years from some year selected as the base year. A set of price index numbers can be computed for any given complex of product prices, for example, wholesale prices, retail prices, agricultural prices, or others. The implicit price deflator of Table 5-1 provides the broadest possible complex, since it is intended to cover all goods and services making up GNP. With the implicit price deflators, GNP in current dollar terms can be converted into GNP in real terms. Movements in the general price level are called inflation and deflation. Inflation refers to a period of rising prices while deflation means a period of falling prices.

Comparisons of actual GNP with potential GNP provide a meaningful basis for examining economic fluctuations. Potential GNP may be defined as the level of GNP that could be attained if the unemployment rate were no more than 3 or 4 percent. Economic fluctuations in a downward direction—recession and depression—are reflected in a widening gap between actual and potential GNP, while those in an upward direction—periods of rapid expansion—bring about a decreasing gap or, in some cases, even a negative gap. Although a recession may or may not be accompanied by deflation, a depression almost certainly will be because of its greater severity. Rapid expansion is almost always accompanied by inflation; the closer the economy is to a full-employment level of GNP, the greater will be the inflation associated with a given increase in the economy's output.

Since persistent weakness in Canada's balance of payments would make the achievement of our domestic economic goals very difficult, Canada's international payments position warrants special attention. Or, to put it another way, the satisfactory achievements of our basic domestic objectives entail a viable balance of international payments. In brief, monetary and fiscal policies must take the external environment into account.

The effects of recession, depression, and deflation can be classified in two categories, (1) output effects and (2) redistributive effects. Output effects are obvious; actual GNP is below potential GNP and the public has less to consume than it could have. Redistributive effects refer to relative changes in incomes among families and individuals that stem solely from the downturn in economic activity. Those whose net incomes fall relatively more than average incomes fall will be those made unemployed by the decline, that is, those who furnish resources to durable goods and capital goods industries, and debtors. Those whose net incomes fall relatively less than average incomes fall include salaried persons, those living on fixed incomes, and creditors.

Similarly, rapid expansion and inflation will have output effects and redistributive effects. Output effects can occur only if there are unemployed resources in the economy. Expansion occurring from an increase in aggregate demand under full-employment conditions can result in inflation only. Redistributive effects occur as the net incomes of some groups increase more rapidly than those of others. Favoured groups are those who have been unemployed and who obtain employment, those who furnish resources to durable goods and capital goods industries, and debtors. Those who lose relatively are salaried personnel, fixed-income receivers, and creditors.

Exercises and Questions for Discussion

1. "Since unemployment was at a high level during the Great Depression, there was a scarcity of goods. This implies that prices should have been relatively higher in this period, not lower." Evaluate this statement.
2. Why are some economists not concerned about a moderate amount of inflation? Explain.
3. Give several possible reasons why recessions are no longer necessarily accompanied by deflation. Explain each one carefully.

4. How is real GNP computed? What useful purposes can this concept serve? Explain.
5. Contrast a recession and a depression with an economic expansion. Consider in your discussion the movements of the level of unemployment and the general price level in each. Illustrate each situation graphically.

Selected Readings

Boreham, G. F., *et al.*, *Money and Banking in a Canadian Context*. Toronto: Holt, Rinehart and Winston of Canada, 1969, Chap. 19.

Lee, Maurice W., *Macroeconomics: Fluctuations, Growth, and Stability*, 3rd ed. Homewood, Ill.: Richard D. Irwin, Inc. 1963, Part 3 and Chap. 20.

Slichter, Sumner H., "How Bad Is Inflation?" *Harper's Magazine*, August 1952, pp. 53-57.

White, Derek A., *Business Cycles in Canada*. Ottawa: Queen's Printer, 1967, Staff Study No. 17, prepared for the Economic Council of Canada.

6

Money

What are the causes of recession, depression, deflation, expansion, and inflation? Can they be brought under control so that year in and year out actual GNP is somewhere in the neighbourhood of potential GNP and so that their arbitrary redistributive effects are largely eliminated? We hear and read conflicting opinions on what the government ought or ought not be doing if we are to avoid the Scylla of inflation on the one hand and the Charybdis of recession on the other. In this and the following chapters we try to sort out the main causes of instability and to find the appropriate means of controlling them. In doing so we shall make a detailed study of the monetary system, of the government's expenditure and tax structure and policies, and of the body of economic principles generally referred to as national income analysis. The order of exposition is not necessarily the order of importance of these three subject areas. Rather, it is in an ascending order of complexity.

We concentrate on money in this chapter—stuff that we are so accustomed to handling that we accept it and its uses automatically and unquestioningly. In so doing we may very well miss or lose sight of the important role that it plays in the exchange of goods and services and in economic fluctuations. We shall start by defining the term and then we shall identify the functions of money. Thirdly, we shall examine the determinants of the value of money and then outline a simple framework of monetary theory.

What is Money?

A Definition

Money can be easily and simply defined as a medium of exchange that is generally accepted as such by the public. It is anything that we are willing to accept from others in return for giving up to them items that we possess and that in turn other people are willing to accept in return for items that they give up to us. It is something whose units the community has by custom come to adopt and use as a means of measuring and expressing relative values of different goods and services.

Historically, a rich variety of tangible objects and intangible debts have served as money. These include cloth in Samoa, in parts of Africa, and in parts of China; whales' teeth in the Fiji islands; shells and animals' teeth in a number of Pacific islands; animals such as pigs, buffalo, reindeer, and cattle in almost every continent of the globe; beads in Africa and among American Indians; rice and other grains in Japan, the Philippines, India, Babylonia, Europe, and other agricultural areas; tobacco in Colonial North America; fur in Alaska and Canada; tea bricks in China; salt in Ethiopia and China; bronze in ancient Italy and Rome; slaves in Africa and Ireland; silver and gold throughout the world; and, in the modern world, paper and evidences of debt.[1]

Modern Money

The money in circulation today in most countries is classified into two broad categories: (1) currency in the form of notes and coins and (2) chequable deposits at commercial banks. Frequently we think of money as consisting of currency only, but a little reflection on our use of the chequebook and on the definition of money given above will convince us that deposits are not only money but constitute the most important part of the total money supply of the economy. Note in Table 6-1 that in March, 1970 they represented over 77 percent of the total.

Chequing Account Deposits

Suppose we look more carefully at chequing accounts in commercial or chartered banks, and consider how we use them in economic transactions. When we make a deposit we turn over to the bank assets of ours—currency or cheques made out to us by other people—and these become bank assets. But in accepting our assets the bank incurs liabilities or debts to us that we call chequing accounts. Our chequing deposits carry with them a

[1]*Probably the most extensive historical account of items used as money is that of Paul Einzig,* Primitive Money. *London: Eyre and Spottiswoode, 1949.*

special privilege. If we so desire we can transfer a part of what the bank owes to us to other persons by writing cheques in their favour. When they deposit the cheques the bank owes them that much more and owes us that much less. Bank debts transferred in this manner from one person to another are widely used as a medium of exchange and are well accepted by the public as such. They fulfill all of the requirements necessary to be designated as money.

TABLE 6-1

Canadian Stock of Money and Its Components, March 1970
(Millions of Dollars)

Currency outside chartered banks	
Bank of Canada notes	$ 2,709
Subsidiary coinage	433
Total currency in circulation[1]	3,142
Chartered bank deposits[2]	
Chequable deposits	
Demand	6,132
Personal savings	5,444
Government of Canada	1,084
Total chequing deposits	12,660
Nonchequable deposits	
Personal savings[3]	6,101
Personal fixed term[4]	3,781
Nonpersonal term and notice[4]	3,571
Total nonchequable deposits	13,453
Total currency and Chartered Bank deposits	29,255
Total currency and chequable Chartered Bank deposits	15,802
Total currency and chequable Chartered Bank deposits	
held by the general public[5]	14,718

[1]*The figure for currency in circulation is exaggerated somewhat because some has disappeared from circulation through loss, destruction, and the accumulations of collectors. On the other hand, the figure excludes any foreign currency that may be in circulation.*
[2]*Less Canadian dollar "float".*
[3]*These savings accounts are payable on demand.*
[4]*Most of these deposits are redeemable before maturity.*
[5]*Excludes deposits owned by the Government of Canada.*
Source: Bank of Canada, Statistical Summary, April 1970, pp. 257 and 265.

Before leaving this subject, it should be pointed out that some Canadian economists include all chartered bank deposits (chequable and nonchequable) in their definition of money supply; others exclude only those owned by the federal government. (For the differences involved, see Table 6-1 .) A few go further and include all deposits and deposit substitutes (shares and certificates redeemable on demand) offered by trust companies, mortgage loan companies, credit unions, *caisses populaires*, and government savings institutions.[5]

[5]*For a discussion of the issues raised in this section, see Gordon F. Boreham,* et al., Money and Banking: Analysis and Policy in a Canadian Context. *Toronto: Holt, Rinehart and Winston of Canada, 1969, pp. 30-37.*

We need not explore this matter further. Suffice to say that there is nothing that is "by nature" money and that the exact meaning of money stock is more a matter of taste than scientific necessity. And that even though most economists exclude the so-called "near moneys" from their definition of money supply, they do not ignore their effects on the behaviour of the rate of spending.

Currency

The major part of the currency component of the Canadian money supply consists of Bank of Canada notes, as is indicated in   Table 6-1 . Bank of Canada notes, like chartered bank deposits, represent debt. They are certificates of indebtedness of the Bank of Canada[6] to those who have possession of them, but since they are declared by the Canadian government to be "legal tender" for all debts, public and private, what would you exchange them for if you went to the Bank of Canada to claim what is owed to you?

Coins, the remaining part of the currency component, are circulated by the federal government and are for convenience in making change and in operating coin machines. The values of the metals that they contain must always be less than or equal to their value as money. If this were not so they would not remain in circulation, since it would pay people to obtain them at their money value, melt them down, and sell the metal at the higher commercial value.[7]

[6]*The Bank of Canada is a government owned institution. It is examined in detail in Chapter 8.*

[7]*This is why silver coins have gone out of circulation. In 1966, as a result of the growing demand for silver for commercial purposes and for use in coin, the world market price for silver rose above $1.66 per ounce. As a consequence, the market value of the silver in the Canadian silver dollar (which contained six-tenths of an ounce of silver), and in the half-dollar, the quarter and the dime now exceeded the monetary value of these coins. The difference between the market cost of the materials and the monetary value of the coins represented a loss to the government. Moreover, it had now become profitable, though still illegal, for persons to melt silver coins and sell them for bullion on commercial markets. In the light of these developments, and aware of the implications that a continued rise in the market price of silver would make the supply of coins inadequate, Parliament enacted legislation in 1967 that authorized the minting of new dollars, half-dollars, quarters and dimes with no silver content. The new coins, which were put into circulation on September 1, 1967, are made of pure nickel. Parenthetically, a comparable situation and solution obtained in the United States in 1965.*

Functions of Money

Money performs three major functions in an economic system. In the first place, it serves as a *medium of exchange*. Secondly, it serves as a *unit of account*, or as the unit in terms of which economic values are measured. Thirdly, it serves as a *liquid store of value*. These functions are closely related and they overlap, as we shall see as we examine each in detail.

Medium of Exchange

Money as a *medium of exchange* is a great technological convenience in any society in which exchanges commonly occur. The alternative is a *barter system*, in which goods and services are exchanged for goods and services. The inconvenience of such a system is well illustrated by the example of the traveller in Africa who wanted a boat. A boat owner was found who was willing to trade a boat for a certain amount of ivory. The traveller had no ivory but through inquiry a man with ivory was found who wanted cloth for the ivory. Unfortunately, the traveller had no cloth; all he had was a quantity of wire. But luck was with him. He found a trader who had cloth and wanted wire in exchange. The traveller traded wire for cloth and cloth for ivory. He then exchanged the ivory for the boat, finally fulfilling his original desire.

Barter arrangements would be even more inconvenient in a complex, modern economy in which most of us complete only a small part of any specific productive process. Who, for example, would be willing to trade groceries or housing or clothing directly to an economist in exchange for a few lectures on how the economic system works? However, in a money economy the economist is able to gather together groups of persons either desiring or forced to learn economics. He sells his services to them for money and in turn uses the money to purchase the things he wants. The greater the degree of specialization in an economy, the more convenient money is for exchange purposes.

Measure of Value

The units of a monetary system are used as a measure of value for goods, services, and resources. The value of a loaf of bread is measured as 35 cents; that of an automobile as $4500; that of a haircut as $2.50; and that of an hour of skilled labour as $5. We use such measurements for purposes of comparing values and as a means of keeping accounting records. Comparative values expressed in monetary units provide the basis for most of our economic decision-making and exchange. As consumers we compare the market values (prices) of the different goods and services available and we make our choices as to how to allocate our incomes among them. As resource owners we compare the values placed on units of the resources we own in their various alternative uses and we sell or hire them out accordingly. The decisions of businessmen with respect to what products to sell and what resources to purchase are based on comparative values. Revenues expressed in money terms compared with money costs indicate what output levels yield the greatest profits.

Unfortunately, monetary units are not perfect for measuring values. During periods of inflation the dollar represents smaller and smaller physical quantities of goods and services, and during periods of deflation it represents larger and larger quantities. Thus we often find ourselves using a rubber yardstick for economic and accounting measurements. However, we can and do make use of price index number techniques to compensate for the variations that occur.

Liquid Store of Value

Most people find it desirable to accumulate and hold a stock of assets over time. The stock is held in many different forms—real estate, business assets, common stocks, bonds, homes, and personal property of different kinds. Ordinarily a part of it will be held in the form of money.

We speak of different kinds of assets as having different degrees of *liquidity*, the term "liquidity" referring to the ease with which one kind can be converted into another. Anyone who has tried to sell a house knows that it is rather illiquid; it takes time to find the buyer willing to pay what the house is worth. Common stocks or bonds are much more liquid. But money is the most liquid of all assets, since it can be converted immediately into other desired forms.

We hold money as a *liquid store of value* for several reasons. We need to keep enough on hand to see us through from one pay cheque to another, to take care of our ordinary day to day *exchange transactions*. We like to keep a little more than that on hand in order to take advantage of any special opportunities that may come our way. Further, we like to be in a position to meet *unforeseen emergencies and contingencies*. Once we have reached an income level that enables us to hold a stock of money that we consider sufficient for these purposes, we begin to think in terms of *investment* and to keep a stock of money on hand to invest at propitious times in promising stocks and bonds or other properties.

The Value of Money

What gives money its value? Is it the gold that the government has stored away in the vaults of the Bank of Canada? Many people think that gold "backing" provides the key to the value of our money, and at one time, they may have been right. When we had gold coins circulating freely the commercial value and the money value of the metals could never be far apart. But the value per unit of our present money supply is independent of any gold backing. For example, can you redeem a five dollar bill, a five dollar bank deposit, or five dollars in coin for five dollars worth of gold?[8]

In any sort of meaningful sense the value of money is the goods and services that a unit of money will purchase; that is, its purchasing power. Whether money is "backed" by gold or anything else for that matter is immaterial. If the general price level rises, the purchasing power or the value of the dollar falls; and if the price level falls, the purchasing power or the value of the dollar rises. Since the value of money varies inversely with the price level, we must pursue the question of what determines the price level.

The Equation of Exchange

Everything about our study of economics thus far suggests that the prices of goods and services depend upon the demands for them on the one hand and on the quantities of them made available on the other. In the preceding chapter, for the economy as a whole we put this in terms of aggregate demand and aggregate supply. We shall be concerned with a slightly different form in this section, but the underlying aggregate demand and aggregate supply analysis will be evident.

The main determinants of the value of money or of the general price level can be demonstrated readily with an old expository device known as *the equation of exchange*. In its simplest form it states

$$MV = PT.$$

Let the time period under consideration be one year. M is the average stock of money in circulation—total currency and chartered bank deposits; V is the velocity of circulation, or the number of times the average dollar is spent per year; and T represents the physical volume of goods and services traded per year. Since pairs of socks, automobiles, hamburgers,

---

[8]*The gold redemption of Dominion of Canada notes was formally abandoned on April 10, 1933. Parenthetically, stringent restrictions were imposed on gold dealings in 1931. These were subsequently eased, and on March 22, 1955, the Canadian government eliminated all remaining obstacles to private gold transactions.*

and the like cannot be added to form any kind of meaningful total, it is the same kind of abstraction as is the measurement along the output axis in Figure 5-3. We can think of it as homogeneous baskets of all kinds of goods and services, a basketful being the quantity that will sell for, say, $100 in a year that we choose as a base year. P is the price level, or the price of a basket of goods—or, in reality, a price index number.

The equation of exchange is a truism saying that

Total Spending = Value of Goods and Services Sold.

The average stock of money, M, multiplied by the velocity of circulation, V, is the total spending that occurs per year. The physical volume of trade, T, multiplied by the price level, P, is the value of goods and services sold per year. The equation is a truism, since what people spend as purchasers (MV) must equal the value of goods sold, or what people receive as sellers, (PT). But it brings together in the proper relation the determinants of the value of money.

The value of money is shown by the price level, which depends upon the relation between total spending on the one hand and the physical volume of trade on the other. Suppose, for example, that M increases but that V and T remain constant.[9] The increase in the money supply means an increase in the total spending side of the equation of exchange. Both mathematics and common sense let us know that if the left-hand side of the equation increases, so must the right-hand side; an increase in total spending necessarily means an increase in the value of goods sold. Since we have assumed that T is constant, the rise in the value of goods sold can occur only through an increase in the price level, P. To put it another way, the increase in the money supply increases spending in the economy. With more dollars chasing the same volume of goods and services, shortages occur at the original price level. These, in turn, cause the price level to rise as purchasers bid against one another for the short supplies.

In a similar way the impact of changes in V and in T on the price level and, therefore, on the value of money is easily determined. If V falls, with M and T remaining constant, P must fall and the value of money rises. If M and V remain constant and T rises, then P must fall and the value of money increases. In fact, M, V, and T may all be changing simultaneously, with the net effect on P depending upon the directions and the comparative magnitudes of the changes.

---

[9]*This does not imply that V and T must always remain constant when M increases. We are simply following the procedure of changing one independent variable at a time in order to determine the impact of each such change on a dependent variable.*

Inflation

Suppose we examine inflation, or a period in which the value of money is declining, in terms of the equation of exchange. At the outset it is apparent that if P is to rise, MV or total spending, must be increasing relative to T. An absolute increase in total spending may ensue from an increase in the stock of money, from an increase in velocity, or from both. Also, M may increase while V declines, but if total spending is to increase, the rise in M must more than offset the decline in V. This may work the other way. Total spending may be increased by a rise in V even though a decrease in M occurs simultaneously, provided the proportional rise in V is greater than the proportional decline in M.

Ordinarily there will be some direct response of both T and P to an increase in total spending, the amount of the response depending upon the extent to which the economy's resources are employed. The closer the economy is to full employment, the less will be the relative response of T to an increase in total spending and the greater will be the relative response of P.

Historically, Canada experienced its last period of significant inflation from August 1939 to December 1948. This period embraced World War II and its aftermath and provides an excellent example of the points discussed in the preceding paragraph. Letting P refer to the wholesale price level (1935-39 = 100), there was an increase of 113 percent for the entire period, or alternatively, the value of money at the end of the period was roughly one half what it was at the beginning of the period. What were the causes of the change? In order to finance World War II the stock of Money (M) was almost tripled during the period, being increased by 194 percent. Direct data on the physical volume of trade (T) are hard to come by; however, industrial production in the economy almost doubled. If we can assume that industrial production was representative of the economy's entire output of goods and services, then T can be said to have doubled also. The velocity of circulation (V) was lower at the end of the period than at the beginning, falling by slightly less than 10 percent. For the period as a whole, then, there was a large increase in total spending stemming from a very large increase in M tempered somewhat by a decrease in V. The increase in T was much less proportionally than was the increase in total spending; consequently, there was a very large rise in P and a correspondingly large decrease in the value of money.

Recession and Depression

Recession and, perhaps, depression occur when total spending declines relative to the volume of goods and services available to be purchased.

Reductions in total spending may result from reductions in M, in V, or in both. As total spending declines, sellers of goods find that they cannot sell as much as before at the previous price level and T declines also. During a recession the entire impact of a relative decline in total spending may rest on T, with no decline in the price level; however, during a depression P will fall also because of surpluses in sellers' inventories over a prolonged period of time. For reasons that we will discover later, declining economic activity usually causes further decreases in M, thus making matters worse. To compound the problem, further reductions in V are likely to be induced, too, by declining economic activity, for as recession, depression, and deflation occur people become more reluctant to spend what they have. Why buy now when prices are likely to be lower next week? Besides, it's necessary to save now for when times get worse, isn't it? Thus dollars are held longer than before and V falls.

The king-sized Great Depression of the 1930's was ushered in by a contraction lasting from April 1929 to March 1933. Over this period the stock of money, M, declined by about one-sixth and the velocity of circulation fell by slightly more than one-third. The physical volume of trade fell by something like one-third; thus the relatively greater decline in total spending pulled the price level, P, down by nearly one-third also. The point is simply this: the fall in aggregate demand or total spending pulled both the volume of trade and the price level down. The value of money, of course, increased.

Quantity Theory of Money

It is apparent from the foregoing analysis that the stock of money plays a key role in economic fluctuations or economic instability. The monetary theory that attributes prime importance to the average quantity of money in circulation and to changes in its magnitude has become known as the *quantity theory of money*. Put succinctly, the theory states that the price level and the level of economic activity tend to move in the same direction as the quantity of money in circulation. Special note should be taken of the word "tend," which indicates that exceptions may occur. It is possible, for example, for the volume of trade to increase at a slightly greater rate than total spending and, even though M may be increasing, for the price level to be falling. This occurred in Canada from 1925 to 1929.

The velocity of circulation further loosens the link between the quantity of money and the price level. As a matter of fact, changes in velocity can themselves change the price level with no help from changes in M. Suppose, for example, that the general public comes to expect or to believe that inflation will occur. Money, which decreases in value as the price level rises, becomes less attractive as a part of people's asset holdings than goods of various kinds; consequently, they are more inclined to exchange dollars for goods. The increase in total spending is accomplished through an increase in velocity and will have its effects on the price level—and, perhaps, the volume of trade—even though M has not increased. (Can you explain the effects of expectations on the part of the public that a recession is imminent?)

Usually in the course of economic fluctuations M and V change in the same direction; however, it is possible for a change in M to be nullified in whole or in part by a change in V in the opposite direction. When both change in the same direction, the quantity theory prediction that the price level will also change in the same direction will hold, except in the unusual case in which T changes relatively more than does total spending. Even when a change in M is accompanied by a change in V in the opposite direction, we usually expect that the former will outweigh the latter and that total spending will change in the same direction as does M. Ordinarily, the more stable the quantity of money, the more stable velocity will be.

If we are to press further into the causes of economic instability and the means of controlling it, the quantity theory of money indicates that we should inquire into the determinants of the money supply and especially into the forces that cause it to change up or down over time. Referring to Table 6-1 , we see that the currency component of the money supply can be fairly easily explained. The bulk of the currency consists of Bank of Canada notes, with the total dollar amount of these determined by Bank authorities. The coin component is under the control of the federal government represented by the mint. Thus the total currency component, representing a small part of the total money supply, is under the control of government agencies and has not in the recent past been subject to marked manipulation. It has grown rather steadily over time. The deposit component of the money supply is much more important and more complex. An explanation of it will require that we examine the structure and operation of the banking system. This is done in the following two chapters.

Summary

Money is anything used as a medium of exchange that is generally accepted by the public as such. In Canada it includes at least currency and chequing account deposits. Currency consists of coins issued by the federal government and paper bills issued by the Bank of Canada. Chequing account deposits are chartered bank liabilities or debt to depositors and are freely transferable from one person to another. Many Canadian economists favour a broader definition of the money supply. They would include nonchequable deposits at the chartered banks. Some would go further and include transferable and nontransferable deposits at other domestic financial institutions. The main functions of money in an economic system are to serve (1) as a medium of exchange, (2) as a measure of value, and (3) as a liquid store of value.

The value of money refers to what money will buy—that is, what it is worth as a medium of exchange—and does not depend on the value of the substance of which it is made. The value of money varies inversely with the general price level of what is purchased in the economy. Determinants of the price level and of the value of money are total spending on the one hand and the physical volume of goods to be purchased on the other. These factors are brought together conveniently in the equation of exchange. Increases in total spending may result from increases in the stock of money in circulation, from increases in its velocity of circulation, or from both. Decreases in total spending stem from decreases in the same magnitudes. When the rate of increase in total spending exceeds the rate of increase in the volume of goods to be purchased, inflation occurs and the value of money declines. Similarly, when total spending declines at a more rapid rate than the volume of goods and services to be purchased there will be deflation and a rise in the value of money. Deflation may or may not take place during recession but it will most surely occur during depression.

The quantity theory of money assigns a key role to money in both the cause of economic fluctuations and their control. It states that the price level and the level of economic activity tend to move in the same direction as the quantity of money in circulation. Thus it becomes important to inquire into the determinants of the money supply. The currency component of the money supply is determined primarily by the Bank of Canada. Determinants of the deposit component come under scrutiny in the next two chapters.

Exercises and Questions for Discussion

1. "As a bearer of options, money increases the freedom of choice of consumers." Explain.
2. Since all our money is debt, does it follow that all debt is money? Discuss.
3. "If the monetary authorities increase the money supply, production in the economy will increase." Evaluate this statement.
4. The Canadian dollar is now worth less than it was several years ago. What

changes in the variables making up the equation of exchange could account for this? What might have caused each variable to change?

5. In the recession of the late 1950's prices continued to rise. What are the possible determinants of this phenomenon?

Selected Readings

Boreham, G. F., *et al.*, *Money and Banking: Analysis and Policy in a Canadian Context.* Toronto: Holt, Rinehart and Winston of Canada, 1969, Chaps. 1, 2 and 3.

Carroll, Sheldon, "The Bank of Canada's Numismatic Collection," *The Canadian Banker*, Spring 1968, pp. 58-62; *ibid*, Summer 1968, pp. 47-53.

Friedman, M., and A. J. Schwartz, *A Monetary History of the United States, 1867-1960.* Princeton, N.J.: Princeton University Press, 1963, Chap. 10.

Friedman, M., Harold Wincott, F. W. Tooby, "The Money Supply Debate," *The Banker*, December 1968, pp. 1094-1115.

Galbraith, J. A., "The Concept and Measure of Money Supply," *The Canadian Banker*, Winter 1965, pp. 28-35.

Radford, R. A., "The Economic Organization of a P.O.W. Camp," *Economica*, November 1945, pp. 189-201.

7

Banks and the Money Supply

When you paid your tuition and your room and board, you wrote a cheque on the bank in which you have a chequing account. You write cheques for other sizable expenditures and from time to time when you need currency you cash a cheque. You may even have borrowed from a bank in order to buy an automobile or some other costly item that you could not do without and that your immediate liquid assets would not cover. But as indispensable as banks are to your personal economic activities, it probably never crossed your mind that banks create the major part of our money supply and that they play an important role in the ups and downs of the economy. In this chapter we shall study the banking system as a creator and destroyer of money. We shall then relate these activities to economic fluctuations.

Chequing Account Deposits as Money

What kinds of business enterprises are banks that they can create and destroy money? What are the mechanics of bank deposit transfers from individual to individual? These are the questions to which we address ourselves in this section.

Banks as Business Enterprises

An ordinary commercial bank is a business enterprise, organized, as a corporation, for the purpose of earning income for its owners. Banks sell two major kinds of services to the general public. They provide money to business firms and individuals that are good credit risks and in need of purchasing power as well as to governments. This is effected through bank lending, although banks may also purchase relatively small amounts of corporate stock. The interest that banks charge on the loans they make constitutes their main source of revenue. The second kind of service that the bank provides to the public is the provision of facilities for making payments through the transfer of ownership of bank deposits, or banks' debts to individuals. All of us use these instruments consistently. Some banks absorb the cost of these operations from their other income, but most levy a service charge of a specified amount per cheque.

The Balance Sheet

In analyzing the monetary activities of banks we shall be concerned with changes in their assets and liabilities; consequently, we shall find a T-account or balance sheet framework indispensable. This device is illustrated in Figure 7-1 and is based on the bookkeeping identity:

Assets = Liabilities + Net Worth.

Assets are listed on the left-hand side of the balance sheet while liability and net worth items appear on the right. Suppose now that the Western Bank has just been formed with an initial issue and sale of $50,000 worth of common stock,[1] the stock being paid for in currency. This transaction is represented by (1) in Figure 7-1 . The currency or cash becomes the property of the bank and is listed as an asset. The bank does not yet have liabilities. The owners' equity in the business, or the net worth, is represented by $50,000 worth of capital stock.

Changes in the balance sheet will occur as the bank prepares itself for business. Suppose that it spends the $50,000 in cash for a building and for the necessary banking equipment. The purchase is recorded as transaction (2) in Figure 7-1 . Cash is decreased by $50,000 and a new asset account, Building and Equipment, amounting to $50,000, comes into being. The Western Bank is ready for business.

[1]*In Canada, the minimum authorized capital stock for a commercial bank is $1,000,000.*

WESTERN BANK

BALANCE SHEET

ASSETS		LIABILITIES AND NET WORTH	
Cash	(1) + $50,000 (2) − $50,000 (3) + $20,000	Demand deposits Giroux Wilson	 (3) + $10,000 (3) + $10,000
Building and Equipment	(2) + $50,000	Capital stock	(1) + $50,000

Figure 7-1
The balance sheet of a bank.

Primary Deposits

Further changes in the balance sheet of the bank will occur as it begins to carry on its banking operations. Two persons, Mr. Wilson and Mr. Giroux, decide to make use of the bank's facilities and each makes a cash deposit of $10,000. The changes are shown in Figure 7-1 as transaction (3). Cash rises by $20,000 and a $10,000 deposit is established for each man. The cash has become the property of the bank and is therefore an asset. In return for the cash the bank incurs a liability of $10,000 to Giroux and of $10,000 to Wilson. For illustrative purposes, we shall assume that the bank offers only *demand deposits*. Such accounts are payable on demand and have full chequing privileges.

The deposits of Wilson and Giroux were made in cash and, as such, are called *primary deposits*. When these are established the money supply of the economy is not affected. The cash turned over to the bank is withdrawn from circulation and is replaced by an equivalent amount of demand deposits. The process of money creation by banks will appear shortly.

Transfer of Deposit Ownership

When one person writes a cheque to another, certain bookkeeping mechanics on the part of banks are involved. To illustrate these, the simplest possible example, a *monopoly-bank system*, will be used first. We shall then build up a more complex example in which the economy uses a *multibank system*.

The Monopoly-Bank System

If the Western Bank is the only bank in the economy, the transfers of deposit ownership associated with the use of demand deposits as a medium of exchange are accomplished through bookkeeping entries on the part of the bank. This is illustrated in Figure 7-2 . The bank initially has cash assets of $20,000 resulting from the deposits of Giroux and Wilson. The deposit liabilities of the bank are, correspondingly, $10,000 for each of them. The Building and Equipment asset account is $50,000 and the bank's Net Worth account is also $50,000.

WESTERN BANK			
			BALANCE SHEET
ASSETS		LIABILITIES AND NET WORTH	
Cash	+ $20,000	Deposits Giroux	$10,000
			(1) + $ 1,000
		Wilson	$10,000
			(1) − $ 1,000
Building and equipment	$50,000	Capital stock	$50,000

Figure 7-2
Deposits as money: the single-bank case.

If Wilson buys some article from Giroux priced at $1,000 and writes a cheque to him for that amount, Giroux will take the cheque to the bank for deposit in his account. The cheque informs the bank that Wilson "demands" that $1,000 of its debt to him be transferred to Giroux, and this is precisely what the bank does. It reduces on its books the amount owed Wilson by $1,000 and increases the amount it owes Giroux by the same amount. These changes are shown in Figure 7-2 by transaction (1), and this is the end of the matter.

The Multi-Bank System

Payments made by means of deposit transfers become more complex when more than one bank serves the economy. Suppose that in addition to the Western Bank the Northern Bank is in operation. Wilson has deposited $10,000 in cash in the Western Bank and Giroux has deposited the same amount in the Northern Bank. The appropriate balance sheets are shown in Figure 7-3 .[2]

Again Wilson buys a $1,000 item from Giroux and pays for it with a cheque drawn on the Western Bank. Giroux takes the cheque to the Northern Bank, endorses it, and deposits it in his account. The Northern Bank increases its debt to Giroux by $1,000 and sends the cheque to the Western Bank for collection. The Western Bank interprets the cheque as a request to pay $1,000 of what it owes Wilson to Giroux and to mean that

[2] *We have omitted both the Building and Equipment and the Net Worth accounts, since these are not necessary for our purposes.*

WESTERN BANK		BALANCE SHEET	
ASSETS		**LIABILITIES**	
Cash	$10,000 (1) − $ 1,000	Deposits Wilson	$10,000 (1) − $ 1,000

NORTHERN BANK		BALANCE SHEET	
ASSETS		**LIABILITIES**	
Cash	$10,000 (1) + $ 1,000	Deposits Giroux	(1) + $ 1,000

Figure 7-3
Deposits as money: the multi-bank case.

Giroux, by his endorsement, has turned over his claim to the Northern Bank. The Western Bank therefore pays $1,000 in cash to the Northern Bank, and in so doing it discharges $1,000 of its deposit obligation to Wilson. Transaction (1) in Figure 7-3 illustrates the appropriate balance sheet changes.

In an economy in which there are many banks, each with many depositors, cash transfers among banks can be minimized by *clearing operations*. Individuals with accounts at bank A will be writing cheques to individuals who maintain accounts at other banks. Individuals who maintain accounts at other banks will be making payments by cheque to individuals who maintain accounts in bank A. Instead of sending out currency immediately for every cheque returned to it for collection, bank A waits until the end of the day (or some other appropriate time period) and totals up the amount it owes other banks. Other banks do the same thing. It may develop that bank A owes bank B $10,000, that bank B owes bank C $10,000, and that bank C owes bank A $10,000. If this is the case, when all three banks become aware of who owes what to whom they simply cancel out their debts to each other and no cash transfers are necessary.

In practice, a group of banks among which many interbank transactions occur may designate one bank as a *clearing house* to facilitate clearing payments. Each bank maintains a deposit at the clearing house bank for this purpose. In Figure 7-4 , the Western Bank and the Northern Bank are assumed to have each deposited $5,000 in cash with the Eastern Bank, which serves as the clearing house. These deposits are liabilities for the Eastern Bank, but for the Northern Bank and the Western Bank—the depositors—they are assets; that is, they are amounts that the Eastern Bank owes them. Now suppose that Wilson, who banks with the Western Bank, writes a $1,000 cheque to Giroux, who banks with the Northern Bank. Giroux takes the cheque to the Northern Bank for deposit. The Northern Bank increases Giroux's deposit by $1,000 and at the same time increases on its books its Deposit at Eastern account by $1,000. It then sends the cheque to the Eastern Bank for clearance. The Eastern Bank decreases the Western Bank's deposit with it by $1,000 and increases the Northern Bank's deposit with it by $1,000. It then sends the cheque to the Western Bank, which reduces Wilson's deposit by $1,000 and at the same time reduces on its books its Deposit at Eastern account by the same amount. The whole series of changes is shown by transaction (1). The Western Bank in this case is said to have an *adverse clearing balance*. This example can be easily expanded to include many banks using the clearing house facilities.

EASTERN BANK

BALANCE SHEET

ASSETS		LIABILITIES	
Cash	$10,000	Deposits	
		Western	$ 5,000
			(1) − $ 1,000
		Northern	$ 5,000
			(1) + $ 1,000

WESTERN BANK

BALANCE SHEET

ASSETS		LIABILITIES	
Cash	$ 5,000	Deposits	
Deposit at		Wilson	$10,000
Eastern	$ 5,000		(1) − $ 1,000
	(1) − $ 1,000		

NORTHERN BANK

BALANCE SHEET

ASSETS		LIABILITIES	
Cash	$ 5,000	Deposits	
Deposit at		Giroux	$10,000
Eastern	$ 5,000		(1) + $ 1,000
	(1) + $ 1,000		

Figure 7-4
Clearing operations.

A careful reexamination of the foregoing examples will reveal that none of them has changed the amount of money in circulation. In every case a total of \$20,000 in cash was withdrawn from circulation, placed in the banks' vaults, and there it stayed throughout the transactions illustrated. In lieu of the cash, \$20,000 in demand deposits was placed in circulation. Primary deposits simply result in an exchange of cash or currency for an equivalent amount of demand deposits for use as a medium of exchange.

Advantages of Deposits as Money

The use of demand deposits for exchange purposes has several advantages. In the first place, a cancelled cheque, endorsed by the person to whom it is made out, provides a convenient, though not in all cases legal, receipt for a payment made. Second, demand deposits are not as easily misplaced, lost, or stolen as is currency. Can you imagine sending a \$100 bill through the mail? Third, cheques can be written for exact amounts of transactions, thereby doing away with the necessity of making change. Fourth, demand deposits are convenient for making large payments—a satchel full of bills and coins is awkward to carry around.

Deposit Creation and Deposit Destruction

Banks can go beyond the mere placing of primary demand deposits in circulation in lieu of currency; they are able to create additional or *secondary deposits* that do not require the withdrawal of an equivalent amount of currency from circulation, and they can also destroy these deposits. This means that banks can create and destroy money. If banks are not regulated, the possibility is introduced that they may expand or contract the money supply in a way that will contribute to economic instability. Throughout the remainder of this chapter we shall assume that banks are not regulated. This will enable us to see more clearly the economic forces affecting banking operations and the effects of banking practices on economic activity. It will also give us a greater appreciation of the need for and the problems associated with the regulation of the system. We shall look first at a monopoly-bank system and then at a multibank system.

The Monopoly-Bank System

Money creation and destruction for a monopoly-bank system is essentially the same as for an entire multibank system except that it is simpler because adverse clearing balances do not occur. Consequently, we assume here that the monopoly bank carries out all the banking operations of the economy.

One Hundred Percent Reserves

The monopoly bank of Figure 7-5 initially has had $100,000 in currency deposited in it, giving rise to $100,000 in cash assets and $100,000 in deposit liabilities. This currency is available to the bank for any contingency, but principally it is available as a reserve to meet depositors' claims against it. As such it forms part of the bank's *cash reserves*. Actually, the *cash reserves* of a bank consist of more than its holdings of currency; the deposits that it has at the Bank of Canada, to be discussed in the next chapter, are also part of its cash reserves.

The ratio of a bank's reserves to its deposits is called the *reserve ratio* and is ordinarily expressed as a percent. In all the cases that we have considered thus far the reserve ratio has been 100 percent. As long as the reserve ratio of the monopoly bank is 100 percent, no money is created. But 100 percent reserves are not likely to be found in practice.

Fractional Reserves and Deposit Creation

The managers of the monopoly bank soon discover that there is no need to maintain a reserve ratio of 100 percent. When one depositor writes a cheque to another the bank simply makes a bookkeeping entry, decreasing the deposit of the former and increasing that of the latter, and reserves are undisturbed. Occasionally a depositor writes a cheque to "cash" when he needs currency for some specific purpose. Such a cheque, say for $100, will decrease its writer's deposit by $100 and the bank's cash by the same amount. But when the individual spends the currency, those who receive it are likely to redeposit it in the bank, increasing their deposits and the

MONOPOLY BANK				BALANCE SHEET	
ASSETS			**LIABILITIES**		
Reserves		$100,000	Deposits		$100,000
	(1) − $	5,000		(2) + $	5,000
	(2) + $	5,000			
L & I	(1) + $	5,000			

Figure 7-5
Money creation by a monopoly bank.

bank's reserves by $100. Only if people are expected to turn completely away from the use of demand deposits as money is it important that the bank have reserves of 100 percent. For the monopoly bank the $100,000 in reserves is far more than enough to take care of depositors' requests for currency.

It seems possible—and profitable—that some of the $100,000 can be put to work earning interest. There are always businesses or individuals desirous of obtaining loans and willing to pay interest for them. Here is a ready-made source of loans. A local clothing store wants to order its fall suits and needs $5000 for a three-month period. A loan officer of the bank assures himself that the clothier is a good credit risk and approves the loan at 7 percent interest.[3] The borrower signs a promissory note to the bank for this amount and, for the moment, let us suppose he takes the loan in cash. In Figure 7–5, the balance sheet changes are shown by transaction (1). Reserves are decreased by $5000 and in their place the promissory note becomes a $5000 asset. The account in which assets of this type are carried is called *Loans and Investments*, or *L & I* for short.

The loan increases the money supply of the economy by $5000. Demand deposits remain at $100,000, but the net amount of currency that has been withdrawn from circulation and that is resting in the bank's vaults is now only $95,000. There is now $100,000 in demand deposits in circulation in lieu of the $95,000 in currency that makes up the bank's reserves. When the bank increases the money supply its reserve ratio drops below 100 percent and it is said to be operating on *fractional reserves*.

The money supply increase generated by a bank loan may take place through an increase in the volume of demand deposits rather than through a return of currency to circulation. Suppose the clothier pays out the $5000 in currency to a wholesaler for fall suits. Since there is only one bank in existence, the wholesaler also uses the bank. He sacks the currency, takes it to the bank, and deposits it to his account, thereby increasing the cash of the bank by $5000, bringing total cash of the latter back to $100,000—and increasing the bank's deposits by $5000—bringing its total deposits up to $105,000. These changes are represented by transaction (2) in Figure 7-5 . In lieu of $100,000 in currency, $105,000 in demand deposits is now in circulation.

In the usual case loans are not made in currency at all. When the clothier or anyone else borrows from a bank the loan is usually taken directly in the form of an increase in a deposit account, or an increase in the bank's

---

[3]*Simple interest at 7 percent on a $5000 loan for a three-month period amounts to*
$$\$5000 \times \tfrac{3}{12} \times .07 = \$87.50.$$
This sum of money is income to the bank, used to pay expenses and, hopefully, dividends to stockholders. As such, it need not enter into the balance sheet transactions with which we are primarily concerned.

liability to the borrower. In return the borrower signs a promissory note to the bank increasing the bank's L & I account. Transaction (1) in Figure 7-6 illustrates the point. The borrower incurs a debt to the bank in exchange for a bank debt to him. The borrower's debt to the bank is not generally acceptable to the public as a means of payment and is therefore not money; however, the bank's debt to the borrower is transferable and is acceptable as a means of payment, and thus it is a part of the economy's money supply.

MONOPOLY BANK					
					BALANCE SHEET
ASSETS			**LIABILITIES**		
Reserves		$100,000	Deposits		$100,000
L & I	(1)	$ 5,000		(1)	$ 5,000
	(2)	$895,000		(2)	$895,000

Figure 7-6
Deposit creation by a monopoly bank.

Additional loans made by the bank will generate additional deposits. If the bank were to make additional loans to other businesses and to private individuals totaling $895,000, the results would be as shown by transaction (2) in Figure 7-6 . L & I is increased by that amount and the loans are given to the borrowers in the form of demand deposits. The monopoly bank has now created $900,000 in money that did not exist before it began its lending activities. The deposits arising from lending activities—the $900,000—are called *secondary* or *derivative deposits*.

Deposit Contraction

Deposit contraction or the destruction of demand deposits is the opposite of deposit creation. Figure 7-7 shows the monopoly bank with reserves of $100,000, loans and investments of $900,000, and deposits of $1,000,000. (Can you break up the $1,000,000 in deposits into primary deposits and secondary deposits and explain the basis of the distribution?) The clothing store's note for $5,000 is due. In anticipation of paying off the note, the clothier has accumulated more than this in his account and he writes a cheque for $5,000 to the bank. The bank marks the note "paid," turns it over to him, reduces its L & I account by $5,000, and reduces the deposit account of the clothier by $5,000 (see transaction (1) in Figure 7-7). Further repayment of other loans that were made by the bank will bring about a further reduction in demand deposits or the money supply.

MONOPOLY BANK			BALANCE SHEET	
ASSETS			**LIABILITIES**	
Reserves	$100,000		Deposits	$1,000,000
			(1) − $ 5,000	
L & I	$900,000			
(1) − $ 5,000				

Figure 7-7
Deposit contraction by a monopoly bank.

One of the rights of depositors is to demand and receive currency for their deposits whenever they so desire. If a bank is operating on fractional reserves, as is the monopoly bank of Figure 7-7 , it is obvious that if all depositors go to the bank and insist on exchanging their deposits for currency, the bank cannot meet their demands. Once it has paid out $100,000 in currency its reserves are exhausted and the rest of its depositors are left high and dry. Mass behaviour of this kind on the part of depositors is called a *run on the bank*. In periods of economic stability it is unlikely to occur, but if the public loses confidence in the bank's capacity to meet its demands for currency, as it did in the United States between 1929 and 1933,[4] a run may develop.

Capacity for Money Creation

The rules governing money creation and destruction by the bank can be summed up briefly. If the dollar amount of new loans and investments being made exceeds the dollar amount of those being paid off or liquidated, new money is being created. If, on the other hand, the dollar amount of new loans and investments being made is less than the dollar amount of those being paid off or liquidated, money is being destroyed. Are there any limits to the volume of demand deposits that can be created?

Business prudence will determine how far the bank will go in creating money, and the reserve ratio turns out to be the critical factor. The larger the dollar volume of the bank's loans, the more income it can earn, interest on loans being the bank's main source of income. But given the amount of the bank's reserves, the larger the dollar volume of its loans and, con-

---

[4]*In one six-month period alone, December 31, 1932 to June 30, 1933, 3,876 commercial banks failed in the United States. Although there have been 21 bank failures in Canada between 1867 and the present, the last one, and the first in a decade, was in 1923.*

sequently, its deposits, the smaller its reserve ratio will be. The smaller its reserve ratio, the more vulnerable the bank becomes to depositors' demands for currency. In the absence of governmental determination of what the minimum reserve ratio will be,[5] the bank must strike some sort of balance between the income incentive on the one hand and prudence on the other. As long as people have as much confidence in demand deposits as in currency as a medium of exchange, the limits on deposit creation are extremely high, or, put the other way around, the reserve ratio can be extremely low.

Once we know the reserve ratio desired by the monopoly bank, its present level of deposits, and the amount of reserves that it has, we can easily determine the amount of *additional* money that it can create. Suppose, for example, that the bank desires to maintain a *reserve ratio* of not less than R percent. Suppose, further, that the *present level of deposits* is D dollars and that *total reserves* are C dollars. If the bank's deposits are all primary deposits, then

$$C = D.$$

The *required reserves* for the present level of deposits is only $R \cdot D$, so, letting X represent excess reserves, we find that

$$X = C - R \cdot D. \tag{7.1}$$

These excess reserves are available to support the creation of secondary deposits through loans and investments by the bank. Letting $\triangle D$ represent the total possible *deposit expansion* or *creation*, we obtain

$$\triangle D \cdot R = X$$

or

$$\triangle D = \frac{X}{R}. \tag{7.2}$$

MONOPOLY BANK			
			BALANCE SHEET
ASSETS		**LIABILITIES**	
Reserves	$10,000	Deposits	$40,000
L & I	$30,000		

Figure 7-8
The limits of deposit creation by a monopoly bank.

[5] *As we shall see in the next chapter, minimum reserve ratios for the banking system are set by law.*

This is a perfectly general principle for a monopoly-bank system which states that if the bank has excess reserves, it can create additional deposits in the amount of the excess reserves times the reciprocal of the reserve ratio. The formula holds also for the computation of the necessary deposit contraction for a *reserve deficiency* of X dollars.

As an illustration of how to use the deposit-change formula, consider Figure 7-8 . Reserves of the monopoly bank, or C, are $10,000. Total deposits, or D, are $40,000. Suppose the desired reserve ratio, R, is 10 percent. First, we compute the excess reserves, and since

$$X = C - R \cdot D$$

then

$$X = \$10,000 - 0.1 \cdot \$40,000 = \$6,000.$$

The possible deposit expansion is

$$\triangle D = \frac{X}{R}$$

so

$$\triangle D = \frac{\$6,000}{0.1} = \$60,000.$$

The monopoly bank can create an additional $60,000 in demand deposits.

The Multibank System

The principles of deposit creation and destruction developed for the monopoly-bank system are applicable to the multibank system generally found in modern economies. They are applicable only to the system as a whole, however, rather than to individual or single banks in the system. In the multibank system, individual banks are subject to *adverse clearing balances*, a phenomenon not possible in the monopoly-bank system.

Single-Bank Expansion

By how much can a single bank of a multibank system expand its deposits when it has excess reserves? The question can be best answered by an example. Suppose that bank A in Figure 7-9 is only one of many banks in a multibank system and that initially it has reserves of $100,000, loans and investments of $900,000, and total deposits of $1,000,000. Now suppose that someone makes a primary deposit of $10,000 in the bank, increasing both reserves and deposits by $10,000, as shown by transaction (1) in the figure. Using equation 7-1 , we find that if bank A desires to maintain a reserve ratio of at least 10 percent, its excess reserves are \$9,000.[6] According to equation 7-2 , these should support the deposit expansion of \$90,000 shown by transaction (2). After the expansion, reserves of \$110,000 are supporting deposits of \$1,100,000, the reserve ratio is 10 percent, and everything seems to be in order.

BANK A				BALANCE SHEET	
ASSETS			**LIABILITIES**		
Reserves		\$100,000	Deposits		\$1,000,000
	(1) +	\$ 10,000		(1) + \$	10,000
	(3) −	\$ 90,000		(2) + \$	90,000
L & I		\$900,000		(3) − \$	90,000
	(2) +	\$ 90,000			

Figure 7-9
Adverse clearing balances and deposit creation in a multi-bank system.

But we have not yet taken into account the possibility that one bank of a multibank system may have adverse clearing balances. The people who have borrowed the extra \$90,000 from bank A may use their deposits to make payments to people who keep their accounts in other banks. If the entire \$90,000 were paid to people who keep their accounts in other banks, those banks would have claims against bank A's reserves amounting to \$90,000, thus reducing the reserves of bank A to \$20,000. The reserve ratio would be 2/101, or 1.98 percent. This situation is represented in Figure 7-9 as transaction (3). Obviously, one bank of a multibank system cannot expand as much on the basis of given excess reserves as can a monopoly bank that does all the banking for the entire economy.

When we allow for all possible adverse clearing balances, the maximum expansion of deposits that a bank's excess reserves will permit is an amount equal to its excess reserves. Any expansion beyond that amount leaves the bank open to adverse clearing balances that will reduce its reserve ratio below the desired level. In Figure 7-10 , for example, we show again the same initial balance sheet for bank A. Transaction (1) shows a primary deposit of \$10,000, leading to excess reserves of \$9,000. Suppose now that loans and deposits are both increased only by the amount of the excess reserves, as shown by transaction (2). If these borrowers pay out all they have borrowed to individuals who keep their accounts in other banks, clearing operations will reduce bank A's deposits as well as its reserves by

[6]*There is nothing magic about the 10 percent figure for the desired reserve ratio in either this or the monopoly bank examples. We use 10 percent in order to make computations easy. At the same time, it is not too far from actual reserve ratios of banks.*

BANK A				BALANCE SHEET		
ASSETS				**LIABILITIES**		
Reserves		$100,000		Deposits		$1,000,000
	(2)	$ 10,000			(1) +	$ 10,000
	(3) −	$ 9,000			(2) +	$ 9,000
L & I		$900,000			(3) −	$ 9,000
	(2) +	$ 9,000				

Figure 7-10
The limits of deposit expansion by one bank of a multibank system.

$9,000, as transaction (3) indicates. The reserves remaining are $101,000, supporting $1,010,000 in deposits. This time bank A is able to meet the adverse clearing balances *and* to maintain a reserve ratio of 10 percent. As a general principle, then, we can state that *when a single bank in a multibank system has excess reserves, its loans and deposits can be expanded by an amount equal to the excess reserves.*

Deposit Expansion by the System

By how much can deposits for the banking system as a whole be expanded when excess reserves appear? To keep the analysis as simple as possible we shall use an example in which deposit expansion takes place in one bank at a time serially. We shall assume that all who borrow from one bank make payments to individuals who maintain their deposits in only one other bank; for example, those who borrow from bank A make payments to people who keep their accounts in bank B; those who borrow from bank B make payments to individuals who keep their accounts in bank C; and so on. All banks are assumed to desire a 10 percent reserve ratio.

Consider now in Figure 7-11 the effects of a primary deposit of $10,000 at bank A on possible loan and deposit expansion. The bank designates $1,000 of the $10,000 in currency as desired reserves, leaving it with excess reserves of $9,000. As a single bank of a multibank system, bank A, then, may make loans, thereby creating new deposits, of $9,000. The expansion is illustrated by the plus transactions for bank A in Figure 7 −11. Now let those who borrowed from bank A make payments to individuals who keep their deposit accounts at bank B. When the latter deposit their cheques, bank B's deposits increase by $9,000. Bank B sends the cheques to bank A for collection. Bank A's deposits (of those who wrote the cheques) are reduced by $9,000, and when it sends bank B $9,000 in currency its reserves are reduced by that amount also. Correspondingly, bank B's reserves are increased by the same amount. These

BANK A
BALANCE SHEET

ASSETS		LIABILITIES	
Reserves	$10,000	Deposits	$10,000
	− $ 9,000		+ $ 9,000
L & I	+ $ 9,000		− $ 9,000

BANK B
BALANCE SHEET

ASSETS		LIABILITIES	
Reserves	+ $ 9,000	Deposits	+ $ 9,000
	− $ 8,100		+ $ 8,100
L & I	+ $ 8,100		− $ 8,100

BANK C
BALANCE SHEET

ASSETS		LIABILITIES	
Reserves	+ $ 8,100	Deposits	+ $ 8,100
	− $ 7,290		+ $ 7,290
L & I	+ $ 7,290		− $ 7,290

BANK D
BALANCE SHEET

ASSETS		LIABILITIES	
Reserves	+ $ 7,290	Deposits	+ $ 7,290

BANK E
BALANCE SHEET

ASSETS		LIABILITIES	

Figure 7-11.
The limits of deposit expansion by a multibank system as a whole.

changes are shown by the minus $9,000 entries in bank A's balance sheet and by the plus $9,000 entries in bank B's balance sheet.

Bank B now finds itself with a $9,000 increase in both its reserves and its demand deposits. Its position is just as it would be if a $9,000 primary deposit had been made. Of the $9,000 increase in reserves, 10 percent or $900, will be designated as desired reserves for the $9,000 increase in deposits, leaving $8,100 as excess reserves. The excess reserves permit bank B as a single bank of a multibank system to expand its loans and therefore its deposits by $8,100. This situation is shown in   Figure 7-11 by the plus $8,100 items in bank B's balance sheet. Suppose that the borrowers from bank B make payments to people who maintain deposit accounts at bank C. The cheques are deposited at bank C, thereby increasing deposits by $8,100. Bank B will now experience adverse clearing balances. Collection by bank C from bank B increases the former's reserves by $8,100 and decreases the latter's reserves and deposits by the same amount. Bank B's decreases and bank C's increases are shown on their balance sheets by the appropriate minus and plus designations.

The impact of bank A's initial $9,000 in excess reserves is becoming apparent. Bank A expanded loans and deposits by the amount of its excess reserves. Bank B expanded loans and deposits by an additional $8,100— bank B's excess reserves. Bank C expands loans and deposits by $7,290— the amount of its excess reserves—and can expect to lose this amount of reserves to bank D. Bank D expands loans and deposits by $6,561. The process continues through bank after bank. Each successive bank, upon acquiring additional reserves and deposits, retains 10 percent (or whatever the desired reserve ratio is) of the newly acquired reserves as desired reserves against the newly acquired deposits. This enables each to make loans equal to its excess reserves, or 90 percent of its newly acquired reserves, and to expand deposits by the same amount. Thus the lending and deposit-creating ability of each successive bank is equal to 90 percent of that of the preceding bank, and eventually it approaches zero.

The total increase in deposits that can originate from the original $9,000 in excess reserves approaches $90,000. This is the sum of the deposit increases of all banks. Mathematically, it is a converging geometric progression, and as the increases approach zero the sum of the increases can be expressed as:

$$\$9,000 + 9,000 \cdot \tfrac{9}{10} + 9,000 \cdot (\tfrac{9}{10})^2 + 9,000 \cdot (\tfrac{9}{10})^3 \ldots$$

$$= \$9,000 \cdot \frac{1}{1 - \tfrac{9}{10}} = 9,000 \cdot 10 = \$90,000$$

We have taken a long and complex, but necessary, route to show that the multibank system as a whole behaves according to the same principles as the monopoly bank. Given excess reserves in the system, the possible deposit expansion for the system as a whole is found by using the equation

$$\triangle D = \frac{X}{R}. \tag{7.2}$$

No one individual bank of the system can expand by this amount—one bank can expand only by the amount of its excess reserves—but the sum of individual bank expansion triggered by excess reserves is equal to the excess reserves multiplied by the reciprocal of the reserve ratio.

Deposit Contraction by the System

Deposit contraction is the opposite of deposit expansion for the multibank system. If the banks of the system decide that higher reserve ratios than they currently hold are in order, or if withdrawals of cash by depositors leave them with reserve deficiencies, they will contract their deposits. As was explained earlier, this is accomplished by letting the dollar volume of old loans being paid off exceed the dollar volume of new loans being made. This reduces the deposits of banks, but it does not reduce their reserves. Equation 7-2 is also the formula for deposit contraction for the system as a whole. If X is a reserve deficiency, deposits must be contracted by X times $\frac{1}{R}$.

MULTIBANK SYSTEM				CONSOLIDATED BALANCE SHEET	
ASSETS			**LIABILITIES**		
Reserves	$100,000		Deposits	$1,000,000	
	− $ 10,000			− $ 10,000	
L & I	$900,000			− $ 90,000	
	− $ 90,000				

Figure 7-12
Deposit contraction by a multibank system.

Suppose that Figure 7-12 depicts a consolidated balance sheet for all banks of a multibank system. Initially it shows reserves of $100,000, loans and investments of $900,000, and deposits of $1,000,000. The desired reserve ratio is assumed to be 10 percent. Depositors now withdraw a net amount of $10,000 in currency from the banks. Reserves decrease by $10,000 and so do deposits; consequently, the reserve ratio drops below the desired 10 percent level. The reserves required to support $990,000 in deposits would be $99,000, but the reserve account stands at only

$90,000. The $9,000 reserve deficiency will induce the banking system to contract loans and deposits by an additional $90,000, bringing total deposits down to $900,000 and the reserve ratio up to the desired 10 percent.

Economic Fluctuations and the Banking System

The principle of deposit expansion and contraction by the banking system shed additional light on economic fluctuations. They provide an explanation of why an increase in total spending may feed on itself and may lead to serious inflation, as occurred from 1946 through 1948. They also help to explain a recession-depression spiral like that of 1929-1933.

Expansion and Inflation

Whatever it is that triggers the increase in total spending that ushers in an expansion, whether it is an increase in M or an increase in V, the expansion itself induces the banking system to increase the money supply, generating still further increases in total spending, in the money supply, and so on. Both the banking system and the public are responsible for this self-generating upward spiral. When banks are increasing the amounts of their loans outstanding they are increasing the money supply—and the economic climate during expansion encourages increases in lending activities. During periods of expansion and prosperity, the public desires to increase its volume of borrowing for at least two reasons. First, expanding business activity calls for an expanding volume of loans to finance larger inventories and the other expenses associated with it. Second, consumers are less reluctant to go into debt during an expansion period, since expansion and inflation work in favour of debtors. On the supply of loans side, banks worry less about defaults on loans during periods of expansion. They are willing to expand loans and increase deposits, letting the reserve ratio fall, in order to increase their interest income.

Recession and Depression

The shoe is on the other foot during periods of recession and depression. On the demand for loans side, business firms and individuals are less eager to borrow as business activity contracts. Business firms desire to cut back their inventories and have less need for loans to finance these and other expenses. Individuals fear the burden of a large debt during recession and depression and are generally more reluctant to borrow. On the loan supply side, banks are seeking safety when economic activity is contracting and want to increase their reserve ratios to achieve a greater measure of it. Thus as old loans are paid off new loans will not be made in sufficient quantities to offset them. The money supply shrinks, decreasing total spending still further, which may lead to further decreases in the money supply, and so on into a depression spiral.

An uncontrolled, unregulated banking system operates in a *destabilizing* manner over the course of business fluctuations. When total spending tends to decrease, the banking system decreases the money supply, thus accelerating the rate of decline. When total spending begins to increase, the banking system increases the money supply, thus augmenting the rate of increase. This is not to accuse bankers of diabolical intent; they operate their businesses like the managers of other types of enterprises operate theirs—to make profits. But because of the very special nature of the banking business, the production of its services—the extension of loans or credit—brings about significant changes in the money supply of the economy. Admittedly, there are a few other types of businesses where this is the case also, but at the present time at least, none is as important in this respect as banks.

Summary

Commercial banks are business enterprises engaged in providing two major kinds of services to the public: (1) they sell loans for which they are paid interest and (2) they provide the mechanism for transferring ownership of demand deposits from one person to another, for which they are usually paid service charges.

Demand deposits are bank liabilities or debts to individuals or organizations and they serve as a medium of exchange when the ownership of them is transferred from one to another by means of cheques. When deposits are transferred between persons using the same bank no currency changes hands—only a bookkeeping transfer is required. When deposits are transferred between persons using different banks, the bank from which the deposit is transferred has an adverse clearing balance and must transfer assets to the bank receiving the deposit. To minimize and to facilitate clearing payments, banks utilize a clearing house, one bank in which the others maintain deposits primarily for clearing purposes.

Banks create deposits or money when they make loans and investments. Deposits arising from loans and investments are called secondary deposits. Deposits made in currency are called primary deposits. The latter do not affect the total quantity of money in circulation; they simply substitute demand deposits for currency. The cash assets of a bank plus the deposits it has at the Bank of Canada are called its reserves. The ratio of its reserves to its total deposits is its reserve ratio. If all deposits were primary deposits, the bank's reserve ratio would be 100 percent, but when the bank makes loans, extending them to the borrower in the form of additional or secondary deposits, the reserve ratio is less than 100 percent and the bank is said to be operating with fractional reserves. The difference between the actual reserves that a bank has and the reserves it needs to maintain some desired reserve ratio is called its excess reserves. The amount of money that the banking system can create is equal to its excess reserves multiplied by the reciprocal of the average desired reserve ratio in the system. The banking system is increasing the money supply whenever the volume of new loans and investments being made exceeds the volume of old loans and investments being paid off or sold.

Contraction of the money supply by the banking system is the opposite of money creation. It occurs whenever the volume of old loans and investments being paid off or sold exceeds the volume of new ones being made by banks in the system. A reserve deficiency in the banking system will bring about a contraction of deposits amounting to the deficiency multiplied by the reciprocal of the reserve ratio.

When viewed in relation to business fluctuations, the banking system left uncontrolled and unregulated operates in a destabilizing way. During expansion and inflation the system creates additional money, thus increasing the rate of expansion. During recession and depression the system contracts the money supply, increasing the rate at which total spending falls.

Exercises and Questions for Discussion

1. A fractional reserve banking system depends on the willingness of the public to keep most of its money in banks. Explain why this statement is true.
2. Is it correct to say that banks lend out the money that is deposited with them? Explain.
3. The banking system does not actually create money, since loans are not considered as part of the money supply. The only way money can actually be created is for the government to print new paper money." Evaluate this statement.
4. If a banking system did not have clearing houses, would it still be possible for the system to create demand deposits? Explain.
5. What would be the seasonal (for example, Christmas) effects on the banking system's ability to create money? Elaborate.
6. If you were asked to tell banks what reserve ratio to maintain, on what economic factors would you base your decision? Under what circumstances would it be higher? Lower?

Selected Readings

Boreham, G. F., *et al.*, *Money and Banking: Analysis and Policy in a Canadian Context.* Toronto: Holt, Rinehart and Winston of Canada, 1969, Chap. 7.

Galbraith, J. A., "A Table of Banking Multipliers," *Canadian Journal of Economics*, November 1968, pp. 763-771.

McLeod, A. N., "The Mysteries of Credit Creation," *The Canadian Banker*, Winter 1959, pp. 20-28.

The Royal Bank of Canada, "How the Canadian Money Supply is Affected by Various Banking and Financial Transactions and Developments," Economic Research Department, Montreal, Autumn 1969, pp. 3-61.

Tobin, J., "Commercial Banks as Creators of Money", in D. Carson (ed.), *Banking and Monetary Studies*, pp. 408-412.

8

The Central Bank and Monetary Policy

In the two preceding chapters we studied the nature of money, its functions, and the ways in which it is created and destroyed. We must now carry our study somewhat further and discuss how the central authorities can seek to combat economic fluctuations by monetary action.

In order to understand the contribution of monetary policy to economic stability we shall look first at the structure of the Canadian banking system. Next we shall discuss the functions of a central bank, particularly as they are performed by the Bank of Canada. Third, we shall consider the tools available to Bank of Canada authorities for controlling the money supply. Finally, we shall see how the latter are co-ordinated to combat instability.

Structure of the Banking System

The Canadian banking system has two main parts: the Bank of Canada, which is the nation's central bank; and the privately-owned commercial banks which are under central-bank control. Other financial institutions, such as credit unions and *caisses populaires*, trust and mortgage loan companies, and insurance companies, carry on one or more banking functions—deposit, discount or investment—but are not allowed to call themselves banks. Although these non-bank financial intermediaries are not subject to *direct* regulation by Bank of Canada authorities, it is increasingly recognized that they are affected by monetary policy in the same way as the commercial banks.

Commercial Banks

Commercial banking in Canada is conducted by ten "chartered" banks, so called because each of them operates under the authority of a charter granted to it by the federal government.[1] Five of the banks are nation-wide institutions, three operate mainly in the Province of Quebec, one operates only in the Province of British Columbia at the present time, and one, a wholly owned subsidiary of a New York bank, has offices in six large cities. Typically, towns having populations of 10,000 or more are serviced by branch offices of two or more different banks. At the end of 1969 there were 6,038 branches spread throughout Canada (as well as 251 branches in foreign countries), thus providing an average of one banking office for each 3500 people in Canada. This represents a much higher density of banking services than in the United States where the comparable average is about 6300 people for each office.

Besides carrying chequing accounts, commercial banks accept savings deposits, make loans and investments, and provide a variety of services for businessmen and the general public. However, their special importance in our economy arises principally from their relation to chequable deposits. Not only do they "carry" these deposits, but by their lending and investing operations they actually create them.

The Bank of Canada

The Bank of Canada was incorporated under the Bank of Canada Act, 1934, and commenced operations on March 11, 1935. Initially the Bank was a privately owned institution although control was divided between the stockholders and the federal government (i.e. the Cabinet appointed the first Governors and directors and was to approve all future appointments of Governor and Deputy-Governor). A 1936 amendment to the Bank of Canada Act, however, made the government a majority share-

---

[1]*All bank charters in Canada must be renewed simultaneously at ten-year intervals, a statutory provision which provides the occasion for an extensive periodic review of chartered bank operations with a view to making improvements for the future. This decennial revision is a unique feature of Canadian banking. The latest revision of the Bank Act—the charter of all Canadian commercial banks—took place in 1967.*

holder and a further amendment in 1938 brought about the complete nationalization of the Bank.[2]

The head office of the central bank is situated in the City of Ottawa, but the Bank has the power to establish branches and agencies within Canada and, with the approval of the Cabinet, to set up branches and agencies outside the country. At the present time, the Bank maintains an agency at Halifax, Saint John (N.B.), Montreal, Ottawa, Toronto, Winnipeg, Regina, Calgary, and Vancouver and is represented in St. John's and Charlottetown.

The Bank's capitalization is $5 million; in addition, it has a wholly paid up Rest Fund (or surplus) of $25 million. All Bank profits are paid to the Receiver General of Canada and placed to the credit of the Consolidated Revenue Fund. In 1969 the net earnings of the Bank amounted to $228.7 million as compared with $186.1 million in 1968.

Originally it was provided that the Bank should maintain a minimum reserve of 25 percent of its note and deposit liabilities in gold coin and bullion, but this requirement was suspended in May, 1940, under authority of the War Measures Act. The suspension of the reserve requirement was continued under Section 25 of the Currency, Mint and Exchange Fund Act from 1952 until 1967. In March 1967 the gold reserve requirements for the Bank of Canada were formally abandoned when Section 23 of the Bank of Canada Act was repealed.

The responsibility for the affairs of the Bank rests with a Board of Directors composed of the Governor as chairman, the Deputy-Governor and twelve directors. The Deputy Minister of Finance sits on the Board but has no right to vote. The Board normally meets eight times a year. Between its meetings an Executive Committee, made up of the Governor, the Deputy-Governor, two directors and the Deputy Minister of Finance (again without the right to vote) acts for the Board and has all the powers of the latter. It is required to submit the minutes of its proceedings to the next Board meeting. A Bank by-law stipulates that the Executive Committee shall meet at least once each week.

The directors are appointed for three-year terms by the Minister of Finance subject to Cabinet confirmation. They, in turn, appoint the Governor and Deputy-Governor, also with the approval of the Cabinet, for seven-year terms during good behaviour. This latter provision means that they can be removed from office only by special legislation or a joint

[2]*The 1936 amendment provided for (1) the issue of $5.1 million additional capital stock, to be purchased by the Minister of Finance and held by him on behalf of the Government and (2) the appointment by the government of the necessary number of additional directors. The 1938 amendment provided for the redemption at $59.20 per share (par value $50.00) of all shares held by the public and the reduction of the total capitalization to 100,000 shares.*

address of both houses of Parliament. The other members of the Executive Committee are selected by the directors as well. All directors, including the Governor and Deputy-Governor, are eligible for re-appointment on the expiration of their terms of office.

Central Bank Functions

Since the concept of a central bank is more easily described than defined, we shall explain it by discussing the main central bank functions performed by the Bank of Canada. These are: (1) to serve as a bankers' bank, (2) to provide facilities for the final settlement of interbank debts, (3) to act as fiscal agent for the federal government, (4) to furnish the economy with the supply of currency (but not total money supply) that it desires, and (5) to exercise control over the volume of deposits created by the banking system. All of these functions are revealed by a study of the balance sheet of a central bank.

A Banker's Bank

In its role of the chartered banks' bank the Bank of Canada serves chartered banks in much the same way that chartered banks serve the public. Chartered banks may obtain deposits both by turning currency over to the central bank and by borrowing from it. Except for the vault cash necessary to carry on day-to-day operations, chartered banks carry their cash reserves on deposit at the central bank. Reciprocally, a chartered bank's cash reserves consist of whatever it has on deposit at the Bank of Canada plus its vault cash. As a rule, the chartered banks carry about two thirds of their reserves with the Bank of Canada.

Chartered bank *cash deposits* at the Bank of Canada are illustrated in Figure 8-1 . Chartered banks A and B each have cash reserves in the form of currency of $100,000 initially and the central bank balance sheet is initially blank. Both banks now deposit their currency holdings at the central bank, increasing its cash asset account by $200,000, in return for which the Bank of Canada sets up a liability or deposit account of $100,000 for each chartered bank. For the central bank what is owed bank A is a liability, while for bank A it is an asset. In fact, bank A is entitled by law to consider its deposit at the Bank of Canada as reserves. The same applies for bank B and other chartered banks. All that has happened in the balance sheets of banks A and B is that cash reserves in the form of currency are replaced by reserves in the form of deposits owed them by the central bank. Reserves of chartered banks are unchanged by

BANK A

BALANCE SHEET

Reserves	$100,000	Deposits	$1,000,000
L & I	$900,000		

BANK B

BALANCE SHEET

Reserves	$100,000	Deposits	$1,000,000
L & I	$900,000		

BANK OF CANADA

BALANCE SHEET

Cash	+ $200,000	Deposits	
		Bank A	+ $ 100,000
		Bank B	+ $ 100,000

Figure 8-1
Chartered bank deposits at the Bank of Canada.

the deposits of currency held by the banks in the Bank of Canada.

When a chartered bank borrows from the Bank of Canada, *reserves that did not exist before are created by the borrowing.* There are two methods used for borrowing. First, the chartered bank simply gives its promissory note to the central bank for the amount borrowed, using Government of Canada bonds and notes due it as security. Loans made to chartered banks in this way are called *advances.* Second, the chartered banks may take some of the notes due it[3] and endorse them to the central bank, making the notes the property of the latter but leaving the chartered bank liable for them if payment is not met when the notes fall due. This process is called *discounting.* Interest charged the chartered banks for loans by the Bank of Canada is called the *Bank Rate,* regardless of which process is used. In practice, lending by the Bank of Canada has come to take the form exclusively of secured advances.

[3]*The Bank of Canada Act specifies which of these are eligible and which are not.*

CHARTERED BANKS

BALANCE SHEET

Reserves	$100,000	Deposits		$1,000,000
	+ $ 10,000	Advances from		
L & I	$900,000	Bank of Canada	+ $	10,000

BANK OF CANADA

BALANCE SHEET

Cash	$100,000	Deposits		
Advances to		Chartered banks	$	100,000
Chartered banks	+ $ 10,000		+ $	10,000

Figure 8-2
Chartered-bank borrowing from the Bank of Canada.

Chartered-bank borrowing by means of advances secured by Canadian government obligations is illustrated in Figure 8-2 . A consolidated balance sheet for chartered banks is shown along with that of the Bank of Canada. The initial positions of both are represented by the figures without plus signs, while the plus figures indicate the changes brought about through the borrowing process. The borrowing of $10,000 by chartered banks creates a $10,000 liability account (due the Bank of Canada) for them; this account is called *Advances from Bank of Canada*. The $10,000 in promissory notes made out to the Bank of Canada by the chartered banks in the process are Bank of Canada assets and are listed under the heading *Advances to Chartered Banks*. The central bank makes the loans by increasing the amount it owes the chartered banks by $10,000; that is, by increasing chartered-bank deposits at the Bank of Canada by that amount. The $10,000 increase in chartered-bank deposits in the Bank of Canada is, of course, a $10,000 increase in chartered-bank cash reserves and is so listed on their balance sheets. The borrowing transaction has increased the assets and the liabilities of both chartered banks and the Bank of Canada by $10,000. Of great importance, as we shall see later, is the fact that $10,000 in *additional reserves* has been created for chartered banks.

Ultimate Clearing House

Since chartered banks carry their cash reserves as deposits at the Bank of Canada, the latter is in a natural position to provide for the final settlement of bank balances. These are illustrated in Figure 8-3 . Banks A and B are chartered banks with reserves deposited at the central bank. Again the initial positions of all three banks are shown without plus or minus indications, with the plus and minus figures denoting the changes that occur. We will employ this procedure throughout our discussion. Now suppose that someone with a deposit at bank A makes a $1,000 payment by cheque to someone who deposits the cheque at bank B. Bank B's deposits and reserves are both increased by $1,000 and the cheque is sent to one of the 51 clearing houses provided by the Canadian Bankers' Association. Here, the clearing house manager prepares a statement showing the amount that bank A owes bank B and sends it to the nearest Bank of Canada agency. On receipt of the statement the information is dispatched

BANK OF CANADA			
			BALANCE SHEET
Cash	$200,000	Deposits	
		Bank A	$100,000
			− $ 1,000
		Bank B	$100,000
			+ $ 1,000

BANK A			
			BALANCE SHEET
Reserves	$100,000	Deposits	$800,000
	− $ 1,000		− $ 1,000
L & I	$700,000		

BANK B			
			BALANCE SHEET
Reserves	$100,000	Deposits	$800,000
	+ $ 1,000		+ $ 1,000

Figure 8-3
The Bank of Canada as the ultimate clearing house.

by the agent to the Bank of Canada in Ottawa which then transfers $1,000 on its books from bank A's deposit to bank B's. In the process the cheque is returned to bank A which must decrease its deposits and reserves by $1,000 each. At this point, the clearing operation is complete.

Banking Functions for the Government

The Bank of Canada functions as a fiscal agent for the federal government, or as the government's banker, carrying out in this role two principal types of banking operation. First, government deposits on which government cheques are drawn are maintained at the central bank, and, second, the government borrows from the central bank from time to time.

CHARTERED BANKS

BALANCE SHEET

Reserves	$100,000	Deposits	$900,000
	− $ 10,000		− $ 10,000
L & I	$900,000		

BANK OF CANADA

BALANCE SHEET

Cash	$100,000	Deposits	
		Chartered Banks	$100,000
			− $ 10,000
		Gov't. of Canada	+ $ 10,000

Figure 8-4
Government deposits at the Bank of Canada acquired through tax collections.

One method by which the government acquires deposits at the Bank of Canada is illustrated in Figure 8-4 . Suppose that the Government of Canada collects $10,000 in taxes from the general public. Taxpayers write cheques to the government for that amount and the government deposits the cheques at the central bank. The latter transfers $10,000 from the deposit accounts of the chartered banks on which the cheques were written to the deposit account of the government—chartered banks and the federal government are customers of the Bank of Canada just as businesses and individuals are customers of chartered banks. The cheques are sent to the appropriate chartered banks, and chartered-bank reserves as well as deposits (those of the taxpayers) are reduced by $10,000. The net effect of the whole set of transactions is a deposit transfer at the central bank from chartered banks to the government, along with a corresponding decrease in chartered-bank reserves and the deposits at chartered banks. It is worth noting here, however, that the federal government maintains deposit balances with the chartered banks as well as with the Bank of Canada and permits the Bank, with the concurrence of the Minister of Finance, to transfer balances between the central bank and the chartered banks for cash-reserve management reasons.

The federal government borrows from the Bank of Canada by selling government bonds or treasury bills to it, and this process enables the central bank to *create* deposits for the government. Direct government borrowing from the Bank of Canada is illustrated in Figure 8-5 .[4] If $10,000 in government securities is acquired by the Bank of Canada, a government securities asset account of that amount is established. The central bank pays for the securities by increasing its deposit liabilities to the government (that is, by creating new government deposits) in the amount of $10,000. (If the government were now to spend what it has borrowed, what would be the possible impact on the total amount of money that the banking system could create?)

BANK OF CANADA			BALANCE SHEET
Cash	$100,000	Deposits	
		Chartered banks	$100,000
Government		Government	
securities	+ $ 10,000	of Canada	+ $ 10,000

Figure 8-5
Government deposits at the Bank of Canada acquired through borrowing.

Two further services of the Bank of Canada may be noted within this context. In the first place, the Bank acts as agent and adviser for the federal government in the management of the public debt. It announces new issues of government securities, receives subscriptions and payments, makes allotments, and arranges conversions. In addition, it redeems and exchanges securities and is instrumental in the transfer of short-term securities. Secondly, the Bank serves as the government's agency in gold and foreign exchange transactions and provides the government with information and advice on foreign exchange matters.

---

[4]*It may be useful to add that the Bank of Canada has not made cash advances to the Government of Canada for many years.*

Currency Supply Functions

We noted previously that the major part of the currency supply in Canada consists of Bank of Canada notes. What are Bank of Canada notes and how do they get into circulation?

A Bank of Canada note is just what the name implies. It is a certificate of indebtedness of the Bank to the bearer of the note, a kind of promissory note payable to the bearer instead of to a specific person. It constitutes a first lien upon all the assets of the Bank, and is payable in whatever form of money the bearer desires. He can convert it into bank deposits or coins of any kind.

The amount of Bank of Canada notes in circulation depends upon the proportion of the total money supply that the general public desires to hold in that form. Suppose, for example, that an individual goes to his bank to cash a cheque for $1,000 and the bank has no Bank of Canada notes—or, as is more likely, the withdrawal will pull the amount that it holds in its vaults below the amount that it desires to hold. As Figure 8-6 shows, the chartered bank goes to the central bank and exchanges $1,000 of its deposits there for Bank of Canada notes. Chartered bank deposits at the Bank are decreased by $1,000. Concurrently, a $1,000 liability

---

CHARTERED BANKS

BALANCE SHEET

Reserves	$100,000	Deposits	$900,000
	− $ 1,000		− $ 1,000
L & I	$800,000		

BANK OF CANADA

BALANCE SHEET

	Deposits	
	Chartered bank	$100,000
		− $ 1,000
	Notes in	
	circulation	+ $ 1,000

Figure 8-6
How Bank of Canada notes are put into circulation.

account, Notes in Circulation, is created at the Bank of Canada. The chartered bank turns the $1,000 in notes over to its customer, reducing his account by $1,000 and its reserves by the same amount. (Can you construct an example illustrating the opposite of this process—the retirement of Bank of Canada notes?) If the banking system were fully loaned out, that is, if there were no excess reserves in the system before the process was started, a multiple contraction of deposits would be generated because the conversion of reserves to central bank notes results in a deficiency in chartered-bank reserves. In practice, as we shall see later, the Bank of Canada can offset the effect of changes in note circulation on cash reserves by several means.

Money Supply Control Functions

Control of the economy's supply of money is without question the most important of the Bank of Canada's functions. It is so important that we shall examine it in considerable detail later in the chapter. At this juncture it will be given brief mention in very general terms only. This is not to say that the functions already discussed are unimportant; rather, it means that in performing its other functions the Bank of Canada is in a unique position to control the volume of chartered bank deposits and, hence, the money supply. Control of the money supply is important because it provides a partial means of controlling economic fluctuations.

In considering the instruments of control we shall argue frequently as though central bank officials can determine precisely when the money supply should be expanded and when it should be contracted and that the appropriate expansion or contraction follows immediately. This is not entirely so—it is not always easy to determine when and by how much the money supply should be changed. Further, control is not always direct nor is it complete. Lags occur between the initiation of action on the part of the monetary authorities and the resulting changes in chartered bank deposits. Further, chartered bank deposits do not constitute the entire money supply. Finally, taxation and government expenditure programs may make it extremely difficult for Bank of Canada authorities to change the money supply in the direction and magnitudes that they desire— fiscal operations and central bank operations are not always mutually consistent.

Instruments of Control

Bank of Canada authorities have five major instruments available for controlling the volume of credit extended by banks: (1) open-market operations; (2) transfers of Government of Canada funds; (3) changes in "bank" rate; (4) changes in secondary reserve requirements; and (5) moral suasion.

The first four tools go to the heart of the money-creating and destroying capabilities of banks operating on fractional reserves. They either change the *required amount of reserves* that must be held against deposits or they change the *quantity of reserves* available to the banking system. Changes in either of these lead to changes in the permissible level of bank lending and to consequent changes in the volume of deposits in the system. Use of the tools to contract or to restrict the expansion of chartered bank deposits is known as a *tight money policy*. When they are used to encourage expansion of such deposits an *easy money policy* is said to be in effect.

Open-Market Operations

Open-market operations have been the prime tool of monetary control since the establishment of the Bank of Canada. The term refers to the purchase and sale of marketable government bonds and treasury bills by the Bank of Canada. Marketable bonds and treasury bills, representing the bulk of the Canadian government debt of approximately $23 billion, are bought and sold in securities markets among institutions and individuals at whatever prices they will bring, much in the same manner as are corporation bonds. If persons or institutions wish to sell their holdings of government securities, they can sell them for whatever they (or their brokers) can get someone to pay. The existence of this large supply of government securities, issued and originally sold by the Canadian government at past dates, makes open-market operations possible.

Both the central bank and chartered banks at any given time hold government securities as a part of their assets. In the Bank of Canada balance sheet of Figure 8-7 it is assumed that the central bank holds $300,000 worth of government securities initially. Chartered banks have invested $200,000 in government securities, and in this and subsequent diagrams we break government securities away from the loans and investments account, showing each category of assets separately. Previously we have included chartered-bank holdings of government securities as a part of their loans and investments accounts.

If Bank of Canada authorities want to implement a tight money policy, they engage in open market sales of government securities.[5] The impact

---

[5]*To simplify the analysis we shall assume that open-market transactions of the Bank of Canada are made with chartered banks only; however, open-market sales are in fact made to the public including chartered banks, and open-market purchases are made from the public, including chartered banks. When transactions are made with the nonbank public the end results are approximately the same as they would be had they been made with chartered banks, except that the routes for getting to those results are more devious.*

CHARTERED BANKS

BALANCE SHEET

Reserves	$100,000 − $ 10,000	Deposits	$1,000,000 − $ 100,000
L & I	$700,000 − $100,000		
Government securities	$200,000 + $ 10,000		

BANK OF CANADA

BALANCE SHEET

Government securities	$300,000 − $ 10,000	Deposits Chartered banks Government	$100,000 − $ 10,000 $200,000

Figure 8-7
Effects on chartered bank deposits of open-market sales of government securities.

of sales amounting to $10,000 is recorded in   Figure 8-7. We assume that the required reserve ratio is 10 percent. The government securities asset account of chartered banks is increased by $10,000. Chartered banks pay for the securities by writing cheques on their accounts at the Bank of Canada, thus decreasing their deposit at the latter along with their reserves by $10,000. The government securities account of the central bank is decreased by $10,000. The purchase leaves chartered banks with a reserve deficiency of $10,000; consequently in order to re-establish a reserve ratio of 10 percent, chartered banks must reduce the volume of their loans outstanding and their deposits by $100,000. Thus *open-market sales lead to a contraction of the money supply that is a multiple of the amount of the sales.*

An easy money policy is implemented through *open-market purchases* of government securities by the Bank of Canada, as illustrated in Figure 8-8 . Again let the required reserve ratio be 10 percent and the initial positions of chartered banks and the Bank be represented by the figures without plus and minus signs. A $10,000 purchase of government securities from chartered banks by the central bank decreases the chartered banks' government securities account and increases that of the Bank of Canada by that amount. The latter pays for the bonds by increasing chartered-bank deposits by $10,000. This, of course, increases chartered-bank reserves by $10,000 and permits a $100,000 increase in chartered-bank loans and deposits. *Open-market purchases make possible an increase in the money supply that is a multiple of the amount of purchases.*

How can the Bank of Canada induce chartered banks to buy or sell government securities at the appropriate time? Chartered banks typically desire to maintain some sort of balance between earning assets that produce higher income yields but that may be somewhat more risky and those that produce lower yields but are more secure. Loans to private individuals illustrate the first type and holdings of government bonds or other govern-

CHARTERED BANKS		
		BALANCE SHEET
Reserves	$100,000 + $ 10,000	Deposits	$1,000,000 + $ 100,000
L & I	$700,000 + $100,000		
Government securities	$200,000 - $ 10,000		

BANK OF CANADA		
		BALANCE SHEET
Government securities	$200,000 + $ 10,000	Deposits Chartered banks	$100,000 + $ 10,000
		Government	$100,000

Figure 8-8
Effects on chartered bank deposits of open-market purchases of government securities.

ment securities the latter. An increase in the yield on government securities relative to that on commercial loans will change the relative attractiveness of the two types of assets, inducing banks to make adjustments in favour of larger amounts of government securities. The process also works in reverse.

The Bank of Canada will increase the yield obtainable on the bonds it offers for sale in order to induce chartered banks to purchase them. This is accomplished by a reduction in the asking price for the bonds. Suppose that a bond with a face value of $100 carries an interest rate of 4 percent, that is, it pays interest of $4 per year, and it matures in one more year. As this bond is bought and sold, its market price may fluctuate, but it pays interest of $4 per year and at the end of one more year the government will redeem it at its face value of $100. If government bonds now owned by chartered banks are currently yielding 4 percent on what the banks have invested in them, and if the Bank offers $100 face value bonds like the one described above at $99 each, purchases of such bonds will yield chartered banks 5.05 percent on their investment.[6] This is obviously an attractive offer and will induce chartered banks to increase their holdings of government securities.

Chartered banks can be induced to sell government securities to the central bank by the opposite technique. The central bank will increase its offering price for the bonds until it becomes attractive enough for chartered banks to sell. By apporpriate price manipulations the central bank can get chartered banks either to buy or sell whatever quantities of government securities are deemed desirable.

It looks as though open-market operations are a losing proposition for the Bank of Canada, since it appears to buy at high prices and sell at low prices. Although this may be the case, it does not necessarily happen in precisely this way. To sell bonds, the Bank needs only to sell below the current market price, and this says nothing about the prices at which the bonds were originally acquired. They may have been acquired originally for less. The same reasoning applies to purchases. But even if the central bank were to lose on open-market transactions, this would be of no consequence. Control over the money supply is its most important objective. Profit-making is secondary.

Two final comments should be made. One of the strong points of open-market operations is that it brings about definite changes in chartered-bank reserves and, if carried far enough, can bring about increases or decreases of almost any desired magnitude.[7] Fine adjustments or changes in the amount of chartered-bank reserves can be easily and quickly induced through changes in the selling or purchase prices of government securities. A second point in its favour is that it is not disruptive of chartered-bank expectations—they are not forced or coerced by Bank of Canada authorities to do anything. The Bank *makes it attractive* for chartered banks to buy or sell government securities, whichever is desirable, on a *voluntary* basis.[8]

Changes in the Government's Deposit Balances

Originally, transfers of government funds between the Bank of Canada and the chartered banks—draw-downs and re-deposits—were mainly

[6]*Investment in the bond yields interest of $4 plus appreciation of $1 in the price of the bond for a total of $5. The $5 yield divided by the $99 investment in the bond is the rate of return on the investment; that is, 5.05 percent.*

[7]*The limiting factor here is the amount of government securities held by the Bank of Canada available to be sold. This having been said, however, it remains a fact that this limit has never been approached in practice.*

[8]*Compare this with the legal compulsion to comply with an increase in the secondary reserve ratio requirement.*

undertaken to prevent the uneven flow of government receipts and expenditures from affecting the volume of cash reserves held by the banking system. In the last few years, however, government deposit transfers have become a major means of central bank control of cash reserves. If the Bank of Canada transfers more funds to the federal government's account at the central bank than are necessary to compensate for government cheques currently being cleared, the effect is to decrease chartered bank cash. If it reduces the size of the government's balance with the Bank of Canada, the result is an increase in the banks' cash reserves.

Suppose the central bank wishes to effect a tight money policy and transfers $10,000 of government funds from the chartered banks to the Bank of Canada. The result is recorded in   Figure 8-9 . The Bank of Canada's balance sheet shows a decrease in its deposits due to chartered banks and an increase in its deposits due to government. The chartered banks' reserve balances decrease by $10,000, as do their deposits due to government. With reserves of $90,000, a legal reserve requirement of 10 percent and deposit liabilities of $990,000, it is clear that the banking system has a reserve deficiency of $9,000. To eliminate this deficiency, the chartered banks must reduce the volume of their loans outstanding and their deposits by $90,000. *Thus a transfer of government funds from the chartered banks to the Bank of Canada leads to a contraction of the money supply that is a multiple of the "draw-down."*

Suppose now the Bank of Canada wishes to follow an easy money policy and transfers $10,000 of government funds from the central bank to the

CHARTERED BANKS
BALANCE SHEET

Reserves	$100,000 − $ 10,000	Deposits Government	$100,000 − $ 10,000
L & I	$900,000 − $ 90,000	Non-government	$900,000 − $ 90,000

BANK OF CANADA
BALANCE SHEET

	Deposits Chartered banks	$100,000 − $ 10,000
	Government	$100,000 + $ 10,000

Figure 8-9
Effects on chartered bank deposits of "draw-downs."

chartered banks. Chartered bank balances with the Bank of Canada are increased by $10,000, bank reserves are enhanced by a like amount, and the cash ratio of the banks rises above 10 percent. These are illustrated in Figure 8-10 . Excess reserves of $9,000 will permit an expansion in loans and investments and in deposits of $90,000. *Thus a transfer of government cash balances from the central bank to the chartered banks leads to an expansion of the money supply that is a multiple of the "re-deposit."*

CHARTERED BANKS

BALANCE SHEET

Reserves	$100,000 + $ 10,000	Deposits Government	$100,000 + $ 10,000
L & I	$900,000 + $ 90,000	Non-government	$900,000 + $ 90,000

BANK OF CANADA

BALANCE SHEET

Deposits Chartered banks	$100,000 + $ 10,000
Government	$100,000 − $ 10,000

Figure 8-10
Effects on chartered bank deposits of "re-deposits."

To sum up, the central bank may engage in monetary management by regulating the location of the government's deposit holdings. Of course, the central bank loses the use of this instrument when government balances in total are too low to permit adequate transfers. On the other hand, the Bank of Canada can flush up government cash balances by purchasing securities directly from the government or outstanding securities from the government's Securities Investment Account[9] or foreign exchange held by the Exchange Fund Account.[10]

[9]*The Securities Investment Account has been used for several purposes: (1) to change bank cash; (2) to stabilize Government of Canada bond prices; (3) to invest temporary excess cash balances of the federal government; and (4) for debt management purposes.*
[10]*The Exchange Fund Account, which was set up by the Canadian government in 1935, is used to influence conditions in the foreign exchange market. The Bank of Canada is the government's agent for operating both the Exchange Fund Account and the Securities Investment Account.*

Changes in the Bank Rate

In theory, when chartered banks are short of funds to meet the needs of their customers, they borrow from the central bank in order to increase their lending power. We shall suppose that chartered banks are initially in the position shown in Figure 8-11, with reserves of $100,000, loans and investments of $920,000, deposits of $1,000,000, and advances from the Bank of Canada of $20,000. Of the $100,000 in chartered bank reserves, $20,000 was obtained by the borrowing from the central bank. The minimum cash reserve ratio is assumed to be 10 percent. The *bank-rate*— the rate of interest that the Bank of Canada charges those who borrow from it[11]—is assumed to be 4 percent initially.

Assume now that bank rate changes are used to put a tight money policy into effect. An increase in the bank rate to 5 percent makes borrowing more costly to chartered banks and, presumably, induces them to contract the average amount of their borrowing. If it induces them to reduce their level of borrowing by half, then $10,000 of chartered-bank deposits at the central bank are used to pay off $10,000 in the latter's advances. On the balance sheet of chartered banks, central bank loans are reduced by $10,000 and so are chartered-bank reserves, since the decrease in char-

---

CHARTERED BANKS
BALANCE SHEET

Reserves	$100,000 − $ 10,000	Deposits	$1,000,000 − $ 100,000
L & I	$920,000 − $100,000	Advances from Bank of Canada	$ 20,000 − $ 10,000

BANK OF CANADA
BALANCE SHEET

Government securities	$ 80,000	Deposits	$100,000 − $ 10,000
Advances to chartered banks	$ 20,000 − $ 10,000		

Figure 8-11
Effects on chartered bank deposits of an increase in the bank rate.

---

[11]*Lending by the Bank of Canada is restricted to loans to the chartered banks, the Government of Canada, the Montreal City and District Savings Bank, and designated money market dealers (in the form of "repurchase" agreements).*

tered-bank deposits at the Bank of Canada is a decrease in chartered-bank reserves. Chartered banks now have only $90,000 in reserves supporting $1,000,000 in deposits. The reserve deficiency of $10,000 calls for a $100,000 contraction in chartered-bank loans and investments and in deposits, thus putting the tight money policy into operation.

For an easy money policy the Bank of Canada lowers the bank rate. Chartered-bank borrowing from the central bank becomes less costly, presumably bringing about an increase in the average level of such borrowing. An increase in chartered-bank borrowing means an increase in chartered-bank deposits at the central bank, and this in turn means an increase in chartered-bank reserves. Excess reserves acquired in this way permit an increase in chartered-bank deposits (via an increase in loans and investments) equal to the increase in reserves multiplied by the reciprocal of the reserve ratio.

In practice, chartered banks have been reluctant to borrow from the Bank of Canada except to meet temporary reserve deficiencies, and once borrowing has occurred there is a strong tendency on the part of chartered banks to repay promptly.[12] Consequently, although changes in the bank rate may have some impact on chartered-bank borrowing, the effect has not been a major one.

Still, it is also true that changes in the bank rate can serve as a sign to the financial community as to the intentions or expectations of the central bank. Or, to put the same point another way, bank rate changes provide evidence of official determination to counteract inflationary or deflationary pressures. Accordingly, a change in bank rate often results in a changed attitude toward loan expansion by the banks.

Changes in Secondary Reserve Requirements

Before considering secondary-reserve ratio changes, a brief digression may be appropriate. When the Bank of Canada was created in 1934, monetary control was not an immediate problem. It seemed then inappropriate and futile to try to fix a range for the banks' cash ratios. But the principle of monetary management was incorporated in the Bank of

---

[12]*In this connection, it should be pointed out that the arrangements governing chartered bank access to central bank credit were revised in 1969. Under the new procedure, a central bank advance can be taken for a period of either 2 or 3 juridical days; formerly Bank of Canada advances were made for a minimum period of seven days and chartered banks were obliged to pay interest for the full term. Also deserving of mention is the fact that the first central bank advance taken in an averaging period—chartered banks are now required to maintain their statutory cash requirements on a half-monthly basis—bears interest at the* published *bank rate; if a second or subsequent advance is required the rate in principle will be higher and will be negotiated.*

Canada Act. It took the form of a clause requiring the chartered banks to keep a cash reserve of not less than 5 percent of their deposit liabilities payable in Canadian dollars in the form of Bank of Canada notes and deposits with the Bank of Canada. A 1954 amendment to the Bank of Canada Act set the legal minimum cash reserve ratio at 8 percent and empowered the central bank to vary this ratio between 8 and 12 percent. The provision of a variable cash reserve requirement was designed to add a new instrument to those available to the Bank of Canada to enable it to perform its statutory duty of regulating the supply of money "in the best interest of the economic life of the nation". Let us illustrate the effects of a change in cash reserve requirements.

Suppose that chartered banks are initially in the position shown in Figure 8- 12 , with reserves of $100,000, loans and investments of $900,000, and total deposits of $1,000,000. Suppose now that the limits within which the minimum reserve ratio can be varied by the central bank are from 5 to 20 percent (for obvious reasons, it is more convenient to work with reserve ratios that are multiples of five) and that the present ratio is 10 percent. As long as reserves remain at $100,000, chartered banks have created as much money as they are capable of creating.

CHARTERED BANKS

BALANCE SHEET

Reserves	$100,000		Deposits	$1,000,000
L & I	$900,000			− $ 500,000
	− $500,000			

REQUIRED RESERVE RATIO
Initial	10%
Raised to	20%

Figure 8-12
Effects on chartered bank deposits of an increase in the required cash-reserve ratio.

To effect a tight money policy using this instrument by itself, the central bank can raise the legal reserve ratio as high as 20 percent. If it does this the $100,000 of chartered-bank reserves will no longer support $1,000,000 in deposits; only $500,000 in deposits can be supported. Banks must let old loans be paid off faster than new loans are made until a net amount of $500,000 in old loans has been liquidated. This will have the effect of reducing deposits by the same amount, as is indicated in Figure 8-12 .

An easy money policy via reserve ratio changes is put into effect by the central bank through decreases in the minimum reserve ratio requirement. In Figure 8-13 we start from the same initial position as before, with a

```
┌─────────────────────────────────────────────────────────────────────────┐
│  CHARTERED BANKS                                                          │
│                                              BALANCE SHEET                │
│                                                                           │
│     Reserves        $100,000         Deposits         $1,000,000          │
│     L & I           $900,000                          + $1,000,000        │
│                    + $500,000                                             │
│                                                                           │
│     REQUIRED RESERVE RATIO                                                │
│     Initial          10%                                                  │
│     Reduced to        5%                                                  │
└─────────────────────────────────────────────────────────────────────────┘
```

Figure 8-13
Effects on chartered-bank deposits of a decrease in the required cash-reserve ratio.

designated reserve ratio of 10 percent, $100,000 in reserves, $900,000 in loans and investments, and $1,000,000 in deposits. If the required reserve ratio were now reduced to 5 percent, reserves required to support $1,000,000 in deposits would be only $50,000, leaving $50,000 as excess reserves. Using the standard formula, we find that excess reserves of $50,000 will permit an expansion in loans and investments and in deposits of $1,000,000—that is, $50,000 multiplied by the reciprocal of 5 percent. Thus total reserves of $100,000 will support $2,000,000 in deposits: cutting the reserve ratio in half doubles the potential chartered-bank deposit expansion.

On the basis of explanations given at the time of its introduction, it is clear that the power to change chartered-bank reserve requirements was not regarded by the Bank of Canada as a regular substitute for the technique of open-market operations, but rather intended to help deal with a sudden inflationary surge. In the event, the Bank of Canada did not see fit to exercise its authority to alter the cash-reserve ratio, and this instrument was finally abandoned in the 1967 amendments to the banking acts.

The 1967 Bank Act revision provided for a split cash reserve requirement. A 12 percent minimum cash reserve now applies to chartered bank demand deposits (i.e., current accounts and personal chequing accounts) and a 4 percent minimum to deposit liabilities payable after notice. As noted above, these ratios are not subject to variation at the discretion of the Bank of Canada. At the same time, the central bank was given the legal authority to impose on the chartered banks a minimum secondary reserve requirement in the form of cash (additional to the cash that forms part of the required cash reserve) treasury bills, and demand loans to money-market dealers (day-loans) and to vary this requirement between 0 and 12 percent of Canadian deposit liabilities. The maximum increase may not exceed 1 percent per month, the banks must be given one month's notice of any increase in the ratio, and, after a period where no secondary reserve has been required, the initial rate may not exceed 6 percent.

Two observations are worth stressing here. In the first place, although the Bank of Canada cannot now change the legal cash-reserve ratio, fixed minimum cash-reserve requirements still serve a very useful purpose by providing a fulcrum upon which open-market operations and bank-rate policy can acquire the necessary leverage.

Secondly, the basic difference between a variable cash-reserve ratio and a variable secondary-reserve ratio is the effect on bank earnings, since cash reserves are nonearning assets. Minimum liquid-asset ratios are designed to immobilize a part of the chartered banks' holdings of short-term securities so that they cannot be converted into cash. Thus, the effect of raising the secondary-reserve ratio is the same as if the cash ratio were raised, except that the banks would earn interest on that part of their reserves held in the form of treasury bills and day loans.[13] Furthermore, this technique is intended to make it more onerous for the banks to switch out of securities into loans; if the banks wish to expand their loans and the liquid-asset ratio is at the minimum set by the central bank, they will be required to dispose of their less liquid securities on which the capital-loss deterrent to selling will be greater. To put it differently, by raising the secondary-reserve ratio the Bank of Canada could reduce the ability of the chartered banks to continue financing loan expansion through liquidation of treasury bills and day-loans, and thus compel them to begin rationing their loans more stringently and sooner than they might otherwise have done. Conversely by lowering the ratio or eliminating the requirement entirely the central bank could expand the scope for chartered bank liquidation of short-term assets to accommodate a demand for bank loans.

In sum, it seems likely that variations in the minimum secondary-reserve ratio will be a more frequently used element in the ordinary management of monetary policy in the future than has been the discretionary power to alter the minimum cash reserves of the banks in the past. It may be useful to add that the secondary ratio is being used as a means of government financing, as witness the recent increase in the ratio from 8 percent to 9 percent effective July 1, 1970. This was done solely to provide a haven for additional Government of Canada treasury bills issued in May when federal cash balances were being run down by foreign exchange purchases.

---

[13]*It is important to appreciate that an increase in the secondary-reserve ratio would not in itself affect the money supply. In general, the banks would meet the higher secondary requirement by selling securities and use the proceeds of these sales to acquire treasury bills or day-loans to money market dealers, or both. As a result, the overall level of bank deposits would remain the same and the money supply would be unchanged. Nevertheless, it is expected that an increase in the secondary-reserve ratio would compel the banks to scrutinize loan applications more carefully and would temper the extension of credit to private borrowers.*

Moral Suasion

Another instrument of control used by the Bank of Canada is *moral suasion*—i.e. informal advice to, and special arrangements with, the chartered banks and at times other lenders. By conferences, oral and written statements, and mere circular letters, the central bank attempts to persuade the chartered banks and sometimes other financial institutions to expand or contract the volume of credit by increasing or decreasing their loans according to circumstances. It should be emphasized, however, that such lenders are not obliged by law to follow the central bank's recommendations.

Moral suasion is also the source from which spring many selective credit controls. Under selective credit controls the central bank takes action to alter the amount (or terms) of credit available for specific groups of people that desire to use it for a particular purpose. In other words, a selective credit control curtails the demand for credit rather than the supply, as occurs under the application of more general controls.

Perhaps the best way to bring out the use of moral suasion as an instrument of credit control is to give a few examples:

1. In February, 1951, following discussions with the Bank of Canada, the chartered banks agreed to accept a "credit ceiling" and to restrict their less essential loans (loans to finance companies, loans intended for speculation, capital loans, etc.). This understanding was suspended in May, 1952.

2. In the late autumn of 1955, a number of conferences were held between the central bank and the chartered banks to discuss the impending threat of inflation. In consequence, the banks agreed to (a) scrutinize loan applications more carefully; (b) refrain from making capital loans to, or purchasing directly securities from, any one business corporation in amounts exceeding $250,000; (c) maintain on a monthly average basis a 15 percent minimum ratio of liquid assets to deposits.

3. In the fall of 1956, a conference between the Bank of Canada and members of the governing bodies of the Montreal, Canadian and Toronto Stock Exchanges was held, at which the central bank emphasized the need for restraint in the extension of stock market credit. After discussion, the three exchanges agreed that it would be inappropriate for the volume of stock market credit to expand any further under prevailing conditions and a notice to this effect was issued by these exchanges to their members.

4. During the autumn of 1967 the larger chartered banks competed vigorously for large blocks of short-term corporate funds. In fact, the competition for fixed-term deposits became so aggressive that it appeared to

be uneconomic to Bank of Canada officials. Moreover, they believed that it threatened to introduce some instability and distortions into the financial system. Accordingly, they expressed their concern to the banks and a more normal relationship of interest rates came about soon thereafter.

5. Other uses of moral suasion occurred in 1969 when the central bank sought to soften the impact of monetary restraint. The Bank of Canada asked the chartered banks to (a) have a special concern for borrowers in the less prosperous parts of the country; (b) pay particular attention to loan requests from small businesses; (c) maintain a reasonable continuity of lending on housing mortgages; (d) give priority in the use of their funds to the credit-worthy needs of their Canadian customers.

As the examples mentioned suggest, the Bank of Canada has, over a period of time, acquired effective influence over the banking community. In the main, the use of persuasion to initiate monetary restraint has met with success. Nevertheless, the use of moral suasion on several occasions has been seriously questioned; this poses the problem as to where the limits of central bank advice should properly be set. We need not go into this complex subject here. It is sufficient to note that moral suasion has proved to be a valuable adjunct to the mechanistic instruments of money and credit control.

Monetary Policy for Stability

The tools of monetary control should be used in a coordinated way to combat economic fluctuations. Central bank activities of this kind are referred to as *monetary policy*. A tight money policy is appropriate for controlling inflation, while recession and depression call for an easy money policy. But things are not always so simple. Though monetary policy can contribute to economic stability, it is not likely to be sufficient in and of itself to bring about simultaneously full employment, economic growth, and price-level stability. As we shall see later, monetary policy must be coordinated with fiscal policy and other appropriate measures to reach an acceptable measure of success in achieving those and other economic goals. But for the present we are concerned primarily with monetary policy.

Combating Inflation

The implementation of a tight money policy to control inflation starts logically with open-market operations or with draw-downs. The Bank of

Canada can engage in the sale of government securities or in the transfer of government funds from the chartered banks to the central bank, thus reducing reserves of chartered banks. If chartered banks have excess reserves, open-market sales or draw-downs will reduce them, curtailing the potential ability of the banking system to expand its loans and deposits. Once all excess reserves have been absorbed, further open-market sales or draw-downs will induce contraction of the money supply.

Concurrently with open-market sales or with draw-downs, an increase in the bank rate serves as a second order or back up control measure. Conceivably, chartered banks, as they lose reserves through their purchases of bonds, can replenish those reserves by borrowing from the central bank. An increase in the bank rate will reduce their incentive to increase their level of borrowing and will thus reinforce the effectiveness of either open-market sales or draw-downs, or both.

Direct action to reduce chartered-bank excess reserves can, of course, be taken via increases in the required secondary-reserve ratio, but this tool should be used sparingly. If banks were confronted with frequent changes in the secondary-reserve ratio, the effectiveness of the device would soon be lost. It would be necessary for banks to hold adequate liquid assets to meet the highest anticipated reserve ratio, and this would mean that the level of loans would no longer be responsive to (frequent) changes in the ratio.

Combating Recession and Depression

The order in which the control instruments should be used to implement an easy money policy during recession and depression are the same as for the tight money policy. The first line of defense is either open-market purchases of government securities by the central bank from chartered banks or transfers of government balances from the Bank of Canada to the chartered banks to increase the volume of chartered bank reserves and to make deposit expansion more attractive to them. Additionally, the bank rate could be lowered and so could the required secondary-reserve ratio, but neither of these is likely to be as effective in inducing chartered banks to increase their lending, or even to halt their contraction of loans and of deposits, as an increase in chartered-bank reserves via open-market purchases or by means of redeposits.

Monetary policy aimed at combating recession and depression has certain fundamental weaknesses. The difficulty lies in securing an expansion of loans and of deposits by chartered banks during a period of recession or depression. Banks are reluctant to lend because of the repayment risks when economic activity is declining. Since the pace of business activity is slowing down, the public has less desire to borrow. Open-market purchases by the Bank of Canada or redeposits offer the greatest possibility of combating these tendencies, but even in this case chartered banks may not be able to expand loans if there is no demand for loans.

The chances of stemming recession by means of monetary policy will be enhanced if it is put to work promptly. The more serious the recession is allowed to become, the greater the barriers to preventing monetary contraction. The sooner the central bank acts, the less opportunity there is for public confidence to be shaken, and the easier it will be to prevent a contraction in loans and deposits and, perhaps, to encourage some expansion.

Recent Monetary Policy in Canada

Our experience with monetary policy as a means of stabilizing the economy is still rather limited. The Bank of Canada Act is now a little over 35 years old, but effective monetary policy has been slow in developing. When the Bank of Canada commenced operations in 1935, the control of money and credit involved the implementation of an appropriate anti-depression monetary policy. As Graham Towers, then Governor of the Bank of Canada has expressed it:

> "The pre-war period of our operations began after recovery from the worst effects of the depression had started but unemployment was still very evident and in the circumstances an 'easy money' policy was appropriate. For that reason the Bank of Canada carried on 'open market' purchases of government securities which increased the cash reserves of the chartered banks and maintained their liquidity somewhat above the normal level so that they would have an incentive to expand credit in the form of loans or security purchases, as opportunities were presented. The overall result of monetary action in these years was quite substantial as is indicated by the fact that total Canadian bank deposits and note circulation in August, 1939, were about 14% higher than in the former peak year of 1929."[14]

Clearly during the first several years of its existence, economic conditions did not require uncommon brilliance in technique from the fledgeling central bank.

During World War II and its aftermath the Bank of Canada was severely handicapped in pursuing sensible monetary policy. The government was engaged in large-scale borrowing to finance the war. Desiring to maintain a good market for government bonds without increasing the interest rates

[14]*Bank of Canada*, Press Release, *April 21, 1949, speech by Mr. G. Towers, Governor of the Bank of Canada, delivered at a meeting of the Institute of Chartered Accountants of Ontario.*

yielded by them, the fiscal authorities induced the Bank of Canada to agree to engage in open-market purchases of these securities in sufficient quantities to prevent their prices from falling (and their yields from rising). As larger and larger quantities were placed on the market by the government this amounted to an easy money policy throughout the war. In retrospect Governor Towers has said that:

> "The overriding necessities were such that the most a central bank could hope for was that the costs of the war should be covered by taxation to the maximum extent the public would bear and that everything possible would be done to encourage savings. Financing directly or indirectly through the banks had to be looked upon as a last resort, but to the extent that it was inevitable central bank policy had to adapt itself to this situation."[15]

After the war the easy money policy was continued despite the emergence of unexpectedly strong and persistent inflationary forces. As Governor Towers explained it, a restrictive monetary policy was not adopted because "it was felt that the degree of possible benefit to our price and cost structure would not be commensurate with the damage done in hampering reconversion and holding back capital development".[16] Bank of Canada efforts at controlling the first period of post-war inflation consisted of: (1) a 1947 recommendation that the chartered banks scrutinize closely the inventories and receivables of their customers; (2) a minor modification in the policy of supporting bond prices early in 1948 (the Bank ceased its practice of publishing daily a list of bids and offers for federal securities); (3) in February, 1948 the central bank suggested that current conditions "made it undesirable for capital expenditures to be financed through expansion of bank credit."[17] As already explained, quantitative credit controls were not used as a restraining influence because of the Bank of Canada's conception of its responsibility for bond prices.

The first post-war surge of inflationary pressure came to an end in the third quarter of 1948, and prices levelled out until the second quarter of 1950, when serious inflationary forces returned. On October 17, 1950, the Bank of Canada raised its discount rate from 1½ percent to 2 percent and issued the following statement:

> "At the time the reduction in Bank Rate took place in 1944, the Bank expressed the view that it did not then see any prospect of an economic

---

[15]*Bank of Canada*, Press Release, *October 18, 1954, speech by Mr. G. Towers, delivered to the Canadian Club, Montreal, Quebec.*

[16]*Statement of Mr. G. F. Towers, at a hearing of the Standing Committee on Banking and Commerce of the House of Commons, March 18, 1954.* Minutes of Proceedings and Evidence, *No. 16, pp. 694-95.*

[17]*Bank of Canada*, Annual Report, *1948, p. 7.*

situation in the post-war period of a character which would call for a policy of raising interest rates. The change to a 2% Bank Rate is an indication that the earlier view no longer holds good under today's conditions. . . ."[18]

This increase in bank rate meant that the central bank, in its open-market operations, would allow the fluctuating forces of demand and supply to be reflected more readily in variations in securities prices. This change in bank rate marked the beginning of the official rediscovery of money in Canada.

As noted earlier, a "credit ceiling" was imposed upon the chartered banks in February, 1951. One inference to be drawn from this action is that "the Bank of Canada was no more willing to make open-market operations an effective instrument of control in the post-Korean period than in the immediate post-war years."[19] The credit ceiling was removed in May, 1952, but with the threat of inflation still present, the central bank pursued a policy of moderate monetary restraint until the autumn of 1953, when for the first time in the post-war period it was faced with a downward readjustment of economic activity. The Bank of Canada, however, delayed in moving to monetary ease until after mid-1954, when it permitted the chartered banks to keep much of the cash freed by the latter moving from the traditional 10 percent cash ratio to the new legal minimum of 8 percent.[20] This monetary expansion, as measured by the Bank's ability to purchase government securities without having to reduce other assets, continued until August, 1955, when the Bank of Canada began to "lean against the wind" as inflationary pressures became manifest. The monetary authorities resorted to a more rigorous policy of monetary restraint via open-market sales, bank rate increase, and moral suasion as the inflation gathered momentum and by mid-1956 the monetary expansion had been checked. This policy was pursued until the autumn of 1957, when another recession began. After a brief interlude of monetary ease by way of open-market purchases and moral suasion during the recession of 1957-1958, restraint was resumed. And apart from minor fluctuations, the total stock of money remained fairly constant until late 1960, when recessionary tendencies reappeared. Monetary policy eased considerably during 1961 and throughout the first part of 1962 as the Bank became a heavy net purchaser of securities.

[18]*Bank of Canada*, Press Release, *October 16, 1950.*
[19]*R. C. McIvor*, Canadian Monetary Banking and Fiscal Development. *Toronto: Macmillan Company of Canada Ltd., 1958, p. 221.*
[20]*The effective lowering of the minimum bank cash ratio on July 1, 1954, immediately gave the chartered banks about $200 million in excess reserves. In the following six months only $91 million of bank cash was absorbed by the central bank.*

Monetary restraint was resumed in June, 1962 following a sharp decline in the official foreign exchange reserves. By September, however, the recovery of the foreign exchange reserves and the restoration of confidence in Canada's ability to maintain the exchange value of the Canadian dollar at the level established in May, 1962 (C$ = .925 U.S.), had proceeded far enough to permit some relaxation of monetary policy. Accordingly, central bank policy shifted from restraint to ease and became increasingly easier throughout 1963 and 1964 by means of open-market purchases and bank-rate cuts. In 1965, however, as the Canadian economy moved toward full utilization of resources, monetary policy tightened and the rate of increase in the money supply levelled off in the latter part of the year. A period of subdued economic growth, which lasted from the spring of 1966 to the final months of 1967, brought about some easing in monetary policy, which was also appropriate to Canada's external financial position; open-market purchases, decreases in bank rate, and moral suasion were the tools used to ease monetary conditions.

As 1968 opened, Canada faced an exchange crisis. Accordingly, the Bank of Canada moved to make monetary policy extremely tight. By mid-year the exchange crisis was over and monetary policy was made less restrictive. The cash reserve position of the banking system was eased and the bank rate was reduced in three steps from 7½ to 6 percent. When it became clear in the autumn of 1968 that the anticipated moderation of inflationary pressures was not occurring, monetary policy was again directed towards restraint, and it has continued to retain that posture. The recent tightening of monetary policy has involved open market sales, draw-downs, increases in bank rate and in the minimum secondary-reserve ratio, and moral suasion.

Though generally working in the proper direction for economic stability, monetary policy has exhibited certain shortcomings. In the first place, economic fluctuations still have a way of slipping up on us. Economic forecasting techniques seem to be improving, but they are not yet infallible. It is difficult for the monetary authorities to determine precisely when a tight money policy or an easy money policy ought to be inaugurated. Once a recession or an inflation is underway, the proper course of action becomes obvious, but precisely when should it be started and precisely when should it be terminated? Secondly, monetary policy by itself may not be able to accomplish the job of stabilization. Fiscal policy, to be discussed in the following chapters, may be needed to supplement it.

A third dilemma for those responsible for monetary policy (and for fiscal policy-makers as well) is whether full employment and price stability are compatible objectives. In the period from 1958 to 1963, unemployment rates averaged about 6½ percent of the civilian labour force whereas the annual rate of increase of the consumer price index was about 1.2 percent. As 1970 began, consumer prices were rising at a rate of approximately 4.5 percent and unemployment (seasonally adjusted) stood at about 5 percent of the labour force. Can policies designed to increase total spending and thereby to increase employment bring unemployment rates down to acceptable levels without generating an unacceptable rate in inflation? We shall return to this question after we have studied government finance and fiscal policy.

Summary

The Bank of Canada is the keystone of the Canadian banking system. It carries out five closely related functions in its role as a central bank. It serves as a bankers' bank, as a final clearing house for the chartered banks, as the government's banker, and as a control agency over the paper currency and the bank deposit components of the money supply.

In carrying out monetary policy, or controlling the volume of bank deposits in a way intended to promote economic stability, Bank of Canada authorities employ five primary tools. These are moral suasion, changes in the required secondary-reserve ratio, changes in bank rate, changes in the location of the government's deposit balances, and open-market operations. The latter two appear to be the most effective of the five and represent the first line of defence against recession or inflation. Raising or lowering the bank rate is a companion tool to open-market operations and to draw-downs or redeposits. All three devices affect the total volume of deposits through their impacts on the quantities of cash reserves available to the chartered banks. The fourth instrument, changing the required secondary-reserve ratio, should in all probability be used sparingly. Moral suasion may be used to regulate both the supply of, and the demand for, money and credit.

The emergence of monetary policy as a force of major economic significance is a current phenomenon, dating essentially from the mid-1950's. During the first two decades of its existence, the Bank of Canada pursued an easy money policy. The government's fiscal policies were regarded as the prime instrument of economic stabilization. Only in the last 15 years has the Bank of Canada come to play an equally important role in government-anticyclical policy. The impact of fiscal policy on the economy is considered in Chapter 11.

Exercises and Questions for Discussion

1. "The Bank of Canada's liabilities form the base of the economy's money supply." Explain this statement.
2. Does the fact that it is the "lender of last resort" hinder the use of discretionary pressures by the central bank? Discuss.
3. Under what circumstances might each of the tools of monetary policy be ineffective?
4. If inflation is occurring, are there ever any arguments that might be made against restrictive monetary policy? Elaborate.
5. Discuss the "proper use" of the secondary-reserve ratio, the bank rate, and open-market operations during (a) a recession, (b) an inflation, and (c) an inflation with high unemployment. Consider in your discussion the effects of each policy.
6. Why does the current market price of government securities fluctuate? What is the relevance of this fact to monetary policy?

Selected Readings

Bank of Canada, *Submission to the Royal Commission on Banking and Finance*. Ottawa, May, 1964.

Boreham, G. F., *et al.*, *Money and Banking: Analysis and Policy in a Canadian Context*. Toronto: Holt, Rinehart and Winston of Canada, 1969, Chaps. 8, 9, 10, 11, and 26.

Brewis, T. M., *et al.*, *Canadian Economic Policy*, rev. ed. Toronto: Macmillan, 1965, Chaps. 10 and 11.

Gordon, H. S., *The Economists Versus the Bank of Canada*. Toronto: Ryerson Press, 1961.

McIvor, R. C., *Canadian Monetary Banking and Fiscal Development*. Toronto: Macmillan Company of Canada Ltd., 1958, Chaps. 10 and 11.

Neufeld, E. P., *Bank of Canada Operations and Policy*. Toronto: University of Toronto Press, 1958.

9

Government Economic Activities: The Expenditures Side

Economists have long advocated that governments use tax and expenditure policies—or fiscal policies—in such a way that they promote economic stability and growth.[1] But those in control of governmental policy-making have been cool to proposals that taxes and expenditures be deliberately manipulated for this purpose. Prime Ministers Pearson and Trudeau were able in some measure to overcome that coolness and to succeed in using fiscal policy in limited doses for growth[2] and stabilization ends.[3]

In order to understand how fiscal policy operates we need to develop as clear a picture as we can of the economic operations of the various levels of government. In this chapter we shall concentrate on expenditures and in the next on receipts.

---

[1]*The brilliant British economist John Maynard Keyes was a leading exponent of this point of view. His classic work,* The General Theory of Employment, Interest and Money *(New York: Harcourt, Brace & World, Inc., 1936), widely heralded as creating a revolution in economic thinking, was instrumental in making it an acceptable part of the general body of economic theory.*

[2]*See budget speech delivered by Hon. W. L. Gordon, Minister of Finance, in the House of Commons, April 26, 1965; Queen's Printer, 1965, pp. 16-17.*

[3]*See budget speech delivered by Hon. E. J. Benson, Minister of Finance, in the House of Commons, March 12, 1970; Queen's Printer, 1970, p. 7 and p. 51.*

Rationale of Government Economic Activities

Almost all of the activities of government have economic aspects. These activities have evolved over time in any given society in response to needs felt either by the general public or by the group in control of the government. In our own society we say that governments should "promote the general welfare." This conveys the very important idea that acting through governments people should be able to obtain certain benefits that they either cannot obtain or can obtain less efficiently as individuals.

In an economic sense governments provide certain of the goods and services that we consume. As a matter of fact, in Canada government-provided goods and services, measured by the government expenditures made to put them in the hands of the public, account for almost 22 percent of GNP. This is the *public sector* of the economy as contrasted with the *private sector*, in which private enterprise produces goods and services. One important issue debated today both in Canada and throughout the world is that of how large, relatively, the public sector of an economy should be. The goods and services provided by government are frequently classified into three categories: (1) those collectively consumed; (2) those individually consumed; and (3) those semicollectively consumed. In addition to producing goods and services, governments also act to transfer purchasing power among individuals and families. A discussion of the three classifications of goods and of *transfer* expenditures will not resolve the debate, but it should clarify some of the issues involved in it.

Collectively Consumed Goods and Services

One service provided by all national governments to their citizens is national defence. How much is it worth to you as an indivdual? If you were asked to contribute to national defence on a yearly volunteer basis, what would your contribution be? Is there any way of determining for each individual in the economy the value of national defence to him? Another government service provided for the general public is space research—or have you ever thought of this activity as being a service to the public? The new technological knowledge gained from the development of space hardware and the knowledge gained from space exploration are expected to benefit the general public. But how valuable is the yearly effort to you personally?

Characteristics

The prime characteristic of *collectively consumed goods* is that their benefits are not divisible among the private economic units that consume them. A good or service provided for a group of consumers is collectively consumed if it is not possible to exclude one of the group from receiving its benefits. Can the protection afforded Canadian citizens by the armed forces be denied you? Can anyone be arbitrarily denied the benefits of space research? This principle of nonexclusion is brought home even more effectively by the classic example of the Bahamian fishermen who joined together and built a lighthouse on a coral reef where many had been shipwrecked. Once the lighthouse was in operation, anyone sailing those waters had access to its services—there was no way of restricting its light to those who planned it and built it.

It is possible for collectively consumed goods and services to be provided by private groups operating on a voluntary basis, but such groups are limited in an important way. A vigilante group organized to combat mercury pollution in the Ottawa River provides benefits for all the commercial fishermen who fish in that part of our country. But suppose that one fisherman decides that he will not pay his share of the costs. Can he be denied the benefits that arise from an absence of mercury pollution? Or suppose that a gigantic private concern were to furnish national defence with a mercenary army; could it deny you protection if you fail to pay your share of the cost? The problem encountered by private businesses in producing collectively consumed goods is that they face a "free rider" problem. It cannot coerce individuals into paying for them if those individuals do not wish to do so.

The Major Examples

Governmental units with their powers of coercion are in a unique position to provide collective goods and services; they can force everyone in the group to pay a share of the costs. People can be "free riders" only by evading taxes, a practice that can lead to unsettling if not disastrous results for those who attempt it. The major government services that fit squarely into this category are national defence, the whole system of law and order, and regulatory services of various kinds.

From the standpoint of costs, national defence (or its counterpart, armed aggression) is the most important collectively consumed item in most countries of the world. Historically, the provision of this service was a primary reason why people banded together in the first place. In primitive societies tribes came into being because people thought they could protect themselves—or prey on others—more effectively as a group than they could as individuals. And so it has been done through the ages.

As the individuals of a society engage in their daily activities they inevitably encroach upon the rights and privileges of others, giving rise to a desire on the part of most people for a system of law and order. Much of this encroachment is intentional as some people attempt to take advantage of others or to advance their own well-being at the expense of others. Robbery and murder—or, more generally, force and fraud—are cases in point. Other encroachments are accidental, as, for example, when street or highway traffic becomes congested enough to interfere with its free flow. In protecting themselves from both types of encroachment people have found that governments with their coercive powers are particularly well suited to provide the services of law and order. Laws are established against the unrestricted use of force and fraud by individuals. They are also established to provide for an orderly flow of traffic and for other purposes in which it is thought that the common interest is served. These laws provide the fabric of the social order and in most countries they are enforced by the police and by the courts. Their benefits are available to all whether or not all are willing voluntarily to contribute to their support.

As we have noted already, an economic system left to its own devices is likely to perform less than perfectly, giving rise to the possibility that certain regulatory services will be in the interests of the general public. Among the more obvious flaws of an unregulated free enterprise economic system are (1) the tendency for economic units to monopolize and (2) the tendency for economic fluctuations to occur. In an attempt to minimize the damage wrought by these, people—ordinarily through government— provide themselves with regulatory services, the benefits of which are available to all; for example, the government attempts to curtail monopoly by means of anticombines laws. With such agencies as the Canadian Transport Commission, the National Energy Board, the Canadian Radio- Television Commission, and provincial corporation commissions, governmental units regulate the operations of so-called natural monopolies, presumably in the public interest. By means of the monetary policies discussed previously and the fiscal measures now under consideration, the federal government attempts to promote economic stability.

In a very fundamental sense the system of law and order and the regulatory activities engaged in by government can be viewed as the rules of a game. Without a set of rules some mayhem is likely to result. The application of judiciously selected laws and regulations may increase the efficiency with which resources devoted to the economic game are used. But, as in any game, it is possible to make the rules so complex and so burdensome that they hinder rather than facilitate the attainment of the desired objectives.

Individually Consumed Goods and Services

Goods and services provided by governments are by no means confined to those that are collectively consumed. Governments at one time or another or in one place or another have actively operated almost every type of business, and all present-day governments provide a host of goods and services that are consumed individually. An *individually consumed good or service* is one that can be divided among consumers and the benefit received by each can be separated out and measured. Most goods and services produced in the private sector of the economy are of this nature. For example, hamburger consumption benefits consumers as individuals only. Nonconsumers are excluded from sharing in this particular gastronomical delight.

We can make a sizable list of individually consumed goods and services produced by governmental units. Postal services are a clear-cut example, as are transit services, electrical services, and garbage collection services owned and operated by municipalities. By and large, in Canada government activity in this area is confined to industries ordinarily thought of as public utilities—industries thought to be natural monopolies—and public or government ownership and operation of them is an alternative to private ownership and operation, subject to government regulation. However, it is by no means necessary that governments confine their activities as producers of individually consumed goods to public utility or natural-monopoly industries. In any society inclined toward socialism the list will extend well beyond these. Steel production, oil production, and hotel services in many countries provide examples, and in the Soviet Union the list includes almost all industries in the economy.

Semicollectively Consumed Goods and Services

Many goods and services provided consumers through governmental units lie somewhere between the purely collective and the purely individual categories, and we refer to these as being *semicollectively consumed*. Consider the nation's highway network. Certainly persons benefit individually from their use of the system. But what of the little old lady living in the middle of the city who owns no autumble and who never ventures beyond the neighbourhood shopping centre? Is the highway system of any significance to her? As a matter of fact, she has access to many things at the shopping centre that would be denied her if the highway system did not exist.

The little old lady is said to receive *social* or *spill-over* benefits from the highway system. These are benefits that accrue to other persons over and above the direct benefits received by those who consume the product or use the service individually. The satisfaction levels of the former are influenced by the consumption levels of the good or service by the latter.

Another important example of a semicollective service produced by governmental units is education. The prime beneficiary of this service is the individual who goes through the prescribed curricula and who receives the appropriate diploma. The greater part of the benefits redound separately to individuals. Yet, there are social benefits for the entire society. An educated populace is essential for the existence of a smooth-working political democracy; crime rates are generally lowest where educational levels are highest; an educated labour force is a more productive work force; and the list can be extended. To those who doubt the social benefits of education, a visit to those parts of the world where literacy rates are below the 50-60 percent level would prove enlightening.

Semicollectively produced goods and services are not provided exclusively by government. Many are produced privately. Oil and gas pipelines are privately owned and operated and so are the trucking companies that move goods over the highways. Yet all of these provide social benefits. Are there any significant differences between the benefits derived from government-owned and operated highways and those from privately owned and operated pipelines to the little old lady in the middle of the city?

The Public Versus The Private Sector

What part of GNP should be produced by the public sector and what part by the private sector of the economy? We are not likely to resolve this question here, but suppose we look at some of the implications of the foregoing classification of goods for it.

The case for governmental units to engage in production is strongest for collectively consumed goods and services. Many of these would not be produced at all if they were not produced by government, even though their value to society as a whole may exceed their costs. A private producer faces the "free rider" problem and may lack the coercive power to extract payments from the public sufficient to cover costs of production. The government, on the other hand, can coerce all who stand to gain into paying taxes. In fact, through its coercive powers, the government is in a position to force taxpayers to pay for services that are worth less to them than they cost.

Individually consumed goods and services are at the other end of the spectrum. Whether or not these should be produced by the government or by private producers depends upon (1) the comparative efficiency of the two alternatives, and (2) the value judgments of the general public.

These determinants are difficult to separate in fact. Those whose value judgments favour leaving the bulk of productive activity to the private sector of the economy argue that this sector utilizes resources more efficiently than the public sector. Those with socialistic value judgments argue that the private sector tends to waste resources and that through government ownership and operation of production facilities a greater measure of efficiency is achieved. If we could actually run tests and determine which sector does a given job with the greater efficiency, the allocation of individually consumed items to the public sector or to the private sector would be much easier. But no one has been able to establish measures of comparative efficiencies to everyone's satisfaction, and so the classic debate continues. In Canada our value judgments have favoured leaving the production of most individually consumed goods and services to the private sector. In the Soviet Union value judgments are such that most goods and services are produced in the public sector.

In an economy oriented toward free enterprise, there is much controversy over whether goods and services semicollectively consumed should be produced by the private sector or by the public sector. The greater the social benefits yielded by an economic activity, the better the case that can be made for the socialization of it. But again, the real problem is that of measuring the social benefits. Some activities—primary and secondary education, for example—we have chosen to socialize; but it is by no means clear that this choice is the best among the possible alternatives.

The general economic principle for determining whether specific goods or services should be produced by the government—or the extent to which they should be produced by the government—is easy enough to state but difficult to use as an operating rule. Resources used by the government to provide goods and services have alternative uses in the private sector of the economy. Thus the government should use resources to provide goods and services only to the extent that at the margin the resources will contribute more to consumer well-being than they would if they were used by the private sector. The difficulty lies in determining the value to consumers of the resources used by the government.

Transfer Expenditures

Not all government economic activities and expenditures create goods and services consumed by the citizenry; that is, governments may make payments to persons who render or provide no goods or services in return. Welfare expenditures fall into this category, as do interest payments on government debt. Some individuals either cannot or will not accumulate sufficient stocks of resources to provide income during such periods of economic adversity as old age, mental and physical incapacity, sickness, unemployment, and the like. In many cases the fault is thought to lie with society as a whole rather than with the individual, but whether or not this is so, all advanced nations call on those who are more affluent to help those who are needy. Governments simply transfer purchasing power from taxpayers to those to whom payments are made. Interest payments on government debt, similarly, represent transfers of purchasing power from taxpayers to bond-holders (interest receivers). Through *transfer expenditures* of this kind consumer demand for privately produced goods and services may be redirected—say away from mink coats toward shoes; however, there is no transfer of production processes from the private to the government sector of the economy.

Expenditures of the Federal Government by Function

We turn now to the public sector of the economy in order to get some feel for the vast army of economic activities in which our government is involved. The expenditures of the federal government are examined in this section. The expenditure format used in Table 9-1 is that employed by the Minister of Finance in his annual budget proposals to Parliament. It provides a functional breakdown of proposed federal expenditures. In other words, it brings together all departmental spending on similar functions. Expenditures from the various trust funds, such as the Old Age Security Fund, the Unemployment Insurance Fund and the Canada Pension Plan Fund are excluded from budgetary expenditure. Also excluded are loans and advances to Crown corporations, government funds, foreign governments and international organizations.

Health and Welfare

Expenditures for health and welfare[4]—most of them of a transfer rather than of a direct income-creating nature—account for almost 25 percent of total estimated budgetary expenditures for fiscal 1971.[5] If budgetary and Old Age Security Fund expenditures are combined, outlays for health and welfare purposes will claim nearly 35 percent of total expenditure. Total federal outlays for health in fiscal 1971 are expected to amount to $1,277.8 million. The hospital insurance program, by which

[4]*Since collectively consumed goods and services provided the public by governments are not sold to the public through markets, there is no objective way of determining their total value to the public. The standard procedure is to value them at what they cost. Thus health, and welfare services are assumed to be worth what they cost—total health and welfare expenditures.*

[5]*In usual terminology, by the term 1971* fiscal year *is meant the fiscal year ending on March 31, 1971.*

TABLE 9-1

Federal Expenditures by Function for Fiscal Year
Ending March 31, 1971
(Millions of Dollars)[1]

FUNCTION			
Health and Social Welfare			$3,149.8
Public health		$ 28.3	
Medical care		477.6	
Medical research council grants		34.0	
Hospital care services		720.4	
Hospital construction grants		5.5	
Other health		12.0	
Income maintenance		771.1	
Payments to families	$620.3		
Payments to unemployed	150.8		
Social assistance		366.0	
Canada Assistance Plan	338.1		
Aid to handicapped	11.1		
Other social assistance	16.8		
Veterans' services		423.2	
Indian, Eskimo affairs, health services		252.3	
Housing, urban renewal		53.7	
Administration		5.7	
Defence			1,816.6
Economic Development			1,817.8
Primary industry		638.4	
Agriculture	373.4		
Fisheries	48.6		
Forestry	22.8		
Minerals	38.2		
Water resources	57.6		
Energy	86.6		
Other primary	11.2		
Secondary industry		129.1	
Service industry		11.2	
Foreign trade		37.6	
Labour force		470.9	
Adult training allowances	352.8		
Immigration	27.6		
Employment services	49.7		
Other labour	40.8		
Function			
General research		181.4	
Regional development		325.3	
Public Debt Costs			1,799.7
Fiscal Transfer to Provinces			1,063.3
Transportation and Communications			958.8
Air services		132.4	
Water transport		143.4	
Rail transport		107.2	
Road transport		53.0	
Post Office		396.0	
Telecommunications		16.7	
Other transportation		110.1	

TABLE 9-1 CONTINUED
Federal Expenditures by Function for Fiscal Year
Ending March 31, 1971
(Millions of Dollars)[1]

Education Assistance		$450.6
Bilingualism	$ 53.5	
Post-secondary education grants	377.3	
Student loans	19.8	
Foreign Affairs		269.4
Diplomatic relations	58.4	
International organizations	18.3	
Foreign aid	192.7	
Culture and Recreation		254.5
Archives, galleries, theatres	15.3	
Parks, historical sites	33.9	
Film, radio, television	179.3	
Other	26.0	
Internal Overhead Expenses		744.5
Government support services	410.9	
Employee pension, insurance plans	278.6	
Contingencies vote	55.0	
Outlays on General Administration and Protection		584.6
Collection of revenue	165.9	
Legislative expenses	30.2	
Territorial relations	60.3	
Information Canada	7.4	
National Capital Commission	28.0	
Justice	18.2	
Correctional services	84.4	
R.C.M.P.	140.7	
Consumer services	25.4	
Racetrack supervision	—	
Total Budgetary Expenditures		12,909.8
Old Age Security Fund Expenditure		1,905.0

[1]*Figures may not add owing to rounding.*
Source: Canada, Estimates for the Fiscal Year Ending March 31, 1971, *Ottawa, Queen's Printer, February 26, 1970, Table 5.*

the federal government shares with the provinces the cost of providing specified hospital services to insured patients, is the largest item in the category, followed by payments for provincially administered medical care programs. Other health expenditures are for medical research, training for the health profession, hospital construction, attacks on such health hazards as air, water and soil pollution and impure foods and drugs, medical and associated health care costs for recipients of provincial welfare assistance, and mental health programs.

Welfare expenditures in fiscal 1971 are expected to amount to $1,872.0 million. This outlay reflects the change in the public's attitude, in that the provision of a decent, minimum standard of living for the population as a whole has now become a major national goal. Payments to families (family allowances, youth allowances, family assistance) and to the unemployed together claim more than 40 percent of total welfare expenditures. Supplementing these income maintenance programs, are payments to provinces under the Canada Assistance Plan for aid to the aged, the blind, the disabled, and the unemployed. Other federal expenditures are for veterans' services, housing and urban renewal, and social benefits for native peoples.

It is worth noting again that Old Age Security expenditures, including the monthly guaranteed income supplement to certain Old Age Security pensions, and Canada Pension Plan outlays, including supplementary payments to widows, orphans and disabled contributors, are essentially governmental in character, designed to help people make financial provision for their retirement and to protect themselves and their dependents or survivors against loss of income in the event of the disability or death of the head of the family.

Economic Development

The second major category of federal budgetary expenditures, about 15 percent of the total, consists of various outlays designed to increase the economic well-being of certain sectors in the economy and of regions of slow growth. In 1971 agricultural expenditures, intended primarily to aid farm incomes and facilitate the production and marketing of farm products, (mainly wheat) was the largest item in the class, followed by expenditures for the development and utilization of manpower, including grants for research in connection with better planning. Estimates classified under "regional development" consist of expenditures on conservation and reclamation projects, development of primary industries, and comprehensive development plans (Fund for Rural Economic Development and ARDA agreements). Other expenditures aimed at economic expansion were for general research (mainly by DBS and the National Research Council), secondary industry (mostly for product innovation), and foreign trade (mostly for market development).

National Defence

Annual expenditures of more than $1,750 million have been required in recent years for Canada's defence. This has amounted to an average of 21 percent of total budgetary outlays for the last decade; about 18 percent for the last 5 years; about 15 percent in fiscal 1971. It should be added, however, that the percentage decline is due more to an increase in total federal expenditure than to a reduction in military spending.

Most of the outlays were for men and material for the current operations of the armed forces. Some went for research and development of equipment and weapons systems. Other defence expenditures were for military construction, family housing for military personnel, mutual aid (NATO, NORAD), civil defence (Emergency Measures Organization), and a host of administrative items.

Public Debt

Public debt charges consist of interest on the federal debt, the annual amortization of bonds and discounts and commissions, the cost of issuing new loans and other costs incurred in servicing the public debt. In dollar terms this is the fourth largest category of federal expenditures. Like expenditures to provide social security, these are transfer payments; new income does not come into being at the time they are made. Rather, dollars of purchasing power are transferred from taxpayers to bondholders. (What would be the impact of interest payments on the federal debt if taxes were levied on the general public in exactly the same distributive pattern as that of the interest payments made to the public?) About 5 percent of the total yearly interest paid on the federal debt goes to government trust funds and to government agencies that have invested funds in government securities. This interest outlay is an intergovernmental transfer of funds rather than a cash payment to the public.

Another important point is this: when considering the magnitude of these public debt charges and the burden they place upon the federal treasury, we should bear in mind that a substantial portion of the debt is attributable to, or is invested in, productive or earning assets. Therefore, in calculating the net burden of the federal government's annual interest charges, the income derived from loans, investments and other productive assets should be taken into account.[6]

Payments to the Provinces

Budgetary expenditures for payments to the provinces are estimated at $1,063.3 million for fiscal 1971. Payments are made under the Federal-Provincial Fiscal Arrangements Act (1967-1972), the Established Programs (Interim Arrangements) Act, statutory subsidies, and through

[6]For the details, see Canada, House of Commons Debates, Volume 114, No. 85, 2nd Session, 28 Parliament, Thursday, March 12, 1970, Ottawa, Queen's Printer, pp. 164-65.

transfers of certain public utility tax receipts.[7] Payments to municipalities take the form of grants in lieu of taxes on federal property.

As already mentioned, the federal government also makes payments or *grants-in-aid* to the provinces and municipalities for specific purposes such as hospital insurance, social assistance, vocational school training and various resource projects. These so-called conditional grants are not classified as "payments to other levels of government" but are included under the categories dealing with the subject to which they apply.

Transportation and Communications

The sixth-ranking transportation and communications classification brings together a heterogeneous collection of expenditures. Expenditures in the transportation area include the various subsidies paid to the railways and to regional air carriers, the steamship subventions for coastal services, the capital subsidies paid to encourage the construction of commercial ships and fishing vessels in Canadian yards, and payments into the Railway Grade Crossing Fund. The expenditures in this group also include federal efforts to complete the Trans-Canada Highway, the Northwest Highway system (Alaska Highway), and to provide roads to areas of potentially rich natural resources (Roads to Resources Program). Other important expenditures are for construction and maintenance of airports and related facilities, maintenance of the Coast Guard fleet, aids to navigation, harbours and rivers engineering services, marine surveys, other roads and bridges, and deficits of transportation agencies operated by the government (mainly the Canadian National Railways, Newfoundland Ferry & Terminals and the St. Lawrence Seaway Authority).

In the communications area are the services of the Post Office, the Telecommunications and Electronics Branch of the Department of Transport in aid of marine and aeronautical navigation, and the research satellite program of the Department of Communications. The operation of postal services represents about 40 percent of the total expenditures in this category.

Internal Overhead Expenses

The government's contribution to the public service superannuation account is the largest item in this category. This item is followed by contributions to the death benefit account, the Unemployment Insurance Fund, the Canada Pension Plan and the Quebec Pension Plan, and the government's share of surgical-medical insurance premiums. The costs of

[7]*The subject of federal payments to the provinces is taken up at length in Chapter 10.*

the Public Service Commission and the Public Service Staff Relations Board are also covered here. A final item is the liability account "reserve for salary revision."

General Administration and Protection

Government expenditures which are classified under the heading of "Legislation and Administration" include the costs of the Department of National Revenue; of Parliament (parliamentary salaries and allowances, Library of Parliament, etc.); payments to the governments of the Territories; Information Canada, a centralized, government-controlled information agency; and the National Capital Commission which is responsible for the development, conservation and improvement of the National Capital Region which covers Ottawa and 1800 square miles surrounding it.

Expenditures under the heading of "Protection of Persons and Property" include the costs of operating the federal courts; the Canadian Penitentiary Service; the Royal Canadian Mounted Police force which is responsible for the enforcing of federal statutes, the suppression of smuggling and traffic in narcotic drugs, and the protection of governmental property; and of protecting the consumer against fraud and deception in the market place and against unsafe or hazardous products.

Education

Federal aid to education is estimated at almost $451 million for 1971. Of this figure, approximately 85 percent is in the form of operating grants to provinces for post-secondary education; that is, the educational institutions and courses requiring for admission at least junior matriculation or its equivalent. These grants are tied in with federal-provincial fiscal arrangements, and are disbursed by the provincial governments at their discretion. A student loan program, designed for graduate or undergraduate students in any form of post-secondary educational institution, is operated by the chartered banks under the Canada Student Loans Act. The federal government guarantees these loans and pays the interest while the student is studying and for six months after graduation or discontinuance of his studies. The government also makes various grants and subsidies in aid of bilingualism to Canadian universities and educational institutions.

Culture and Recreation

The federal government assists in the development of a wide range of cultural and recreational facilities through its own agencies and through grants to private organizations and other levels of government. In the recreational area the government operates national parks and historic sites and makes grants for the promotion of physical fitness and amateur sport (Fitness and Amateur Sport Program). In the cultural area are the services of the Canada Council (for the encouragement of the arts, humanities and social sciences), the Canadian Film Development Corporation (for the development of a feature film industry in Canada), the National Art Centre (for the encouragement of the performing arts), the National Film Board (acts as official government photographer), the National Library, the Public Archives, and the National Museums of Canada (including the National Gallery). Lesser amounts were earmarked for the advancement of Indian and Eskimo culture, for the operation of campgrounds and picnic areas in the Yukon and Northwest Territories, for research and support grants to arts and cultural services organizations and activities, and for the Boy Scouts, Girl Guides and Boys' Clubs of Canada.

Foreign Affairs

The government will spend some $270 million in fiscal 1971 for the protection and advancement of Canadian interests abroad. The bulk of this amount is for foreign aid. Through the Canadian International Development Agency, Canada provides funds for economic, technical and educational assistance to underdeveloped countries. Food aid is also a significant element of Canada's development assistance program. In addition to foreign aid, expenditures for the conduct of international affairs fall under this heading—for the operations of the Department of External Affairs and international organizations and commissions.

Expenditures of Provincial and Municipal Governments by Function

The economic activities of governments are by no means limited to those of the federal government. Provincial and municipal government expenditures in 1968 amounted to $18,265 million compared with federal expenditures of $12,296 million. There is, however, a major difference between the type of expenditures made by provincial and municipal governments and those made by the federal government. Federal government expenditures generally, though not exclusively, are for services devolving upon the population of Canada as a whole, whereas those of provincial and municipal governments are confined more narrowly to serving smaller groups or individuals falling within their respective jurisdictions. Many provincial and municipal government expenditures are in the area of semicollectively and even privately consumed goods and services, while the bulk of federal expenditures provide collectively consumed goods and services.[8]

Education

Provincial and municipal expenditures for education are almost twice those for any other item. Table 9-2 indicates that over $2,325 million was spent for education in 1965 (the latest figures available). In most provinces the responsibility for producing primary and secondary educa-

TABLE 9-2

Provincial and Municipal Expenditures by Function, Fiscal Years Ended Nearest to December 31, 1965
(Millions of Dollars)

FUNCTION	EXPENDITURES[1]
Education	$2,325.7
Transportation and Communications	1,436.9
Health, hospitalization, and sanitation	1,342.2
Protection	580.5
Social welfare	512.4
General government expenditure	431.5
Debt charges (excluding debt retirement)	361.1
Natural resources and primary industries	286.9
Recreation and culture	187.3
Contributions to own government enterprises	95.6
Other	323.4
Total expenditure[2]	$7,886.6

[1]Excludes intergovernmental transfers.
[2]Figures do not add owing to rounding.
Source: Dominion Bureau of Statistics, Consolidated Government Finance, February, 1969, Table 7.

tion rests with locally elected or appointed school boards, while teacher training, post-secondary vocational enducation and higher education is the domain of provincial governments.

Transportation and Communications

The construction and maintenance of streets, roads and highways has long been considered a basic function of government. In Canada provincial

[8]See James M. Buchanan, The Public Finances, rev. ed. Homewood, Ill.: Richard D. Irwin, Inc., 1965), pp. 417-20.

and municipal governments have shouldered the bulk of the burden[9] receiving some help from the federal government through a system of matching grants-in-aid. Federal participation in road building was increased greatly following a federal-provincial agreement in 1949 for construction of the Trans-Canada Highway. In 1958, a federal-provincial cost-sharing program was undertaken, designed to provide access roads to areas potentially rich in natural resources or to areas with tourist potential. This program expired on March 31, 1970. In addition to roads and highways, some provinces operate facilities for rail, water, road and air transportation. In the communications field, several provinces and many municipalities provide public telephone service. Provincial and municipal expenditures for transportation and communications totalled nearly $1,437 million in 1965.

Health, Hospitalization, and Sanitation

Expenditures on health, hospitalization, and sanitation were almost at the same level as those for transportation and communications in 1965. The responsibility for health services rests largely with provincial governments, with municipalities often being delegated a considerable degree of authority. In 1965 the provincial share of combined provincial and municipal net general expenditure on health services was 93.4 percent.[10] The provision of health services by governmental units rather than by the private sector of the economy presumes that the general public obtains social benefits from higher standards of public health, hospitalization and medical care and that private facilities would not be available in adequate quantities. All provinces operate medical care and hospital insurance plans. The assumption of responsibility for sanitation and for sewage disposal by provincial and municipal governments is also based on the belief that these services would be inadequately supplied by private producers.

Protection

The protective function of government is manifested by the courts, the police department and the fire department. The British North America

[9]*The British North America Act of 1867 makes every province responsible for local public works. Only works declared by Parliament to be for the general advantage of Canada or of two or more provinces come within federal jurisdiction. Thus, most roads and highways within a province are the sole responsibility of the junior governments to construct, maintain and finance.*

[10]*Canadian Tax Foundation*, Provincial Finances, 1969, *Toronto, July 1969*, *p. 131.*

Act provides that the salaries, allowances and pensions of judges of the superior, district and county courts in each province (except the courts of probate in Nova Scotia and New Brunswick) are to be fixed and provided by the Parliament of Canada, while justices of the peace, magistrates and judges of the juvenile, family and welfare courts are a provincial responsibility. Two provinces, Quebec and Ontario, maintain their own law enforcement agencies, while the others engage the services of the R.C.M.P. to enforce provincial statutes and the *Criminal Code*. In general, most of the larger urban municipalities are responsible for maintaining an adequate police force of their own according to their needs. Similarly, local governments are responsible for fire protection and street lighting. Combined provincial and municipal expenditures relating to the protection of persons and property exceeded $580 million in 1965.

Social Welfare

Social welfare expenditures of provincial and municipal governments are transfer expenditures; that is, no direct productive service is performed by the recipients of the funds at the time the expenditures are made. Mention has already been made of the fact that old age security, family allowances and unemployment insurance are exclusively federal programs. The Canada Assistance Plan provides for the replacement of four federal-provincial shared-cost programs (for the aged, the blind, the disabled, and the unemployed) by one general coordinated program for assisting all needy persons regardless of the cause of the need. Provincial and municipal programs cover mothers' allowances, child protection and child care and homes for the aged and infirm. In addition, the provinces and municipalities provide general assistance to the needy.

Other Expenditures

In addition to the services discussed above, Table 9-2 indicates that provincial and municipal governments carry on a number of economic activities of a smaller magnitude. The conservation and development of natural resources, including minerals, wildlife, and timber, required quantitatively $287 million in 1965. Other functions are trade and industrial development, including financial assistance to industry; housing and urban renewal projects; and development of parks and recreational and cultural facilities. Expenditures are also made to pay interest on provincial and municipal debt and for general legislative and administrative functions.

Trends in Government Expenditures

Total expenditures of federal, provincial, and municipal governments in 1968 were $30,461 million. GNP in 1968 was $71,454 million. This means that total government expenditures (including intergovernmental transfers[11]) amounted to almost 43 percent of the value of the economy's gross output of goods and services in that year. It will be of interest to trace briefly the history of government participation in economic activity as indicated by its expenditures.

Changes in Magnitude

The major historical data for the period 1926-1968 by level of government are presented in   Table 9-3. We notice immediately the inexorable upward movement of government expenditures. Over the 42-year period covered in the table total expenditures rose from $854 million to $30,461 million. What are the causes of the upward trend?

Inflation

Among the several possible causes *inflation* is an obvious one. When we examine the changes in the price level from 1926 to 1968 we find that an increase of slightly over 200 percent has occurred, or in terms of 1968 dollars, the 1926 level of government expenditures is somewhat in excess of $1,400 million. Although inflation has been a factor in increasing the level of government expenditures, clearly it has not been the major factor.

Population Growth

Another possible cause of rising government expenditures is *population growth*. The population of Canada rose from 9,451 million in 1926 to 20,772 million in 1968, an increase of approximately 120 percent. This factor too has had important effects on total expenditures, but it is far from being the complete explanation. Government expenditures per capita during the period have risen several times over.

[11]*In 1969 D.B.S. published a complete revision of their national accounts. Unfortunately government expenditure data excluding intergovernmental transfers on the revised national accounts basis is available only on a government sector or consolidated basis. Thus the figures in   Table 9-3,, which are on a revised national accounts basis for the three levels of government, include intergovernmental transfers and hence involve a certain amount of double counting. To get some idea of the orders of magnitude involved, total government expenditure, excluding intergovernmental transfers, totaled $23,701 million in 1968 compared with the $30,461 million mentioned above.*

War

A significant cause of increasing government expenditures has been for the purpose of *defence* and for *international peace-keeping*. The rapid technological developments of the past three decades have caused huge increases in the costs of military equipment and weapons systems and in the costs of training personnel to operate them. Further, each war has generated its own set of extra, continuing expenditures, veterans' benefits and interest on a larger federal debt being the principal items.

TABLE 9-3
Total Federal, Provincial and Municipal Government Expenditures[1]
Including Intergovernmental Transfers, Selected Years, 1926–1968

| Year | Provincial and Municipal | | Federal | | Total | | |
	Millions of Dollars	Percent of Total	Millions of Dollars	Percent of Total	Millions of Dollars	Percent of GNP	GNP[1]
1926	633	74.1	321	25.9	854	16.6	5,146
1928	603	63.7	344	36.3	947	15.7	6,050
1932	770	66.6	387	33.4	1,157	30.3	3,814
1942	775	17.1	3,765	82.9	4,540	44.2	10,265
1944	880	14.2	5,320	85.8	6,200	52.3	11,848
1948	1,714	46.8	1,952	53.2	3,666	24.2	15,127
1952	2,709	37.6	4,492	62.4	7,201	30.0	24,042
1958	4,995	44.7	6,176	55.3	11,171	32.8	34,094
1962	8,845	54.2	7,486	45.8	16,331	38.6	42,353
1963	9,636	55.9	7,608	44.1	17,244	37.9	45,465
1963	9,636	55.9	7,608	44.1	17,244	37.9	45,465
1964	10,466	56.6	8,011	43.4	18,477	37.1	49,783
1965	11,923	58.2	8,551	41.8	20,474	37.3	54,897
1966	14,080	59.1	9,761	40.9	23,841	38.8	61,421
1967	16,136	59.3	11,016	40.6	27,152	41.4	65,608
1968	18,265	60.0	12,196	40.0	30,461	42.6	71,454

[1]*Current dollars.*
Source: Dominion Bureau of Statistics, National Income and Expenditure Accounts, *1926—1968, Ottawa, Queen's Printer, August, 1969.*

Government Services

A growing population, an advancing technology, increasing urbanization, greater affluence, and other factors have generated a growing demand over time for *government services*. Until the 1940's social assistance programs did not reach beyond limited amounts of public assistance—Old Age Pension Act and Blind Persons Act—and workmen's compensation for disabilities. Social security expenditures now run in excess of $3 billion annually for all levels of government combined, and as medicare plans get into full swing further large increases are inevitable. Ependitures on economic opportunity or "war on poverty" programs have been increasing in recent years, and, with the focusing of more and more attention on the problem arising in the ghettos of our cities, and on the problems facing the Indian, Eskimo and Métis peoples, we can expect these to increase even more rapidly in the future.

Apart from welfare and economic opportunity programs, governments are being called upon to improve and expand still other services. Intracity and intercity transporation problems have become more and more pressing; street and highway expenditures are rising; increasing crime rates call for expanded police protection; and so it goes through a long list of services for which government at all levels has come to assume responsibility. As evidence of this trend, government expenditures as a percentage of GNP have been increasing since 1948, as shown in Table 9-3 .

Federal versus Provincial/Municipal Expenditures

The second major fact evidenced in Table 9-3 is that federal expenditures have become smaller relative to provincial and municipal expenditures. The shift in relative importance occurred in the early part of the 1960's, and federal expenditures have shown a very appreciable decline since then. The shift is largely accounted for by enlarged provincial responsibility for public welfare and by the increased costs of education. Both sets of expenditures have been increasing over the last 10 years, but provincial and municipal expenditures the most.

Summary

Government expenditures and receipts exert a significant impact on the level of economic activity, and by appropriate manipulation of them, that is, through fiscal policy, governments can make positive contributions to economic stability.

Government-produced goods and services consumed by the general public are said to come from the public sector of the economy while goods and services produced and sold by private businesses are said to come from the private sector. There is much debate over the appropriate relative sizes of the two sectors. Generally speaking, from the point of view of economics, whether or not any specific good or service should be produced by the public sector or by the private sector depends upon which can do the job more efficiently. But this is often difficult to determine, and value judgments rather than objective facts tend to establish one's position in the debate.

Goods and services may be classified as (1) those that are collectively consumed, (2) those that are individually consumed, and (3) those that are semicollectively consumed. Collectively consumed goods and services include national defence, law and order, regulatory services, and the like, that, once provided for a group of consumers, cannot be denied to any one in the group. If these were not produced by government, it is possible—and in many instances likely—that they would not be produced at all. Individually consumed goods and services, on the other hand, are enjoyed separately by consumers and are produced in the main by the private sector of the economy; however, in some instances government units produce and sell them, postal services and municipally owned utilities being cases in point. Semicollectively consumed goods and services, which are partly of an individually consumed nature but from which substantial social benefits are obtained by persons who do not consume them directly, form a great gray area about which the debate takes place.

Not all government expenditures are for the provision of goods and services for the citizenry. Some represent transfer expenditures for which the recipients provide no current services, the leading examples being social security and welfare payments along with interest payments on government debt to those who hold Government of Canada securities.

The budget presented by the Minister of Finance provides an overview of federal expenditures for various functions. The largest expenditure category is health and welfare. Economic development expenditures rank second, closely followed by expenditures for national defence. Other functions in their order of magnitude for fiscal 1971 were public debt costs; fiscal transfers to provinces; transportation and communications; internal overhead expenses; general administration and protection; educational assistance; foreign affairs; and culture and recreation.

Provincial and municipal expenditures are largely for goods and services benefiting those in a particular jurisdiction. Those for education comprise the largest category, followed by transportation and communications; health, hospitalization, and sanitation; protection of persons and property; social welfare; general government; debt charges; natural resources and primary industries; and recreation and cultural services. There are a great many other provincial and municipal expenditures of smaller magnitudes.

Since the mid-1920's two major trends may be discerned in government spending in Canada. First, expenditures have increased rapidly. Secondly, an upward shift in the relative importance of provincial and municipal versus federal spending has occurred since 1961, and it has strengthened in recent years. The first trend is attributable to inflation, population growth, war, and to a broadening and deepening of the range of services provided as society has become more affluent. The second reflects the heavy entry of provincial governments into public welfare programs along with the enormous increases in the cost of education.

Exercises and Questions for Discussion

1. Suppose your municipal government owns and operates the electric company that serves you. Do you think the government should involve itself in this sort of productivity? Defend your answer.
2. "Semicollectively consumed goods and services must be provided by government, since the private sector would be less efficient in providing them." Evaluate this statement.
3. Are all transfer expenditures based on value judgments? Discuss.
4. "Government expenditures since the earliest twentieth century have increased tremendously. This is direct evidence that control of the Canadian economy has gone from private hands to those of big government." Analyze this statement critically.
5. List the expenditure categories of the federal and municipal governments.
   a. Which expenditures must be borne by government? Why?
   b. Which are for things that might be provided by the private sector of the economy? Why?
6. What is the present role of the federal government in providing funds for education? Do you think it should be larger or smaller? Give your reasons.

Selected Readings

Buchanan, J. M., *The Public Finances*, rev. ed. Homewood, Ill.: Richard D. Irwin, Inc., 1965, Chaps. 3-5.

Budget Papers presented by the Hon. E. J. Benson, M.P., Minister of Finance for the information of Parliament in connection with the Budget for 1970-71. Ottawa: Queen's Printer, March 12, 1970.

Canadian Tax Foundation, *The National Finances, 1969-70,* Toronto: October, 1969.

————, *Provincial Finances, 1969,* Toronto: July, 1969.

Due, J. F., *Government Finance*, fourth edition. Homewood, Ill.: Richard D. Irwin, Inc., 1968, Chap. 5.

Musgrave, R. A., *The Theory of Public Finance.* New York: McGraw-Hill Book Company, Inc., 1959, Chap. 1.

Sharp, A. M. and B. F. Sliger, *Public Finance.* Homewood, Ill.: The Dorsey Press, 1964, Chaps. 2, 3 and 5.

10

Government Economic Activities: The Revenue Side

The goods and services that governments provide are not costless—and neither are their transfer expenditures. Most of us are aware that as a society we pay for them in one way or another, although we frequently expect that an expansion of some service that will benefit us will be paid for by others. The economics of financing government expenditures is developed in the first two sections of the chapter, while the last two sections examine the tax structures of both the federal government and of provincial and municipal governments.

The Economics of Financing Governments

Government versus Private Use of Resources

Where do governments obtain the resources necessary for producing such services as national defence and education or such capital goods as highways and airports? In a market economy, governments bid, along with private producers, for most of the resources that they use. However, some resources, for example, land for housing and community development, are not always available in the desired quantities at the prices that the government is willing to pay. For these the government uses its coercive powers (of expropriation, in this case) to acquire whatever amounts it wants. Resources used by governments are not available for use by the private sector of the economy, or, alternatively, resources used by the private sector are not available for government use. The real costs of governmental production of goods and services are the values of the foregone alternative products that could have been produced had the resources used by the government been left in private hands. Government-produced goods and services are costless only if the resources used to produce them would have been unemployed otherwise.

Even government transfer expenditures cause resources to be allocated differently from the way they would had the transfer expenditures not been made. The reallocation occasioned by them occurs *within* the private sector rather than *from* the private to the public sector of the economy. The people who are made better off by the transfer expenditures now have a greater influence on demands for goods and services, while those made worse off have less influence. These changes in private demand patterns touch off a corresponding reallocation of resources.

All government expenditures influence the allocation of resources, and the mechanism through which resources are released from one employment and reallocated to another depends upon how those expenditures are financed. The most important methods of financing them are through taxation, through the creation of new money, and through borrowing. An additional method, used particularly for government-produced individually consumed goods and services, is the direct sale of those goods and services to the public.

Taxation

If the federal government decides to expand its activities in the area of national defence, how can it obtain the necessary resources to meet the increase? One way to accomplish the reallocation is to increase the taxes levied on the general public, say through a surtax on individual and corporate incomes. The more the public pays in taxes, the less it has available to spend for goods and services produced and sold in the private sector of the economy. The decrease in demand for privately produced goods and services reduces the demand of private producers for resources. The additional spending power placed in the hands of the government puts the latter in a position to bid the desired resources away from the private sector. In summary, then, through the exercise of its taxing power the government can substitute its demand for resources for that of the private sector and thus bring about a reallocation from the private sector to the public sector.

Taxation can also aid in the process of diverting resources from one group of consumers in the economy to others through government transfer expenditures. Suppose that government officials decide that larger monthly payments should be made to the unemployed—that is, that the unemployed should be given relatively more command over what the resources of the economy are used to produce. Through taxation the demands for privately produced goods and services of those taxed are decreased, and when the corresponding transfer expenditures to the unemployed are put in the hands of the unemployed, the demands of the latter for privately produced goods and services are increased. To the extent that the new demand pattern differs from the old, forces are set in motion to reallocate resources correspondingly.

The use of taxation to finance government expenditures acts as a lubricant to ease the reallocation of resources that government officials intend to bring about. The demands of those taxed are reduced while the demands of government and of those who receive transfer expenditures are increased correspondingly. (When government expenditures are just met by tax collections, would you expect the impact on the level of total economic activity to be positive, negative, or neutral?)

The Creation of New Money

All national governments have found it expedient at some time or another to finance some part of their expenditures by creating new money directly; that is, by printing and spending new currency. Generally speaking, the "solid" citizens of the world tend to frown on this practice in the belief that it is inflationary. Suppose we look first at the diversion of resources from private to public uses and the impact of transfer expenditures when this method of financing is used. We shall then turn to the question of inflation.

The economic processes of resource reallocation vary only slightly from those of the taxation case. To secure resources for government productive processes the government creates money that it then uses to bid for resources. The increase in government demand relative to private demand enables the government to bid resources away from private producers, even though the absolute dollar demand of the latter has not been decreased. Similarly, transfer expenditures financed through the creation of money increase the demand of those to whom the expenditures go relative to the demands of others in the economy, although the absolute dollar demand of the latter has not been decreased. The former are given access to some resources that otherwise would have been controlled by the latter.

But will money creation of this kind be inflationary? If it is used extensively to finance large proportions of government expenditures, it probably will be. Carefully used in a growing economy, it need not be. Larger government demands not offset by smaller private demands will drive price levels up unless at the same time both the productive capacity and the output of the economy are growing. If, however, the economy's available supplies of resources are increasing, or if its techniques of production are improving, leading to an increasing volume of goods and services produced, a larger money supply is in order if price levels are to remain stable. The inflationary danger occurs only if total spending, government plus private, is made to increase at a more rapid rate than the volume of goods and services made available for purchase. If there is a significant amount of unemployment in the economy, mild inflation may be necessary in order to reduce it.

The financing of some part of government expenditures by means of money creation is not necessarily harmful and may even be desirable in a growing economy *if done judiciously*. It will not cause inflation unless it is carried to the point at which total spending (MV) is increasing more rapidly than the volume of trade (T). In the aggregate, this method of financing expenditures differs from taxation in that it does not reduce private demands as an offset to the increase in government demands.

Borrowing

Governments also frequently resort to borrowing as a means of financing expenditures. Borrowing by the federal government is accomplished through the sale of government bonds and treasury bills to the general public, to businesses, particularly financial enterprises, and to such government trust funds as those for Old Age, Unemployment Insurance, and the Canada Pension Plan.

The economic effects of borrowing may be similar either to those of taxation or to those of creating new money, depending upon how lenders would have disposed of their funds had they not bought government securities. Government borrowing may, in fact, be the avenue through which new money is created.

Borrowing to finance government expenditures will have the same economic effects as the use of taxation when those who buy the securities do so in lieu of spending their available purchasing power on goods and services. If they elect to purchase government securities instead of goods and services, private demand is decreased by the value of the securities purchased and government demand is increased by the same amount. Further, if banks purchase government securities when their reserve ratios are as low as they want them to be, they can do so only at the expense of loans to the general public, thus substituting government purchasing power for private purchasing power.

Borrowing by the government to finance expenditures has effects equivalent to money creation when it brings about increased government spending with no corresponding decrease in private spending. Suppose, for example, that the public buys bonds with money that would have been hoarded or held idle otherwise. The rate of total spending in the economy is increased as idle money is put to work.[1] The same occurs when bonds are sold to government trust funds. Money balances that would have been held idle otherwise are put into circulation.

Direct money creation may result when government bonds are sold by the government to the Bank of Canada. In this case the central bank pays for the bonds by creating government deposits for the amounts involved. As these deposits are spent by the government, their recipients deposit them at their own banks, thus increasing chartered bank reserves and deposits. The increases in chartered bank deposits represent, of course, newly created money. Additionally, the set of transactions just described makes excess reserves available to chartered banks, and these can serve as a basis for further money creation.

The Predominance of Taxation

In the mix of taxation, money creation, and borrowing that governments use to finance their expenditures, we find that taxation is by far the most important. There may be greater resort to money creation and borrowing when recession occurs and depression is threatening. During inflationary periods there may be no money creation or borrowing at all—tax receipts may even exceed expenditures. Choices among the methods used, then, are made ideally, if not always in practice, according to the fiscal policies needed to promote economic stability. In keeping with its major role in fiscal policy, taxation will occupy us through the remainder of the chapter.

Principles of Taxation

Writers in the field of public finance have traditionally been concerned with, among other things, the requisites of a "good" tax. What distinguishes a "good" tax from a "bad" one—that is, what makes some taxes more acceptable than others? Among the characteristics frequently listed, the most important ones are (1) adequacy, (2) simplicity, (3) certainty, and (4) equity. As we shall see, these characteristics are not entirely independent of one another.

---

[1]*Actually no new money is created, but the velocity of circulation is increased. The effects are essentially the same as they would be if new money were created while the velocity of circulation were constant.*

Adequacy

The characteristic of *adequacy* requires little explanation. Does the tax do what it is supposed to do? The function of most taxes is to raise revenue, although some, those on tobacco and alcohol, for example, are for the additional purpose of suppressing consumption. If the purpose of a tax is to raise revenue, does it do so in the desired amounts? A tax on caviar is not likely to raise much revenue; a tax on all consumer goods will be much more lucrative.

Simplicity

A *simple tax* is one that can be easily understood by taxpayers and easily administered by the government. Examples of simple taxes are poll taxes and sales taxes. A *poll tax* is a tax of some set amount per year per person. *Sales taxes* are levied in two ways. They may be levied on particular goods on the basis of product units measured in weight or volume—alcohol taxes, for example—or on the basis of product value, say, a certain percentage of the sales price. The former are called *specific taxes* while the latter are referred to as *ad valorem taxes*. Sales taxes are easily collected by the government from the sellers of goods and services, and for this reason they have often been recommended as appropriate taxes for underdeveloped countries to levy. On the other side, probably few people in Canada who have wrestled with Form T1 General will deny either the complexity of the personal income tax or the desirability of simplicity in tax construction.

Certainty

The *certainty* of taxes implies several things, the most important being the consistency of the revenue over time, the impossibility of avoiding or evading the tax, and a knowledge on the part of the taxpayer of the amount of the tax that rests on him. Consistency over time does not mean that the tax structure or the tax rates must remain unchanged. Rather, it means that over time there is stability and orderly change so that both taxpayers and the government know where they stand from year to year. The *avoidance* of a tax refers to the success on the part of taxpayers of finding legal loopholes in the tax that enable them to avoid paying it. *Evasion* is an illegal attempt not to pay the tax. Knowledge on the part of the taxpayer of the amount that he pays seems almost a foregone conclusion, but as we shall see, this is frequently not the case.

Equity

Above all else we want the taxes levied to meet public expenditures to be equitable in terms of the relative loads imposed upon different persons in the economy. But what constitutes equity in taxation? We can say easily and with impunity that persons in like circumstances should be subjected to like taxation, but once we depart from identical circumstances we are in trouble. How can we evaluate and compare the economic circumstances of widely diverse persons engaged in widely diverse activities in widely diverse parts of the country? Satisfactory answers are not easy to find; however, when we observe closely the tax laws enacted by legislatures we find that two rather different equity theories emerge. These are the benefits-received theory and the ability-to-pay theory.

Benefits-Received Theory

Taxation according to *benefits received* means that taxes are levied on individuals according to the benefits each obtains from government expenditures. To apply the theory it is necessary to evaluate the benefits received from government services for every person in the economy. Those receiving equal benefits from government expenditures would be required to pay equal amounts of taxes; those receiving the greatest benefits would pay the largest amounts of taxes; and those receiving the least benefits would pay the least.

There are two major arguments against the widespread use of the benefits-received theory. First, the calculation of the value of the benefits received for every individual in the economy is an impossible task. We need only consider the nature of government-provided collectively consumed goods and services to establish this point. Their very nature precludes determination of their values to particular individuals. Second, general use of the theory would preclude the use of transfer expenditures to redistribute income, thus violating the concepts of equity held by a great many people. Its use in providing welfare services would mean that the poor would be required to pay for their own relief—a result that is patently absurd.

Nevertheless, there are some special areas in which application of the theory leads to results that most people consider to be reasonably equitable. These are the areas in which the goods and services provided by government are to a large extent individually consumed. Highway-user taxes, or taxes on motor fuel, provide an example. Those who use the highways the most buy the most gasoline and thus pay larger shares of these taxes, which are generally earmarked for building and maintaining highways.

Ability-to-Pay Theory

Ordinarily when we think of equity in taxation we think in terms of ability to pay. Roughly, this means that those most able to pay taxes should pay larger amounts than those least able to pay. As we attempt to put the theory into practice two questions arise. First, what constitutes ability to pay? Second, what distribution of the tax load among people of differing ability to pay is equitable?

On the first question, comparative property holdings are sometimes thought to measure comparative abilities to pay. Personal property taxes illustrate this point of view. But this measure is not without shortcomings. Suppose, for example, that one individual owns large amounts of property or capital resources and not much in the way of labour power while another owns much in the form of labour power and not much in the form of property. If both earn the same yearly income, which has the greater ability to pay?

Comparative incomes are likely to provide a better criterion of ability to pay than are comparative property holdings. Both property and labour have value because of their capacities to generate income when they are used in the productive processes. Or, putting it the other way around, comparative incomes take into account the comparative holdings of both property and labour of different persons. Among the problems of using the income measure, the determination of what should and what should not be considered income is undoubtedly the most important. In any case, the topic provokes continuing controversy among economists and among accountants.

Even if incomes could be accurately defined and determined and arrayed according to size, the second question, the assignment of the appropriate tax load to each person, remains. In approaching this question economists classify taxes into three groups: (1) those that are proportional, (2) those that are progressive, and (3) those that are regressive. A *proportional tax* is one that takes the same percentage or proportion of everyone's income. A *progressive tax* is one that takes larger proportions of the income of the rich than it does of the poor. A *regressive tax* is one that takes larger proportions of the income of the poor than it does of the rich. Even in the case of a regressive tax, it is possible that the rich may have larger tax bills than the poor, although this is not necessarily so.

Some disagreement arises with regard to whether greater equity is achieved through the use of proportional taxes or through the use of progressive taxes. No one argues for regressive taxes on the basis of equity. The argument for progressive taxes is that any given proportion of a rich man's income is less important to him than is the same proportion of a poor man's income to the poor man. According to this argument, a man with a $50,000 per year income will miss $20,000 in taxes less than a man with a $5000 per year income will miss $2000 in taxes. This is a difficult proposition to prove; however, it does represent a generally held value judgment. Most people believe that in order to equalize tax loads among different income groups, the tax structure should be progressive.

The Shifting and Incidence of Taxation

What do we know about how much of the tax load each individual in the economy carries? Undoubtedly the correct answer is that we do not know as much as we think we know. Who pays the corporation income tax? If a sales tax is collected by the government from sellers, does this mean that sellers carry the burden or the *incidence* of the tax or are they able to *shift* it in whole or in part to someone else, say to purchasers, by charging higher prices for the product? What is the incidence of a sales tax collected from purchasers instead of from sellers? The answers to these questions are not easily found.

One of the first points that we must get clearly in mind is that *things* do not pay taxes—people do. Yet many taxes are levied on things, partly because of convenience but partly, too, because some people believe that if things, corporations, for example, are taxed, people will somehow escape. Taxes levied directly on persons, individual income taxes and poll taxes, for example, are called *direct taxes*. Taxes levied on things, sales taxes or corporation income taxes, for example, are called *indirect taxes*.[2]

The shifting and incidence of taxes are tricky matters, as is illustrated by the sales tax. In Figure 10-1(a) the initial equilibrium price of cigarettes is p per pack and the original quantity exchanged is X. A sales tax of t cents per pack is placed on the product. Who pays the tax? Where does its incidence lie?

Suppose that the sales tax law specifies that purchasers or consumers must pay the tax. Consumers' incomes and tastes are no different than they were before the tax, so the demand curve, DD, shows the price per pack *including the tax* that consumers are willing to pay for various quantities of cigarettes. Consequently, the price per pack that sellers can receive for each and every one of those quantities will be $D_t D_t$, the prices that consumers will pay *minus* the tax. At the original equilibrium price, *including tax*, consumers want quantity X. At that price, once the tax is

[2]*The distinction between "direct" and "indirect" taxes may be drawn in other ways. Some economists have suggested that (1) indirect taxes are taxes which are shifted, and others that (2) they are taxes which are meant to be shifted. Still others hold that (3) they are simply taxes which are not on income. (These distinctions have been cited by Richard A. Musgrave,* Fiscal Systems. *New Haven: Yale University Press, 1969, pp. 173-74.) While our definition—indirect taxes are taxes which are assessed on objects rather than on individuals—is probably the most useful criterion, it should be pointed out that in the eyes of the Canadian courts a direct tax is generally regarded as one "which is demanded from the very person who it is intended or desired should pay it" (as opposed to an indirect tax which the person paying is able to pass on to someone else). Thus, in Canada, the individual income tax, the corporation income tax, death and gift taxes, property taxes, and provincial sales taxes are usually classified as direct.*

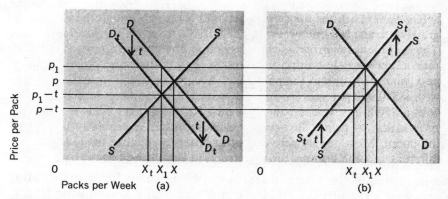

Figure 10-1
The incidence of an excise tax.

levied, sellers would receive $p - t$ and therefore would be willing to place only X_t on the market. A shortage of $X_t X$ packs per week occurs and consumers will bid up the price. When the price *including the tax* reaches p_1, consumers want quantity X_1. At the price $p_1 - t$ that sellers are receiving, they are just willing to place quantity X_1 on the market. So, when the tax is collected from consumers, the new equilibrium price level is p_1 *including the tax* or $p_1 - t$ *not including the tax*. But note that consumers and sellers share the tax. Consumers pay a higher price and sellers receive a lower price for the product than before. An amount pp_1 of the tax is borne by consumers, while the difference between p and $p_1 - t$ is borne by sellers. The incidence is on both. (Suppose that the supply curve in the neighbourhood of the equilibrium price and quantity becomes more and more elastic. What happens to the amount of the tax borne by sellers and buyers respectively? If the demand curve instead of the supply curve becomes more and more elastic, what happens?)

The results would be exactly the same if the law were to state that the tax must be paid by sellers. The initial demand curve, supply curve, equilibrium price, and quantity exchanged are the same in Figure 10-1(b) as they are in Figure 10-1(a). If sellers must turn a tax of t cents per pack sold over to the government, they must still receive for themselves the prices shown by the supply curve in order to be induced to bring the various quantities to market. This means that they must collect the prices shown by $S_t S_t$, which lies above SS by an amount t, from consumers for those quantities. If consumers were to pay the equilibrium price, p, for the product, sellers would receive an amount $p - t$ for themselves; consequently, they would bring only X_t to market. A shortage would exist and consumers would bid up the price. At price p_1, consumers would take quantity X_1 while at price $p_1 - t$ received by sellers, the same quantity would be placed on the market. The new equilibrium price is p_1 for consumers and $p_1 - t$ for sellers. Again the incidence of the tax is on both consumers and sellers, with pp_1 being borne by consumers and with the difference between p and $p_1 - t$ resting on sellers. The reasoning, prices, and quantities in this paragraph are identical to those of the preceding one.

What conclusions can we draw from this discussion of tax shifting and incidence? Some taxes are more likely to be shifted than others. To whom can one shift a poll tax or a personal income tax, for example? Where shifting occurs, the public generally is not well informed as to the incidence of the tax or taxes in question. Taxes for which shifting occurs and for which the incidence is not generally known cannot meet the certainty criterion of a "good" tax. The other features of the tax may, however, be such as to override the importance of the certainty factor.

The Federal Tax Structure

What are the major taxes levied by the federal government and what is the relative importance of each in the overall tax structure? How do they measure up with respect to the adequacy, simplicity, certainty, and equity criteria? The data contained in Table 10-1 will help us attack these questions.

The Individual Income Tax

The federal government relies heavily on the *individual income tax* as a source of revenue. Over 40 percent of the total estimated budgetary revenues of $13,150 million are expected to come from this source. Its adequacy as a revenue source is hardly questionable; therefore, we shall appraise the tax in the light of the other requisites of a "good" tax.

Simplicity

The individual income tax is simple in concept and in practice for those with incomes under $10,000 consisting of wages subject to withholding tax and not more than $2,500 of investment income and who wish to take the standard deductions. Those with larger incomes or with incomes that are generated from several sources run into myriad definitions, exemptions, and deductions so complex that it is usually necessary for them to seek the advice and services of an experienced tax specialist. Problems arise over the definition of income—what is and what is not

TABLE 10-1
Federal Receipts from the Public
Fiscal Years 1967-1971
(Millions of Dollars)

SOURCE	1967	Amount[1] 1968	1969	1970[2]	1971[3]
Budgetary Revenues					
Personal income tax	2,473.8	2,849.6	3,356.4	4,592.0	5,290
Corporation income tax	1,593.2	1,670.6	2,030.0	2,605.0	2,480
Nonresident tax	203.6	220.5	205.6	240.0	255
Social development tax	—	—	63.0	477.0	585
Excise taxes	1,829.2	1,938.1	1,947.7	2,105.0	2,180
Customs duties	777.6	746.4	761.7	815.0	835
Excise duties	461.0	488.6	509.3	525.0	575
Estate tax	101.1	102.2	112.4	104.8	115
Other taxes	0.2	0.3	0.2	0.2	0.2
Total taxes	7,439.7	8,016.3	8,986.3	10,987.0	11,730
Nontax revenues	878.8	1,013.0	1,204.8	1,283.0	1,420
Total budgetary revenues	8,318.5	9,029.3	10,191.1	12,270.0	13,150
Old age Security Revenues					
Personal income tax	576.6	800.1	915.0	1,027	1,170
Corporation income tax	149.5	150.0	183.0	227	230
Sales tax	559.5	544.5	528.1	569	600
Total old age security revenues	1,285.6	1,494.6	1,626.1	1,823	2,000

[1]*Columns may not total due to rounding.*
[2]*Preliminary.*
[3]*Forecast.*
Source: Budget Papers, presented to the House of Commons by Hon. E. J. Benson, Minister of Finance, Ottawa, Queen's Printer, March 22, 1970, p. 225; Canada, House of Commons Debates, March 1, 1970, p. 4747.

to be counted. A variety of confusing criteria are used to determine the legitimacy of various deductions and complex formulae are established for computing deductions—depreciation and medical expenses and charitable donations provide examples—and for claiming foreign tax credits. Complexity arises in part from the way in which the individual income tax provisions of the Income Tax Act have evolved, for over time Parliament has added to the law in a rather piecemeal fashion.

Certainty

The individual income tax measures up fairly well against the test of certainty. Provisions of the tax have been consistent enough over time so that taxpayers know generally what to expect from year to year. Changes, when introduced, have been minor enough, each considered separately, to avoid undue problems in this respect. Further, the individual income tax is a difficult one to shift, as are most direct taxes. The incidence of the tax is largely on the persons taxed.

Equity

A tax is difficult to evaluate accurately on the basis of its equitability because the value judgments of different people concerning what constitutes equity are likely to differ in degree if not in kind. The individual income tax is levied according to ability to pay, thus moving in the direction of what many people consider to be equity.

The individual income tax is progressive—the higher the taxable income of the taxpayer, the higher his tax rate. The tax rate is graduated according to the taxpayer's level of taxable income. For example, for 1969, that part of the taxable income of a single taxpayer up to $1,000 per year was taxed at a rate of 11 percent; that part between $1,000 and $2,000 at 14 percent; that part between $2,000 and $3,000 at 17 percent; and so on, up to a level of $400,000 per year. The entire part of a taxpayer's taxable income in excess of $400,000 per year was taxed at the maximum rate of 80 percent. The rate applicable to the highest bracket of the taxpayer's income is called the *marginal rate of taxation*, and it is worth noting that with a rising marginal rate, the *average rate* rises but lies below the marginal rate. Differences of opinion arise as to the degree of progression that is most equitable—and even as to whether there should be progression. However, there is no great opposition to the general rate structure as it now exists, and this in itself indicates that many people believe it to be a reasonably equitable tax.

The Corporation Income Tax

The second largest revenue source for the federal government is the *corporation income tax*, accounting for almost 20 percent of its estimated 1971 budgetary revenue. The tax is based on the net income of the corporation, or income left after deducting business expenses, including depreciation and interest payments. The tax rate is presently set at 18 percent on the first $35,000 of taxable income and 47 percent on that portion in excess of $35,000. (These rates are before the provincial abatement.) The average rate structure is thus slightly progressive. As in the case of the individual income tax, the yield of the corporation income tax is high, so it may be judged adequate.

Simplicity

On simplicity grounds the corporation income tax is subject to the same criticisms as the individual income tax. There are ambiguities in the definition of what constitutes taxable income and with respect to which deductions are legitimate. There are complexities in computing allowable depreciation deductions, depletion allowances, and investment credits. But these may be of less consequence to the corporation than to an individual, since the former ordinarily has professional advice readily available and usually keeps a much better set of financial records than the latter.

Certainty

The corporation income tax does not come off very well with respect to certainty. It has been and is likely to continue to be a consistent tax over time, but there is much uncertainty, or lack of knowledge, on the part of the public with respect to its incidence, which is probably one of the important reasons for the popularity of the tax. The public has the impression that it is an impersonal "thing"—the corporation—that pays the tax and is quite willing that the "thing" rather than the public itself be taxed. Legislators do not appear to be averse to this line of thought, for corporations have no vote. Although the corporation is treated under law as if it were a person, it is ultimately owned by its shareholders, and these are the ones who pay the bulk of the tax. Stockholders receive the net income of a corporation after expenses have been met and they have little opportunity to shift the tax to others.

Equity

From the point of view of equity, many people believe that the corporation income tax leaves much to be desired. If equity requires that individuals in like income circumstances be treated alike, the tax does not meet the test. If equity requires that the tax structure be progressive with respect to those on whom the incidence of the tax rests, it also has shortcomings.

Suppose that all individuals in an economy earn equal taxable incomes and that initially there is no corporation income tax. Some individuals have invested in corporation stocks and receive a part of their incomes from this source. Others have invested in partnerships and receive their shares of partnership earnings. Still others receive income from their own sole proprietorships. With equal taxable incomes, all will pay equal individual income taxes. Now suppose that a corporation income tax is imposed. Will the income tax load still bear equally on all individuals in the economy?

Suppose now that incomes are not equal but that a general belief prevails that the tax structure should be progressive if it is to be equitable. The corporation income tax treats all stockholders of a given corporation alike regardless of their individual incomes. The corporation income tax on that part of their incomes earned through the corporate device is proportional. The millionaire stockholder is taxed by it at the same rate on the income that his stock earns as the widow who is barely able to live on the dividends earned by her stock.

Not everyone agrees that the corporation income tax has shortcomings on the equity basis. Some people argue that the tax is equitable on the grounds of benefits received. The corporation has certain legal advantages not available to partnerships and sole proprietorships, and the argument runs that the tax is simply payment for the privileges conferred on corporations—but at 18 to 47 percent of net income?

Commodity Taxes

Commodity taxes are levied upon the sales (or output) of goods and generally collected from the vendor. Excise taxes, excise duties and customs import duties are of this type.

Excise Taxes

Excise tax receipts are estimated at $2,180 million for 1971, or about 17 percent of the total budgetary revenue. Of this sum, the *general manufacturer's sales tax* is expected to yield $1,755 million, slightly over 80 percent of the total. The federal sales tax applies to all goods manufactured or produced in Canada or imported into Canada unless the goods are exempted by a provision of the Excise Tax Act. Included in the list of exemptions are: most foodstuffs and drugs; electricity and fuels; materials incorporated into manufactured goods; and production, farming, fishing and mining equipment and machinery. The sales tax, which is at the rate of 9 percent, is applied, in the case of goods manufactured and produced in Canada, on the manufacturer's selling price exclusive of all other excise taxes but inclusive of excise duties. When the goods are imported, the tax is imposed on the duty-paid value.

A number of articles are subject to *special* (*ad valorem* or specific) *excise taxes* in addition to the general sales tax. These include cigarettes, cigars, jewellery, radios, phonographs and television sets, tobacco, toilet articles, and wines.

It should be pointed out that neither the sales tax nor the special excise taxes are levied on goods exported.

Excise Duties

Federal *excise duties* are imposed at specific rates, and apply only to specified domestic products. The present excise duties are levied on alcohol, alcoholic beverages and tobacco, cigars and cigarettes produced in Canada. These duties are not levied on imported alcoholic beverages and tobacco products because the customs import duties more than compensate. Also, these duties are not levied on goods exported.

Customs Import Duties

Most goods imported into Canada are subject to *customs duties* at various rates as provided by tariff schedules. These levies, which once were the chief source of federal revenue, have declined in relative importance as a source of revenue to the point where they now provide less than 7 percent of the total budgetary revenue. Quite apart from its revenue aspects, however, the Canadian tariff, as we shall see later, still occupies an important place as an instrument of foreign commercial policy.

Pros and Cons of Commodity Taxes

In appraising commodity taxes, we find that they meet the test of simplicity. Taxpayers generally understand clearly what is and what is not taxed and, at the federal level at least, such taxes are relatively easy to administer. Generally the government collects them from the seller of the item taxed.

Certainty is another matter. From the point of view of consistency over time, commodity taxes may be certain, although it is by no means a foregone conclusion that they always will be. Legislators and the public are frequently mistaken with regard to the incidence of any given commodity tax. It is generally assumed that the party from whom the collection is actually made bears the incidence of the tax, but, as noted earlier, this is not likely to be the case. Generally the tax is shared in some way by buyers and sellers, depending upon the elasticities of demand and supply.

Are commodity taxes equitable? When we look at the heterogeneous items taxed to provide general revenue, it is obvious that the benefits-received theory of taxation cannot be used to justify taxes of this sort. For the most part, commodity taxes exist because they are good revenue producers, but they are regressive in nature. By and large higher-income groups are likely to spend smaller proportions of their income on the taxed goods than are lower-income groups, since the proportion of income saved by higher-income groups is larger. Consequently, the tax load of the higher-income groups will be less proportionally than that of lower-income groups.

Old Age Security Taxes

The *Old Age Security Taxes* are not included in budgetary revenue but are channelled into the Old Age Security Fund which is separated from the budgetary accounts. At present the taxes are: 3 percent on taxable corporate income, bringing corporate tax rates up to 21 percent (on the first $35,000 of taxable income) and 50 percent (on taxable income in excess of $35,000); 3 percent on sales, bringing the total general sales tax to 12 percent; and 4 percent of personal income, maximum $240 (reached at $6,000 of taxable income). These three special taxes form the basis of what is referred to as the "3–3–4" formula. In fiscal 1971, these three taxes are expected to yield a total of $2,000 million.

Estate and Gift Taxes

Estate and Gift Taxes are levied on transfers of resources or claims to resources from an individual to his beneficiaries. They are not very important as revenue measures but they raise some interesting issues. Federal estate taxes are levied on that of estates exceeding $50,000 (all amounts left outright or in trust by one spouse to the other are excluded from the taxable estate of the deceased spouse) and the rate structure of the tax is highly progressive, ranging from a low of 15 percent on estates having an aggregate taxable value of between $20,000 and $40,000 to a high of 50 percent on estates having an aggregate taxable value of $300,000 or over.[3] Gift taxes are levied on gifts of over $2,000 per year from one person to another (except on gifts between husband and wife) and the rate on the taxable portion of gifts is highly progressive, ranging from 12 percent on taxable amounts up to $15,000, to 75 percent on amounts over $200,000. Equally important, the gift tax is levied on a cumulative basis, that is, the total of taxable gifts made affect the rate of gift tax demandable. In other words, the more gifts made, the higher is the applicable tax range. Furthermore, the gift tax is effectively integrated with the estate tax. This means that the cumulative gift total, plus the tax paid on it, is added back into the estate for purposes of estate tax. The gift tax serves in part to prevent the avoidance of inheritance taxes through gifts made to beneficiaries while the giver is still living. It

[3]*The Estate Tax distinguishes between estates of those who were domiciled in Canada at the time of death and estates of persons who were domiciled elsewhere. In the latter case, property of the deceased situated in Canada is subject to a flat rate of 15 percent. Additionally, the general exemption and the deductions for survivors do not apply.*

also serves to protect the revenue arising from personal income taxes.

Estate and gift taxes are not simple, since extensive and expensive legal determinations are usually required to establish the tax base. Gift taxes are not certain with respect to incidence, since they seem to fall on both the giver and the receiver, the exact amount on each being difficult to determine. They are consistent over time.

The most interesting aspect of these taxes is equity. The controversial issue is whether an individual should be free to bequeath his entire estate to his heirs, thus in many cases placing those heirs in an advantageous economic position, or whether greater equality of opportunity among resource owners should be sought. There is, of course, no clearcut answer to this question. As in most equity questions, value judgments reign supreme. However, any thoroughgoing program for equality of opportunity must contain provisions that prevent certain individuals from being placed by inheritance in especially favoured positions.

Other Federal Taxes

As of January, 1969, *a social development tax* is imposed under the Income Tax Act on the taxable income of individuals at the rate of 2 percent, with a maximum tax of $120. The maximum is reached at $6,000 of taxable income.

Applicable to the 1968, 1969 and 1970 calendar years, a temporary 3 percent surtax on the amount of the "basic tax" (that is, the federal tax before federal abatements), payable in excess of $200 is imposed on individuals. A similar surcharge is imposed on the tax payable by corporations. The temporary surtax on individuals and corporations was introduced as *an economic stabilization measure*, and is expected to lapse at the end of 1970.

Nonresident individuals and corporations are liable for federal income tax at the regular rates only on income from employment in Canada or from carrying on business here. Other forms of income such as interest, dividends and management fees, when paid to nonresidents are subject to a 15 percent withholding tax.[4] Nonresident corporations are also subject to an additional tax of 15 percent on after-income tax earnings minus an allowance for increases in capital investment in property in Canada.

[4]*The rate is reduced to 10 percent in the case of dividends paid by a company that has the required degree of Canadian ownership (i.e., "where 25 percent of its equity and voting shares are owned by Canadians and/or corporations controlled in Canada, or where the voting shares of the corporation are listed on a Canadian stock exchange and no more than 75 percent of its issued outstanding voting shares are owned by a nonresident alone or in combination with related persons"). (D.B.S. Canada Year Book, 1968, p. 1015).*

The purpose of the supplementary tax is to equalize, at least roughly, the tax burden on Canadian firms owned by nonresidents.

Nontax Revenues

The importance of nontax revenue has been growing in recent years and in the 1971 fiscal year is expected to amount to $1,420 million or almost 11 percent of total budgetary revenue. Over 60 percent of this sum is made up of: interest, dividends and surpluses from Crown agencies; interest on loans; earnings of the Exchange Fund and the sinking funds; and bank interest. Some 27 percent is expected to come from gross revenue receipts (after certain expenses are deducted) of the Post Office Department. The balance comes from a wide variety of sources such as: privileges, licences and permits; services and service fees; proceeds from sales; refunds of previous years' expenditures; and the operation of the Royal Canadian Mint.

The Provincial and Municipal Revenue Structure

The revenue patterns of provincial and municipal governments are widely diverse. Rather than attempting to explain each of them we shall aggregate the totals from different revenue sources in this section. Data are not as readily available for provincial and municipal revenues as they are for federal revenues because of problems of compilation. Neither are they as accurate. In Table 10-2 the major sources of provincial and municipal revenue are listed together with the latest available data on the amounts in each category.

Property Taxes

Provincial and municipal revenues from the *property tax* are more than twice those for any other item. Table 10-2 indicates that the property tax accounts for almost 25 percent of total revenues (including intergovernmental transfers) of provinces and municipalities. It is used more by municipal governments and school boards than by provincial governments. For purposes of taxation, property is divided into two classifications, *real property* and *personal property*, with the former consisting of land, buildings, and improvements on these, while the latter is made up of such things as furniture, clothing, and jewellery. There has been a tendency over the years to eliminate personal property, so that today the property tax is levied almost solely upon real estate.

TABLE 10-2
Consolidated Provincial and Municipal Revenues,
For Fiscal Years Nearest to December 31, 1963–1965

| | Millions of Dollars | | |
| | Amount[1] | | |
SOURCE	1963	1964	1965
Taxes			
Real and personal property	1,630.9	1,716.1	1,731.1
Individual income taxes	389.3	507.7	834.3
General sales[2]	620.1	730.4	813.3
Motor fuel and fuel oil sales	539.9	616.1	679.6
Corporation income taxes	412.2	455.1	523.5
Other sales	73.6	77.9	113.7
Estate taxes and succession duties	85.7	92.2	107.9
Business	51.7	54.6	60.5
Other	214.6	325.6	289.8
Totals, taxes	4,018.0	4,575.7	5,153.7
Privileges, licences and permits			
Liquor control and regulation	55.5	60.0	61.9
Motor vehicles	210.8	221.7	243.9
Natural resources	366.6	440.4	508.3
Other	68.3	73.0	77.8
Totals, privileges, etc.	701.3	795.1	891.9
Sales and services	54.0	67.5	111.8
Fines and penalties	10.7	12.3	59.5
Other	749.0	893.5	987.4
Net general revenue	5,532.8	6,344.2	7,204.7

[1]*Columns may not total due to rounding.*
[2]*Includes contributions from government enterprises, non-revenue and surplus receipts and transfers from federal government.*
Source: Dominion Bureau of Statistics, Consolidated Government Finance, *1963, 1964 and 1965.*

Property taxes are simple in that they are easily understood; however, they are difficult to administer. The key administrative agent is the county assessor, whose job it is to assess the property in his county for property tax purposes. The evasion that takes place through failure of taxpayers to declare property and of assessors to locate and evaluate property on a continuing basis is notorious.

Property taxes are reasonably certain taxes. They can be and generally are consistent over time. Further, even though they are indirect, in the sense that they are levied on objects (and thus only indirectly on people), the incidence seems to rest on the owners of the property assessed and taxed. In the short run, particularly, the tax is difficult to pass along to others, except to property renters.

Much could be said about the equity of property taxes—or, rather, the lack of it. Significant inequities stem from assessment shortcomings, such as the difficulty or the unwillingness of the assessor to find, classify, and value property correctly. But even if this were done perfectly, another serious inequity would exist. The property tax discriminates against investment in property as compared with investment in human beings. Suppose that upon finishing high school an individual faces a choice of investing $10,000 in a business or in a university education. If the annual dollar income yield from both investments were the same, investment in the university education would provide the individual with the greater net return because of property taxes. In both cases the annual income would be subjected to the same personal income tax; however, an investment in property would subject the individual to property taxes as well, while an investment in education would not.

Income Taxes and Succession Duties

By 1940, every province was taking advantage of its right under the British North America Act to levy a personal income tax, a corporation profits tax, and succession duties, which are a tax upon the right to succeed to property and are assessed upon the interest or benefit passing at death to an heir or beneficiary.[5] In 1941, in order to secure as much revenue from taxation as was desirable for the prosecution of the Second World War, the provinces agreed to withdraw from the income-tax field—leaving it clear for the federal government—in exchange for federal payments. After the war these "tax-rental" arrangements were renewed, with some variation in terms, in 1947 and 1952, and with substantial differences in 1957. Under these postwar agreements, all provinces except two also vacated the succession-duty field in exchange for annual cash grants from the federal government. Quebec did not participate in the postwar agreements and Ontario did so only to a limited degree.

In 1961, the Tax-Sharing Arrangements Act expired and Parliament passed the Federal-Provincial Fiscal Arrangements Act which applied to the tax years 1962 to 1966 inclusive. Under this legislation each province undertook to impose its own personal and corporation income taxes and the federal government accepted to withdraw from the corporation income-tax field by 9 percentage points of corporate income and from the personal income tax field by 16 percent in 1962 and by an additional 1 percent in subsequent years up to 20 percent in 1966. The federal government offered to collect both income taxes imposed by the provinces,

[5]*The rates of succession duties are generally governed by the total value of the estate, the relationship of the beneficiary to the deceased and the amount going to any one individual.*

provided that provincial personal income tax was expressed as a percentage of federal personal income tax otherwise payable and provincial corporation income tax applied to taxable income was calculated in the same way as for federal income tax purposes. All provinces except Ontario and Quebec accepted the federal offer to collect taxes and Ontario did so on personal income tax. In 1964 an additional withdrawal of 2 percent from the personal income tax field was offered for the 1965 tax year and a further 2 percent for the 1966 tax year so that the total federal withdrawal amounted to 24 percent for the 1966 tax year.

In the federal estate tax field a 50 percent abatement (taxcredit) was provided for provincial succession taxes, or if none was levied, one-half the federal estate tax revenue derived from the province was to be returned to the province. In 1964 the payment or abatement was increased to 75 percent of the federal estate tax. Only the provinces of Ontario, Quebec and British Columbia (as of 1963) levy succession duties.

A new Fiscal Arrangements Act became operative on April 1, 1967 and will run until March 31, 1972. Under this arrangement the federal government increased its abatement of the personal income tax from 24 percent to 28 percent of the federal tax payable in the provinces and raised the abatement of the corporate income tax from 9 percent to 10 percent of taxable income. The 75 percent abatement of the federal estate tax was continued for provinces with succession duties. However, for provinces which levy their succession duties at the same rate as in 1964 (i.e. Ontario and Quebec), the federal government now abates its estate tax by 50 percent of the federal estate tax payable, and makes a cash payment equal to 25 percent of the estate tax payable in the province. For provinces which do not levy a death tax the direct payment is still 75 percent of the federal estate tax due in the province.

While the provincial tax rates are not restricted to the extent of the federal withdrawal, four provinces (Ontario, Prince Edward Island, Nova Scotia and British Columbia) impose a rate of personal income tax that is the same as the standard abatement. For 1970 the effective rate in Newfoundland, Saskatchewan, Manitoba and Alberta is 33 percent of the federal tax payable and in New Brunswick is 38 percent. In this connection, it should be pointed out that the federal abatement is 50 percent for taxpayers in Quebec. The higher abatement in Quebec is in compensation of the fact that the payment of youth allowances and full cost of certain programs in the other provinces have been assumed by Quebec. Accordingly, Quebec, which administers its own personal income tax, imposes its tax under a rate schedule (it progresses from 5.5 percent on the first $1,000 of taxable income to a maximum of 40 percent on the excess over $400,000) which is structured to give effect to the 50 percent federal abatement available to residents of that province. At the present time, four provinces set their corporation tax rate at the basic 10 percent allowed by the federal government. The provincial rates currently payable in the other provinces are: 11 percent in Manitoba, Saskatchewan and Alberta; 12 percent in Ontario and Quebec; and 13 percent in Newfoundland.

It should be added that municipal income taxes were imposed widely for many years until the federal government entered into the Wartime Tax Agreements with the provinces in 1941, primarily in the maritime provinces, and to some extent in Ontario and Quebec. Certain localities have retained the use of a poll tax.

As Table 10-2 indicates, income taxes and death duties accounted for 23 percent of provincial revenues in 1965. Under the Fiscal Arrangements (1967-1972), it is likely that these three items will increase significantly in the next few years, especially in the field of personal income taxes.

Other Provincial and Municipal Revenues

Other provincial and municipal revenues include taxes on retail sales and motor fuel, amusement and business taxes, natural resource charges and motor vehicle user charges, liquor revenue, sales and service charges, and fines and penalties. Of these retail sales taxes, fuel taxes and natural resource charges are by far the most important.

Whereas federal excise taxes are levied on a limited number of products, provincial taxes of this sort are imposed on such a wide range of commodities and services that they are called appropriately *general sales taxes*. All provinces except Alberta impose such taxes at rates varying from 5 percent to 8 percent. Only in five provinces is the designation, sales tax, applied to the levy, the taxes in the other provinces (Saskatchewan, Nova Scotia, Newfoundland, New Brunswick and British Columbia) being designated on the basis of the uses to which the tax revenues are put (e.g. education, health, social security). In their usual form, general sales taxes are *ad valorem* in nature, are imposed technically upon the consumer, the retailer being designated as an agent of the province for purposes of collection.[6] But it is not at all certain that the incidence will rest on consumers. Ordinarily, we would expect the incidence to be distributed between buyers and sellers.

In addition to general retail sales taxes, provinces frequently place specific excise taxes on particular products, partly for regulatory and

---

[6]*The merchants are allowed to deduct a varying but small percentage from their sales tax remittances as compensation for their work as collectors of tax, and are required to observe regular filing dates and maintain records, and the like.*

control purposes and partly for purposes of financing particular kinds of provincial expenditures that benefit consumers of the product being taxed. Provincial excise taxes on tobacco and the pari-mutual betting system at horse race tracks illustrate the former. Motor fuel taxes, land transfer taxes and security transfer taxes illustrate the second.

In all provinces except Prince Edward Island natural resource charges constitute a substantial source revenue. All provinces except Prince Edward Island levy taxes on some or all of the following: the profits of firms engaged in mining operations in general (i.e., metallics, industrial minerals and mineral fuels) or in specific kinds of mining operations; on the assessed value of minerals; on acreage of mining property. Revenue is also obtained in some provinces from rentals of land for mineral production and from royalties on the minerals produced. Three provinces, Quebec, Ontario and British Columbia, impose a tax on the income from logging operations of individuals, partnerships, associations or corporations engaged in this activity.

In all provinces the sale of intoxicating liquor is a provincial government monopoly and the markup on the manufacturers' prices constitutes the effective means of taxation. In addition, there is a licence fee imposed on breweries and distilleries, and on establishments authorized to sell alcoholic beverages on the premises. Permits for the purchase of alcoholic beverages are required in Newfoundland, Prince Edward Island and Nova Scotia. Provincial government revenue from the control and taxation of alcoholic beverages in the fiscal year 1965 amounted to almost $311 million. The revenue from taxation of liquor, apart from its control and regulation, is included in the "other" classification in Table 10-2. Profits from other government enterprises also appear under this heading.

All provinces charge registration and licence fees for motor vehicles and for motor vehicle operators. They represent a special kind of taxes, providing revenues ordinarily earmarked for highway construction and maintenance and for highway safety. Motor vehicle licence fees are more or less the same as property taxes with respect to the primary impact of the tax itself, while operator licence fees resemble poll taxes. In both cases the incidence is generally on the one who pays the fee. Both of these taxes, like motor fuel excise taxes, are generally justified by the benefits-received theory. Those who use the highways the most provide the largest amounts of revenue necessary for their construction and maintenance. Most provinces and municipalities collect miscellaneous other fees from firms and individuals. These include fees for the privilege of acting as a corporation, going fishing, being a barber, being a taxi driver, and so forth.

The items, fines and penalties and sales and services, are self-explanatory.

Revenue from the Federal Government

As already indicated, the federal government is a major source of funds for provincial and municipal governments. The federal government makes three types of general or unconditional payments to provinces: (1) statutory subsidies; (2) equalization grants; and (3) stabilization grants. When the Dominion of Canada was formed in 1867, the powers of the provinces to levy sales taxes and excise taxes were withdrawn. Since they had relied heavily on these sources, the federal government gave them annual subsidies (related to population, cost of government, debt interest, compensation for public lands and special grants) to replace the lost revenue. The amounts were intended to remain fixed, but were gradually increased, and have continued up to the present time. The total in 1965, however, was only $23 million. In essence, equalization grants are designed to equalize the relative revenue position of the various provinces, and thus to aid the poorer provinces. The federal formula for equalization payments is based on 16 provincial revenue sources.[7] Stabilization grants are given to assure the provinces that the current year's revenue at the previous year's tax rates does not fall below 95 percent of the previous year's revenue. Total net general revenues of a province, including equalization and other unconditional grants from the federal government, are used in determining the size of the federal payment. The total of equalization and stabilization grants in 1965 was approximately $277.5 million. These unconditional grants are included in the "other" classification in Table 10-2. The federal government also shares the income tax on power utilities with the provinces; the provinces' share is 95 percent. As a consequence of recent fiscal arrangements, unconditional grants now include "adjustment" payments for post-secondary education.

As noted earlier, the federal government also makes conditional payments or *grants-in-aid* to the provinces for specific purposes such as: hospital insurance; assistance to the aged, the blind and the disabled; airport development; the construction of designated types of highways; and various resource projects. These payments, which were in the neighbourhood of $947 million in 1965, are *not* included in Table 10-2. It should be added that federal conditional grants and shared-cost programs have occasioned some provincial criticisms and misgivings in recent years. It has been argued that the preponderant occupancy of the income tax field in the postwar years by the federal government encouraged the growth of joint federal-provincial programs as the provinces were denied the funds that would have enabled them to provide equivalent programs themselves.

Federal payments to provinces and municipalities in lieu of taxes on

[7]*For a more detailed treatment of the equalization formula, see Canadian Tax Foundation*, Provincial Finances, 1969, *Toronto, 1969, pp. 83-84.*

real federal property were over $36 million 1965. These payments are equivalent to full taxes on land and buildings where normal municipal services are performed. Properties administered by Crown agencies make payments in lieu of taxes directly to municipalities.

Tax Reform

Widespread recognition of defects in the federal tax system led in 1962 to the appointment of the Royal Commission on Taxation, with the late Mr. Kenneth LeM. Carter as chairman. The Commission's massive six-volume, 2600 page report, presented in December 1966, concluded that "the present Canadian system is as good as most other systems" but that it "fell far short of the attainable objectives". The Commission set out to devise a tax structure that would generate a "sufficient flow of revenues", correct most of the defects in the present structure, and which would meet the Commission's two overriding objectives—equity and neutrality. According to the Commission, *equity* requires that individuals in essentially the same economic circumstances bear essentially the same tax burden while individuals in essentially different circumstances bear appropriately different burdens, while *neutrality* requires that the tax system not discriminate between different types of activity to achieve particular objectives.

We need not here go into the hundreds of conclusions and recommendations of the Carter Commission which, if implemented, "would produce a complete transformation of Canada's existing tax system". It is sufficient to note that a vigorous public debate arose over the Commission's report and the government received many letters and briefs concerning it. As a consequence, little action[8] was taken until November 1969 when the federal government introduced its now famous *White Paper*, "Proposals for Tax Reform". Offering his proposals in the White Paper as grounds for debate, the Minister of Finance, launching an experiment in participatory democracy, said that he would be willing to make changes in it "if we are persuaded".[9] It appears that public support for the income tax proposals made by the government last year varies from qualified acceptance to outright condemnation. There has been particularly strong opposition to the government's proposed treatment of the middle income groups —the taxpayers in the $9,000-$16,000 income range—since the bulk of savings and capital accumulation comes from these individuals. It is argued that the added weight of taxation on these groups could not help

[8]*Changes in the estate tax and gift tax were made in October, 1968.*
[9]Ottawa Journal, *"Hundred Tax Reforms Proposed by Benson,"* November 8, 1969, p. 5.

having a dampening effect on incentives to initiative, effort and investment in Canada. Thus, at this point, it is impossible to suggest what proposals for tax reform may or may not be adopted.

Summary

Government expenditures serve to reallocate resources from the private to the public sector of the economy and, within the private sector, away from the rest of the economy toward those receiving transfer expenditures. Determination of who in the private sector must give up reseources, and the impact of government expenditures on economic activity, depend upon how those expenditures are financed.

The primary methods of financing expenditures are through taxation, the creation of new money, and borrowing. Most expenditures are financed by tax receipts, but in the interests of economic stability, judicious use of money creation and borrowing are in order. Financing by means of taxation substitutes government demand for private demand. Financing by money creation increases government demand without decreasing private demand. Borrowing may have effects like those of taxation or money creation, depending upon what would have been done with the money had it not been loaned to the government.

Several criteria may be used in selecting the kinds of taxes to use to raise government revenue. Most experts in public finance agree that taxes should be adequate, simple, certain, and equitable. Adequate taxes are those that provide good revenue yields. By simple it is meant that the taxes are easily understood and easily administered. Taxes are certain when taxpayers can expect consistency over time from them and when they have knowledge of the incidence of the tax. The incidence of a tax refers to who ultimately pays it. Those from whom a tax is collected are frequently able to shift the tax or some part of it to others. Equity in taxation is difficult to define. For some kinds of government expenditure financing is thought to be equitable when taxes are levied according to benefits received, but, in general, equity is thought to lie in the direction of taxation according to ability to pay.

The federal government relies most heavily on income taxes for its revenues, but in addition it levies sales taxes, excise taxes and duties, custom import duties, and estate and gift taxes. Income taxes are levied on both individual and corporation incomes. Those imposed on the latter raise some questions as to whether the corporate form of business organization is discriminataed against compared with other forms. The federal sales tax is a tax of general application in that it applies to all goods manufactured or produced in Canada or imported into Canada unless the goods are exempted. Many classes of goods are exempt from sales taxes. Excise taxes are levied on a hodge-podge of items whereas excise duties are levied only upon alcohol, alcoholic beverages and tobacco products produced in Canada. Most goods imported into Canada are subject to customs duties. While primarily regarded today as a tool of national policy (even though most international tariff arrangements aim at tariff reduction), custom duties are still an important source of federal revenue. Estate and gift taxes are not especially good revenue raisers but they bring up some interesting equity issues.

Provincial and municipal governments obtain the bulk of their revenues from property taxes, income taxes, excise taxes and retail sales taxes. Property taxes are the principal revenue source for municipal governments, while personal and corporation income taxes, retail sales taxes and motor fuel taxes provide most of the receipts of provincial governments. Additionally, nontaxation revenue (liquor profits, privileges, licences and permits, and profits from government enterprises) provides a substantial source of income for provinces and localities.

Federal unconditional grants are also important for some provinces and municipalities.

Exercises and Questions for Discussion

1. "Through money creation the government may increase its expenditures with no decrease in private expenditures. This practice is obviously superior to taxation as a method of financing expenditures, since the government via this method can pursue its activities at no expense to the private sector." Is this argument correct? Explain.
2. In each of the following situations which of the three methods of financing government expenditures would you deem most appropriate? Explain why you recommend the method you have chosen.
   a. Inflation.
   b. Unemployment.
   c. Inflation with unemployment.
3. Suppose that the sales tax in your province is earmarked for welfare expenditures. Can this be justified in the light of either the benefits-received or the ability-to-pay theory? Discuss.
4. "If a retailer is taxed at the rate of 18 cents for every gallon of gas he sells, he merely adds this amount to the price of each gallon; therefore the incidence of the tax is clearly on the consumer." Evaluate this statement verbally and graphically.

5. "The most sensible way for the government to finance its expenditures is to have those who benefit from government-provided goods and services to pay accordingly, as is the case for toll roads and toll bridges." Evaluate this statement.

Selected Readings

Buchanan, J. M., *The Public Finances*, rev. ed. Homewood, Ill.: Richard D. Irwin, Inc., 1965, Chaps. 21, 22, 24, 25, and 26.

Canadian Tax Foundation, *The National Finances*, 1969-70, Toronto, October 1969.

————, *Provincial Finances*, 1969, Toronto, July 1969.

Dominion Bureau of Statistics, *Canada Year Book, 1968*. Ottawa: Queen's Printer, pp. 1005-1056.

Due, J. F., *Government Finance*, 4th ed. Homewood, Ill.: Richard D. Irwin Inc., 1968, Chaps. 5, 6, 13, 14, 17, 18, 19, 21 and 24.

Sharp, A. M., and B. F. Sliger, *Public Finance*, rev. ed. Homewood, Ill.: The Dorsey Press, 1970, Chap. 14.

Appendix to Chapter 10

The 1969 White Paper on Tax Reform

The income tax reform proposals made by the federal government in November 1969 were a major part of a longer-range plan to revise the whole of the federal tax system. Already adopted are revisions of the estate and gift taxes. Still to come are changes in sales taxes and tax administration. The purpose of this appendix is to describe the highlights of the 1969 White Paper.

The aims of the proposed tax reforms may be summarized as follows:
(1) A fairer distribution of the tax burden based upon the "ability to pay" principle,
(2) The ensurance of continuing economic growth and prosperity,
(3) The recognition of growing social needs,
(4) The need to achieve widespread understanding of, and voluntary compliance with the tax laws, (This includes provisions for eliminating loopholes in the law.)
(5) Development of a tax system which would be flexible enough to allow provincial participation.

To accomplish these objectives numerous tax proposals were made. The major ones are discussed below.

1. *Tax Exemptions*

In order to remove or reduce the burden of taxes on the lower income groups:

    (1) The basic personal exemption for a single person would rise from $1,000 to $1,400;

    (2) The proposed exemption for married couples would rise to $2,800 from $2,000.

Thus with the standard $100 exemption in lieu of deductions for medical expenses and charitable donations remaining as is, no taxes for a single person earning less than $1,500 would be paid. Similarly, married couples earning $2,900 would not pay personal income taxes. Accordingly, the impact of this proposal would be to eliminate entirely income taxes for 750,000 Canadians and reduce the tax payments for an additional 3 million taxpayers.

2. *Capital Gains as Income*

After many years of debate in private and governmental circles, the government has officially recommended a tax on capital gains.

    (1) Capital gains will apply to assets having a value of $500 or more.

    (2) Capital losses through the sale of certain assets will be deductible from income.

    (3) Special exemptions would be permitted for taxpayers' homes.

    (4) Capital gains from marketable shares of corporations will be subject to taxation. Moreover, the gains tax will apply to *accrued* gains (every 5 years) as well as to realized gains. Additionally, both realized and accrued losses would be deductible as well.

    (5) Only 50 percent of the gains (losses) on shares of "widely held" Canadian companies, that is, listed companies or companies whose shares are traded over the counter, are taxable (deductible) as (from) income.

The tax on capital gains is not a separate tax; rather, capital gains are to be part of income and taxed progressively in accordance with the new personal income tax rates. It is estimated that once capital gains become included as taxable income, the portion of the total income of the well-to-do that will be taxable will be substantially increased, so that by 1976 (based on 1969 incomes) the capital gains should add $345 million to personal income taxes.

3. *Deductions*

Proposals have been made which would:

    (1) Provide employees with a general deduction of 3 percent of employment income up to a maximum of $150;

(2) Provide, as an aid to working mothers, that the maximum expenses deductible would be the lower of $500 per child under 14 years of age or $2,000 per family. Moreover, this is in addition to the normal exemption for children.

The effect of the first proposal would be to benefit more than 6.5 million persons, the majority of whom earn less than $10,000 per annum. The second proposal should serve to increase the real incomes of working mothers who at present are not able to deduct child care and other legitimate expenses of the working mother. In turn, the proposal may be expected to increase the female participation rate in the labour force.

4. *More Comprehensive Definition of Income*

In addition to the inclusion of capital gains as income the White Paper also proposes that:
(1) Unemployment insurance benefits become taxable (and contributions to the fund be deductible);
(2) Fellowships, scholarships, bursaries and research grants not related to services become taxable; with the exception of allowances paid to those living away from home, training allowances under the Adult Occupational Training Act become taxable also;
(3) The income of visiting teachers and professors, previously exempt from Canadian income taxes for two years, become taxable;
(4) Members of the Armed Forces be taxed as are other Canadians rather than under special regulations as now exist;
(5) Various fringe benefits received by employers or by owners of a business become included as income. (This would include, for example, the use of a business car for personal use. Moreover, entertainment costs, such as yachts, lodges, airplanes, etc. would no longer be deductible to employers.)

5. *Personal Income Tax Rates*

It is estimated that the proposed new exemptions and deductions from income will exceed the proposed additions to income by a wide margin, and, if present rates are left unchanged, it would mean a loss of revenue of approximately $800 million (in terms of 1967 incomes). Thus, the government has proposed a new rate schedule which is shown in the following table. The existing rates are shown in the same table. Five years after the White Paper becomes effective as law, the top federal rate would be 40 percent. With a 28 percent provincial rate, the combined maximum rate would be 51.2 percent. The federal tax rate now includes the old age security tax, social development tax, the current surtax and the 20 percent reduction on the "basic" tax (allowable up to $20). Thus the new rate schedule greatly simplifies the present system.

The new rates take into account the increase in exemptions, deductions, the new income concepts and various other changes so that total revenues are virtually the same. With the new rate system proposed, however, and taking into consideration the new employment expense allowance of $150, single persons earning less than $3,400 per year and married persons earning $9,100 will pay less. Those earning more than these amounts will pay more than currently exist.

6. *Corporation Income Taxation*

Proposals are made which would eliminate the present two-rate treatment of corporation income. A distinction would be made between two types of corporate structures for tax purposes.

A. *Private (closely-held) Corporations*

In this type of corporation in which there is a close relationship between the shareholders and the management, the proposal is that:
   (1) The federal income tax paid by such corporations be treated as a prepayment of the personal income tax on behalf of individual resident shareholders;
   (2) Under certain conditions:
      (a) The corporation could choose to be taxed as a partnership of its shareholders if the tax rate on personal income was less than the 50 percent corporate tax;
      (b) The shareholders would pay a tax on a sum that would include their dividends plus a related amount of corporate tax already paid. Shareholders could then claim a tax credit for the tax already paid and could qualify for a refund if their own personal tax rates are lower than the corporate rate;
   (3) The lower rate of 21 percent on the first $35,000 of taxable corporate income would be removed gradually over a period of 5 years.

The effect of this proposal is that the benefits of low rates of tax would accrue to the shareholder with small income rather than corporations with small incomes.

B. *Public (widely-held) Corporations*

In this type of corporations where the link between shareholders and management is more tenuous, it is proposed that:
   (1) One half the corporation tax paid by corporations would be regarded as a prepayment of individual tax for shareholders;
   (2) Shareholders receiving dividends from profits would be liable for a tax on the dividend plus an amount of "creditable" tax

TABLE 10-3
Present and Proposed Schedule of Rates Applied to Taxable Income

	Present					Proposed				
	Federal Tax		Combined Federal and 28% Provincial Tax			Federal Tax		Combined Federal and 28% Provincial tax		
Taxable Income Bracket	Tax at the beginning of the bracket	Tax Rate on income in bracket	Tax at the beginning of the bracket	Tax Rate on income in bracket	Taxable Income Bracket	Tax at the beginning of the bracket	Tax Rate on income in bracket	Tax at the beginning of the bracket	Tax Rate on income in bracket
$	$	%	$	%	$	$	%	$	%
0-909	0.00	11.72	0.00	14.80	0-500	0	17	0.00	21.76
909-1,000	106.55	13.92	134.55	17.00	500-1,000	85	18	108.80	23.04
1,000-1,643	119.20	16.08	150.00	20.00	1,000-1,500	175	19	224.00	24.32
1,643-2,000	222.57	16.50	278.57	20.42	1,500-2,000	270	20	345.60	25.60
2,000-3,000	281.50	18.75	351.50	23.51	2,000-3,000	370	21	473.60	26.88
3,000-4,000	469.00	20.25	586.60	25.57	3,000-4,000	580	22	742.40	28.16
4,000-6,000	671.50	22.50	842.30	28.66	4,000-5,000	800	24	1,024.00	30.72
6,000-8,000	1,121.50	19.50	1,415.50	26.78	5,000-7,000	1,040	26	1,331.20	33.28
8,000-10,000	1,511.50	22.50	1,951.10	30.90	7,000-10,000	1,560	28	1,996.80	35.84
10,000-12,000	1,961.50	26.25	2,569.10	36.05	10,000-13,000	2,400	30	3,072.00	38.40
12,000-15,000	2,486.50	30.00	3,290.10	41.20	13,000-16,000	3,300	33	4,224.00	42.24
15,000-25,000	3,386.50	33.75	4,526.10	46.35	16,000-24,000	4,290	36	5,491.20	46.08
25,000-40,000	6,761.50	37.50	9,161.10	51.50	24,000-	7,170	40	9,177.60	51.20
40,000-60,000	12,386.50	41.25	16,886.10	56.65					
60,000-90,000	20,636.50	45.00	28,216.10	61.80					
90,000-125,000	34,136.50	48.75	46,756.10	66.95					
125,000-225,000	51,199.00	52.50	70,188.60	72.10					
225,000-400,000	103,699.00	56.25	142,288.60	77.25					
400,000-	202,136.50	60.00	277,476.10	82.40					

(1) Fully effective
Source: Minister of Finance, Proposals for Tax Reform, Ottawa, 1969, pp. 24-25.

equal to half the dividend and would be given credit for that amount of tax.

7. *Mineral Industries*

Two main changes are proposed:
  (1) One would replace the three-year tax exemption for new mines with a special rule beginning in 1974 which would permit capital costs of fixed assets purchased for the development and operation of a new mine to be charged off against the income of that mine as quickly as desired;
  (2) A second would alter depletion allowances. Existing maximums would continue to apply (about one-third of production profits) but a taxpayer could run out of depletion allowances unless he continues to explore for and/or develop Canadian minerals.

Before leaving this summary of the White Paper, it should be pointed out that many of the government's assumptions and conclusions have been criticized. For example, the White Paper estimates that the proposed tax system would, after a five-year run-in period, add $630 million to government revenues. Other projections on a similar basis (1969 incomes) have shown substantially higher figures. For another view of the topics considered in this appendix, see Canadian Bankers Association, *Bulletin*, Toronto, June 1970. See also I. H. Asper, *The Benson Iceberg*. Toronto: Clark Irwin, 1970.

11

Fiscal Policy and the National Debt

The vast amounts of money spent and collected by government units are eloquent testimony of the impact of government on economic activity. Both government spending and revenue collection—primarily tax collections—not only affect what goods and services resources are used to produce but they also affect in a very significant way the *level* of economic activity. Government expenditures and tax receipts are not closely tied to one another. In any given year expenditures and tax revenues may be the same, in which case the government is said to have a *balanced budget*. However, it is entirely possible, and indeed quite likely, that expenditures will exceed tax collections, thereby creating a *budget deficit or deficit spending*, or that expenditures will be less than tax collections, creating a *budget surplus*. The use of budget deficits, surpluses, and the balanced budget in order to affect the level of economic activity, or for economic stability, is the essence of *fiscal policy*.

Fiscal Policy for Stabilization

Federal government fiscal policy as a companion tool to monetary policy for achieving economic stability and growth has been discussed seriously by economists only since the Great Depression. The deliberate application of fiscal policy for this purpose has been quite limited. The public works and price support (for wheat) programs of the federal government after 1935 provide one example. To find another of major proportions one must search in vain up to the recession of 1957-1958 when the scales of old age pensions, family allowances and certain other federal government transfer payments were increased, tax rates were reduced and public investment (largely in housing) on a substantial scale took place. Similarly, personal income tax rates were cut in fiscal 1965, in spite of a federal deficit, for the conscious and deliberate purpose of providing an expansionary impetus to the economy. The powerful stimulus of government spending to economic activity, although it was not intended for this purpose, was amply demonstrated in World War II and the Korean War. Thus, although fiscal policy as a tool for stimulating economic activity has not been extensively tested, its potential for this purpose is certainly clear.

In this section we shall examine the impact of fiscal policy on the level of economic activity. We shall consider in turn which policies are called for during periods of full employment when there is no inflation, during periods of recession and depression, and during periods of rapid inflation.

Full Employment with No Inflation: The Balanced Budget

What fiscal policy is appropriate when the economy's resources are near the full employment level and when, at the same time, no significant inflation is occurring? In terms of the equation of exchange, in a situation of this kind, total spending in the economy, both public and private, is changing in the same direction and at the same rate as the volume of trade. Both of these will be expanding even though there is full employment.[1]

If private spending alone is expanding enough to maintain full employment without inflation, it would appear that fiscal policy should be more or less neutral. This means that, as a first approximation, a balanced budget is in order. The government should add to the spending stream the same overall amount that it removes from the spending stream through tax collections; that is, it should supplant the reduction in private spending with an equivalent amount of government spending.

There are qualifications to the supposed neutrality of the balanced budget. Things are not quite as simple as they seem. From whom were taxes collected? Were they collected from people who otherwise would have spent the money or from those who would have hoarded it? Further, what are the purposes of the expenditures? Will they generate new economic activity, for example, a road that opens up new trade possibili-

---

[1]*Output would be expanding because the economy ordinarily is (1) adding to its stock of capital resources in terms of both quantity and quality, (2) improving its techniques of production, and (3) improving the quality and, perhaps, the quantity of its labour force during times of full employment.*

ties, or are they made for services immediately consumed or for more or less nonproductive activities such as relief payment transfers? Generally speaking, the approximation of fiscal neutrality from a balanced budget is probably not too wide of the mark, but we should keep in mind that this policy is not always or necessarily neutral in its effects.

Recessions and Depressions: The Budget Deficit

If a recession is underway or if unemployment seems to be at excessively high levels, what fiscal policy is recommended? Both total spending and output of the economy are too low, and thus an increase in total spending is in order. Such an increase will raise the price level, make business more profitable, and expand the volume of trade and employment. The appropriate fiscal policy, then, is a budget deficit—government expenditures should exceed tax revenues. A budget deficit increases total spending, since government spending in the deficit situation more than offsets the negative effects of tax collections on private spending.

The method of financing the deficit will determine how large the impact of a deficit will be on total spending. The government may finance its deficit by *creating new money*, either through borrowing from the central bank, through direct printing by the treasury department, or through borrowing from chartered banks when the latter have excess reserves. Or it may finance the deficit by *borrowing a part of the existing money supply*; that is, by borrowing from the general public.

Creation of New Money

The government may create new money to finance a deficit through the issuance and sale of new bonds and treasury bills to the central bank in exchange for new Bank of Canada notes or for new deposits at the central bank.[2] The spending of these notes or deposits by the government creates new deposits in chartered banks in the names of those to whom the government makes payments. But even more important, the accompanying transfer of Bank of Canada notes or deposits from the government to the reserve accounts of chartered banks increases the excess reserves of the latter, making it possible for them to expand their loans and deposits by more than the amount borrowed and spent by the government.

Additionally, if the government finances the deficit by selling new bonds to chartered banks, new money in the form of bank deposits may be created. If chartered banks have excess reserves—and this is the usual case during recession—they pay for the bonds by creating new deposits for the government. As the government spends them these deposits become

---

[2]*The government borrows by issuing and selling new government bonds and treasury bills.*

deposits for the recipients of government payments, and a net increase in the money supply has occurred. Government expenditures so financed serve to increase total spending in the economy, since they are not offset by a decrease in private spending.

Financing a deficit by the creation of new money is a double-edged sword. Total spending is increased in the first instance by government spending that is not offset by tax collections from the general public. Second, the larger stock of money in the economy serves as a further stimulus to spending.

Borrowing from the Public

If the deficit is financed by the issuance and sale of new government bonds to people who would have spent the money for consumer goods and services or for capital goods, there will be no net effect on total spending. This method of financing government spending is similar to taxation, since just enough private spending is absorbed by the bond sales to offset the government spending. A deficit financed in this way serves only to increase the national debt and does not stimulate the economy.

If the borrowing is accomplished by the issue and sale of bonds to persons, businesses other than banks, and institutions (including government trust funds) that would otherwise have held idle money, total spending will be increased, although the money supply will not be. Idle money is drawn into the spending stream, increasing the velocity of circulation. Since private spending is not reduced, government spending in the amount of the deficit constitutes a net addition to total spending in the economy. The borrowing does add to the national debt, however.

Ordinarily, when the government engages in deficit spending and covers the deficit through borrowing, without creating new money in the process, a combination of the two foregoing possibilties occurs. Some bonds are purchased by the public with money that would otherwise have been spent in some other way. Some people, some businesses, and some institutions will purchase bonds with money that would otherwise have been hoarded or left idle. Total spending in the economy is increased, but not by as much as it would be if the deficit were financed by the creation of new money.

Inflation: The Budget Surplus

When resources are fully employed and the economy is plagued with inflation, the appropriate fiscal medicine is a budget surplus to reduce total spending. If tax collections exceed government expenditures, the reduction in private spending caused by tax collections is not fully offset by the government expenditures. Total spending will be less than it would be if the budget were balanced. This policy will attack directly the cause of the inflation, which is a rate of increase in total spending that exceeds that rate of increase in the volume of goods and services available to be purchased.

The Surplus Impounded

A budget surplus will have the greatest impact on total spending if the government simply impounds it. In the first place, the surplus in and of itself reduces total spending, but if the surplus is impounded, the quantity of money in circulation will be decreased, thus causing total spending to be reduced even further. Since the taxes giving rise to the surplus are paid with cheques drawn by the public on chartered banks, the net effect is to reduce bank deposits outstanding by the amount of the surplus. Further, as the cheques in the amount of the surplus are deposited by the government with the Bank of Canada and are impounded there, chartered bank deposits at the central bank are transferred from chartered banks to the government's account. This reduces chartered bank reserves, and to the extent that it reduces them below required or desired levels, it induces banks to make further contractions in their deposits outstanding.

Retirement of Government Debt

Legislators and the public may want a surplus to be used to pay off government debt, that is, to purchase and retire outstanding government bonds. If the surplus is used in this manner, total spending may or may not be reduced, depending upon who owns the bonds that are retired. There are three possibilities: the bonds may be held by (1) The Bank of Canada, (2) chartered banks, and (3) the nonbank public.

If a budget surplus is used to retire government bonds held by non-bank persons or business institutions who would then hold idle the money received for the bonds, the reduction in total spending occasioned by the surplus is the same as it would be if the surplus were impounded by the government. The stock of money in the economy is not changed by the surplus accrual and debt retirement;[3] however, the velocity of circulation is decreased. Both the initial surplus and the reduction in the velocity of circulation operate to reduce total spending.

[3]*Can you trace the changes in the balance sheets of the Bank of Canada and chartered banks to show that this is so? As a starting point, assume that a surplus of $1 billion is run by the government. How does this affect chartered banks and central bank balance sheets? Now the government purchases government bonds from the nonbank public who maintain deposits in chartered banks. How does this affect chartered bank and Bank of Canada balance sheets?*

Suppose the budget surplus is used to retire government securities held by the Bank of Canada. Government deposits at the central bank are used to purchase the bonds from the latter and the Bank of Canada balance sheet shows equal reductions in its *government deposit* liability account and its *government securities* asset account. The total effect of the accumulation of a budget surplus and the use of the surplus to pay off government bonds held by the central bank is precisely the same as it is when the government impounds the surplus.

Suppose now that the government uses the budget surplus to retire government bonds held by chartered banks, that is, it uses its deposits at the Bank of Canada to buy bonds from chartered banks. On the central bank balance sheet, government deposits decrease and chartered bank deposits increase by the amount of the surplus so used. On chartered bank balance sheets government securities accounts decrease and reserve accounts increase by the amount of the surplus so used. Thus chartered bank reserves are raised to the level at which they stood before the budget surplus was accrued, permitting chartered bank loans and deposits to expand to the level at which they stood *before* the budget surplus was built up. The primary reduction in total spending caused by the surplus is still effective, but since there is no net reduction in the money supply, secondary reductions in spending from this source are eliminated.

Implementation of Fiscal Policy

We consider now how fiscal policy should be put into effect. Should surpluses and deficits be effected by changes in government expenditures, in tax collections, or both at the same time?

As a matter of fact, the structure of federal expenditures and of the tax system is such that expenditures and tax receipts change automatically in the right direction when economic fluctuations occur. The factors that cause these automatic changes to occur are referred to as *built-in*, or *automatic, stabilizers*. Over and above the automatic stabilizers, the government can take *discretionary action* to increase or decrease taxes and/or expenditures in the proper direction.

Built-In Stabilizers

Some of the expenditures of the federal government, and of provincial governments too, will tend to rise during periods of recession and depression and to fall during periods of high employment and inflation even though Parliament and provincial legislatures take no action to increase or to decrease them. Government transfer payments make up the bulk of expenditures of this kind. Disbursements of unemployment compensation and outright relief increase. Greater payments are made for farm price supports. Old age assistance payments increase as many people over 65 years of age, otherwise eligible but who had not been receiving them because their earnings in employments were too large, now are laid off and are placed on the eligibility lists. All of these expenditures tend to decrease automatically during prosperous times.

Most of the built-in stabilizing effects of government budgets are on the tax side. Given an existing range of taxes and tax rates, depression and recession will reduce total tax receipts while high employment and inflation will increase them. Individual income taxes, corporation income taxes, excise taxes, and sales taxes are the principal ones involved. Although unemployment insurance contributions are not generally referred to as taxes they are similar to taxes in many ways.

The individual income tax is the most important built-in stabilizer. As individual incomes increase during inflation the increase in the tax base itself increases the government's receipts from the tax—but an additional feature is operative—because the tax rate is progressive, more and more income is taxed at the progressively higher rates. The larger individual incomes grow, the greater becomes the proportion of total personal income that must be paid in taxes. These same forces work in reverse to decrease tax receipts in greater proportion than the decrease in income during recession and depression.

The corporation income tax, too, is highly sensitive to changes in the level of economic activity. During periods of recession and depression, corporation incomes tend to fall more rapidly than does gross national product. The opposite tends to be the case during periods of expansion. The corporation income tax also has an element of progressivity in its rates. These two factors together tend to make corporation tax receipts respond to changes in economic activity in greater proportion than the changes that occur in gross national product.

Sales taxes and excise taxes are not as sensitive as income taxes to changes in the level of economic activity. Nevertheless, they vary in the right directions for built-in stabilization. During periods of expansion sales and excise tax collections increase because the spending of the public on taxed items is increasing. The opposite occurs during recession and depression.

In periods of rising economic activity and high employment, unemployment insurance contributions increase and surpluses accumulate in the Unemployment Insurance Fund; inflationary pressure is reduced correspondingly. When recession sets in, unemployment insurance contributions decline in total and government unemployment payments rise. Thus while the worker does not receive his full pay when he is unemployed,[4] he does receive some compensation, and this prevents economic activity from declining as rapidly as might otherwise be the case.

Discretionary Fiscal Policy

Built-in stabilizers alone ordinarily will not generate sufficiently large deficits or surpluses to prevent economic fluctuations from occurring. If economic stability at high levels of employment is to be attained, some additional *discretionary* changes in taxes and/or in expenditures usually are necessary.

Changes in Expenditures

Not all government expenditures can be manipulated in order to increase deficits or surpluses. Some functions of government are continuing ones requiring rather stable expenditures year in and year out. Among these are: interest on the national debt, veterans' benefits and services, general government, and education. The magnitudes of some other functions, while not necessarily stable over time, are determined by forces other than whether or not the economy is undergoing economic fluctuations. Examples include national defence, fiscal transfers to provinces, and international affairs, but there is enough leeway in many government activities to permit some bunching of expenditures in periods of recession while reducing them to some minimum level in periods of high employment and inflation. The most important categories of expenditures of this type are (1) social security and welfare expenditures and (2) government investment in public works projects such as dams, highways, school buildings, government buildings, and the like.

Social security and welfare expenditures can be broadened in scope in periods of recession and high employment. Social security coverage (The Canada Pension Plan, Old Age Security Plan, Unemployment Insurance System, etc.) can be expanded and payments increased. Direct welfare payments (to families, to unemployed, to handicapped, etc.) can be liberalized and, as the U.S. War on Poverty well illustrates, a multitude of antipoverty programs can be initiated—area redevelopment programs,

[4]*The government White Paper for Reform of the Unemployment Insurance Act, tabled in the House of Commons on June 15, 1970, proposed, among other things, that the weekly maximum benefits of $42 per week for a person without dependents be raised to 67 percent of average weekly earning up to a maximum of $100 per week. Legislation based on this White Paper is expected to be introduced during the fall (1970) session of Parliament.*

retraining and mobility programs, headstart programs for disadvantaged chilolen, community action and community change programs, and others.

There are several things to be said for government investment in construction projects to create budget deficits during recession. First, it provides direct stimulation of capital goods industries, and it is these that exhibit the most marked contraction in recession. Second, an expansion of government projects will employ directly some of the unemployed. Third, the government goods can be obtained at lower cost during recession, since many of the resources used would otherwise remain unemployed. Fourth, from a psychological standpoint, employment and income earned from projects of this kind are preferable to direct welfare payments.

There are also some drawbacks to such discretionary expenditure changes for public works. One of the most serious is the problem of timing. For projects of any size, a lag of several months will generally elapse between approval of the project by the appropriate legislative body and the actual start of construction—recessions are notoriously poor about holding still until action against them can be taken. Final plans must be drawn; bids must be obtained; and contracts must be let, assuming that expenditures have been authorized for the items to be constructed. Then, once a project is underway, expenditures cannot be turned off at precisely the right time. If a year or more is necessary to complete the project, the recession may have ended and the instability problem may have become one of inflation. If so, carrying the project through to completion may add fuel to the inflationary fires.

Another common argument against increases in government expenditures to incur deficits is that the practice tends to exhibit a ratchet effect. Once expenditures are increased, it is difficult to reduce them again. Social security coverage has been broadened and benefits have been increased, but no reductions have occurred. When any agency of the government has its scope of activities and its budget expanded, reductions at a future date become very difficult to accomplish. In any case, so the argument runs, the *level* of government expenditures should be based on whether or not the activities in which the government is engaging are desirable and economically sound in their own right rather than on whether or not a deficit or a surplus is needed for purposes of economic stabilization.

Changes in Taxes

Taxes seem to provide more promise for discretionary changes than do expenditures. If a deficit is desired to combat recession, both personal and corporation income tax rates can be lowered. Their exemptions and deduction features can be liberalized. Additionally, excise tax rates can easily be decreased or removed entirely. All of these can be changed in the opposite direction to eliminate a deficit or to run a surplus, although tax increases are harder to accomplish politically than are tax decreases.

Discretionary fiscal policy based on changes in taxes rather than in expenditures has the virtue of permitting government functions and government activities to be determined on their own merits apart from the pressures of recession or inflation. Highway construction or conservation projects, for example, can be considered on the basis of whether they represent the most productive uses of the resources that would be required to carry them out. Social security and welfare coverage and payments can be based on value judgments as to what is socially desirable rather than on the extent to which they make a direct contribution toward stemming recession.

The principal problems associated with tax variation are those of timing and the possible generation of uncertainty on the part of taxpayers. As already mentioned, the fiscal year in Canada runs from April 1 to March 31. Thus tax changes of any considerable magnitude have to be decided sometime in February or March for announcement in the annual budget speech which usually takes place between March 15 and April 15. Of course, the Minister of Finance can introduce a supplementary budget or issue a financial statement proposing tax changes any time Parliament is in session. In fact, tax changes have been introduced outside the annual budget on six occasions since World War II—in September 1950 and December 1957, when tax changes were announced in a financial statement, and in December 1960, December 1966, November 1967 and October 1968, when supplementary or "baby" budgets were brought down. Nevertheless, there is a strong reluctance to make important tax changes at times other than the spring budget.[5] Given the need for federal budgetary flexibility, some experts advocate "formula flexibility", which involves linking tax changes to changes in various aggregate price and income indices. For example, if the national unemployment rate exceeded 5 percent for three months in a row, it might be mandatory to lower personal income tax rates by 10 percent. Or again, if the price level rose at an annual rate in excess of 3 percent a year for three months in a row, a tax increase would automatically go into effect. While the idea has possibilities, the Report of the Royal Commission on Taxation concluded that "formula flexibility by itself is undesirable".[6] In the same context, other experts advocate "standby authority", which would enable the cabinet to introduce tax changes without prior legislative approval. This idea has

[5]*In this connection, it should be pointed out that the present Minister of Finance has indicated that he intends to present only one budget a year (see House of Commons Debates*, Official Report, *Thursday, March 12, 1970, p. 4750).*

[6]*Canada*, Report of the Royal Commission on Taxation, *Volume 2, Ottawa: Queen's Printer, 1966, p. 84.*

possibilities also, but so far Parliament has not been willing to provide these standby powers. Not much need be said of uncertainty. It goes almost without saying that frequent changes in tax rates complicate tax planning both for individuals and for businesses.

Changes in Both Expenditures and Taxes

Changes in both expenditures and taxes each have their virtues and their flaws as means of implementing fiscal policy to combat economic fluctuations. If either practice is used alone, the magnitudes of the changes that must be brought about may from time to time be unduly large. Parliament may balk at approving extraordinary large changes in either expenditures or taxes. Private individuals or businesses may find that large tax changes generate enough uncertainty to interfere with sound economic decision-making. To mitigate the shortcomings of each when used alone, some combination of expenditure and tax changes of a discretionary nature may be in order to obtain deficits or surpluses large enough for fiscal policy to be effective. To enumerate the drawbacks of discretionary fiscal policy is not to discredit it. Rather, it serves the purpose of challenging us to devise ways to circumvent or eliminate the obstacles standing in the way of its use.

The National Debt

Historically the federal government has generated larger and more frequent deficits than surpluses even though the deliberate use of discretionary fiscal policy has been very limited.[7] This is evidenced by the growth of the national debt over time. There has been much public concern over the size of the debt, with people commonly expressing two major fears. One is that the debt will become so large that the government will go "bankrupt". The other is that the present generation of taxpayers, by resorting to borrowing to finance government expenditures, is passing along the cost of those expenditures to future generations of taxpayers. Let us look first at the facts regarding the growth and size of the national debt. After examining these we shall consider the problem of transfers from taxpayers to bondholders within a given year and over a period of years. Finally, we shall consider the available alternatives to an increasing federal debt.

[7]*From 1867 to 1970 the federal budget has gone into the red on 78 occasions. On only 25 occasions have the nation's budgetry accounts been on the black side of the fine edge of balance. In other words, deficits have outnumbered surpluses just over three to one.*

The Magnitude of the Debt

The net debt of the federal government, which is referred to as the national debt, grew from $75.7 million in fiscal 1867 to an estimated $16,881 million in 1970. Table 11-1 shows the amounts for selected years to 1970. From 1867 to 1913 the total debt rose by 445 percent; since 1913 it has increased by 527 percent. The change in the net debt figure from one fiscal year to another represents the budgetary surplus or deficit for the year plus any adjustments made in respect of prior years' transactions. In effect, the national debt represents the accumulated overall deficit of the federal government since the nation's beginning.

As we review the history of the 1913-1970 period we gain some insight into the causes of the changes in the debt. We can surmise that during World War I there was much deficit spending leading to the large debt increase from 1913 to 1919. Until the onset of the Great Depression, the 1920's were generally prosperous, and budget surpluses after 1923 permitted paying off some $276 million of the debt. The depression years of the 1930's brought deficit spending on a substantial scale—one of the first conscious uses of deficit spending to promote recovery from depression—and the debt increased correspondingly. The phenomenal debt increase from 1939 to 1946 is explained by World War II. Parliament and the general public were not willing to see tax levels raised sufficiently to cover the enormous (for that time) expenditures associated with the war.[8] Following World War II there was a sharp contraction of government spending and the government ran very large budgetary surpluses. For 1950 through 1954 the surpluses were appreciably reduced as government spending sharply increased, but eight successive years of budgetary surpluses enabled the government to pay off over $2,200 million of the debt. Since 1954, however, budgetary surpluses on a public accounts basis (as opposed to a national accounts basis) have occurred in only two years— 1957 and 1970.

The "Bankruptcy" Fear

Dire predictions concerning the consequences of the increasing size of the national debt are not hard to find. The general public, businessmen, editors and the financial community, in particular express fear that deficit spending and debt accumulation are leading the government down the road to "bankruptcy". Are these fears real or imaginary?

[8] *If the war had been financed largely by taxation, do you think the quantities of resources available to produce private goods and services would have been smaller than they were; that is, would the general public have been worse off than it actually was?*

TABLE 11-1
National Debt[1] for Selected Years, 1867-1970

Fiscal Year[2]	Amount (Millions of Dollars)	Per cent of GNP
1867	75.7	20.7
1873	99.8	N.A.
1885	196.4	N.A.
1900	265.5	26.6
1913	314.3	11.9
1919	1.574.5	31.5
1923	2,453.8	55.1
1930	2,177.8	38.1
1939	3,152.6	56.1
1946	13,421.4	112.9
1954	11,115.9	44.2
1960	12,089.2	32.0
1961	12,437.1	31.8
1962	13,228.1	31.2
1963	13,919.7	30.6
1964	15,070.1	30.3
1965	15,504.4	28.2
1966	15,543.4	25.4
1967	15,964.9	24.3
1968	16,759.7	23.5
1969	17,335.8	22.2
1970	16,880.8	20.3

[1]*The national debt is the difference between the gross liabilities of the federal government (unmatured and outstanding security issues plus liabilities on insurance and pension funds) and "net recorded assets." For the most part, these consist of assets which yield interest, profits or dividends, and all cash balances.*
[2]*As of March 31.*

Source: Dominion Bureau of Statistics, Canada Year Book, Ottawa: Queen's Printer, various years. Budget Papers, March 12, 1970, p. 214. Dominion Bureau of Statistics, National Accounts, Income and Expenditure, 1926-1968; O. J. Firestone, Industry and Education, Ottawa: University of Ottawa Press, 1969, pp. 261-62.

Government Debt versus Business Debt

We cannot progress toward answering the question just posed until we determine what people mean by bankruptcy. The meaning for a private business is clear enough: the business incurs losses to the extent that it cannot meet its creditors' demands with the result that its assets are sold and the proceeds are distributed to these creditors. Can this happen to a government? Obviously it cannot. In the first place, a government is not a business enterprise operated for profits, or incurring losses, so bankruptcy is an inappropriate term to apply to it. Further, a national government can create the means of paying the interest and/or the principal on its debt. Private businesses cannot do this. What is it then that *really* concerns people who express fears of bankruptcy?

Excessive External Debt

We draw a distinction between the debt owed by a government to its own people and that owed by it to foreigners. The former is called the *internal debt* of the country while the latter is an *external debt*. Payments on the interest and the principal of a country's internal debt do not reduce the total amounts of resources available for the economy to use; that is, they do not cut down on the current size of the country's gross national product. Such payments transfer command over those resources from the rest of the economic units in the economy to those who receive the payments.

Payments on the interest and principal of externally held debt will reduce the amounts of resources that can be used currently to produce goods and services for domestic use. The payments enable foreigners to buy goods and services from the country; that is, to exercise command over some part of the economy's resources. Thus, from the point of view of the economy as a whole, the internal debt is not necessarily currently burdensome *per se*,[9] but the external debt is. Payments made on the latter reduce the current goods and services available for the country to use.

A country accumulating external debts may find that the servicing payments on the debt become more and more burdensome, although this is not necessarily the case and, presumably, never should be. If the money borrowed from foreigners is invested in an economically sound way, that is, so as to increase the country's productive power by more than enough to service the external debt, it is not really burdensome at all from a long-run point of view. If it is not used to increase the country's productive capacity, the servicing payments will reduce the country's living standards over the long run below what they would have been otherwise. The external debt of Canada is negligible, so any fears on this point by Canadian citizens are groundless. Such fears may be very real, however, for an under-developed country that has borrowed heavily from abroad and that has not used what it borrows to increase its capacity to produce.

Refusal to Pay Interest and Principal

Is there any likelihood that the national debt will reach such a magnitude that the government will default on its interest payments and on bond retirements? Table 11-1 provides data pertinent to this question. Although

[9] *Collection of taxes and payments of interest and principal may not transfer purchasing power in the most desirable directions, and they may lead to less efficient resource use in the economy, but these effects are not inevitable.*

the debt has been increasing in absolute amounts, gross national product has been increasing at a faster rate. As a percentage of the value of the economy's annual total output, the debt decreased tremendously from 1946 to 1970. The larger the gross national product relative to the debt, the easier it becomes for the government to levy and collect the taxes necessary to service the debt. Thus, from this point of view, the magnitude of the debt is of much less consequence now than it was 25 years ago. Certainly there is no indication that the government has now or is likely to develop a financial position so shaky as to make defaulting on debt servicing a possibility.

As a matter of fact, as long as the government pays enough interest on government securities to make them attractive to investors, it will never need to pay off the principle unless it so desires. The debt can be carried on at its present level or at higher or lower levels in perpetuity. As old bonds mature new ones can be issued and sold, and the proceeds of the new issue can be used to pay off the maturing issue. Paying off the debt does not really present a serious problem, since it need not be done.

Fear of Inflation

Will not the deficits that create the rising national debt cause inflation, reducing the value of the currency until the public loses confidence in it as a medium of exchange? As we have seen, the financing of a deficit through borrowing creates new money when chartered banks have excess reserves and when bonds are sold either to chartered banks or directly to the Bank of Canada by the federal government. Whether or not inflation occurs depends upon the rate at which new money is created. With regard to the equation of exchange, if the increase in the money supply causes total spending to increase at the same rate over time as the volume of trade increases, no inflation is generated. If the creation of new money increases total spending faster than the volume of trade is increasing, inflation will indeed occur. But note that whether or not inflation occurs does not depend upon the *size of the debt*; rather, it depends upon *how rapidly the debt is increased*.

Fears that the national debt is approaching a level at which financial chaos will result thus appear to be unfounded. Inflation is probably the most serious financial consequence of debt accumulation, and even this need not occur. There may be problems associated with paying interest on the debt, but these are not problems of the ability or capacity of the government to pay; rather they are transfer problems and will be considered shortly.

The Transfer-of-Cost Fear

Many people believe that when the government finances some part of its expenditures by borrowing the present generation is obtaining those government services at no cost and that the burden will fall upon some future generation of taxpayers. An analogy usually is made with a private family. Suppose a man and his wife increase their current consumption by going in debt. Before the debt matures the couple die, leaving the debt to be paid by the estate—that is, by the couple's heirs, say their children. The couple lived beyond their means at the expense of the future generation.

Is this line of reasoning applicable to government borrowing? Suppose we consider the cost for the economy as a whole when the government resorts to borrowing to finance current expenditures. We shall look at three cases. In the first we shall suppose that there is full employment and that the government spends on a worthless project. In the second we shall assume that there is unemployment and that the government spends on a worthless project. In the third and fourth cases we shall assume that the government expenditure is a capital-creating one and that, alternately, there is unemployment and then full employment.

The Worthless-Project-Full-Employment Case

Suppose that certain government expenditures financed by borrowing are a total waste—for example, an irrigation system is built in a desert area where nothing will grow regardless of the amount of water used. Prior to the expenditures the resources of the economy were fully employed. What is the cost of the system and who pays for it? The cost of the project is clearly the value of alternative products that could have been produced with the resources used to build it. The primary economic cost is here and now, regardless of how the expenditures are financed. There will be secondary costs on future generations if the resources sucked into the building of the project could have been utilized to increase the economy's stock of capital had the project not been undertaken. Future stocks of capital will be smaller if the propect is built than they would be if it is not. Thus the future output of the economy available to future generations would be smaller.

The Worthless-Project-Unemployment Case

Suppose that there are unemployed resources in the economy when the irrigation system is constructed and that the project draws only on these. In this case there is no primary economic cost, since no alternative products are forgone in order to build the system. There may even be secondary benefits or gains in the future from the activity. Incomes paid the owners of the resources used will be spent either in whole or in part, thus increasing demand for other products and drawing other unemployed resources into employment. The economy's output will be increased, thus permitting more capital accumulation than would occur otherwise. Future output will exceed what it would be in the absence of the project, and, rather than having a burden imposed on them, future generations benefit.

The Worthwhile-Project-Full-Employment Case

Suppose that the government activity financed by borrowing is one that creates capital—a hydroelectric project, for example—and it draws resources from the production of goods and services in the private sector of the economy. The current or primary economic cost is again the value of other products forgone by the diversion of resources into the construction of the project. The capital created by the government expenditure is expected to make positive contributions to future income flows generated by the economy. If the forgone private goods were consumer goods or less productive capital goods, future output would be increased by the project, making future generations better off.

The Worthwhile-Project-Unemployment Case

If the hydroelectric project financed by government borrowing is undertaken during a period when there is unemployment and if the resources that it employs are drawn from the ranks of the unemployed, the primary cost of the project is zero. No private goods need to be forgone in order for it to be constructed. Future generations will have the benefit of the project's output and thus, rather than having to bear the cost of an extravagance of the present generation, they stand to gain from an investment made for them by the present generation.

Implications for the Transfer-of-Cost Fear

All four of the hypothetical cases point to a fundamental economic fact of life. The cost of producing anything today depends upon what must be forgone to produce it. If the government does the producing instead of private businesses, the principle is not altered. We are confronted here with a straightforward application of the alternative-cost doctrine. Whether the government project is financed by taxation, by borrowing, or by printing of new money is important only insofar as the method may determine from which private productive activity—if any—resources are to be drawn. Thus the fear of a transfer of cost from the present generation to future generations seems to be unfounded with respect to the internal debt of a country except for a situation in which the government uses resources less efficiently than they would have been used by the private sector of the economy.

Although a transfer of cost from present to future generations does not seem likely under most circumstances, there will be a transfer of *income* within a given future generation as the debt is serviced. Those who own the government securities will receive income from those who pay the taxes from which interest on the securities is paid. If bondholders are rich and taxpayers are poor on the average, this transfer may violate equity value judgments. If bondholders and taxpayers are by and large the same people, the only costs that are involved are those of collecting the taxes and of paying the interest.

Alternative to Increasing the National Debt

The increasing size of the national debt is mute testimony to the prevalence of budgetary deficits over the long run. To be sure, the largest deficits and the largest increases in the debt have occurred during war periods. Nevertheless, since 1946 the debt has increased by almost $3,500 million. Why should deficits occur on the average during periods other than those of serious national emergencies?

Over the long run, budgetary deficits may be expected to exceed surpluses because deficits provide a means of increasing the quantity of money in circulation. In a growing economy the volume of goods and services available to be purchased—the T in the equation of exchange—is increasing. In order to prevent the general price level, P, from falling, total spending, MV, must increase in approximate proportion to the increases in T. This means that the money supply must be expanded.

But is borrowing by the government the only way of increasing the money supply by the necessary amounts? We indicated earlier that an alternative is available. Instead of issuing interest-bearing bonds and increasing the quantity of money by selling those bonds to the Bank of Canada and to chartered banks with excess reserves, the government could (and has on occasion in the past) simply print and spend new paper money.

The printing of new paper money to finance a deficit has the virtue of not increasing the interest-bearing debt of the federal government. It achieves approximately the same results as does borrowing through the sale of government bonds to the central bank; that is, it increases the money supply. Nevertheless the idea of the government printing new paper money to finance a deficit is appalling to most people—primarily because they have seen countries misuse the printing press, flooding themselves with money and creating runaway inflation and financial chaos. The conclusion is that the printing press is at fault when the blame should be placed on those responsible for using it. Guns or automobiles are also dangerous in the hands of irresponsible people.

The practice of actually printing new money when an increase is needed in the money supply as sound economically as the practice of creating new bank deposits through the sale of government bonds to the central bank and to chartered banks with excess reserves. The soundness (or unsoundness) of either method rests entirely with those responsible for using it—that is, with federal Department of Finance officials, Bank of Canada officials, and Parliament. The direct printing of new money has the virtue of increasing neither the national debt nor the annual interest charges on that debt. Its use requires both responsible conduct and a great deal of knowledge on the part of the Finance Department and Parliament, but these requirements already rest on both.

There appear to be two reasons why many people prefer the debt-increasing method of financing deficits. First, it is not generally understood that the money supply is increased in the process. This reason obviously has no merit. Second, those who do understand the process of money creation hope that adverse reactions to the total size of the national debt will serve to control the extent to which new money is created. The debt itself is thought to force those responsible for increasing the money supply to act with restraint.

Two final observations are worth stressing here. First, over time the national debt could be paid off rather easily if this were genuinely desired. All the elements of the process have been discussed above. Growth in the volume of goods and services being produced in the economy generates a need for a growing money supply. The additional money could be created by the government via use of the printing press and injected into the economy through debt retirement, or the paying off of maturing government bonds, in whatever amounts are consistent with economic stability. Second, this method is not associated with the acceptance of "social credit" economic theory.[10] It is presented solely as an alternative to borrowing to finance budgetary deficits.

[10]*For a discussion of social credit theory, see Scott Gordon, "The A Plus B Dogma of Social Credit"*, The Financial Times, *July 16, 1962.*

Summary

Fiscal policy refers to the use by the federal government of tax and spending practices to influence economic activity. In general, a balanced budget tends to be neutral in its effects on total spending. Budgetary deficits tend to increase total spending in the economy and constitute the appropriate fiscal policy for combating recession and unemployment. Budgetary surpluses tend to reduce total spending and are, therefore, the recommended policy for halting inflation.

The inflationary or expansionary effects of budget deficits depend upon how they are financed. The primary methods of financing deficits are (1) through the issue and sale of government bonds and (2) through the printing of new paper money. The maximum effects will be obtained if the deficit is financed by the issue and sale of government bonds to the Bank of Canada, or, alternatively, through the printing of new paper money. If the deficit is financed by borrowing, it is also possible that bonds may be issued and sold to chartered banks and/or to the general public. Some expansionary effects will occur if the banks that purchase the bonds have excess reserves and if the public buys bonds with money that would otherwise have been hoarded.

Surpluses exert their maximum effect in curbing inflation when the excess of tax collections over government expenditures is simply impounded by the government or is used to pay off bonds held by the central bank. If the excess is used to pay off bonds held by chartered banks, the money supply will be decreased only if banks elect to hold the amounts so paid as excess reserves. If a surplus is used to pay off bonds held by the general public, total spending will be decreased only if the amounts so paid are hoarded.

Fiscal policy is implemented by the government either through built-in stabilizers or through discretionary changes in taxes and/or expenditures. Both the tax and the expenditure structure are such that total tax collections and government expenditures tend to vary automatically in the right direction for economic stability, but these built-in stabilizers can be supplemented with discretionary tax and expenditure changes by the government to bring about the desired results.

The national debt has been growing as the amounts of federal budget deficits have exceeded the amounts of federal budget surpluses. Much of this growth has resulted from such national emergencies as war, but some can be expected to result from growth in the output of the economy over time. The increasing size of the debt has caused many people to fear that the government will go "bankrupt." It has also induced a fear that the present generation is transferring the cost of present government services to future generations. Neither of these fears seems to be well grounded.

Continued growth of the national debt is not really necessary, since the alternative exists of printing new paper money to finance deficits of appropriate sizes for economic stability. This alternative is not held in high repute by a public that tends to confuse the means with the degree of responsibility to be exercised by those who use it. If responsibly used, the practice is, in most respects, equivalent to borrowing and has the further virtue of increasing neither the national debt nor its interest load. It could even be used as a means of reducing the size of the debt over time.

Exercises and Questions for Discussion

1. Is an increase in government expenditures always inflationary if full employment prevails in the economy? Explain in detail.
2. "The budget deficit of Canada has grown larger and larger. Interest payments are now nearly two billion dollars. Our country is moving toward bankruptcy." Evaluate this statement.
3. What are the problems associated with the use of fiscal policy to control economic fluctuations? Should it be abandoned? What improvements can you think of in the means of implementing fiscal policy?
4. Suppose the economy is suffering from prolonged inflation (depression). What fiscal policy would you recommend to alleviate this situation? If a budget deficit is warranted, which method of financing would you employ?
5. In 1967 Canada was experiencing some inflation. At the same time, the government was running a budget deficit. Was this policy economically sound? What factors were responsible for this situation?

Selected Readings

Brewis, T. N., *et al.*, *Canadian Economic Policy*, rev. ed. Toronto: Macmillan Co. of Canada, 1965, Chap. 11.

Buchanan, J. M., *The Public Finances*, rev. ed. Homewood, Ill.: Richard D. Irwin, Inc., 1965, Part VI.

Buchanan, J. M., and R. E. Wagner, *Public Debt in a Democratic Society*. Washington, D.C.: American Enterprise Institute for Public Policy Research, 1967.

Canada, *Report of Royal Commission on Taxation*, Volume 2. Ottawa: Queen's Printer, 1966, Chap. 3.

Economic Council of Canada, *Conference on Stabilization Policies*. Ottawa: Queen's Printer, 1966.

Miller, H. L., "The New and the Old in Public Debt Theory" in N. F. Keiser, *Readings in Macroeconomics*. Englewood Cliffs, N.J., 1970, pp. 446-454.

Sharp, A. M. and B. F. Sliger, *Public Finance*, rev. ed. Homewood, Ill.: The Dorsey Press, 1970, Chap. 10-12.

Taylor, K. W., "Fiscal Policy" in J. J. Deutsch, *et al.*, *The Canadian Economy, Selected Readings*. Toronto: Macmillan Co. of Canada, 1961, pp. 291-298.

12

National Income and Product Concepts

Whenever economists, journalists, government officials, and others attempt to evaluate the performance of the economy they ordinarily do so in terms of national income or national product concepts. National income and product data are used to determine whether economic growth is taking place and, if it is, the rate of growth. They also indicate the size and frequency of economic fluctuations. Additionally, on the basis of these concepts comparisons may be made between the actual and the potential performance of the economy.

Thus far in our discussions of economic fluctuations we have focused on the concept of gross national product. Actually, there is a group of related concepts, ranging from gross national product at one end to disposable income at the other, that is useful for analyzing economic performance as well as for collecting economic data.[1] This group of concepts provides the subject matter of the present chapter and lays the foundation for the more comprehensive analysis of national income in the chapters that follow. We shall consider three way of viewing the value of the economy's output: (1) the value-of-product approach, (2) the income-received approach, and (3) the disposable-income approach. Except for minor statistical discrepancies, the three methods yield the same result.

[1] *In Canada the Dominion Bureau of Statistics is the primary agency for collection of national income data. Some of the concepts defined in this chapter differ slightly from those of the DBS, but their magnitudes can be easily determined from the bureau's data.*

Value-of-product Approach

The *value-of-product* approach to the national income and product concepts is the most common one and is the easiest to understand. This is the one we have used implicitly wherever we have made use of the concept of gross national product. Basically it consists of valuing goods and services at their market prices, but as we shall see there are some things that cannot be valued in this way. In this section we shall refine the concept of gross national product, introduce and explain net national product, and examine the nature of intermediate goods along with problems of double counting.

Gross National Product

Gross national product, or GNP, is a convenient starting point for measuring the economy's output. It is defined as the total value of all goods and services produced in final form in a given period (usually a year or quarter) by residents of Canada. Units of each of the different goods and services comprising GNP are valued at their market prices, with the exception of some government goods and services, as noted later, and then are totalled to arrive at a figure for GNP. Expenditures made by the buyers of GNP commonly are classified into three categories: (1) personal consumption expenditures, (2) gross investment expenditures, and (3) expenditures for government goods and services. We can view these classifications, alternatively, as the values of (1) consumption goods and services, (2) gross capital formation, and (3) government goods and services. As shown in Table 12-1, GNP for 1968 was approximately $71.5 billion.[2]

The gross national product must not be confused with the gross domestic product (GDP). The latter is the value of all goods and services produced within the borders of Canada without regard to whether the income generated in their production is paid to or accrues to Canadian residents or to residents of other countries; the former measures the total output of residents of Canada.

Consumption Goods and Services

Consumption goods and services are those placed in the hands of con-

---

[2]*In mid-1969 the Dominion Bureau of Statistics released the summary results of a comprehensive revision of the National Income and Expenditure Accounts. The statistical revisions and changes in definitions and structural presentation introduced in that publication (National Income and Expenditure Accounts, 1926-1968) are the ones used throughout the book.*

sumers during the year to be used directly in satisfying consumer wants. They are divided into four groups: (1) durable goods, (2) semi-durable goods, (3) nondurable goods, and (4) services. *Durable goods* include such items as automobiles, furniture, and household equipment (e.g., stoves)—products that are expected to last the consumer for several years. The *semi-durable goods* group is composed of items used up more rapidly —clothing, costume jewellery, household furnishings (e.g., drapes), and the like. *Nondurable goods* include such items as food, drugs, and gasoline—products that are likely to last for only a short time. A wide variety of *services* can be listed. Some, such as repair and maintenance services, are readily identified and their values easily determined. The quantities of others, such as domestic and health services, are more difficult to estimate. All of these items are valued at their current market prices in estimating personal consumption, or C, for any given year. In 1968, C was approximately $42.4 billion, as indicated in Table 12-1.

TABLE 12-1
National Income and Product Concepts, 1968.
(Billions of Dollars)

Value of Product		Income Earned		Disposable Income	
Classification	Amount	Classification	Amount	Classification	Amount
Consumption (C)	42.4	Indirect taxes less subsidies[2]	8.9	Household disposable income	46.4
Net Investment[1] (L)	8.6	Corporate profits	6.6		
Government (G)	12.1	Proprietors' income	5.6	Government disposable income	14.0
		Interest income	2.6	Corporate disposable income	2.7
		Compensation of employees	39.4		
Net national product	63.1	Net national income	63.1	Net disposable Income[3]	63.1
Depreciation[1]	8.4	Capital consumption allowances	8.4	Capital consumption allowances	8.4
Gross national product	71.5	Gross national income	71.5	Gross disposable income	71.5

[1]*Includes statistical discrepancy. Gross investment (EI) is the sum of net private, public and foreign investment and depreciation.*
[2]*Includes statistical discrepancy and inventory valuation adjustment.*
[3]*Corporate disposable income only; that is, undistributed profits. All partnership and single proprietorship disposable income is included in household disposable income.*
Source: Computed from Dominion Bureau of Statistics, National Account Income and Expenditure, 1926-1968. Ottawa: Queen's Printer, August, 1969, Summary Tables A and B.

Gross Investment Goods

The gross investment category is made up predominantly of capital goods purchased by business to be used in the further production of consumer goods. This category also includes all government expenditures for capital goods (with the exception of military equipment which is treated as a current expenditure). We frequently represent the entire group by the abbreviation *GI*. Capital goods are further subdivided into a *nonresidential group*, consisting of plant and machinery, and a *residential group*, consisting of dwelling units. In addition, we shall include two other groups in the gross capital formation category. One is the *net changes in business and government inventories*, and the other is the *net foreign trade balance* of the country. Table 12-1 shows *GI* for 1968 at $8.6 billion.

Net additions to inventories held by business firms and governments during the year are, of course, a part of the year's value of production. Reductions in such inventories during a given year represent goods sold that were produced in previous years and must therefore be deducted from the total value of goods sold in order to compute the value of the given year's output. Increases in business and government inventories during the year can be called investment goods legitimately because business and government units must have committed funds to bring about the increases or must have invested in them just as they invested in plant and equipment. These inventories contribute to the consumption of goods and services in future years as surely as do plant and equipment. Decreases in such inventories during a given year are negative investments. Their sale releases the investable funds that were tied up in them.

The net foreign trade balance may be either positive or negative. It is found by subtracting the value of goods and services imported from the value of goods and services exported. If the net balance is positive, that is, if we have sold a greater value of goods and services abroad than we have bought, we have in effect some future goods and services coming to us from abroad or we have made an investment that will pay off in goods and services at some future date. If it is negative, that is, if the value of imports exceeds the value of exports, then we can think in terms of our owing some future goods and services to other countries. In other words, a negative foreign trade balance may be regarded as disinvestment. In this context it is worth noting that our net foreign balance—statisticians at D.B.S. use the term *net balance on current account*—has shown a deficit for every year since 1953.

Government Goods and Services

Goods and services currently produced by the government for the use of the general public have been discussed in detail previously. A large part of these are not sold in market places, that is, they are not directly priced; consequently, it is necessary to estimate their value. What, for example, is the yearly value of the services of judicial and postal systems, and the national defence or of parks and recreational areas. The usual procedure is to value these at what it costs to provide them. The value of government noncapital goods and services, then, is taken to be total current government expenditures—federal, provincial, and municipal—leaving out expenditures of a transfer nature that do not result in the creation of any new good or service. Government transfer expenditures (with the exclusion of transfer costs on the sales and purchases of existing fixed assets which are classified as part of government capital formation) represent a redistribution of purchasing power from taxpayers to those who receive the payments[3] rather than payments made for something produced during the year. We represent the value of government noncapital goods and services for the year with the letter G, and for 1968 it was estimated at $12.1 billion.[4]

The component parts of GNP can now be summed up conveniently in symbolic form. Let GNP represent the dollar value of GNP for the year, C the value of goods and services produced and sold for consumption, GI gross private and public investment goods produced, and G the value of currently produced government goods and services. Thus:

$$GNP = C + GI + G \qquad (12.1)$$

These components are shown graphically by the large rectangle on the left in Figure 12-1. The approximate magnitudes of each one, as well as for GNP for 1968, are listed in the value-of-product columns of Table 12-1.

Net National Product

GNP overstates the performance of the economy, for the entire amount of GNP is not available to use year after year unless productive capacity is not being maintained. Consider any given year. The total stock of capital on hand at the beginning of the year can be thought of as a gigantic machine, represented by the entire large rectangle on the left in Figure 12-2. In the process of producing GNP through the course of the year some of the economy's capital wears out, is used up, or becomes obsolete.

[3]*Transfer expenditures are discussed later in the chapter.*
[4]*This figure is for all levels of government, federal, provincial, and municipal.*

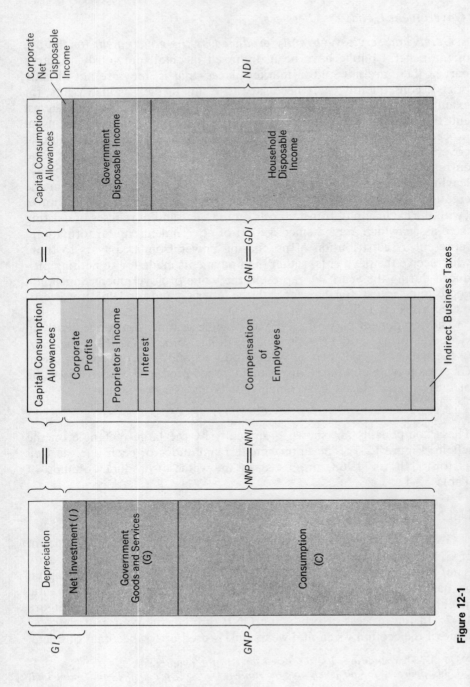

Figure 12-1

Gross national product, gross national income, and gross disposable income, their relations and component parts.

We refer to all of this as *depreciation* of capital. If nothing were done about depreciation, the economy's stock of capital would be smaller at the end of the year than it was at the beginning by the amount of the depreciation. If this process were to continue over the years, eventually the stock of capital would disappear.

Now consider *GNP* for the year—the total value of the economy's output. Or is it? The component parts of *GNP* are *C, G*, and *GI*. Can we count all of this as the year's production? Some part of the *GI* component is required to take care of depreciation of capital, or to replace what wears out or becomes obsolete and to bring the stock of capital back to a condition equivalent to what it was at the beginning of the year. Thus the actual net usable production of the economy for the year is not *GNP*. It is *GNP* minus that part of *GI* used to take care of depreciation. We call this remainder *net national product*, or *NNP*. In Figure 12-2, net national product for the year is the value of consumption goods and services produced, government goods and services, and *net investment goods*, the latter defined as gross investment goods minus the amount used to take care of depreciation. Algebraically,

$$NNP = C + I + G \tag{12.2}$$

Suppose that during a given year the *GI* component of *GNP* is not sufficient to take care of depreciation of capital equipment. How do we compute *NNP*, or the net production of the economy? Nothing new or unusual is really involved; in equation 12.2, *I*, or net investment, is negative, thus *NNP* is less than the total of *C* and *G*. The economy is consuming private and government goods and services in excess of its production for the year. It is able to do this by converting some of its stock of capital—the depreciation not covered by *GI*—into goods and services. In essence, the general public "eats" a part of the economy's stock of capital, but the eaten part is not net production for the year.[5]

Before leaving this item, it should be pointed out that Canada's official statisticians do not calculate the net national product measure, as do American Department of Commerce statisticians because, at present, various valuation adjustments arising from differences in the concepts of income and depreciation as reflected in business accounting records and the corresponding concepts used in national accounting cannot be separated from the allowance for capital depreciation. Thus, the national

---

[5]*This and the preceding paragraph hint at what is necessary for economic decline or for economic growth to take place. Since we are presently concerned only with the nature of the national income and product concepts, we shall not follow up on the hints at this point. They will be developed later in the analysis of national income determination.*

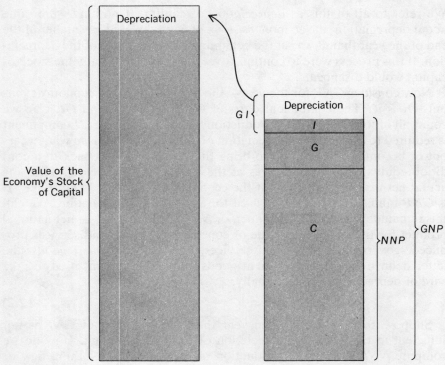

Figure 12-2
The relation between gross national product and net national product.

accounts item "capital consumption allowances and miscellaneous valuation adjustments" technically cannot be subtracted from gross investment (or gross fixed capital formation) to arrive at net investment (or net fixed capital formation). Nevertheless, this item, which amounted to $8.4 billion in 1968, may be subtracted from the year's *GNP* of $71.5 billion to give us a rough estimate for net national product (*NNP*) of $63.1 billion.[6] It may be useful to add that *NNP* has been consistently about 88 percent of *GNP* since 1962.

---

[6]*As noted earlier, Canada's national accounts have recently undergone a substantial revision. One of the major alterations is the change from "capital cost allowances" to "book depreciation" for calculating capital consumption allowances for business corporations. Additionally, it has now become possible to calculate depreciation on all government fixed assets on a replacement cost basis. These changes have brought the capital consumption allowance estimates much closer to the national accounting concept of consumption of capital assets.*

Double Counting

When *GNP* and *NNP* are computed by means of the value-of-product approach, double counting must be avoided. *Double counting* refers to counting at each stage the value of products used at several stages of a production process.[7] Goods that are likely to be double counted are *intermediate goods*, or goods produced to be used in the further production of higher-order goods. Suppose, for example, that the value of an automobile is counted as a part of *GNP* or *NNP*. Steel, glass, copper, rubber, paint, and other items were produced as intermediate goods during the year to be used in the manufacture of the automobile. The purchase price or value of the automobile includes the value of the intermediate materials used in its production. If the value of these materials were counted *in addition to* the value of the automobile, it would be double counted.

Frequently, to avoid double counting of items that go into the production of final goods, national income statisticians use a *value-added method* of computation. As we follow a basic product through its stages of production some value is added to it at each stage. The sum of the values added are the same as the value of the final product as it emerges in final form. Suppose, for example, that we follow a bushel of wheat through the stages of production transforming it into bread. In Table 12-2 a bushel of wheat is sold by a farmer to a miller for two dollars. The miller processes the wheat into flour and sells it to a baker for three dollars. The baker makes the flour into bread and sells it for four dollars. The value of the product is shown at each stage of the production process in the centre column of the table while the value is recorded in the right-hand column. If the values of the wheat, the flour, and the bread were all counted, double counting would occur. If we total the value added at each stage of the production process however, we obtain a sum equal to the value of the final product.

TABLE 12-2
Use of Value-Added Computations to Avoid Double Counting

STAGE OF PRODUCTION	VALUE OF PRODUCT	VALUE ADDED
Wheat	$2.00	$2.00
Flour	3.00	1.00
Bread	4.00	1.00
	Sum of values added	$4.00

[7]*Strictly speaking, the problem is as much one of triple counting or quadruple counting, and so on, as it is of double counting. The term "double counting" is used as an umbrella to cover all of these.*

The Income-Received Approach

Every dollar's worth of goods and services produced during a year generates a dollar in income for those who furnish the resources required for its production. Suppose that a family spends $25,000 to have a new house built this year. Where does the $25,000 go? Part of it goes to carpenters, bricklayers, plumbers, and other workers in payment for labour services they have put into the house. Part of it goes to the suppliers of various kinds of materials. Part of it goes to the contractor who coordinated the use of resources and who may have used some of his own capital equipment on the project. The entire $25,000 paid for the house, the value of the product, becomes income received by those who contributed resources to its construction.

Gross National Income and Net National Income

If we extend the example of the new house to the entire range of goods and services comprising *GNP*, we arrive at a gross income figure for the entire economy. Suppose we call this *gross national income*, or *GNI*.[8] Gross national income is, of course, of the same magnitude as *GNP*. The production and sale of *GNP* generates an equivalent amount of income, *GNI*, for those who produce it.

Just as some capital equipment used up in the production of *GNP* is not a part of the year's net production, so some income used in the generation of *GNI* is not a part of the year's net income. The amount of income so used is that necessary to take care of depreciation, and we call it *capital consumption allowances*. It does not become net income for resource owners. Deducting the capital consumption allowances from *GNI*, we arrive at a net national income, or *NNI*, magnitude that is identical to that of *NNP*.[9]

---

[8]*D.B.S. does not define or use such a concept. However, it is easily determined from D.B.S. data and is useful for completing the logical framework for national income and product accounting.*

[9]*Our definition of NNI is larger than the D.B.S. definition of national income by an amount equal to indirect business taxes. In our judgment our definition is more consistent with and lends itself better to the analytical framework of national income analysis than that of D.B.S. It is easily determined from D.B.S. data. For a more traditional treatment of the national accounts, see Boreham, Gordon F., et al.;* Money and Banking: Analysis and Policy in a Canadian Context. *Toronto: Holt, Rinehart and Winston of Canada, 1969, Chap. 15.*

The Components of NNI

The net national income generated in the production of *NNP* is separated into five parts: (1) compensation of employees, (2) corporate profits, (3) indirect business taxes, (4) proprietors' income (including rental income), and (5) net interest. We met this classification earlier as the *functional distribution of income*. It represents a partial breakdown of income into categories according to the types of resources generating each category, but it does not go all the way in this respect. This will become evident as we discuss the list. The magnitudes of the parts are given in the centre column of Table 12-1 and are represented pictorially in Figure 12-1.

Compensation of Employees

Included in *compensation of employees* is most but not all of the income earned by labour resources in the production of *NNP*. It consists of the wages and salaries and income in kind (e.g. free board and lodging) paid all employees (including members of the armed services) as well as supplements to earnings such as employer contributions for social insurance, pension plans, welfare funds, and the like. The earnings of labour resources not covered in this category are those of the self-employed. These are picked up in some of the categories listed below. From Table 12-1 we see that for 1968 compensation of all Canadian wage-earners and salaried employees was about $39.4 billion and was by far the largest of the five components of *NNI*.

Corporate Profits

Corporate profits as defined by D.B.S. form the next largest category of income earned by resource owners. The resource owners to whom they accrue are the owners of the assets of corporations—stockholders—and they are defined as the difference between corporate gross income from the sale of goods and services and the expenses of corporations as they are identified in current accounting practices. Corporate profits, defined in this way, are not the same thing as economic profits. In computing economic profits we treat average returns to stockholders on their investment as expenses, and *economic profits* is the amount left of the corporate profits after this is done. In accounting practice average returns to stockholders are not considered as a cost of engaging in business activity. Nevertheless, the entire amount of corporate profits can be thought of legitimately as being earned by the resources of corporation stockholders. Whatever is left of gross earnings after all accounting expenses are met is ultimately theirs. Of course, dividends paid to nonresidents out of these profits must be deducted, since we are deriving the net *national* product.

Indirect Business Taxes

Indirect business taxes consist largely of sales and excise taxes collected by businesses from purchasers of goods and services and turned over directly to the government and of property taxes paid by businesses. They also include a number of miscellaneous fees and payments paid to the government by business, although the total amount of these is comparatively small. Parenthetically, profits of provincial liquor control boards have recently been reclassified in the national accounts from government investment income to indirect taxes. Apparently, our statisticians believe that such profits are more closely akin to taxation than to income from commercial activities.

We do not treat indirect taxes in the same way as D.B.S. in setting up the various national income and product concepts. D.B.S. does not include this amount as a part of net national income. Rather, it deducts indirect business taxes from *NNP* to arrive at what it calls *net national income at factor cost*. We add the indirect business taxes to D.B.S. *net national income at factor cost* to arrive at what we call *net national income,* thus *our* net national income is equal in amount to *NNP.*

The justification for our treatment of indirect business taxes as a part of *NNI* is a simple and logical one. The *entire amounts* paid by buyers for *NNP* are earned by resource owners, regardless of whether the latter ever see the money. In this respect indirect business taxes are no different from the part of individual income taxes withheld by employers and paid directly to the government. The indirect business taxes paid by businesses to the government are partly the earnings of labour resources and partly those of capital resources, the amounts attributable to each depending upon the incidence of the taxes. Indirect taxes thus become disposable income for the government just as do any other tax receipts. They are in no way removed from the income flow of spending and are therefore identical to other kinds of government tax receipts.

Proprietors' Income

Consider now the total receipts of single proprietorships and partnerships. Although a large part of these are paid out to resource owners, becoming earnings in some other form, a small part, termed *proprietors' income*, remains. This is what the owners of the businesses have for themselves and is usually thought of as their "profit". The owners of single proprietorships and partnerships own capital resources used in the business and also furnish their own labour resources to the business during the year, so this net income or "profit" is really income earned by their labour and capital combined. A breakdown of this component into wage and salary, rent, interest, and return on investment entails such difficulties that D.B.S. does not attempt it and reports the entire amount under two broad headings: (a) accrued net income of farm operators from farm production; (b) net income of nonfarm unincorporated businesses. In a word, *proprietors' income* represents the net income of all unincorporated business.

It is worth noting here that *rental income*—the net amount earned by the owners of real property from renting the property out to others— until recently classified in the national accounts with interest income, is now included with the net income of nonfarm unincorporated business. This change "recognizes the fact that net rental income is not really rent in the strict economic sense of the term but a special name given to the residual income derived from activity in the real estate industry".[10]

Net Interest Income and Miscellaneous Investment Income

This category includes interest received by persons, excluding interest paid by governments and by consumers on the nonproductive portion of consumer debt (these two forms of interest are excluded because they do not represent a cost payment to a factor of production for a current contribution towards production); profits received by government business enterprises, as well as interest received by governments on their loans and advances and on their pension and social insurance funds, excluding interest on government debt; and withholding taxes on interest, dividends, rents, and royalties paid to nonresidents.

Transfer Payments

As we total up the amounts received during a year by businesses, private individuals, and the government in an attempt to arrive at *NNI* or *GNI* we must be careful to leave transfer payments to one side. *Transfer payments* are those made by one economic unit to another during the year *for which no services are performed by the ones receiving the payments*—that is, no contribution to the year's production is rendered for the payment. Such payments may be either (1) government transfer payments or (2) private transfer payments.

Government Transfer Payments

We met *government transfer payments* before. They are payments made

[10]*D.B.S.*, National Income and Expenditure Accounts, 1926-1968. *Ottawa: Queen's Printer, August, 1969, p. 9.*

by the government to individuals or businesses who make no contribution to the economy's output of goods and services. Old age pensions, family allowances and welfare assistance provide the clearest examples. They represent purely and simply a transfer of purchasing power from the tax-payer to the recipient. The payment is not made for work performed or for the placement of resources in the productive process.

Interest payments on government debt are classified by D.B.S. as trans-fer payments; however, there is some disagreement among economists concerning whether or not this is correct procedure. Some argue that such payments simply represent a transfer of purchasing power from taxpayers to bondholders. Others argue that bonds sold by government units pro-vide funds that are invested in government capital—for example, the St. Lawrence Seaway Authority,—and that the investment yields returns to society at least sufficient to pay the interest. Both arguments have some merit. Some government borrowing is undoubtedly invested so that it yields a return. Just as surely some of it is not, and the interest paid on this part is of a transfer nature. We shall beg the question and follow the D.B.S. procedure of treating interest on government debt as a transfer payment.[11]

Private Transfer Payments

Private transfer payments are those made between private economic units for which nothing new is created. Suppose that Smith purchases a used car produced in some previous year from Jones. Nothing is added to *NNP* for the current year and consequently nothing is added to *NNI* by the transaction. The additions to *NNP* and *NNI* occasioned by the produc-tion and sale of the automobile occurred in the year in which it was origin-ally produced and sold, not this year. All that has happened this year is that an already existing piece of property has changed hands or has been transferred from one party to another. In addition to transactions in goods produced previous to the year in question, gifts from one person to another during the year are private transfer payments.

Product-Income Relation Restated

After the discussion on the component parts of *GNP* and *NNP* in the preceding section and of *GNI* and *NNI* in this one, a summary of the relations between the two sets of concepts is in order. Table 12-1 and Figure 12-2 are useful for this purpose. *GNP* is the total value of goods and services put in final form by Canadians during a given year. Its pro-

[11]*For a useful discussion of this question, see S. A. Goldberg and F. H. Leacy, "The National Accounts: Whither Now?",* Canadian Journal of Economics and Political Science, *February, 1956, pp. 76-77.*

duction generates an equal amount of total income received, or *GNI*. Plant and equipment wear out or become obsolete in the process of producing *GNP*, so the net value of the economy's output, or *NNP*, is equal to *GNP* minus whatever value of goods and services is necessary to take care of such depreciation. On the income received side, businesses use a part of *GNI*, called capital consumption allowances, to take care of depreciation, so the net income earned by resource owners, or *NNI*, is equal to *GNI* minus capital consumption allowances. Net national income and *NNP* are equal, since depreciation and capital consumption allowances are equal.

Net national product, the net value of the economy's output for the year, is made up of three parts. These are the values of consumption goods, net investment goods, and government goods and services produced and they are summed up in the statement

$$NNP = C + I + G \tag{12.2}$$

The production of *NNP* creates an equal amount of income, *NNI*, for resource owners. The component parts of *NNI* as they are computed by national income statisticians are compensation of employees, corporate profits, indirect business taxes, proprietors' income, and net interest income. This income received can be thought of as ending up in the hands of households, corporate business firms, and the government.

But before discussing this alternative way of viewing the value of the economy's output two points should be made. First, when national income statisticians compute gross national product using the value-of-products approach, and when they compute gross national income using the income-earned approach, some items on one side or the other get lost in the shuffle, resulting in a small statistical discrepancy. To give us a single estimate of the gross national product or income, our statisticians add half the difference to the figure which is low and subtract half the difference from the figure which is high. This addition to the smaller aggregate and deduction from the larger aggregate is referred to as the *residual error of estimate*. Second, to distinguish these methods from each other, our statisticians have given a special name to each; if the national output is calculated by adding up final products less imports (the product approach), it is called gross national expenditure (*GNE*); if it is reached by summing up incomes generated through production (the incomes approach), it is called gross national product (*GNP*).

The Disposable Income Approach

All of the income received during the year is available for spending and as such is called *disposable income*. The net amount of disposable income, or *NDI*, made available during the year is necessarily the same as *NNI*, but its distribution among economic units for spending purposes is not the same as the distribution of *NNI* as it is earned by resource owners. This is because some transfers of purchasing power occur between those who earn the income and those who have it available to spend. Households, corporate business firms,[12] and the government are the recipients of *NNI*. They are also the spenders of *NDI*, but the transfers take place between the time of earning and the time of spending.

Household Disposable Income

Before we can observe what constitutes household disposable income we must determine which parts of the components of *NNI* are received by households *before* any transfers take place. Obviously, all of the compensation of employees component is so received. A part of the corporate profits component is received by households in the form of dividends to stockholders. Proprietors' income is received by households, as is rental income and net interest income. Only the indirect business taxes component bypasses households completely.

What are the transfers that make household disposable income differ from the part of *NNI* that they receive as resource owners? Contributions to social insurance and public service pensions are exacted of employers and employees, thus transferring purchasing power from households to the government. Households must also pay personal income taxes, personal property taxes, inheritance taxes, and such nontax payments as fees, fines, donations, and others to the government. But the transfers are not all in one direction. Some households, notably farmers, those who receive social insurance payments, welfare recipients, and government bondholders, receive transfers from the government. In the final analysis *household disposable income* consists of all income earned by households minus personal taxes and other payments made by them to the government, plus government transfer payments made to them. It is available to households to dispose of as they see fit—to spend or to save.

---

[12]*Ideally,* all business firms *should be included here rather than just corporations. However, the D.B.S., in its national income and product classifications for data gathering and analysis, separates out corporations, placing proprietorship and partnership data with that of persons or households. To avoid confusion in the use of D.B.S. data we shall follow the same practice.*

Business Disposable Income

Before transfers occur business firms are in possession of that part of the corporate profits component of *NNI* that is not paid to stockholders as dividends. The major transfers that occur from this amount are corporation income taxes and any other fees paid to the government by corporations. That part of profits remaining in the hands of the corporation after corporation income taxes have been paid and after dividends have been paid to stockholders is called *undistributed profits*. If we add to the undistributed profits any transfer payments to corporations from the government, say subsidies of one kind or another, we have *corporate disposable income*. This is income available to the corporation to spend as it desires.

Government Disposable Income

The government's direct receipts from the *NNI* pie consist of indirect business taxes. To this we add all tax receipts and other transfers from households and corporations to the government. Then we deduct all transfer payments from the government to households and corporations. The remainder is *government disposable income*, or the amount the government has available to provide the goods and services that it determines we should have.

Relation of NNP, NNI, and NDI Restated

The production of *NNP* generates an equal amount of *NNI* for the resource owners who furnish the resources to produce it. The income received by resource owners is subjected to transfers, and after these have been accomplished it becomes *NDI* in the hands of households, corporate businesses, and the government. The distribution of *NDI* will differ somewhat from the distribution of *NNI*, but no change in total income is brought about by the transfers. These relations are summed up in the statement

$$NNP = NNI = NDI \tag{12.3}$$

Summary

This chapter lays the foundation for the analysis of national income developed in the ensuing chapters. Three sets of national income and product concepts are defined. Through the value-of-products approach we derive the concepts of gross national product and net national product.

From the income-received approach we arrive at the concepts of gross national income and net national income, and from the latter concepts we move to those of gross disposable income and net disposable income.

From the value-of-products point of view *GNP* is the total value of all goods and services produced by residents of Canada in final form in the economy per year. It is composed of three parts: (1) goods and services for personal consumption, or *C*, (2) governments goods and services, or *G*, and (3) gross investment or capital goods, or *GI*. If we deduct from gross investment goods the capital goods needed to take care of the depreciation that occurs as *GNP* is produced, then (3) becomes net investment goods, or *I*, and the sum of the three makes up net national product, or *NNP*. In totalling the values of goods and services to find *GNP* or *NNP*, double counting of intermediate goods must be avoided. Intermediate goods are goods produced to further produce higher-order goods.

If we look at the income generated in the production of *NNP* and *GNP*, we have the concepts of net national income and gross national income, respectively, with *NNP* = *NNI* and *GNP* = *GNI*. The components of *NNI* are (1) compensation of employees, corporate profits, indirect business taxes, proprietors' income, and net interest and miscellaneous investment income. If we add capital consumption allowances to these classifications, we arrive at *GNI*. Capital consumption allowances are the part of income received necessary to take care of depreciation and are equal to depreciation. The receipt of transfer payments must not be counted as a part of *NNI* or *GNI*.

The distribution of *NNI* as it is earned by resource owners is somewhat different from the distribution of *NDI* as it is available to be spent, although *NDI* is equal to *NNI*. Net disposable income consists of (1) household disposable income, (2) corporate disposable income, and (3) government disposable income. Household disposable income is what is left of household earnings after all tax and other payments to the government have been deducted and after transfer payments from the government have been added in. Corporate disposable income consists of undistributed profits plus government transfer payments to corporations. Government disposable income is composed of indirect business taxes plus all other tax revenues and government receipts minus government transfer payments.

Exercises and Questions for Discussion

1. Are the tractors manufactured by Massey-Ferguson final goods? Why are the intermediate goods not included in *NNP* or *GNP*?

2. To compare *GNP* for two successive years we compare the market value of all final goods produced by residents of Canada during those two years. Would a comparison of the physical outputs be a better measure of income growth? Why is this not done?
3. Can an economy's output and income earned be unequal in a given year? Explain.
4. In 1933 during the Great Depression net investment was negative. Does this mean that gross investment was negative also? Why or why not?
5. Which of the following goods or services would be included in *NNP* in 1970? In each case indicate why or why not.
   a. Flour.
   b. Sale of 1968 automobile.
   c. Sale of new wrist watch.
   d. Purchase of 100 shares of Bowater Paper stock.
   e. Services of housewives.
6. Which is the best measure of economic performance, *GNP*, *NNP*, or *NDI*? What reasons can you give for your answers?

Selected Readings

Ackley, Gardner, *Macroeconomic Theory*. New York: Crowell-Collier and Macmillan, Inc., 1961, Chap. 3.

Boreham, Gordon F., and Eli Shapiro, Ezra Solomon, William White, *Money and Banking: Analysis and Policy in a Canadian Context*. Toronto: Holt, Rinehart and Winston of Canada, 1969, Chap. 15.

Dominion Bureau of Statistics, *National Income and Expenditure Accounts, 1926-1968*. Ottawa: Queen's Printer, 1969.

Ross, Myron H., *Income: Analysis and Policy*. New York: McGraw-Hill Book Company, Inc., 1964, Chap. 2.

13

The Level of National Income

The step from the national income and product concepts of the last chapter to the forces that determine the level of economic performance is not a giant one. In fact, in developing the concepts and their relations to each other, the basic forces at work become almost self-evident. Though their broad outlines are simple, the details involved in their operation become rather complex. These details are introduced in this and the following chapter.

The Framework of the Analysis

The foundations of national income analysis were laid by the noted British economist John Meynard Keynes in his celebrated *The General Theory of Employment, Interest and Money*.[1] An expert in the area of monetary theory, Keynes had long been troubled by the failure of the conventional economic theory of his day to come to grips with the causes of large-scale unemployment. His concern led to a whole new line of thinking with respect to the determinants of the level of economic activity, the causes of economic fluctuations and of unemployment, and policy prescriptions to correct some of the inherent defects of an economic sys-

[1] *John M. Keynes*, The General Theory of Employment, Interest and Money. *New York: Harcourt, Brace & World., Inc., 1936.*

tem. Other economists have modified and developed Keynes's approach, adding an important dimension to economic analysis.

The Closed, Private Economy

In this chapter we limit our analysis to a closed, private economy. A *closed economy* is one that is self-contained; it carries on no transactions with other economies. By restricting the analysis to a closed economy we avoid the complications that international trade would introduce. A *private economy* is one in which there is no public or government sector. Such a situation is, of course, a figment of the imagination, but we must learn to crawl before we learn to walk. Once we understand the mechanics of national income analysis for the private economy, the extension to include the public sector is an easy one.

What are the implications of a closed, private economy for the national income and product concepts developed in the last chapter? Net national product consists of two parts instead of three. It is now the net value of goods and services produced for private consumption plus the value of net investment goods, or

$$NNP = C + I \tag{13.1}$$

The only implication for net national income is that the indirect business taxes component drops out. Net disposable income is now concentrated in the hands of households and businesses. Government disposable income has disappeared. In the closed, private economy, then, net national product generates an equivalent amount of net national income, which, after certain private transfers are made, becomes net disposable income, or

$$NNP = NNI = NDI \tag{13.2}$$

Spending, Saving, Investment, and Hoarding:[2] An Overview

What do the holders of the economy's net disposable income do with it? In the first instance they have a choice between spending for consumer goods and services or saving. Households will elect to spend some part of their disposable income on consumption and to save the rest. Businesses as such do not purchase consumer goods and services; therefore, we consider all of their disposable income as being saved. *Savings*, then, are that part of the economy's net disposable income that are not spent on consumption, or, letting S represent savings,

$$S = NDI - C \tag{13.3}$$

Savings may be used to buy new capital goods or investment goods;

[2]*We shall defer discussion of the determinants of these to the latter part of the chapter. Here we are simply attempting to establish the mechanics of what makes income remain constant, rise, or fall over time.*

that is, for the purchase of *net investment* goods. The actual channeling of savings into spending on new or net investment or capital goods is done in several different ways. Households may buy new issues of corporate stock with their savings, thus making available to corporations funds to invest in plant, equipment, and inventories. Sometimes they buy corporate bonds, the proceeds of which are invested in new capital by the corporation. Sometimes savings are deposited into accounts in commercial banks or credit unions and *caisses populaires* or are used to buy life insurance, whereupon these institutions make the funds available to businesses to invest in new capital goods. Additionally, there may be direct spending of business disposable income on investment or capital goods. This is usually characterized as "plowing earnings back into the business."

That part of *savings*—of both households and businesses—that is not spent on *investment goods* is *hoarded*. Care must be taken not to confuse hoarding with savings. They are not the same thing unless no spending for investment goods takes place. That part of *NDI not spent* on consumption is defined as savings. The savings are then available to be spent on investment goods or to be hoarded. That part of savings *not spent* on investment goods is defined as hoarding.

The disposition of net disposable income determines whether net national product will remain constant, rise, or decline over time. Although the production of net national product, the earning of net national income and net disposable income, and the spending of net disposable income are actually all occurring simultaneously, conceptually we can separate earning from spending. From the production of *NNP* an equivalent amount of *NDI* is generated.[3] This *NDI* now calls forth and is spent on the production of a new round of consumption goods and services as well as investment goods. The value of this new amount of consumption goods and services and investment goods—a new *NNP*—will be equal to the original one *if and only if* all current savings from the *NDI* are spent on investment goods and none are hoarded. If some of the savings are hoarded, or not spent for investment goods, then all of *NDI* is not spent and the value of consumption goods and services produced in response to spending will also be less than *NDI* and the original *NNP*. Under these circumstances *NNP* will decline over time. On the other hand, if households and businesses decide to spend *more* than the *NDI* currently earned—that is, if spending on investment goods exceeds the amount saved out of *NDI*, a new *NNP* greater than *NDI* and the original *NNP* will be forthcoming. This means that *NNP* will increase over time. We shall develop these processes in detail through the rest of the chapter.

[3]*Since* NDI *is the same amount as* NNI, *we have left out the intermediate reference to* NNI.

Period Analysis

An expository device called period analysis is useful in illustrating the forces that determine whether *NNP* remains constant, rises, or falls over time. We shall divide time into a succession of periods in order to separate analytically the earning from the spending of income.[4]

A Constant Level of NNP

The circumstances leading to a constant level of *NNP* over time are illustrated in Table 13-1. Suppose that in period (1) $70 billion worth of goods was produced. This amount is shown as *NPP* for period (1), and its production generates $70 billion in net disposable income (not listed separately in the table) available to be spent in period (2). We shall ignore the *NNP* figure for period (2) for the moment—we want to examine the process by which it is determined. Of the $70 billion available for spending in period (2) suppose that households elect to spend $60 billion for consumer goods and services. That part not spent on consumption is $10 billion and constitutes period (2) savings. The savings of period (2) can be spent in whole or in part for new or net investment or capital goods[5] and any remainder is defined as hoarding. Suppose, then, that the entire amount of savings is spent for $10 billion dollars worth of new investment goods.

What is the total of *NNP* for period (2)? Consumer purchases of $60 billion worth of consumer goods means a $60 billion value for this component of *NNP*. Saver purchase of $10 billion worth of investment goods means a $10 billion value of the investment goods component. Net national product for period (2) must be $70 billion worth of product and is the same as it was for period (1). The $70 billion *NNP* for period

[4]*The length of the period need not be specified, since it is an abstraction rather than a description of actual events. The values of* NNP, NDI, *and their components are assumed to represent annual rates – that is, to indicate what they would be for the entire year if they were to continue throughout the year at the same level shown in a given period. The essence of period analysis is that we assume income earned in any one period is disposed of (or partially hoarded) during the period immediately following.*

[5]*Why do we refer to new investment goods? Is it not possible that Mr. Throckmorton will use his savings to purchase stock in the Xerox Corporation from someone else rather than buying a newly issued share of Xerox? Of course, this is possible, but if Throckmorton so invests his savings the person from whom he is buying the stock is at the same time disinvesting. This transaction does not channel savings into investment for the economy as a whole. It simply transfers noninvested savings from Throckmorton to the party from whom he buys the stock. For the economy as a whole, savings can be invested only through the purchase of newly produced investment goods.*

TABLE 13-1
A Constant Level of *NNP* (billions of dollars)

	(1)	(2)	(3)
NNP	70	70	70
C	60	60	60
S		10	10
I		10	10

(2) becomes *NDI* for period (3), and if all period (3) savings are invested —that is, if all of *NDI* for period (3) is spent—*NNP* for period (3) remains at the $70 billion level. The principle illustrated here is that *if current savings are all invested, total current earnings in the economy are all spent and NNP will remain constant over time.*

A Falling Level of NNP

The forces that lead to a decline in *NNP* are illustrated in Table 13-2. Again suppose that *NNP* produced in period (1) is $70 billion. This amount is *NDI* for period (2) and $60 billion of it is spent for consumer goods. Savings for period (2) are $10 billion. So far the example is identical to that for a constant level of *NNP*.

What happens to *NNP* if all savings of period (2) are not spent on investment goods? Suppose that only $5 billion of the savings is invested and that the other $5 billion is hoarded. Net national product for period (2) is $60 billion worth of consumer goods and services plus $5 billion worth of investment goods for a total of $65 billion—lower than it was in period (1) by the amount of the savings that is *hoarded* and *not invested.* The governing principle is that *if all current savings are not invested, total current earnings are not all spent and NNP will decline.*

What is likely to happen in period (3) and subsequent periods as a result of the decline in *NNP* from period (1) to period (2)? This question reaches ahead of what we are trying to establish at the moment. It will be handled in detail in the next chapter. However, we can take a brief look at its implications. Since *NNP* for period (2) has declined to $65 billion, *NDI* available to spend in period (3) has also declined to $65 billion as compared with the $70 billion available in period (2). Households, with less income to spend in period (3) than in period (2), are likely to reduce their over-all level of consumption. Suppose they reduce it by $4 billion to a level of $56 billion. Savings for period (3) are $9 billion. Now suppose that investment for period (3) is again $5 billion. Net national product for period (3) is $56 billion plus $5 billion, or $61. Net national product for period (3) is $61 billion, still lower than it was in

TABLE 13-2
A Declining Level of *NNP* (billions of dollars)

	(1)	(2)	(3)
NNP	70	65	61
C		60	56
S		10	9
I		5	5

period (2). (Compare the *cause* of the decline in *NNP* from period (1) to period (2) with the *cause* of the decline from period (2) to period (3). Are they the same?)

A Rising Level of NNP

The principles that govern the two preceding situations make the one associated with a rising level of *NNP* almost self-explanatory. *If businesses invest more than is being saved out of current income, more is being spent than is being earned in the economy and NNP will rise.*

Using the same starting point as before, we shall assume that investment in period (2) is $15 billion (see Table 13-3). Net disposable income available to be spent in period (2) is $70 billion, of which $60 billion is spent on consumption and $10 billion is saved. Investment for period (2) exceeds current savings by $5 billion. Since period (2) consumption is $60 billion and investment is $15 billion, *NNP* is $75 billion.

If investment in period (2) exceeds the savings of period (2), where do investors get the extra $5 billion to spend on investment goods? The answer is not hard to find. There are two sources of funds for investment readily available in addition to those provided by current savings. One such source is past accumulations of *hoarded savings*. Just as these were taken out of the spending stream in the past—as they were in the declining *NNP* case—so can they be reinjected into the spending stream, augmenting current savings at any time the hoarders so desire. The second source is *newly created money*, ordinarily in the form of new chequable deposits. If current savings are not sufficient to meet the demands of those wanting to invest in new capital goods, investors may go to the banks to borrow. If banks have excess reserves, new loans can be made and new deposits are created for the borrowers, thus increasing the funds available to investors over and above current savings.

Again, anticipating the analysis forthcoming in the next chapter, suppose we glance ahead at period (3). Net disposable income for period (3) is $75 billion, equal to the *NNP* of period (2). The rise in income available for spending in period (3) over that available in period (2) will

TABLE 13-3
A Rising Level of *NNP* (billions of dollars)

	(1)	(2)	(3)
NNP	70	75	79
C		60	64
S		10	11
I		15	15

surely stimulate additional spending on consumer goods and services. Suppose that the level rises to $64 billion for period (3). Savings in period (3) are $11 billion. If investment continues at the $15 billion level, *NNP* for period (3) is $79 billion.

Determinants of NNP and NDI

Although the general outlines of national income analysis are contained in the preceding section, a number of details must be filled in if we are to develop a useful theory that will round out our understanding of what determines the level of *NNP* or *NDI*, what causes them to fluctuate and to grow, and what government policies are likely to contribute to stability and growth. Much remains to be said about the nature of consumption, savings, and investment, as well as their interactions in the determination of net national product. We must begin to fill in the gaps.

Consumption

What are the main determinants of the annual spending of households in Canada on goods and services for personal consumption? Why, for example, as shown in Table 13-4, did expenditures of this type fall from $4,583 million in 1929 to a low of $2,974 million in 1932 and then increase over the years to $42,360 million in 1968. Why do households consume a larger proportion of their disposable income in some years than they do in others; for example, compare 1950 with 1951. Again, examine Table 13-4. There appear to be two primary determinants of the level of consumption. One is the level of disposable income available to households. The other is the psychological desire of consumers to spend on consumption as opposed to their desire to save some part of their disposable incomes. We shall refer to this desire as their *propensity to consume*.

TABLE 13-4
Net National Product, Household Disposable Income, and Consumption, Selected Years, 1929-1969
(millions of dollars)

Year	Net National Product or Net Disposable Income[1]	Household Disposable Income[2]	Consumption
1929	5,413	4,572	4,583
1933	2,960	2,978	2,974
1935	3,751	3,294	3,331
1940	5,927	4,798	4,464
1945	10,821	8,354	6,972
1950	15,995	12,704	11,991
1951	18,760	14,803	13,399
1955	24,368	18,639	17,902
1960	32,739	25,893	24,705
1965	48,097	35,787	33,134
1966	54,007	39,499	36,057
1967	57,712	42,791	38,998
1968	63,005	46,384	42,360
1969			

[1]*Equivalent to D.B.S. "Net National Income at Factor Cost" plus indirect taxes less subsidies plus residual error of estimate.*
[2]*Equivalent to D.B.S. "Personal Disposable Income".*
Source: Dominion Bureau of Statistics, National Income and Expenditure Accounts, 1926-1968, *Ottawa, Queen's Printer, 1969.*

The Consumption Function

Ordinarily we expect the level of consumption to vary directly with the level of income available to households to spend—the higher the level of *household disposable income*, the higher the level of consumption. Table 13-4 confirms this expectation. The level of household disposable income in turn bears a direct relation to *net disposable income*, so we can say that consumption is a function of, or depends upon, net disposable income. Its dependence on *NDI* is not quite as strong as its dependence on household disposable income because of possible variations in the business disposable income component of *NDI*. However, in the analytical framework that we construct and use, we can avoid some complexities with little sacrifice of accuracy by relating consumption to *NDI*. This relation is called the *consumption function*, the term "function" being used in the mathematical sense to mean the *dependence* of consumption on *NDI*.

The nature of the consumption function for an economy is illustrated by Table 13-5 and Figure 13-1, but a little background work is in order before we look at the latter explicitly. In Figure 13-1, billions of dollars are measured along both the horizontal and the vertical axes. Now suppose that line OE is drawn upward and to the right from the origin in

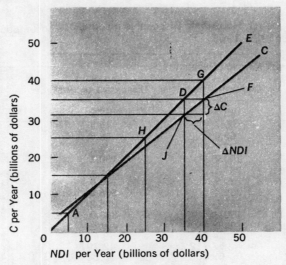

Figure 13-1
The consumption function.

such a way that each point on it represents the same amount measured along the vertical axis as it represents along the horizontal axis. Point *A* is $5 billion; point *H* is $25 billion; point *D* is $35 billion; and point *G* is $40 billion, in all cases both axes or either axis showing the correct measurements.[6] The *OE* line provides indispensable aid in the graphic representation of national income determination, its most valuable property being that for any given measurement along the horizontal axis it provides the same measurement vertically.

A typical consumption function, constructed from hypothetical data, is shown by columns (1) and (2) of Table 13-5 and is plotted as curve *C* in Figure 13-1. In Figure 13-1, net disposable income is measured along the horizontal axis, while expenditures on consumption goods and services are measured along the vertical axis. At an *NDI* level of $35 billion, households would want to spend $31 billion on consumption, and point *J* on the consumption curve is located. If *NDI* were $40 billion, *C* would be $35 billion, and point *F* is located on the consumption curve. Other points tracing out curve *C* are located in a similar manner.

Average Propensity to Consume

The consumption function in Figure 13-1 exhibits a characteristic that merits explanation. At relatively low income levels consumption exceeds

[6]*If the scales of the two axes are the same,* OE *is a 45-degree line, or bisects the angle at the origin of the diagram.*

NDI; at relatively high levels it is less than *NDI*; and the higher the income level, the smaller is the ratio or proportion of consumption to income. To say this another way, at relatively low levels of income the *average propensity to consume* is greater than 1; at relatively high levels of income it is less than 1; and as the income level increases, the average propensity to consume decreases. In this latter statement the *average propensity to consume* is defined as the proportion of the average dollar of disposable income used for consumption purposes. Mathematically it is expressed as

$$APC = \frac{C}{NDI} \tag{13.4}$$

In Figure 13-1 we assume that at income levels below $15 billion the average propensity to consume is greater than 1—that the households of the economy consume a larger value of goods and services than they are currently producing. In order to do this the economy as a whole must transform some of its capital equipment into consumer goods and services or use up some of the inventories of goods and services carried over from previous years that comprise a part of the economy's total stock of capital. It fails to take care of all of the depreciation that occurs during the year. This happened in 1933.

At higher levels of income the pressure to consume is much less severe. People earn large enough incomes so that they need not consume on the

TABLE 13-5
A Hypothetical Consumption Function

(1) NET DISPOSABLE INCOME (*NDI*) (BILLIONS OF DOLLARS)	(2) CONSUMPTION (*C*) (BILLIONS OF DOLLARS)	(3) MARGINAL PROPENSITY TO CONSUME (*MPC*)
5	7	
10	11	0.8
15	15	0.8
20	19	0.8
25	23	0.8
30	27	0.8
35	31	0.8
40	35	0.8
45	39	0.8
50	43	0.8
55	47	0.8
60	51	0.8
65	55	0.8
70	59	0.8
75	63	0.8
80	67	0.8

average as much as they produce. Instead of spending the entire amount of the average dollar on consumption they can afford to save some part of it. And the higher the income level, the greater the proportion of the average dollar they can afford to save—or the smaller the proportion of the average dollar they feel compelled to spend for consumption. In any event, this is what the available data relating consumption to disposable income seem to indicate.

Marginal Propensity to Consume

The marginal propensity to consume, or *MPC*, plays an important role in the analysis of economic fluctuations and their control. Similar to the rest of the marginal concepts that we have used, it is defined as *the change in consumption per unit change in the level of income*, other things being equal. Mathematically it is expressed as

$$MPC = \frac{\triangle C}{\triangle NDI} \qquad (13.5)$$

In Table 13-5, in moving from one income level to the next, the marginal propensity to consume is 0.8, meaning that for each one dollar increase or decrease in *NDI* consumption will change by 80 cents. Consider, for example, an increase in *NDI* from \$35 to \$40 billion. The corresponding increase in consumption is \$4 billion worth of goods and services, the change from \$31 to \$35 billion. Thus

$$MPC = \frac{\$4 \text{ billion}}{\$5 \text{ billion}} = 0.8$$

The table has been constructed using the underlying assumption that the *MPC* is 0.8 throughout the range of possible income levels.

In Figure 13-1 , the marginal propensity to consume for any small change in the level of income is measured by the slope of the consumption curve, *C*, for the change. Suppose again that the level of *NDI* is \$35 billion and that the level of consumption is \$31 billion initially, locating point *J* on the consumption curve. Now suppose *NDI* increases to \$40 billion and consumption increases to \$35 billion, moving up the consumption curve to point *F*. Again

$$MPC = \frac{\triangle C}{\triangle NDI} = \frac{\$4 \text{ billion}}{\$5 \text{ billion}} = 0.8$$

where $(\triangle C)/(\triangle NDI)$ is the slope of line segment *JF*.

Although we have shown the consumption function as a linear relationship, or as a straight-line consumption curve, many economists believe that it is likely to be concave downward, as Figure 13-2 illustrates.

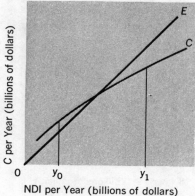

Figure 13-2
A nonlinear consumption function.

In order for the consumption curve to be this shape, the marginal propensity to consume must be higher at low levels of disposable income than at higher levels—at Y_0 the slope of C must be greater than it is at Y_1. Is this plausible? If *NDI* is at depression levels, it seems reasonable to expect that households will spend a very large part of any increase in *NDI* on consumption, or that the *MPC* will be high. An affluent society with a relatively large *NDI* appears to be in a somewhat different position. An increase in *NDI* may not yield such a large increase in consumption because consumption is much less urgent than it is at lower income levels. Even if the consumption curve were concave downward, the theory of national income determination and change is essentially the same as it would be if the consumption curve were linear. Since linear curves are less complex to manipulate, we shall use the straight-line consumption function.

Changes in Propensity To Consume

We must distinguish between movements along a consumption function and shifts in the function itself. So far we have assumed that the over-all *propensity to consume* is fixed, thereby enabling us to identify a given consumption function. At different levels of *NDI* the average propensity to consume and the marginal propensity to consume may vary, but the over-all *propensity to consume* defines the range of consumption reactions of households to the whole range of possible alternative levels of *NDI*—it represents a given state of mind toward all possible alternative income levels.

The given state of mind, or the propensity to consume, may change.

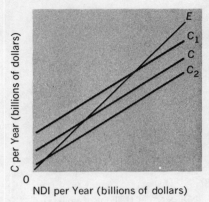

Figure 13-3
Shifts in the consumption function.

Households may be engulfed by a wave of optimism which induces them to consume more at each possible level of *NDI* than formerly and which shifts the entire consumption function upward from, say, *C* in Figure 13-3 to C_1. Or, on the other hand, pessimism—fear of a depression, for example—may shift it downward to a position like that of C_2. Another possibility is that income redistribution from the rich to the poor may occur in a society. Which group is likely to have the higher marginal propensity to consume? If *NDI* is transferred from those with lower *MPC*'s to those with higher *MPC*'s, at each of various levels of *NDI* the level of consumption will be higher than before—the consumption curve will be shifted upward.

Savings

Decisions to save are made by two groups of economic units, (1) households and (2) business enterprises. Household savings decisions must be made concurrently with decisions to consume. Business decisions to save, or to accumulate undistributed profits, are made concurrently with decisions concerning what part of corporate profits are to be paid out to stockholders as dividends. These decisions together define or locate the savings function for the economy.

The Determinants of Savings

When a household makes its consumption and savings decisions the desirability of saving must be weighed against the desirability of consuming, with the objective of reaching that distribution of disposable income between the two that will yield the highest level of satisfaction to the household. What are the factors that tend to make saving desirable? For one thing, an accumulation of savings can provide a degree of security against *unforeseen contingencies*—accidents, sickness, unemployment, death of the family breadwinner, or other adverse circumstances that can happen to anyone anytime. Second, members of households generally look toward *old age and retirement* and save to provide for themselves when they reach this period in their lives. Third, people may save for the explicit purpose of building a *source of additional income*. Toward this end they invest their savings in stocks, bonds, real property, businesses, and other income-yielding assets. Fourth, some people have read Benjamin Franklin's *Poor Richard's Almanac* or have come to value *thrift* as a virtue from other sources. Regardless of their income level they curtail their consumption and put some of their income into savings. Finally, some small part of household savings may be a *residual*, coming into existence simply because the households fail to spend their entire disposable income.

The volume of savings for households as a group will normally vary in the same direction as household disposable income. At relatively low income levels the need to consume is more pressing. But as disposable income increases, and as it becomes easier to fulfill some of the more important immediate wants, households can pay more heed to the various savings motives, holding more and more out of current consumption.

Business savings consist of corporate undistributed profits or of business disposable income. Since businesses do not consume goods and services, all of business disposable income is saved. Businesses save for two reasons. First, as in the case of households, it may be desirable to build some financial security against *unforeseen contingencies*—recessions, strikes, and so on. Second, businesses save in order to *invest in new plant and equipment*. Savings frequently provide a less expensive source of funds for expansion than the issuance of bonds or stocks. The total volume of business savings would be expected to vary directly with business disposable income, rising when income rises and falling when income falls.

Total savings, composed of both household and business savings, bears a direct relation to net disposable income of the economy. The whole is the sum of the parts in this case, since *NDI* consists of household and business disposable income combined. At depression levels of *NDI*, if household spending on consumption is greater than *NDI*, total savings of the economy must be negative.

The Savings Function

The *savings function*, or the relation between the level of savings and the level of *NDI*, is shown graphically in   Figure 13-4(b). The position and shape of the savings curve, *S*, is interdependent with the shape and

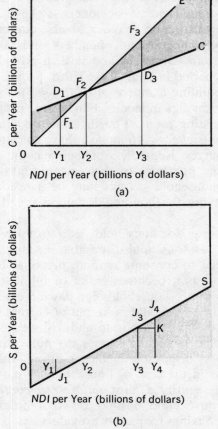

Figure 13-4
The relation between the consumption function and the saving function.

position of the consumption curve, C, of Figure 13-4(a). The *NDI* axes of the two diagrams are identical; however, in Figure 13-4(a) the annual rate of consumption is measured on the vertical axis while in Figure 13-4 (b) the vertical axis represents the annual rate of savings.

Suppose that the consumption curve, C, is given and that we want to derive the savings curve from it. If the level of *NDI* is Y_3, what is the magnitude of savings? The *OE* line of Figure 13-4(a) enables us to answer the question easily and quickly. At income-level Y_3, the level of consumption is Y_3D_3. The distance Y_3F_3 represents the same dollar amount as OY_3—the *OE* curve is constructed to make this so—and therefore is also a measure of *NDI*. Savings at income level Y_3, then, are represented by D_3F_3, the difference between *NDI* and consumption at that income level.

In Figure 13-4(b), at income level Y_3, point J_3 is set so that Y_3J_3 is the same dollar amount as D_3F_3 in Figure 13-4(a) and it locates one point on the savings curve.

Suppose the process is repeated at income level Y_2. Total net disposable income is also measured by Y_2F_2. Spending on consumption, as indicated by the consumption curve, is Y_2F_2 at that income level, so savings are zero. In the lower diagram this is indicated by the point on the *NDI* axis at Y_2.

At income level Y_1, *dissaving* occurs; that is, savings are negative. Spending on consumption exceeds net disposable income. Consumers are either spending past accumlated stocks of household savings or businesses are drawing upon undistributed profits or savings of previous years to pay out more to their owners than their current corporate profits. In the diagam, net disposable income is measured by Y_1F_1 as well as by OY_1. Total spending on consumption is Y_1D_1. Total dissaving is F_1D_1. Point J_1 is located below *NDI* axis in the lower diagram, so that J_1Y_1 is equal to F_1D_1.

Points such as J_1, Y_2, and J_3 trace out the savings function, *SS*, showing the relation of savings to net disposable income at various alternative income levels. In summary, the savings function is obtained by subtracting the consumption curve, *C*, vertically from the *OE* line. At any given level of *NDI* the level of savings is found by subtracting the level of consumption from that level of *NDI*.

Marginal Propensity to Save

The change in the level of savings in the economy per unit change in the level of *NDI* is called the *marginal propensity to save*. This is expressed as $\triangle S/\triangle NDI$ and is the same kind of concept as the marginal propensity to consume; in fact, the two are interdependent. Suppose, for example, that *NDI* increases by one dollar and that the *MPC* is 0.8. The level of consumption increases by 80 cents and the remaining 20 cents is added to savings. The marginal propensity to save, or *MPS*, is obviously 0.2. Mathematically,

$$MPC + MPS = 1 \qquad (13.6)$$

Since the $MPC = (\triangle C)/(\triangle NDI)$ and the $MPS = (\triangle S)/(\triangle NDI)$, then $MPC + MPS = 1$. That is, a one-unit change (or any other change) in *NDI* is necessarily divided between a change in consumption and a change in savings.[7]

[7]*For any change in* NDI,

$$\triangle NDI = \triangle C + \triangle S$$
$$1 = \frac{\triangle C}{\triangle NDI} + \frac{\triangle S}{\triangle NDI}$$

In Figure 13-4(b), for any given small change of *NDI* the slope of the savings curve shows the marginal propensity to save. If, for example, *NDI* rises from Y_3 to Y_4, savings increase by KJ_4. The change in savings per unit change in *NDI* is $(KJ_4)/(J_3K)$, or the slope of the line segment J_3J_4.

Investment

Who determines the annual rate of investment in new plant, equipment, inventories, and other capital goods? Most investment decisions are made by business firms, either those already in business or those in the process of entering. At any given time investment in some industries will be expanding while in others it will be contracting. Households are responsible for almost one quarter of net investment, mostly in the form of net additions to residential structures. The factors that seem to be most important in determining the magnitude of net investment are (1) the interest rate prevailing in the economy and (2) business expectations.

The Interest Rate

What is interest and the interest rate? We usually think of *interest* as the cost of borrowing money—what we must pay the bank or the mortgage company over time over and above the principal sum that we borrow. This is a correct definition but it does not go far enough. Business firms borrow to invest in inventories or in plant and equipment. They also raise funds in other ways, notably by selling stock or equities in the business. Dividend payouts, or the prospective earnings to stockholders in the form of appreciation in the value of their stocks, necessary to induce them to buy those stocks, are also *costs* of obtaining funds for investment. We shall refer to all such costs as *interest*. The *interest rate* is the percentage obtained by dividing the annual interest cost of a principal sum by the principal.

There is, of course, no such thing as "the" interest rate; there is a whole complex of interest rates. More risk is involved in providing investable funds to some businesses than to others, and the more risky business must offer a higher rate of return than others to compensate the supplier of funds for the possibility of not getting back either the full amount of the principal or the interest. Further, long-term use of investable funds usually implies a higher interest rate than short-term use. This is partly because of the greater risk associated with long-term commitments and partly because the supplier of funds loses control of them for a longer period of time. In any case, interest rates differ for different users of investable funds and for different time periods for which funds are committed. When we speak of "the" interest rate we refer to an index number of the complex.

How does the interest rate affect the amount of investment undertaken in the economy? If a business can invest $100 in plant and equipment and if that plant and equipment will yield a net income of $10 worth of goods and services per year—this amount over and above the amount necessary to take care of depreciation on the capital goods during the year—the *yield* on the investment is 10 percent per year. If the business can obtain investable funds from savers (or from itself as undistributed profits or business savings) for 8 percent per year, it is profitable to borrow or otherwise obtain the funds and to make the investment. However, if the cost of obtaining funds from savers is 12 percent per year, the investment will not be made, since it would result in a net loss.

The higher the interest rate, given business expectations, the less investors will be willing to invest. Suppose we know the positive net yield of all of the new investment projects that might be undertaken in the coming year and that we also know the costs of producing the investment goods to fulfill the projects. The total cost of such investment goods is measured in dollars along the horizontal axis in Figure 13-5. Now suppose that we arrange the projects along the horizontal axis so that those providing the highest yields are closer to the origin and those providing lower yields are farther from the origin. The line *MEC* is traced out by the yields as we accumulate the total costs of the projects, moving from the one with the highest yield to those with successively lower yields. A quantity of investment, I_1, will have a yield of r_1 percent or more; a quantity of I_2 will have a yield of r_2 percent or better; and so on, until we reach I, the total amount that will have a positive yield. This curve is called the *marginal efficiency of capital*, or the *MEC* curve.

Now suppose we look at r_1 and r_2 as alternative rates of interest or costs to investors of obtaining investable funds. If the interest rate were r_1, it would pay investors to undertake an amount of net investment of I_1. Investments up to this point would add more to investors' incomes than to their costs, since the yields would exceed the costs of obtaining the funds needed to effect the investments. Similarly, if the interest rate were r_2, investors would undertake investment in the amount of I_2. The amount of investment that would be undertaken, then, is inversely related to the interest rate.

Business Expectations

Business expectations is a blanket term covering everything that affects the general profit outlook of those who make business decisions. During periods of prosperity, such as 1963-1966 profit prospects are excellent and anticipated yields on new investments for the business community at large are relatively high. Exceptionally good expectations encourage larger amounts of investment at each possible level of the interest rate and thus shift the marginal efficiency of capital curve to the right, toward some position such as MEC_1. On the other hand, when profit prospects for business as a whole are adverse, as they were during the recession of 1960-1961, businesses are willing to invest less at each possible level of the interest rate because of smaller anticipated yields on new investment. The marginal efficiency of capital curve will lie farther to the left, toward some position such as MEC_0.

The Investment Curve

If the yearly rate of net investment depends on the interest rate and on business expectations rather than on the level of net disposable income, it is represented by a horizontal line when it is shown graphically on net disposable income diagrams such as those used to show the savings curve. Suppose that business expectations are such that MEC is the appropriate marginal efficiency of capital curve in Figure 13-5 . Suppose also that the going interest rate in the economy is r_1. The level of investment is I_1. Figure 13-6 shows net disposable income on the horizontal axis, as did the savings diagram of Figure 13-4 . The vertical axis measures investment. The investment curve is I_1, lying at I_1 dollars above the horizontal

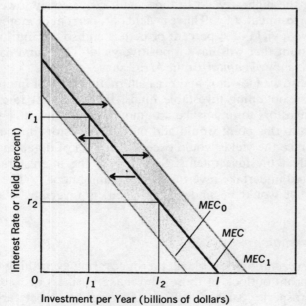

Figure 13-5
The marginal efficiency of capital curve.

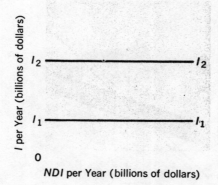

Figure 13-6
The investment curve.

axis for all levels of *NDI*. If the interest rate were to decrease to r_2 in Figure 13-5 , investment per year increases to I_2, shifting the investment curve in Figure 13-6 upward to I_2.

The Equilibrium Level of NDI and NNP

A great part of savings decisions are largely accomplished by a different group of economic units than those who make investment decisions. Further, the factors underlying savings decisions are largely different from those underlying investment decisions. These observations lead to the conclusion that for any given level of *NDI* there is no compelling reason why investors would want to invest exactly the same amounts that savers want to save. If the amount of investment that investors desire to undertake differs from the amount of savings that savers desire to save, changes in *NNP* and *NDI* will be set in motion.

Suppose that the consumption function, the savings function, and the desired level of investment are those illustrated in Figure 13-7 by the *C*, the *S*, and the *I* curves, respectively. The *S* and the *I* curves are placed together in Figure 13-7(b) . One new curve appears in Figure 13-7(a). This is the *C + I* curve, which shows the level of total spending on *both* consumption and investment for each possible level of *NDI*. It is located by adding the level of desired investment to the level of desired consumption for each possible level of *NDI*—that is, it is the vertical summation of the *C* and the *I* curves.

Rising NDI and NNP

If the level of *NDI* were Y_1, would *NNP* and *NDI* rise, fall, or remain constant? At that income level households want to spend Y_1C_1 dollars on

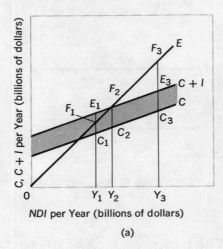

(a)

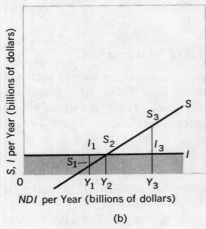

(b)

Figure 13-7
Determination of the level of net disposable income.

consumer goods and services, saving C_1F_1 dollars, as shown in Figure 13-7(a). Investors want to invest C_1F_1 dollars which is more than savers want to save. The consequences are that more will be spent than is being earned currently, inventories of goods and services will be depleted, and production will become more profitable because of rising demand. The economy's output of goods and services will rise in response to the more favourable profit opportunities, bringing inventories back to the desired levels. This, of course, means that *NNP* and *NDI* will rise.

The same situation is illustrated in Figure 13-7(b), since these two diagrams are completely interdependent. In Figure 13-7(b), the savings curve shows that at income level Y_1, the level of savings will be Y_1S_1. Investors desire to invest Y_1I_1 dollars which is more than is currently being saved. If desired investment exceeds savings, then more will be spent than is being earned currently and *NNP* and *NDI* will rise.

Falling NDI and NNP

What forces will be set in motion if the level of *NDI* is initially at Y_3? The level of consumption will be Y_3C_3, leaving savings of C_3F_3. Investment is only C_3E_3. Total spending is Y_3E_3 and E_3F_3 is hoarded. Total spending is less than the amount currently being earned. Falling demand for goods and services make business less profitable and causes inventories to accumulate above desired levels. Production is curtailed, so *NNP* and *NDI* decline.

In Figure 13-7(b) at income level Y_3, savings are Y_3S_3 while investment is only Y_2I_3. Since savings are greater than investment, less is being spent than is being earned; I_3S_3 is hoarded; so *NNP* and *NDI* decline.

Equilibrium NNP and NDI

Net national product and net disposable income will be in *equilibrium* when there are no forces operating to make them rise or fall. In the rising income case, desired investment exceeded current savings, generating rising levels of *NNP* and *NDI*. But as *NDI* increases, savings increase also until at income level Y_2 they are equal, both being C_2F_2 in Figure 13-7(a) or Y_2S_2 in Figure 13-7(b). At this income level the forces generating the rise in income no longer exist and the increase will stop. In the opposite case, desired investment was less than current savings, causing *NNP* and *NDI* to fall. As *NDI* falls, savings decrease until at level Y_2 savings and investment are the same. The forces causing income to fall have faded away and the decrease in income stops. At income level Y_2, at which savings and investment are equal, *NNP* and *NDI* are in equilibrium.

Secular Expansion or Contraction of Productive Capacity

The principles of national income determination have been developed in this chapter as though the total quantity of resources available for use were fixed. This is a reasonable assumption to use for short periods of time, but secularly, or over a period of years, the total quantity of resources will surely change. These changes will usually increase, but on occasion they may decrease, the productive capacity of the economy.

Expansion of Productive Capacity

Throughout the analysis of income determination we have assumed that net investment is positive; that is, that net investment is occurring. What effects will positive net investment have on the economy's productive capacity? Consider Figure 13-8. Suppose we are observing the operation of the economy over a period of one year and that the economy's stock of capital at the beginning of the year is represented by the block labelled *initial stock of capital*. The production of *GNP* for the year, represented by the rectangle so indicated, would by itself reduce the stock of capital by the amount called *depreciation*. Of the *gross investment* component of *GNP*, some part is used to take care of depreciation, or to bring the stock of capital back to its initial amount. The rest of gross investment—*net investment*—represents *capital accumulation* for the year, and when added to the initial stock of capital brings the economy's stock of capital at the end of the year up to that shown as the *final stock of capital.*

Positive net investment then constitutes capital accumulation and a growing capacity of the economic system to produce. This is not inconsistent with the possibility that *NNP* and *NDI* may from time to time decrease. These may increase or decrease, even though the potential capacity of the economy to produce is increasing, as the actual levels of employment of resources of the economy are increased or decreased.

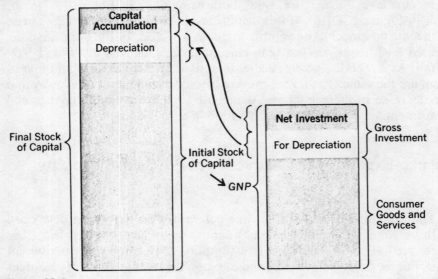

Figure 13-8
Positive net investment and capital accumulation.

Contraction of Productive Capacity

The possibility that net investment in an economy may be negative has been mentioned before. We would not expect long, sustained periods of negative net investment—an economic system where this occurs will not survive. Rather, we would expect short periods of negative net investment for economies undergoing some sort of crisis such as colossal mismanagement or a deep depression.

The circumstances of negative net investment and contraction of an economy's capacity to produce are illustrated in Figure 13-9. Again suppose that we observe the economy's operation for one year. The *initial stock of capital* is represented by the entire large rectangle on the left and is used to produce *GNP*. In the process the quantity of capital indicated as *depreciation* is used up. But this time the *gross investment* component of *GNP* is insufficient to cover all depreciation. That part of it not covered by gross investment is *net capital consumption* and can be thought of as being converted into consumer goods and services that are used up during the year. Thus the *final stock of capital* at the end of the year is less than the initial stock of capital by the amount of capital so consumed. This amount is the *negative net investment*. The shrinking stock of capital constitutes contraction of the economy's capacity to produce. (Can you illustrate and explain the circumstances under which the economy's stock of capital will remain constant over time?)

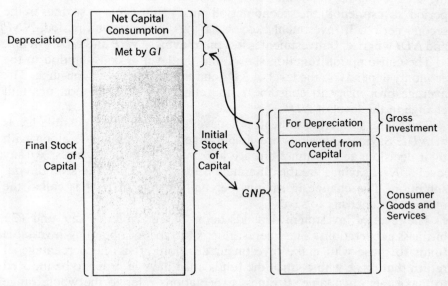

Figure 13-9
Negative net investment and net capital consumption.

Summary

We study in this chapter the private economic forces that lead to a rising, a falling, or an equilibrium level of net national product and net disposable income. The relation of total spending to the amount of net disposable income currently being earned is the key element of the analysis and within this broad framework we examine the interplay among net disposable income, consumption, savings, investment, and net national product.

In the period analysis overview the spending process is separated conceptually from the earning process. That which is earned in one period is conceived of as being available for spending in the next. Of the net disposable income earned in any one period, households will elect to spend some part on goods and services for personal consumption. The remainder is household savings. Household savings together with business savings constitute total savings, the amount of net disposable income not spend on consumption during the second period. Spending for investment goods during the second period is done primarily by business firms, although household spending for new residential construction is considered a part of it. Net national product for the second period is the value of consumption plus the value of investment, and its production generates an equal amount of net disposable income that becomes available for spending in the third period. For net national product and net disposable incomes of the second period to be the same as net disposable income of the first period, investment in the second period must be the same as savings in the second period. If investment exceeds savings in the second period, *NNP* and *NDI* will rise. If investment is less than savings, *NNP* and *NDI* will fall.

The consumption function shows that the level of consumption in the economy depends on the level of *NDI* and the propensity to consume. The average propensity to consume is the change in consumption per unit change in the level of *NDI*.

The savings function indicates the level of savings at all possible levels of *NDI*. Savings decisions are made largely by households, along with their decisions to consume, but are also made by business firms. At any level of *NDI* savings are the difference between *NDI* and the level of consumption. The change in savings per unit change in *NDI* is called the marginal propensity to save.

The level of investment depends upon (1) the interest rate and (2) business expectations. The interest rate is the cost of obtaining investable funds to those who make investment decisions. It is the percentage of return that those who control the funds must have in order to be induced to make them available. Business expectations refer to the whole range of factors affecting the profit outlook for those who make business decisions.

Savings and investment decisions are made largely by different groups of economic units and for largely different reasons. At any given level of *NDI* the amount that investors want to invest is not necessarily the same as the amount that savers want to save. Any divergence between these amounts will cause the level of *NNP* and *NDI* to change until the amount that savers want to save is equal to the amount that investors want to invest. National income—*NNP* and *NDI*—is in equilibrium when this is the case.

Secular expansion or contraction of the economy's productive capacity is dependent on the level of net investment. If net investment is positive, the economy is accumulating capital or adding to its productive capcity. If net investment is negative, capital consumption is occurring and the productive capacity of the economy will be contracting.

Exercises and Questions for Discussion

1. If *I* is greater than *S*, the level of *NNP* and *NDI* will tend to rise until a full-employment equilibrium level of income is attained. Discuss.
2. "If the lower-income groups have a higher average propensity to consume than the higher-income groups and income is transferred from the higher groups to the lower groups, *NNP* will rise." Evaluate this statement.
3. Suppose all consumers decide to save more. What will be the effect on the equilibrium level of *NNP*? Beginning with the original equilibrium, discuss the causal process.
4. "If no hoarding takes place in the economy, investment will never exceed saving and the capacity of the economy will not grow." Discuss this statement critically.
5. Which of the following will affect the position of the consumption function? Why?
   a. An increase in the level of *NDI*.
   b. An increase in the *MPS*.
   c. A decrease in the *MPC*.
   d. A decrease in the *APS*.
6. "If net investment is positive, the equilibrium level of *NNP* will rise in the next period, since the productive capacity of the economy is increased." Evaluate this statement.

Selected Readings

Boreham, Gordon F., *et al.*, *Money and Banking: Analysis and Policy in a Canadian Context*. Toronto: Holt, Rinehart and Winston of Canada, 1969, pp. 444-48 and pp. 464-71.

Dillard, Dudley, *The Economics of John Maynard Keynes*. New York: Prentice-Hall, Inc., 1948, Chaps. 5 and 7.

Heilbroner, Robert L., *Understanding Macroeconomics*. Englewood Cliffs, N.J.: Prentice-Hall, Inc., 1965, Chaps. 4-7.

McKenna, Joseph P., *Aggregate Economic Analysis*, rev. ed. New York: Holt, Rinehart and Winston, Inc., 1965, Chaps. 6 and 8.

14

National Income and Public Policy

When net national product and net disposable income are in equilibrium, is the economic system behaving as we want it to behave? Are the problems of employment, instability, and growth that we have been attacking in the last eight chapters alleviated by the movement of national income to equilibrium levels? Not at all. There is nothing inherently desirable about an equilibrium level of *NNP* or *NDI*. As we shall see, the equilibrium level may be too low or too high. Further, it changes from time to time, leading to recession and depression on the one hand and to inflation on the other. In this chapter we relate national income analysis to the performance of the economy as a whole and we use it to round out our understanding of the causes of poor performance and of policy prescriptions intended to improve it.

National Income and Economic Objectives

As we have considered the performance of the economy as a whole thus far, three important objectives that we would like to see attained stand out. First, we would like to achieve full employment of the economy's resources. Second, we would like to have economic stability—freedom from recession and from inflation. Third, we want the productive cápacity of the economy to grow. How does national income analysis relate to these objectives?

Full Employment and Stability

The objectives of full employment and stability overlap to such a degree that they can hardly be treated separately. The level of resource employment in the economy bears a direct relation to the level of national income

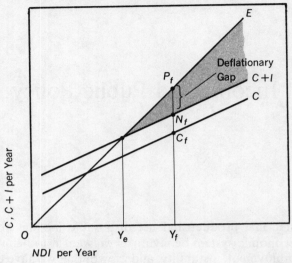

Figure 14-1
A deflationary gap.

up to the level at which full employment occurs. The higher the level of national income, the greater the level of employment up to that point.[1] If national income increases beyond that level, the increases are in money terms only, coming from price increases rather than from actual increases in the volume of goods and services comprising *NNP*.

The Deflationary Gap

Is it possible for national income to be in equilibrium at a less than full-employment level of resource use? It is not only possible, it happens. For *NNP* and *NDI* to be in equilibrium, it is necessary only that current savings be equal to intended investment—that all income currently being earned be spent. Savers decide what part of *NDI* they want to save for one set of reasons and investors decide how much they want to invest for another. If at a full-employment level of *NNP* savers want to save more than investors want to invest, the equilibrium level of *NNP* and *NDI* is necessarily below the full-employment level.

[1]*See pp. 105-112.*

Such a situation is illustrated in Figure 14-1 . Supose that full employment would occur at income level Y_f. But at that level of income savers want to save C_tP_t and investors are willing to invest only C_tN_t Less will be spent than is being earned; *NNP* and *NDI* will fall to the equilibrium level Y_e; and at that level unemployment exists. The deficiency in total spending at Y_t, represented by N_tP_t, is referred to traditionally as the *deflationary* gap. Note that it is identical to the amount that would be hoarded at that level of income.

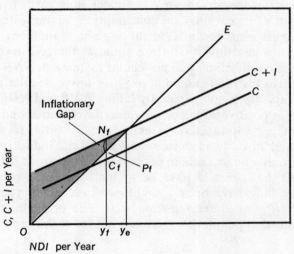

Figure 14-2
An inflationary gap.

The Inflationary Gap

Can the equilibrium level of *NNP* and *NDI* be greater than the level at which full employment would occur? It most certainly can be and was during the immediate post-World War II years from 1946 to the middle of 1948. If at the full-employment level of *NNP* and *NDI* investors want to invest more than savers want to save, total spending will exceed total earning and, through inflation, the money level of *NNP* and *NDI* will rise. Real *NNP* cannot increase, however, if resources are fully employed.

The conditions giving rise to inflationary increases in *NNP* are illustrated in Figure 14-2 . Suppose that Y_f is the full-employment level of *NDI*. Savers want to save only C_tP_t at that level of income but investors want to invest C_tN_t. The excess of desired investment over current savings, P_tN_t, is called the *inflationary gap*.

Economic Growth

Economic growth, measured in terms of rising *NNP*—although more accurately in terms of rising real *per capita NNP*—is not assured by income levels that are merely in equilibrium. Although national income expands when given quantities of resources are used more efficiently, a primary source of growth lies in the accumulation of capital equipment over time—increases in the magnitude of the economy's productive capacity. As we noted at the end of the last chapter, capital accumulation occurs whenever net investment or *I* is greater than zero. If the general public spends all of its earnings on consumption, savings are zero. If at the same time there is no new investment in plant, equipment, and inventories, then savings and investment are equal at the zero level; national income will be in equilibrium; and no secular increase in *NNP* is possible. If savings and investment are equal at *negative levels*, secular contraction of productive capacity accompanied by falling *NNP* and *NDI* will occur.

Even when *I* is positive, some of the underdeveloped economies of the world find that per capita income increases very little, if at all, from year to year, and in some instances may even fall. India, for example, experienced virtually no increase in per capita income from 1900 to 1950, and since 1950 the increases have been small. In Chile between 1955 and 1963 there may have been a slight decrease in per capita income even though *NNP* was increasing somewhat. The problem in these and other countries is that population increases in almost the same proportion as *NNP*.

Destabilizing Forces

Although deflationary and inflationary gaps lead to periods of recession and inflation, additional destabilizing forces are at work. Any given equilibrium level of *NNP* and *NDI* is determined by the existing level of the investment curve and the consumption or the savings function. Changes in one of these may occur, and when they do amplified changes in *NNP* and *NDI* are set in motion.

Changes in Investment

The amount of investment that business firms and households want to undertake is very volatile. Over short time periods business expectations can change rapidly for a variety of reasons. A major work stoppage can bring on a wave of pessimism out of proportion to its real impact on the volume of business being done in the economy. So can the failure of a financial institution like that of Atlantic Acceptance Corporation, a medium-sized sales finance company in 1965, or an important policy proposal like that of the White Paper on tax reform recently made public by the Federal government. External events like the devaluation of the British pound in 1967 and the subsequent weakening of confidence in the stability of the world structure of exchange rates may also have adverse effects. On the other hand, such things as a spectacular technological development, the opening up of new natural resources, or the signing of an international agreement like the automotive trade agreement with the United States in 1965 may have favourable effects on business expectations. Over longer periods nothing buoys expectations like expansion and profits, and nothing is more devastating to them than economic loss and contraction. As expectations change, so does the level of investment.

Changes in the interest rate also affect the level of investment, although it is doubtful that these are as important as changes in expectations. An easy money policy on the part of the Bank of Canada lowers interest rates and investment tends to increase. An easy money policy puts more money into the hands of the general public. It may permit more business borrowing by making excess reserves available to the banking system where none were available before. Both consumption spending and investment spending may increase simply because more money is available. In general, we would expect changes in the interest rate to reinforce changes in business expectations in bringing about changes in the level of investment.

The volatile nature of intended investment moves the latter now above and now below the level of savings. Both the savings and the consumption functions appear to be much more stable over time. As discrepancies between the level of desired investment and current savings occur, corresponding changes in the level of national income are set in motion.

The Multiplier

When changes in investment occur they bring about changes in the equilibrium level of *NPP* and *NDI* that exceed the magnitudes of the changes in investment; that is, they bring about amplified changes in national income, referred to as *multiplier effects*. To learn how they work we shall examine them first by means of period analysis and then by graphic methods.

Period Analysis

Let the equilibrium level of national income be $60 billion initially, as illustrated by periods (1) and (2) in Table 14-1. Suppose the level of consumption in period (2) is $50 billion, leaving $10 billion as savings. Let investment spending in that period also be $10 billion. Investment equals saving; all of the *NDI* earned in period (1) is spent in period (2); the *NNP* produced and the *NDI* earned in period (2) is $60 billion. Let the marginal propensity to consume be $\frac{4}{5}$; that is, a one dollar change in disposable income will bring about an 80 cent change in consumption.

Now suppose that a change in the interest rate or a change in business expectations or both causes investors to increase the amount they desire to invest in new capital goods by $1 billion per period, beginning in period (3). Of the $60 billion earned in period (2), $50 billion is spent on consumption in period (3), leaving savings of $10 billion. But $11 billion is invested, so income earned in period (3) rises to $61 billion. This rise in income in period (3) is equal to the *increase in investment*.

This is not the end of the matter if the level of net investment per period remains at $11 billion. The $61 billion earned in period (3) is the *NDI* available to be spent in period (4). This is $1 billion more than was available to be spent in period (3). Since the *MPC* of the consuming public is $\frac{4}{5}$, then $.8 billion of the increase (1 billion times $\frac{4}{5}$) will be spent on consumption, raising the consumption level of period (4) to $50.8 billion. Savings of period (4) are 10.2 billion. With investment remaining at $11 billion, income earned in period (4) is $61.8 billion— up $.8 billion, or by the *increase in consumption*, over the preceding period.

Another increase in *NNP* and *NDI* occurs in period (5). Of the extra $.8 billion earned in period (4) and available for spending in period (5), $\frac{4}{5}$ of it, or $.64 billion, will be spent on consumption, raising *C* to $51.44 billion. Savings are $10.36 billion and investment is assumed to remain at $11 billion. Thus *NNP* and income earned in period (5) is higher by $.64 billion—the amount of the increase in *C*—than in the preceding period.

The increases in income will continue, becoming smaller and smaller in each successive period and eventually approaching zero. When they become small enough to be negligible, a new equilibrium level of *NNP* and *NDI* is for all practical purposes achieved, as shown for the periods marked (*N*) and (*N* + 1).

In summary, then, the initial increases in investment causes an increase in *NNP* and *NDI* of an equal amount. The increase in income causes an increase in consumption, and the increase in consumption in turn causes a further increase in income that causes an increase in consumption that causes an increase in income, and so on. The new equilibrium level of *NNP* and *NDI* is $65 billion, with consumption at $54 billion, savings at $11 billion, and investment at $11 billion.

TABLE 14-1
Effect on National Income of a Change in Investment[a]
(billions of dollars)

	(1)	(2)	(3)	(4)	(5)	—	(N)	(N + 1)
NNP	60	60	61	61.8	62.44	—	65	65
C		50	50	50.8	51.44	—	—	54
S		10	10	10.2	10.36	—	—	11
I		10	11	11.0	11.00	—	—	11

[a] $MPC = \frac{4}{5}$

$MPS = \frac{1}{5}$

$$m = \frac{1}{1 - MPC} = \frac{1}{1 - \frac{4}{5}} = 5.$$

$$m = \frac{1}{MPS} = \frac{1}{\frac{1}{5}} = 5.$$

How do we determine the level at which national income will again be in equilibrium? As income and consumption increase, savings increase also. However, savings in periods (4), (5), and succeeding periods are less than investment. Not until income approaches $65 billion and the amount consumed approaches $54 billion will savings rise to the point at which they are as large as the amount that investors desire to invest. This can be verified by the laborious task of computing C, S, I, and NNP for a succession of periods following (5) in the same way that they were computed for (4) and (5).

There is, of course, an easier way to find the new equilibrium level of income. The change in NNP generated by the change in investment is a multiple of the change in investment, and the multiplying factor is called appropriately the *multiplier*. In the example the $1 billion change in investment generates a $5 billion change in NNP, so the multiplier is 5.

The size of the multiplier is determined by the marginal propensity to consume and it is found by summing a geometric progression. If the MPC is $\frac{4}{5}$, the effects of a one dollar increase in investment is found as follows:[2]

$$\triangle NNP = \$1 + \$\tfrac{4}{5} + (\$\tfrac{4}{5})^2 + (\$\tfrac{4}{5})^3 + \ldots (\$\tfrac{4}{5})^n = \frac{\$1}{1 - \frac{4}{5}} = \$5$$

The one dollar increase in investment increases NNP and NDI by one dollar, which, in turn, increases consumption by $\frac{4}{5}$ of a dollar, which increases NNP and NDI by the same amount, and so on. As the increases approach zero, the sum of the increases approaches $1(1-\frac{4}{5}5)$, or $5. Since a one dollar change in investment changes NNP by $5, the multiplier is 5. Whatever the MPC, the multiplier will be

[2] *This formula for finding the sum of a geometric progression can be found in any high school or college algebra textbook.*

$$m = \frac{1}{1 - MPC} \tag{14.1}$$

or, since $MPS = 1 - MPC$,

$$m = \frac{1}{MPS} \tag{14.1a}$$

and for any change in investment,

$$\triangle NNP = m. \triangle I \tag{14.2}$$

Applying this to the example of Table 29–1, we see that

$$\triangle NNP = 5 \times \$1 \text{ billion} = \$5 \text{ billion}^3$$

The multiplier works for decreases in investment as well as for increases. If the change in the level of investment had been a negative $1 billion, the new equilibrium level of income would have been $55 billion, a decrease of $5 billion. It will be instructive to work out with period analysis similar to that of Table 14-1 .

Graphic Analysis

The effects of a change in the level of investment on *NNP* and *NDI* are shown graphically in Figure 14-3 . Although either (a) or (b) of the figure can be used alone to illustrate the analysis, in the interests of completeness and clarity we shall use both. For identification purposes we shall call diagrams such as Figure 14-3(a) *total spending diagrams* and those such as Figure 14-3(b) *savings and investment diagrams*. Suppose initially that the consumption function is represented by C; the corresponding savings function is S; the level of investment is I; and the consequent total spending curve is $C + I$. *NNP* and *NDI* are in equilibrium at level Y_e. All that is being earned is being spent.

What are the effects of an increase in investment amounting to $\triangle I$? Both the investment curve of Figure 14-3(b) and the $C + I$ curve of Figure 14-3(a) are displaced upward by the amount $\triangle I$ to the new positions I_1 and $C_1 + I_1$, respectively. At the original income level Y_e, desired investment exceeds current savings or, what amounts to the same thing, more is being spent than is being earned. This means that *NDI* rises, and as it rises consumption and savings rise too as we move along the C curve and the S curve to the right. When *NDI* has risen to the level Y_1 savings are again equal to investment; earnings are again as great as total spending; and *NNP* and *NDI* are again in equilibrium.

---

[3]*What would the multiplier be if the* MPC *were* ⅔? *How would the $1 billion increase in investment affect* NNP *in the example of Table 14-1 if this were the* MPC?

Can the multiplier be illustrated graphically? Consider the savings and investment diagram. The slope of the savings curve or the *MPS* for the increase in *NDI* is measured by $(\triangle S)/(\triangle Y)$. Equation 14.1a defines the multiplier as the reciprocal of the *MPS*, or

$$m = \frac{\triangle Y}{\triangle S} \qquad (14.3)$$

From equation 14.2 we see that the change in *NNP* must be the change in investment multiplied by the multiplier, or

$$\triangle Y = m \cdot \triangle I \qquad (14.4)$$

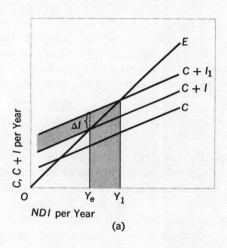

(a)

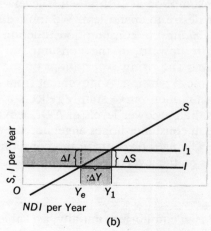

(b)

Figure 14-3
The effects of a change in investment.

Solving this equation for m, we find that

$$m = \frac{\triangle Y}{\triangle I} \tag{14.5}$$

Since $\triangle I = \triangle S$ for the change in income, if we substitute $\triangle S$ for $\triangle I$ in equation 14.5 the equation becomes identical to 14.3; that is, the actual multiplier in this case—the reciprocal of the slope of the savings curve— conforms to the previously established definition of the multiplier.

A decline in the level of investment resulting from an increase in the interest rate or adverse business expectations or both should present no analytical difficulties. The I curve and the $C + I$ curve shift downward by the amount of the change. At income level Y_e savings exceed intended investment, and spending is less than current earnings. The level of national income falls until savings decrease to an amount equal to the new and lower level of investment. The new equilibrium level of NDI is lower than the original level by an amount equal to the change in investment multiplied by the multiplier.

Changes in Consumption

Changes in the equilibrium level of national income result from changes in the propensity to consume as well as from changes in the level of investment, although the consumption function tends to be much more stable than the level of investment. A change in the propensity to consume is reflected by a shift in the consumption function up or down. The consumption function shifts upward when there is a desire on the part of consumers to spend more on consumption at each possible level of NDI and it shifts downward with their desire to spend less. We must distinguish carefully between a movement *along* the consumption function and a *shift* in the function itself, a *shift* upward in the consumption function may be triggered by rising hopes and rising expectations on the part of consumers with respect to economic expansion. A movement from a lower to a higher point on a given consumption curve simply reflects a desire to consume more at higher levels than at lower levels of NDI, leaving out of account the kind of buoyancy in consumer hopes engendered by a period of rapid economic expansion. Changes or shifts in the consumption function will have multiplied effects on the level of NNP and NDI.

Period Analysis

Suppose that NNP is in equilibrium initially, as **Table 14-2** shows from period (1) to period (2). In period (3) the expectations of consumers improve, shifting the consumption function upward and increasing the level of consumption by $1 billion at the $60 billion level of *NNP* and *NDI*. Savings of period (3)—found by subtracting consumption of period (3) from income earned in period (2)—decline by the same amount that consumption increases. The level of investment remains constant and the *MPC* is assumed to be $\frac{4}{5}$.

The increase in consumption causes *NNP* to expand. In period (3) the initial $1 billion increase in consumption increases *NNP* and therefore *NDI* by the same amount. Of the additional income earned in period (3) and available to be spent in period (4), $.8 billion will be spent on consumption, since the marginal propensity to consume is $\frac{4}{5}$. The expansion sequence is identical to that occurring as the result of an increase in

TABLE 14-2
Effects on National Income of a Change in Consumption[a]
(billions of dollars)

	(1)	(2)	(3)	(4)	(5)	—	(N)	(N+1)
NNP	60	60	61	61.8	62.44	—	65	65
C		50	51	51.8	52.44	—	—	55
S		10	9	9.2	9.36	—	—	10
I		10	10	10.0	10.00	—	—	10

[a]$MPC = \frac{4}{5}$.
$MPS = \frac{1}{5}$.

$$m = \frac{1}{1 - MPO} = \frac{1}{1-\frac{4}{5}} = 5.$$

$$m = \frac{1}{MPS} = \frac{1}{\frac{1}{5}} = 5.$$

investment. The increase in income of each period increases consumption of the next period by $\frac{4}{5}$ of that increase in income. Each increase in consumption increases *NNP* and income earned for the period in which it occurs by the amount of the increase in consumption. As the increases approach zero, *NNP* approaches the new equilibrium level shown by periods (N) and (N + 1).

Again we find that a multiplier determined by $1/(1 - MPC)$ or $1/MPS$ is at work. With an *MPC* of $\frac{4}{5}$, the increase in *NNP* and *NDI* from the initial equilibrium level to the new equilibrium level is five times the consumption level increase that generated it. Thus the *consumption multiplier* and the *investment multiplier* are numerically the same.

Graphic Analysis

The graphic picture of a change in the propensity to consume is contained in Figure 14-2. The initial equilibrium level of *NDI* is Y_e. At this level of income in the total spending diagram the $C + I$ curve crosses the

OE curve, showing that total spending, Y_eB_e, is the same as *NDI*. In the savings and investment diagram savings and investment are equal and are measured by Y_eI_e.

An increase in consumption, $\triangle C$, shifts the *C* curve upward and the *S* curve downward by the amount $\triangle C$. This also shifts the $C + I$ curve upward by $\triangle C$. At income level Y_e, after the change in consumption, savings and investment are A_eB_e and A_eC_e, respectively, in the total spending diagram, and they are Y_eS_e and Y_eI_e, respectively, in the savings and investment diagram. Since desired investment is greater than current savings, total spending is greater than the current level of earnings, causing *NNP* and *NDI* to rise. As income rises savings rise also, until at income

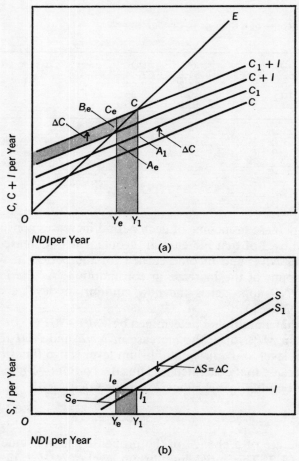

(a)

(b)

Figure 14-4
The effects of a change in consumption.

level Y_1 savings and investment are equal at an amount Y_1I_1 in Figure 14-4(b) or A_1C_1 in Figure 14-4(a). Again all that is being currently earned is being spent, so Y_1 is the new equilibrium level of income.

Problems of the Private Sector

The analysis thus far serves to point up the economic problems of the private sector of the economy taken as a whole. A stable system, automatically generating full employment and economic growth, it is not. The system may be in equilibrium with a deflationary gap. In this case there will be unemployment and a subnormal growth rate. Or it may be in equilibrium with an inflationary gap, generating full employment but subjecting itself to the inequitable consequences and dangers of inflation. Or it may be unstable because of changes in the level of investment and changes in the propensity to consume, together with the multiplier effects of both.

In the discussion of changes in investment and in the propensity to consume we considered a single change in investment and the resultant multiplier effects and then we considered a single change in the consumption function with its resultant multiplier effects. Actually, during a period of economic expansion there may be a series of upward shifts in the level of investment, each one subject to multiplier effects and generating increases in income greater than the increases in investment. Less likely, but still possible, are upward movements of the consumption function, with multiplier effects that amplify the increases in national income over and above the increases in consumption. And all of these may work in reverse during a period of economic contraction. Small wonder that we worry continually about economic fluctuations or instability!

Having developed multiplier theory showing multiplier effects amounting to several times the initial changes in investment or consumption, depending upon the magnitude of the *MPC*, we must now back down to some extent. In developing the theory we assumed that a change in the level of investment or in the level of consumption set the process in motion. Then we assumed that no outside or additional disturbing forces were permitted to interfere with the process until it had completely run its course. The world does not run in this manner. As the multiplier effects of a change in investment or consumption are in process, other changes may occur that prevent them from exerting their full impact. Counteracting changes in investment or consumption may occur, or there may be changes in the *MPC* that change the magnitude of the multiplier. The multiplier is not a precise tool of analysis, at least not with the present state of economic knowledge. It should be thought of as a force tending to amplify the direct effects of changes in investment and consumption on national income.

Monetary and Fiscal Policy

In isolating the forces leading to problems of unemployment, lagging growth rates, and instability in the private sector of the economy we have also isolated the points at which the problems can be attacked. The appropriate agency to attack them is, of course, the government, and the means of attack are monetary policy and fiscal policy. Both of these tools were examined earlier, and the task at hand is to fit them into the framework of national income analysis.

Monetary Policy

How does monetary policy operate within the framework of national income analysis? It would be expected to work by way of either the level of investment or the consumption function. It affects the level of investment through changes in the money supply and in the interest rate. It may have a direct impact on consumption spending.

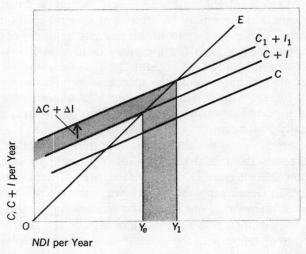

Figure 14-5
Monetary policy to combat unemployment.

Suppose that a deflationary gap exists, as Figure 14-5 illustrates, with the total spending curve initially at $C + I$, the equilibrium level of NDI at Y_e, and the full-employment level at Y_1. We learned previously that in circumstances of this kind an easy money policy is in order. The monetary authorities engage in open-market purchases of government securities, lower the Bank rate, reduce the Government's deposit balances at the

Bank of Canada (redeposits), and, if desirable, lower the required secondary reserve ratio.

The major impact of an easy money policy tends to be on the level of intended investment, since business firms account for the largest part of chartered bank loans. It may encourage business firms to modernize or expand plant and equipment by more than they would have in the absence of the easy money policy. It may also induce them to build larger inventories than they would have otherwise. This is because larger amounts of investable funds are made available to them at lower interest rates. Consumers may also be encouraged to borrow and spend more, particularly on consumer durable goods such as automobiles, household appliances, and the like, than they would have otherwise. To the extent that these results occur, the total spending curve shifts upward toward $C_1 + I_1$, reducing the deflationary gap and moving the equilibrium level of income toward the full-employment level.

Monetary policy can also be used to reduce the equilibrium level of income if an inflationary gap exists. A tight money policy on the part of the monetary authorities is appropriate. To initiate it the Bank of Canada would engage in open-market sales of government securities, increases in the Bank rate, transfers of Government funds from the chartered banks to the central bank (draw-downs), and if desirable, increases in required secondary reserve ratios. These measures decrease chartered bank reserves and raise the interest rate, cutting down on the availability of investable funds. Consumption and investment are discouraged, both by the smaller quantity of money available to be spent and by the increase in the interest rate. The $C + I$ curve shifts downward, thus decreasing the equilibirum level of national income and reducing inflationary pressures.

Government Economic Activity

The introduction of fiscal policy into national income analysis becomes more complex, since the government produces directly a part of net national product and can coerce people into turning over a part of their incomes to the government in the form of taxes. The analytical model that we have been using must be expanded to include the government's economic activities. Net national product becomes the sum of the values of consumer goods and services, business investment goods, and government goods (including capital goods) and services; that is,

$$NNP = C + I + G$$

Correspondingly, the component parts of net disposable income now become household disposable income, business disposable income, and government disposable income, or

$$NDI = DI_h + DI_b + DI_g$$

The production of *NNP* generates, as before, an equivalent amount of *NDI*.

The expanded analytical model is illustrated in Table 14-3, in which national income is in equilibrium. Suppose that *NNP* in period (1) is $70 billion, generating $70 billion of *NDI* to be disposed of in period (2). With the government in the picture, not all of *NDI* is in the hands of households and business firms. Some of it—net tax collections or total tax

TABLE 14-3

National Income in Equilibrium
(billions of dollars)

	(1)	(2)	(3)
NNP	70	70	70
T		10	10
C		50	50
S		10	10
I		10	10
G		10	10

collections (and other receipts of the government) minus transfer payments to household and businesses—becomes *government disposable income*. We assume in Table 14-3 that this amount is $10 billion, as represented by *T* for period (2). Disposable income left in the hands of households and businesses in period (2) but not listed explicitly in the table will be $60 billion. Of this amount suppose consumers elect to spend $50 billion on consumption, leaving $10 billion saved. Suppose, further, that all savings are invested and that the government's disposable income or net tax collections is all spent, providing $10 billion in government goods and services to the public. The value of all goods produced in period (2) and the total income generated in its production is the sum of the values of consumption, investment, and government goods and services, or $70 billion. All that is being earned is being spent. A repetition of this pattern in period (3) and succeeding period means that national income is in equilibrium.

It becomes immediately apparent in Table 14-3 that it is not strictly necessary that *I* = *S* and *G* = *T* in order for national income to be in equilibrium. Suppose, for example, that in period (2) we find *T* = $10 billion and *S* = $10 billion but that *I* = $9 billion and *G* = $11 billion. Substituting these values for those in the table, we see that *NNP* for period (2) is $70 billion, or the same as it was in period (1). Equilibrium exists, since *NNP* is neither growing nor contracting. Strictly speaking, then, national income is in equilibrium, or total spending is equal to the amount being earned, when *investment spending plus government goods and services provided* are equal to *savings plus taxes.*

Equilibrium in the expanded model is represented graphically in Figure 14-6. Looking first at the total spending diagram, we see that the vertical distance between the OE and the C curves at any given level of NDI must be *savings plus taxes* at that level of income. Consider an NDI level of Y_2, represented also by the distance Y_2F_2. Some of that amount of disposable income is paid to the government as taxes and is thus not available for households to consume. Of what is left after taxes are paid, some part is saved and the rest is consumed, thus the difference between NDI and consumption must be the combined amount of taxes and savings. Taxes plus savings are H_2F_2, plotted in the savings and investment diagram as Y_2L_2. The entire $S + T$ curve is obtained by subtracting the C curve

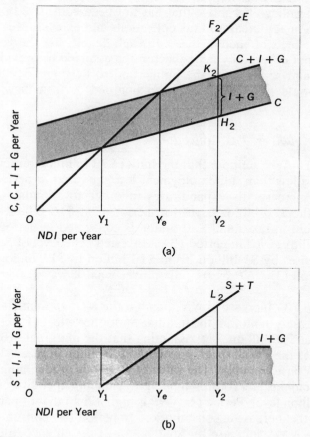

Figure 14-6
The national income model with the government sector included.

vertically from the *OE* curve. The equilibrium level of national income is Y_e, the level at which total spending is the same as total earnings, or at which $I + G = S + T$.

Fiscal Policy to Control Recession

What fiscal policy measures are in order if actual national income is below its potential level—if the equilibrium level is below the full-employment level? From past discussion we know that a budgetary deficit is called for and that this can be achieved through (1) an increase in government expenditures with tax collections constant, (2) a decrease in tax collections with expenditures constant, (3) an increase in expenditures accompanied by a decrease in tax collections. Method (3) is simply a combination of (1) and (2) and does not require separate analysis. There is, however, another fiscal policy alternative that has not been considered previously. It consists of equal increases in tax collections and expenditures. We shall examine the effects of each of these. In each deficit case the government expenditure not covered by tax collections is assumed to provide government goods and services for the public and to be financed either from funds that would otherwise have been hoarded or from newly created money.

Expenditure Changes, Tax Collections Constant

In Table 14-4 we suppose that the initial $70 billion equilibrium level of income is a less than full-employment level and that in period (3) the government increases its expenditures in order to stimulate economic activity. Of the $70 billion earned in period (2), $10 billion is paid to the government in taxes and $50 billion is consumed in period (3). All of the $10 billion saved in period (3) is invested. The level of government expenditure rises by $1 billion, from $10 billion to $11 billion, thus increasing period (3) *NNP* by $1 billion over what it was in the preceding period.

The period (3) increase in *NNP*, and in the *NDI* available to be spent in period (4), sets in motion the familiar multiplier effect. Taxes in period (4) remain at $10 billion, but, assuming that the marginal propensity to consume is $\frac{4}{5}$, the extra $1 billion of *NDI* brings about an $.8 billion increase in consumption. Savings increase to $10.2 billion. (Why?) Investment remains at $10 billion and government expenditures continue at the $11 billion level. Period (4) *NNP* is higher than that of period (3) by $.8 billion—the increase in consumption. In period (5) consumption, and consequently *NNP*, increase by $6.4 billion. In each succeeding period consumption and *NNP* increase by $\frac{4}{5}$ of the increase of the immediately

TABLE 14-4
Effects on National Income of an Expenditure Increase[a]
(billions of dollars)

	(1)	(2)	(3)	(4)	(5)	—	(N)	(N+1)
Y	70	70	71	71.8	72.44	—	75	75
T		10	10	10.0	10.00	—	10	10
C		50	50	50.8	51.44	—	54	54
S		10	10	10.2	10.36	—	11	11
I		10	10	10.0	10.00	—	10	10
G		10	11	11.0	11.00	—	11	11

[a]$MPC = \frac{4}{5}$.
$MPS = \frac{1}{5}$.
$m = \dfrac{1}{1 - MPC} = \dfrac{1}{1 - \frac{4}{5}} = 5$.
$m = \dfrac{1}{MPS} = \dfrac{1}{\frac{1}{5}} = 5$.

preceding period. The increases eventually approach zero, and *NNP* approaches the new equilibrium level shown by periods (N) and $(N + 1)$. approaches the new equilibrium level shown by periods (N) and $(N + 1)$ in which taxes plus savings are equal to government expenditures plus investment.

The *government expenditures multiplier* is the sum of the increases in *NNP* resulting from a one dollar increase in government spending, this sum being the same kind of geometric progression as that of the multiplier derived from a change in investment or a change in consumption; that is,

$$m = \frac{1}{1 - MPC} = \frac{1}{MPS}$$

and, if the *MPC* is $\frac{4}{5}$, the multiplier is 5. The $1 billion increase in government expenditures would bring about $5 billion rise in the level of *NNP* if the multiplier effects could work themselves out before other changes intervene. The increase in economic activity associated with the increase in *NNP* brings with it an increase in the employment level.

The effects of an increase in government expenditures are shown graphically in Figure 14-7 . The equilibrium level of national income is initially Y_e, the income level at which $C + I + G$ curve cuts the OE curve and at which $I + G = S + T$. All that is being earned is being spent, but the unemployment rate is assumed to be higher than that desired. The government now increases its spending on goods and services by $\triangle G$ in order to run a deficit. This shifts the $C + I + G$ curve upward by $\triangle G$ to $C + I + G_1$. The $I + G$ curve is shifted upward by the same amount to $I + G_1$. At the equilibrium level of income Y_e, investment spending plus government spending now exceeds savings plus investment. In the total spending diagram these are A_eH_e and A_eB_e, respectively, while in the savings–investment diagram they are Y_eK_e and Y_eJ_e, respectively. Total spending exceeds the total amount being earned; national income expands; and savings increase until at income level Y_1 government spending plus investment is no greater than tax collections plus savings.

Changes in Tax Collections, Expenditures Constant

Suppose we look now at the effects on national income of a decrease in tax collections, assuming that government expenditures are held constant. As in the last subsection, we assume that any government deficit is financed with newly created money or with funds that would have been hoarded

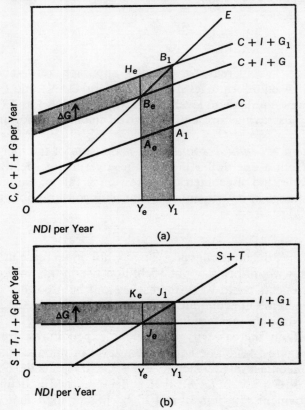

Figure 14-7
The effects of a change in G with T Constant.

otherwise. We also assume that the entire amount of the tax decrease is left to consumers to spend; that is, it increases household disposable income by the amount of the decrease.[4] Again we suppose that national income is initially in equilibrium at a less than full-employment level; that initially $T = G$ and $S = I$, or $S + T = G + I$; and that the marginal propensity to consume is $\frac{4}{5}$.

In Table 14-5 the impact of a $1 billion decrease in tax collections is shown by means of period analysis. Income is in equilibrium at $70 billion from period (1) to period (2). In period (3) the tax decrease is

TABLE 14-5
Effects on National Income of a Tax Decrease[a]
(billions of dollars)

	(1)	(2)	(3)	(4)	—	(N)	(N+1)
Y	70	70	70.8	71.46	—	74	74
T		10	9.0	9.00	—	9	9
C		50	50.8	51.44	—	54	54
S		10	10.2	10.36	—	11	11
I		10	10.0	10.00	—	10	10
G		10	10.0	10.00	—	10	10

[a]$MPC = \frac{4}{5}$.
$MPS = \frac{1}{5}$.
$m_t = \dfrac{1}{1 - MPC} - 1 = \dfrac{1}{1 - \frac{4}{5}} - 1 = 4.$
$m_t = \dfrac{1}{MPS} - 1 = \dfrac{1}{\frac{1}{5}} - 1 = 4.$

effected, leaving private disposable income for that period at $61 billion rather than at the $60 billion level of period (2). Of the extra $1 billion of private disposable income available in period (3), $.8 billion will be spent on consumption, raising the level of period (3) consumption to $50.8 billion. Savings are $10.2 billion, investment remains at $10 billion, and government expenditures are constant at $10 billion. Net national product for period (3) will be $70.8 billion—greater than it was in the preceding period by the amount of the increase in consumption in period (3). The pattern of increases for succeeding periods is the familiar one. The new and higher equilibrium level of income is approached as $S + T$ approaches $I + G$ or as total spending is approached by total earnings of

[4]*This would tend to be the case if the tax cut were made in the personal income tax only. If corporation income taxes and excise taxes were decreased, business disposable income and household disposable income would both be increased and the analysis would be correspondingly more complex. We shall keep our case as straightforward as possible.*

resource owners. The new equilibrium level of income is shown in the columns headed (N) and $(N+1)$.

The multiplier for a tax change is smaller than that for a change in investment, in consumption, or in government expenditures. The reason for this is easily seen. A \$1 billion increase in investment, in consumption, or in government expenditures in and of itself initially increases *NNP* by \$1 billion, while a \$1 billion decrease in tax does not. The decrease in taxes increases private disposable income, which then increases consumption by an amount equal to the increase in private disposables income (or the decrease in taxes) multiplied by the marginal propensity to consume. Thus the initial effect of a \$1 billion tax decrease on *NNP* when the *MPC* is $\frac{4}{5}$ will be only \$.8 billion, or $\frac{4}{5}$ of the tax decrease.

In effect, the geometric progression that we use to compute the tax-change multiplier is without the initial term in the series of numbers that we have been adding together. Whereas the sum of the geometric progression initiated by a government expenditure increase of one dollar when the *MPC* is $\frac{4}{5}$ is

$$1 + \tfrac{4}{5} + (\tfrac{4}{5})^2 + (\tfrac{4}{5})^3 + \cdots$$

that from a one dollar decrease in taxes is

$$\tfrac{4}{5} + (\tfrac{4}{5})^2 + (\tfrac{4}{5})^3 + \cdots$$

The initial one dollar increase at the beginning of the first summation is missing in the second, so that the total tax-change multiplier is 1 less than the investment, consumption, and government expenditure multiplier. Letting m represent the latter and m_t the tax-change multiplier, we can say while

$$m = \frac{1}{1 - MPC} = \frac{1}{MPS} \qquad (14.1)$$

that

$$m_t = \frac{1}{1 - MPC} - 1 = \frac{1}{MPS} - 1 \qquad (14.6)$$

If the *MPC* is $\frac{4}{5}$, then $m = 5$ and $m_t = 4$. So, for a tax decrease of \$1 billion, the increase in *NNP* will be \$4 billion if the tax-change multiplier can work itself out before other changes occur.

Figure 14-8 presents the graphic picture of the effects of a tax change. Suppose that Y_e is the equilibrium level of net disposable income, public and private. Total spending on consumption, investment, and government goods and services is $Y_e B_e$—indicated by the intersection of the $C + I + G$ curve and the OE curve—and is, of course, equal to *NDI* level Y_e. In the savings–investment diagram $S + T$ and $I + G$ are both at level $Y_e I_e$. We assume that at income level Y_e there is enough unemployment to cause concern.

What are the effects of a tax decrease of $\triangle T$? First, it increases consumption by an amount equal to the extra income left in the hands of consumers multiplied by the marginal propensity to consume; that is, by $\triangle T \cdot MPC$. The consumption function is shifted upward by this amount from C to C_1, thereby moving the $C + I + G$ curve upward by the *same amount* to $C_1 + I + G$. Offhand it would appear that the $S + T$ curve would be shifted downward by the amount of the tax decrease, but this is not quite so. Of the $\triangle T$ dollars left in the hands of the public, a part, equal to $\triangle T \cdot MPS$, will be saved. Thus the $S + T$ curve can be thought of as shifting downward by $\triangle T$ then upward by $\triangle T \cdot MPS$. This is, of course, a net shift downward of $\triangle T \cdot MPC$ to position $S_1 + T_1$.

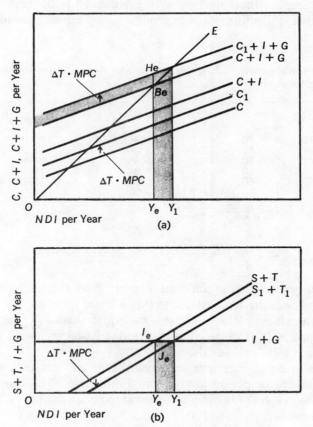

Figure 14-8
The effects of a change in T with G Constant.

At income level Y_e more is now being spent than is being earned. The amount being earned is Y_eB_e and the amount being spent is Y_eH_e. Or in terms of Figure 14-8(b), savings plus taxes are Y_eJ_e while investment plus government spending are Y_eI_e. Income increases until at level Y_1 savings have increased enough so that savings plus taxes are equal to investment plus government spending. All is being spent that is being earned and income is again in equilibrium at a level nearer to the full-employment level.

Equal Tax and Expenditure Changes

Thus far in analyzing the effects of government spending and taxation on the level of economic activity a balanced government budget with tax collections equal to expenditures has been treated as though it were neutral. This implies that, starting with a balanced budget, increases or decreases in tax collections and expenditures by equal amounts would

TABLE 14-6
Effects on National Income of an Equal Tax and Expenditure Increase[a]
(billions of dollars)

	(1)	(2)	(3)	(4)	—	(N)	(N+1)
NNP	70	70	70.2	70.36	—	71	71
T		10	11.0	11.00	—	11	11
C		50	49.2	49.36	—	50	50
S		10	9.8	9.84	—	10	10
I		10	10.0	10.00	—	10	10
G		10	11.0	11.00	—	11	11

[a]$MPC = \frac{4}{5}$.
$MPS = \frac{1}{5}$.
$m_b = m - m_t = 1$.

have no effect on the level of national income. With the tools of national income analysis we can demonstrate that this is not quite so. If tax collections and expenditures are increased by equal amounts, the level of national income will increase. If they are decreased by equal amounts, national income will decrease also.

The effects of equal increases in expenditures and tax collections are analyzed by means of period analysis in Table 14-6. The initial equilibrium $70 billion level of income is assumed to be a less than full-employment level. However, the government has a balanced budget with $G = T$, and at the same time $I = S$. The MPC is assumed to be $\frac{4}{5}$.

The increase in income is initiated in period (3). A $1 billion increase in taxes in that period leaves the private sector of the economy with $1 billion less in disposable income. If the *MPC* is $\frac{4}{5}$, consumption is reduced by $.8 billion and savings are reduced by $.2 billion. A corresponding increase in government expenditures of $1 billion raises *G* by that amount. Since investment spending has not been changed, the total value of goods produced in period (3) and the consequent income generated in that period is $C + I + G$, or $70.2 billion, an increase of $.2 billion over that earned in the preceding period.

In subsequent periods the increases in income increase consumption, which increases income, and so on, with each increase in consumption and income in any given period equal to that of the preceding period multiplied by the *MPC*. In period (4), for example, the amount available for spending is $.2 billion more than was available for period (3). Of this amount $1.6 billion will be spent on consumption, increasing consumption and income for period (4) by that amount. The sum of the increases in income in billions of dollars as the increases approach zero is

$$.2 + .2(\tfrac{4}{5}) + .2(\tfrac{4}{5})^2 + .2(\tfrac{4}{5})^3 + \cdots = .2\,\frac{(1)}{1 - \tfrac{4}{5}} = .2 : 5 = 1.0$$

The total increase in national income is just equal to the amount by which taxes and government expenditures are increased. The multiplier for this method of increasing the equilibrium level of national income is 1.[5]

Figure 14-9 presents the graphic analysis of the effects of equal tax and expenditure changes on the equilibrium level of income. Initial equilibrium is at level Y_e. With $S + T$ equal to $I + G$ and with $C + I + G$ crossing the OE line at that income level, total spending is just equal to total earnings per period.

How do we show the effects of an increase in tax collections of $\triangle T$ and of an increase in government expenditures of $\triangle G$? The increase in tax collections alone would shift the $S + T$ curve upward by $\triangle T$. However, since it also decreases private disposable income by $\triangle T$, savings at all possible income levels are decreased by $\triangle T$ multiplied by the *MPS*. Consequently, the *net upward shift* of the $S + T$ curve will be $\triangle T - (\triangle T \cdot$

---

[5] *Another way to compute the multiplier is to add together the government expenditures multiplier for the expenditure increase and the tax-change multiplier for the tax increase. With an MPC of $\frac{4}{5}$, then*

$$m = \frac{1}{1 - \tfrac{4}{5}} = 5 \quad and \quad m_t = \frac{1}{1 - \tfrac{4}{5}} - 1 = 4$$

so, letting m_b represent the balanced-budget multiplier

$$m_b = m - m_t = 5 - 4 = 1$$

The government expenditures multiplier will always be opposite in sign to the tax-change multiplier in computing the balanced-budget multiplier. (Why?)

MPS), leaving the curve in the position $S_1 + T_1$. The increase in government expenditures amounting to $\triangle G\ (= \triangle T)$ shifts the $I + G$ curve of Figure 14-9(b) upward by that amount to $I + G_1$. Since the $I + G$ curve is shifted upward by a greater amount than is the $S + T$ curve (the extra amount being $\triangle T \cdot MPS$), more is being spent than is being earned at income level Y_e and income will rise to some amount Y_1. At Y_1, $S_1 + T_1$ is equal to $I + G_1$.

In terms of Figure 14-9(a) an increase in government expenditures of $\triangle G$ by itself would shift the $C + I + G$ curve upward by that amount. But the tax increase of $\triangle T\ (= \triangle G)$ would shift the C curve downward by $\triangle T : MPC$. Consequently, the net upward shift of $C + I + G$ to $C_1 + I + G_1$ is equal to $\triangle G - \triangle T \cdot MPC$. At Y_e total spending exceeds total earning and Y will rise to the new equilibrium level Y_1.

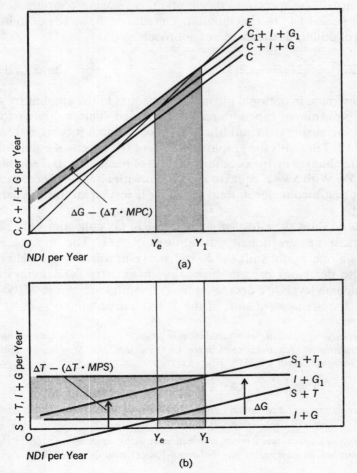

Figure 14-9
The effects of equal changes in G and T.

A Comparison of the Fiscal Policy Alternatives

By way of a brief summary, any one of the three fiscal policy routes may be used to change the equilibrium level of national income. They are not all equally efficient, since the multiplier effects differ for each of the three. In the final analysis, the selection among the alternative routes to fiscal stimulus or constraint depends heavily on pragmatic considerations such as "prior commitments" or "long-range ideology" of the government. Additionally, the scope and method of expansionary fiscal policy can also be constrained by factors such as anxiety over upward price pressures and balance of payments difficulties.

The multiplier effects are greatest for government expenditure changes used alone; they are less for tax changes used alone; and they are least for expenditure changes combined with equal changes in the same direction in tax collections. The multiplier for changes in government expenditures is the same as that for changes in investment and in consumption; that is $1/(1 - MPC)$. The tax-change multiplier is 1 less than that; that is, $1/(1 - MPC) - 1$. When expenditure changes are accompanied by tax changes of the same magnitude and in the same direction, the multiplier is 1— the change in the equilibrium level of national income is equal to the tax expenditure change.

There can be no question that federal fiscal policy contributed to the stability of the Canadian economy in the period 1945-1963. Looked at in broad terms over the shorter period since 1954, it appears that fiscal policy was pointed in the right direction and of the right magnitude about half the time, and was perverse in only three of the ten years considered, namely, 1959, 1960 and 1963.[6] Impressed by the 10-billion dollar cut in income taxes in the United States in 1964, the Canadian government reduced personal income tax rates in 1965, in spite of a budget deficit for the conscious and deliberate purpose of providing an expansionary impetus to the economy. Parenthetically, the U.S. tax cut of 1964 produced highly stimulating effects in the Canadian economy, "perhaps adding as much as a billion dollars to total demand in Canada in 1965-66".[7] Beginning in 1966, a restrictive fiscal policy was adopted to help close the inflationary gap of overall expenditures. Tax rates were raised and the rate of increase of government expenditure was cut. Fiscal restraints have recently been applied to the extent that the federal government surplus in

[6]*See the Royal Commission on Taxation*, Report. *Ottawa: Queen's Printer, 1966, Vol. 2, Chap. 3; and R. M. Will*, Canadian Fiscal Policy 1945-1963 (Study Number 17), *Queen's Printer, 1966, Chap. 5.*

[7]*Arthur J. R. Smith, "The Economic Council's Views on the 70's".* The Canadian Banker, *November-December 1969, p. 10.*

1969 was running at an annual rate of over $1 billion or about 1.3 percent of GNP. As 1970 opens, the Canadian government appears to be moving into a range of fiscal restraint approximating that which prevailed at the period of peak fiscal stringency during the Korean War in 1951.

Obstacles to the Use of Monetary and Fiscal Policies

The explanation above may give the impression that our monetary and fiscal authorities should have no great difficulty in stabilizing the economy. However, a number of conditions exist which tend to make effective use of monetary and fiscal policies difficult. Among the problems with which the monetary authorities must contend are the following: (1) The largest component of our money supply—chartered bank deposits—is dependent on the extent to which the banks extend loans and make investments and is thus in part removed from the control of the central bank. (2) Non-bank financial intermediaries are not directly subject to Bank of Canada regulation. Hence the indirect effect of central bank operations on non-bank iintermediaries' cash reserves is not as swift or as sure as the direct effect on chartered bank reserves. (3) The uneven impact on total borrowing of quantitative monetary controls may provide a "political" offset to policies of monetary restraint, for unsatisfied borrowers, who plead unfair discrimination, are not given to suffering in silence, as indicated by the widespread criticism of "tight money" during the mid-1950's. (4) The reduced dependence of businesses on external financing also lessens the effectiveness of traditional monetary restraints. (5) More important, the Bank of Canada has only a limited degree of independence to pursue any basic course of policy which does not evolve in relatively close accord with monetary conditions in the United States due to the interconnectedness of our respective price levels, interest rates and exchange rates.

Obstacles to applying fiscal controls include the following: (1) Since it is generally politically inexpedient to increase taxes and politically advantageous to lower them, such considerations may tend to become more powerful than the desire to secure economic stability. (2) Tax structures are very complicated and Parliament does not care to enter into this complicated matter any more often than necessary. Moreover, whenever taxes are to be changed, various pressure groups seek to exert influence in their own favour. Here again political considerations make it difficult to offset fluctuations in employment and prices, and to stimulate economic growth. (3) Under our federal system of government there are many expenditure and revenue programs. Hence, no one overall fiscal policy can be established. Thus provincial and municipal governments may carry on policies exactly opposite to that necessary for successful economic stabilization. (4) It is difficult to adjust government spending to fit stabilization needs. No government is likely to reduce defence spending or welfare payments as an anti-inflationary measure for obvious reasons. Similarly, major public works under construction must be completed even if the expenditures involved increase inflationary pressures.

Clearly there are inherent limitations to the ability of fiscal and monetary policies to advance us toward our macroeconomic objectives. Nevertheless stabilization policies which are soundly conceived, and wisely applied, can be of vital importance for the economy as a whole.

Coordination of Monetary and Fiscal Policy

Before leaving our study of the stabilizing tools at the command of the government, we should emphasize once more that monetary and fiscal policies are complementary instruments. Where there is a clearly visible need to expand or restrain the economy, both can be used in the same direction. They can also be used in more subtle ways in order to accommodate special sectoral problems within the total economy. It may be, for example, that a balance-of-payments crisis[8] coincides with a period of considerable slack in the economy, as happened in Canada in 1962. In such a situation fiscal policy may be employed (*via* a series of tax cuts, etc.) in order to provide the major expansionary force, while monetary conditions may be tightened in an effort to attract a net inflow of capital large enough to cover the current account deficit and rebuild the depleted foreign exchange reserves. Given other circumstances, it might be preferable to shift a larger share of the burden of restraint to fiscal devices and thus allow some easing in monetary and credit conditions.

Summary

National income tends to move toward an equilibrium level, but there is nothing inherently "good" about equilibrium. An equilibrium level of income does not guarantee that there will be full employment, economic

[8]*Balance of payments disequilibria are discussed in Chapter 17 of this book.*

stability, and economic growth. Leaving government to one side, the savings function and the level of investment determine the equilibrium level of income. It may be an income level at which there is unemployment or it may be one that will generate inflation. If at the full-employment level of income more is saved than investors want to invest, there is a deflationary gap and national income will fall to a less than full-employment level. If at the full-employment level investors desire to invest more than is currently being saved, there is an inflationary gap and national income will rise in dollar terms but not in real terms. National income may also by chance be at a level at which there is full employment and price stability.

A change in the level of investment and/or a change in the position of the consumption function changes the equilibrium level of national income by more than the initial change in either the one or the other. Such changes are subject to multiplier effects. Instability of investment or of consumption over time leads to amplified changes in national income.

The multiplier, numerically equal to $1(1 — MPC)$ or $1/MPS$, is a number that when multiplied by the initial change in the level of investment or consumption shows the change in *NNP* and *NDI*.

Monetary policy can be used to control fluctuations in national income or to move the equilibrium level up or down, depending upon the economic objectives sought. Monetary policy operates on the positions of the consumption function and the investment curve, with an easy money policy tending to increase them and a tight money policy tending to make them contract. Any changes induced in either by monetary policy will produce amplified effects on national income by way of the multiplier.

Fiscal policy provides an additional means of governmental control over the level of national income. If expenditures are changed while tax collections are held constant, national income will tend to change in the same direction as the expenditures change, since *G* is a component of *NNP*. But the change in *G* will also generate the same kinds of *multiplier effects* on the equilibrium level of national income as do changes in the other two components of national income—consumption and investment.

Changes in tax collections with government expenditures constant bring about changes in private disposable income that in turn induce changes in the position of the consumption function. The shifts in consumption in turn exert multiplier effects on the equilibrium level of national income. However, the multiplier for tax changes is always 1 less than that for changes in investment, consumption, or government expenditures.

Changes in government expenditures accompanied by tax changes of the same magnitude and in the same direction have a multiplier effect of 1 on the level of national income. An expenditure increase by itself would have a positive multiplier effect. A tax increase of the same amount would have a negative multiplier effect that is 1 less than that for the tax increase. Subtracting the latter from the former leaves us with a magnitude of 1 for the equal tax-expenditure multiplier.

There are several major obstacles to applying monetary and fiscal controls. However, in spite of these difficulties, stabilization policies have great potentialities for contributing to economic growth and stability, especially if they are properly coordinated.

Exercises and Questions for Discussion

1. What is an inflationary gap? a deflationary gap? What fiscal and monetary policy measures could be used to eliminate each? Discuss the process by which a new equilibrium would be reached after the introduction of each type of policy measure.
2. Suppose the economy is suffering from inflation and yet its growth rate is less than satisfactory. Can the government do anything about these problems? Explain.
3. "If the economy is at full employment and the government needs to make more expenditures for, say, a war, the proper course to follow is to increase government expenditures with an equal increase in taxes." Evaluate this statement.
4. "During inflation most people's real incomes tend to fall. Therefore, the proper policy for the government to follow is one of decreasing taxes or increasing transfer payments to put more money in the hands of consumers." Comment critically.
5. Suppose the government has a balanced budget. If it now decides to increase expenditures and decrease taxes, what will be the effect on *NNP* and *NDI*? Make the necessary assumptions and explain graphically and verbally.
6. An increase in investment will cause a multiple increase in *NNP*. Explain how this occurs. Will the final effect be larger or smaller than our theory would predict? Why?

Selected Readings

Dernburg, T. F., and D. M. McDougall, *Macro-Economics*. New York: McGraw-Hill Book Company, Inc., 1968, Chaps. 5 and 6.

Heilbroner, Robert L., *Understanding Macroeconomics*. Englewood Cliffs, N.J.: Prentice-Hall, Inc., 1965, Chaps. 7, 8, and 10.

McKenna, J. P., *Aggregate Economic Analysis*, rev. ed. New York: Holt, Rinehart and Winston, Inc., 1965, Chaps. 5, 11, and 15.

Shapiro, Edward, *Macroeconomic Analysis*. New York: Harcourt, Brace & World, Inc., 1966, Chaps. 9 and 15.

Part 3

The World Economy

The economy of Canada, or of any other country, does not operate in isolation from the rest of the world. We carry on trade with other countries, opening up new opportunities for increasing the level of want satisfaction that all parties to trade can attain and, at the same time, creating some very serious problems. In Part 3 we examine both the opportunities and the problems.

The opportunities that are opened up by international trade are of the same basic nature as those arising from all voluntary exchanges. We read and hear so much about the problems arising from international trade and so little about the opportunities presented by it that many must wonder why we bother with it at all. Consequently, Chapter 15 is centred around the modification and application of principles already learned to the world economy so that we might see clearly at the outset why world trade is desirable.

The problems arise from the institutional arrangements that the countries of the world have devised for carrying on trade. In order to understand the problems we must understand the institutional arrangements. Thus, in Chapter 16 we examine the financing of international trade. Chapter 17 focuses on the factors that determine exchange rates and the causes of balance of payments surpluses and deficits. Tariff problems provide the subject matter of Chapter 18. Chapter 19 is concerned with one of the most challenging problems of our times—that of the economically underdeveloped countries.

15

The Basis of International Trade

In this and the following chapters the economic horizons are expanded from those of a single economy to those of the world. Most of the principles developed thus far are as applicable to the world economy as they are to the more limited framework within which they were discussed. However, the world economy has certain unique characteristics that make it advisable to treat trade among its nations separately. Its special characteristics are nationalism, a sort of national consciousness or pride, and problems of exchange among different national currencies, both of which induce nations to restrict the free flow of people, capital resources, goods, and services across their borders. The gains possible from international trade are the same as those to be had from any voluntary exchange. But the principle that all parties gain from voluntary exchange is even less understood for the world economy than it is for national and local economies. Thus, some of the possibilities of gains from international trade are spelled out in this chapter in some detail.

Patterns of Trade

With whom does Canada trade and what are the principle items exchanged? Trade patterns are quite complex. We sell merchandise of many kinds to most countries of the world and we buy merchandise from them. In addition, we buy and sell such services as insurance and transportation for goods and services and for people. We invest in businesses in other countries and foreigners invest in Canadian enterprises. International borrowing and lending are commonplace. In this section we shall confine our attention to the more obvious merchandise trade which constitutes about three fourths of the total value of our foreign trade of all kinds.

Trade Patterns by Countries

The countries with whom Canada carries on a significant volume of trade are listed in Table 15-1 and are ranked by the value of Canadian merchandise exports to them. The value of our exports to the United States far exceeds that to any other single country. Exports to the United Kingdom are next in line, while those to Japan and West Germany follow. Australia, the Netherlands and Communist China round out the seven most important merchandise export markets. The relative importance of Canada's exports to the People's Republic of China, however, is a very recent development.

On the import side the United States again leads the list. The United Kingdom is our second most important foreign supplier of goods, followed by Japan and Venezuela. Imports from West Germany are fifth, followed by France and Italy.

The data show that an overwhelming proportion of Canada's international trade is with two countries—the United States and the United Kingdom—and of the two, the United States is by far the more important. Americans buy about 70 percent of our exports and furnish nearly 75 percent of our imports. Britain purchases nearly 9 percent of our exports and supplies about 6 percent of our imports. The balance of our external trade is distributed among more than a hundred countries.

The reasons underlying our massive trade with the United States reside partly in historical factors, such as cultural, political, linguistic and ethnic similarities,[1] but mainly they reflect the high degree of complementarity between the two economies with Canada exchanging mainly raw or partially-processed primary products for highly manufactured capital and consumer goods. Geographic proximity is also important.[2]

In several instances there are rather large differences between the value of our exports to a country and that of our imports from it. The United States, Britain, Japan, and Venezuela provide excellent examples. These differences may, among other things, reflect the multilateral aim of our

[1]For some candid and contemporary Canadian opinions of the United States, see Al Purdy (ed.), The New Romans. Edmonton: M. G. Hurtig Ltd., 1968.

[2]For a useful recent discussion of the trends in Canada's exports and imports, see G. W. Wilson, S. Gordon, S. Judek, Canada: An Appraisal of Its Needs and Resources. New York: Twentieth Century Fund, 1965, pp. 154-67.

TABLE 15-1
Canadian Trade in Merchandise by Country, 1968.
(millions of dollars)

Country	Exports	Imports
United States	8892.0	9057.1
United Kingdom	1209.6	696.1
Japan	606.8	360.2
Federal Republic of West Germany	228.9	298.9
Australia	185.7	76.0
Netherlands	179.5	69.0
Communist China	163.2	23.4
Italy	131.2	114.5
Belgium and Luxembourg	127.4	57.5
Norway	116.3	39.2
India	111.3	38.3
Venezuela	102.5	357.8
U.S.S.R.	88.6	21.7
France	81.4	121.6
Republic of South Africa	68.3	39.3
Mexico	55.4	52.2
Brazil	48.2	38.7
Argentina	48.0	5.4
Cuba	45.0	5.1
Spain	41.1	25.6
Puerto Rico	37.8	2.5
Philippines	34.5	2.8
Jamaica	34.4	33.9
New Zealand	31.8	18.6
Sweden	31.7	78.0
Switzerland	30.8	64.3
All countries	13,220.[1]	12,358.[1]
Re-exports[2]	354	
Total	13,574	12,358
United States	9,180	9,048
United Kingdom	1,226	696
Other countries	3,168	2,614
Total	13,574	12,358

[1]*Columns will not add up to total due to omissions of smaller trade figures.*
[2]*Exports by Canada of nondomestically produced merchandise (i.e. exports of foreign products).*
Sources: Dominion Bureau of Statistics, Trade of Canada, Exports by Countries 1968; DBS, Trade of Canada, Imports by Countries, 1968; Bank of Canada, Statistical Summary, July, 1969.

trade policy. We buy more goods from the United States than we sell to the United States. The United States may in turn buy more from the United Kingdom and other countries of western Europe than she sells to them. In turn, these other countries may buy more from us than they sell to us. Thus, although large differences may exist between the value of our exports to and that of our imports from a specific country, the difference between the value of our total exports to all countries and of our total imports from all countries will not be as great.[3]

[3]*We obtain a better overall look at what a nation earns abroad as compared with what it spends abroad in the next chapter. Table 15-1 is somewhat misleading in this respect, since it lists only the* merchandise items *that are traded.*

Products Traded

The major groups of merchandise items, together with their values, that make up the trade of Canada with other countries are listed in Tables 15-2 and 15-3. Looking first at Table 15-2, we find that metals and minerals head the list of our exports to other countries. When we consider the abundant supply and diversification of mineral resources in Canada, the continuing large-scale investment of capital for exploration and development and the expansion of existing production facilities, and the adoption of new mining techniques, this is not surprising. The most remarkable development in Canadian external trade in recent years has been the rise to prominence of automotive exports. This phenomena reflects the rapid development of the Canadian automobile industry generally and the Canada-United States Automotive Agreement,[4] signed in 1965, in par-

TABLE 15-2
Canadian Merchandise Exports, 1968

Commodity Group		Millions of Dollars
1. Metals and minerals		3,874
Copper, nickel and products	1,064	
Crude petroleum and natural gas	604	
Aluminum and products	463	
Iron ore	443	
Primary iron and steel	354	
Lead, zinc and products	231	
Other metals and minerals[1]	715	
2. Motor Vehicles and parts		2,665
3. Forest products		2,595
Newsprint	990	
Woodpulp	628	
Soft wood lumber	623	
Other products[2]	354	
4. Sundry manufactures		2,090
Aircraft and parts	369	
Other products[3]	1,721	
5. Farm and fish products		1,580
Wheat and wheat flour	743	
Barley, oats and rye	52	
Other farm and fish[4]	785	
6. Chemicals and fertilizers		417
7. Exports of foreign products		354
Total exports		13,574

[1]*Largely asbestos, silver and products, uranium, platinum and abrasives.*
[2]*Mainly pulpwood, plywoods, veneers, hardwood lumber, logs, pit props, poles and paper products.*
[3]*Mainly machinery (both farm and nonfarm) and parts, electrical apparatus, textiles and beverages.*
[4]*Mainly fishery products, other grains, livestock, meat and dairy products and furs.*
Source: Bank of Canada, Statistical Summary. June, 1969, pp. 475-76.

[4]*See p. 410 for a discussion of the automotive program.*

TABLE 15-3
Canadian Merchandise Imports, 1968

Commodity Group		Millions of Dollars
1. Motor vehicles and parts		3,133
2. Industrial materials		2,675
Ores and primary metals & minerals	794	
Chemical materials	540	
Textiles, furs and leather materials	538	
Primary farm materials	54	
Other industrial materials	749	
3. Producers equipment		2,619
Construction, conveying and mining equipment[1]	397	
Tractors and agricultural machinery	353	
Power generation and transmission equipment	288	
Other special industries machinery[2]	420	
Other producers equipment[3]	1,161	
4. Consumer goods		2,037
Food[4]	819	
Durables	648	
Other nondurables and semi-durables	571	
5. Fuels and lubricants		782
6. Transportation equipment and parts (excl. motor vehicles)		525
7. Construction materials		311
8. Special items[5]		275
Total imports		12,358

[1]*Comprises conveying, elevating, material handling, construction, excavating, mining, petroleum and natural gas industries equipment.*
[2]*Comprises mainly wood, paper, metal working, printing, book binding, textiles, leather, food and tobacco industries equipment.*
[3]*Comprises mainly industrial furnaces and linings, other general purpose industrial machinery, communications industry equipment, precision instruments, scientific and medical equipment, hand tools, office equipment and furniture.*
[4]*Includes non-alcoholic beverages.*
[5]*Mainly shipments valued at less than $200 each and Canadian exports returned.*
Source: Bank of Canada, Statistical Summary. June, 1969, p. 477.

ticular. Moving down the list we find that large amounts, measured in value terms, of forest products—newsprint, pulp, lumber—and farm and fish products—grain and cereal preparations—are sold abroad. The tremendous land resources available for producing merchantable timber and for agricultural purposes in Canada and the continuing improvement of forest and agricultural technology makes us relatively efficient in the production of these items. Chemicals and fertilizers and aircraft and parts follow in descending order of value, exports of both go mainly to the United States. Additionally, there is a very long list of other manufactured products that we export, lumped together in the "other" manufacturing classification. Not one of these is as important in value terms, however, as those listed, but in the aggregate they form a large part of our exports.

On the import side, fully manufactured products dominate the scene. The large imports of automobiles and parts, and various kinds of machinery and equipment reflect the relative smallness of our domestic market which makes us relatively inefficient in the production of these items. We import large amounts of industrial and construction materials to be used in manufacturing a number of intermediate and end products. We also import large amounts of consumer goods. The fuels and lubricants group rounds out our classification of imports.

We seem to be both important exporters of and importers of some specific products—automobiles and parts, aircraft and parts, agricultural machinery, and fuels and lubricants are cases in point. Part of the explanation of this apparent paradox lies in the classification of products. Many exchanges of this sort arise from specialization of different countries on specific kinds of goods within each of the categories. General classifications are likely to hide or mask such internal differences. But as far as petroleum and coal are concerned, the explanation lies in high transportation costs. It is cheaper for users in Ontario and Quebec to import American coal, mined in fields just across the Great Lakes, than to buy it many hundreds of miles away from producers in Alberta or Nova Scotia. Similarly, huge oil deposits are located in Western Canada but existing pipelines extend only as far east as Ontario. Accordingly, the large Quebec market is served principally by oil from Venezuela which is cheaply delivered by ocean tanker to Portland, Maine, and thence transported by pipeline to Quebec.

The Gains from Trade

Why do countries carry on trade with one another. Why does Canada import textiles, tractors, mining equipment, durable consumer goods, and a host of other items? Why do we sell automobiles, wheat and newsprint abroad? Surely our production possibilities are diverse enough so that we could produce as many of these things as we really need to live in reasonable comfort. In this section we consider the bases of trade among countries, with the primary objective being to show why trade is advantageous to all the parties that engage in it voluntarily. We are not at this point interested in determining the exact terms at which trade will take place.

Specialization and Exchange

Specialization and exchange are characteristic of the modern economic world. We do not expect any one family to produce all that it consumes. Aside from the personal services that its members render for one another, one family may produce nothing of what it consumes. Its resources usually do not produce a complete product of any kind but contribute to the making of parts of products only. Each family's resources are specialized to these parts of productive processes and the incomes that they earn from placing those resources in employment are used to buy the complete products and services that the family consumes. The resources of many families contribute to the production of the goods and services so purchased.

Similarly, communities and regions of any one country trade with one another, each specializing in the production of certain products or parts of products. One community produces crude oil but another may refine it. One region produces iron ore but another may smelt it. Still another community builds automobiles. All carry on exchange with one another and all buy the finished products.

Nations trade with one another in essentially the same way. We purchase machinery from the United States, textiles from Japan, and bananas from Central America. We sell automobiles, wheat and many kinds of forest products to the countries from which we buy. But why do nations (or regions or individuals) find such specialization and exchange advantageous?

Principle of Comparative Advantage

Specialization of countries in the production of certain goods and services and the resulting exchange among them makes larger supplies available to each country than would be possible otherwise. Thus consumers in each of the countries are able to obtain larger quantities of the goods and services they want than could in the absence of trade. Voluntary trade raises the standards of living of each participating country.[5] The underlying principle involved is called the *principle of comparative advantage*. Essentially it states that if countries (or regions or individuals) specialize in producing the things that they can produce with *relatively* greater efficiency than other countries, trading some of these for other goods and services, all parties to the exchanges can gain. The remainder of this subsection explains and elaborates on this common sense principle.

Alternative Costs Revisited

The principle of comparative advantage depends so heavily on a

[5]*The actions that different countries take to restrict their trade with other countries would appear to refute these statements. Surely the governments of all countries want the highest possible standards of living for their citizens! Unfortunately, the best interests of the general public within a country do not always coincide with the best interests of particular producing groups that want to suppress competition from abroad and who have the ears of lawmakers. Unfortunately, too, we do not seem to be able to devise a system of international payments that will permit a free flow of goods and services among the countries of the world.*

thorough understanding of the *alternative cost doctrine,* or the *principle of opportunity costs,* that a restatement of that concept is in order.[6] Suppose that a country's resources can be used to produce either alarm clocks or eggbeaters and that its resources are fully employed, producing some combination of the two. What is the real cost of an alarm clock? For the consuming public as a whole the cost of an alarm clock can only be the amount of eggbeaters that must be forgone to produce it. A one-unit increase in the production of alarm clocks draws resources away from the production of eggbeaters, reducing the eggbeater output. If a one-unit increase in the output of alarm clocks reduces the output of eggbeaters by three units, then the cost of an alarm clock is three eggbeaters. Similarly, the cost of an eggbeater is one third of an alarm clock. The real cost of a unit of any good or service, therefore, is the quantities of alternative goods and services that must be forgone in order for that unit to be produced.

Production Possibilities without Trade

Now let there be two countries, *A* and *B*, with resources suitable for producing both alarm clocks and eggbeaters. Suppose that resource prices in each country are given and fixed. If they remain constant throughout the analysis, we can measure the total resource supplies in each country in terms of their total value in whatever monetary units are used. To avoid exchange rate problems—to be discussed in Chapter 17—suppose that both countries use dollars. Suppose, also, that in each country the average and marginal costs of producing both alarm clocks and eggbeaters are constant, that is, they do not vary as outputs per unit of time are changed.[7]

If the total resource supplies available per unit of time in country *A* age worth $400; if the money cost of producing an eggbeater is $4; and if the money cost of producing an alarm clock is also $4, the production possibilities of the country are easily determined. If no alarm clocks are produced, the economy can turn out 100 eggbeaters. Or, if no eggbeaters are produced, 100 alarm clocks are possible. If the economy is currently producing 100 alarm clocks and wants 10 eggbeaters, the latter can be obtained by giving up 10 alarm clocks, using the released resources to produce the eggbeaters. The real cost of an eggbeater in country *A* is thus one alarm clock, and the real cost of an alarm clock is one eggbeater. Country *A*'s production possibilities are listed in the "without trade" columns of Table 15-4 for 10-unit changes in the level of production of

---

[6]*See Vol. I p. 145.*

[7]*None of these assumptions is critical to the results that we shall develop. They do reduce greatly the complexity of the analysis.*

both alarm clocks and eggbeaters, but if we so desire we can interpolate the additional production possibilities lying between any two of those listed. In Figure 15-1 the production possibility curve of country *A* is the line *KL*.

Turning to country *B*'s production possibilities, let us suppose that $1500 worth of resources are available, that it takes $15 worth of resources to produce an alarm clock, and that $5 worth of resources are required to produce an eggbeater. If no alarm clocks are produced the

TABLE 15-4
Production Possibilities of Country A

WITHOUT TRADE[a]		WITH TRADE[b]	
ALARM CLOCKS	EGGBEATERS	ALARM CLOCKS	EGGBEATERS
100	0	100	0
90	10	90	20
80	20	80	40
70	30	(1) 70	60
60	40	60	80
50	50	50	100
40	60	(2) 40	120
30	70	30	140
20	80	20	160
10	90	(3) 10	180
0	100	0	200

[a]*Assume that resource prices are given and fixed; that $400 worth of resources are available; that $4 worth of resources are necessary to produce one alarm clock; and that $4 worth of resources are necessary to produce one eggbeater.*
[b]*The terms of trade are one alarm clock for two eggbeaters.*

output of eggbeaters could be 300. If no eggbeaters are produced the resources of the country would permit the production of 100 alarm clocks. In order to increase the rate of alarm clock output by one unit, three eggbeaters per unit of time must be given up. Conversely, a one-unit increase in the rate of eggbeater output requires the sacrifice of one third of an alarm clock per unit of time. Some of the alternative combinations that could be produced are listed in the "without trade" columns of Table 15-5 . All possible combinations are showns by *RS* in Figure 15-2 .

Comparative Costs of Production

How does the cost of producing an eggbeater in country *A* compare with that in country *B*? We have assumed that only $4 worth of resources are required to produce one unit in country *A* while $5 worth are neces-

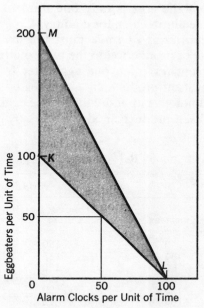

Figure 15-1
Production possibilities of country A before and after trade.

sary in country *B*, so it appears that country *A* can produce them at lower cost. *But the comparative money costs are misleading*—the alternative cost doctrine comes forth to save us from making this common mistake! In country *A* one alarm clock must be given up to obtain an eggbeater, so this is the *real cost* of producing an eggbeater in that country. In country *B only one third of an alarm clock* must be given up to obtain an eggbeater, so the *real cost* of producing an eggbeater is lower in country *B* than it is in country *A*. Country *B* has a comparative advantage in the production of eggbeaters.

The real cost of producing alarm clocks is lower in country *A*. In country *A* an alarm clock requires the sacrifice of one eggbeater. To produce an alarm clock in country *B*, three eggbeaters must be given up. Country *A* has a comparative advantage in the production of alarm clocks.

Production Possibilities with Trade

Suppose that each country specializes in the production of the product for which it has a comparative advantage—country *A* in alarm clocks and country *B* in eggbeaters. Country *A* has a real cost advantage in producing alarm clocks—the cost is only one eggbeater as compared with three eggbeaters for country *B*. Country *B* has a real cost advantage in producing eggbeaters—the cost is only one third of an alarm clock as compared with a whole alarm clock for country A.

Limits within which *terms of trade* must fall are determined by the comparative real costs of production in the two countries. Country A will not be willing to accept *less* than one eggbeater for each alarm clock given up, since it can itself produce an eggbeater by giving up an alarm clock. Country B will not give up *more* than three eggbeaters for an alarm clock because it can itself produce an alarm clock by giving up three egg-

TABLE 15-5
Production Possibilities of Country B

WITHOUT TRADE[a]		WITH TRADE[b]	
ALARM CLOCKS	EGGBEATERS	ALARM CLOCKS	EGGBEATERS
100	0	150	0
90	30	135	30
80	60	120	60
70	90	105	90
60	120	(3) 90	120
50	150	75	150
40	180	(2) 60	180
30	210	45	210
20	240	(1) 30	240
10	270	15	270
0	300	0	300

[a]*Assume that resource prices are given and fixed; that $1500 worth of resources are available; that $15 worth of resources are necessary to produce an alarm clock; and that $5 worth of resources are necessary to produce an eggbeater.*
[b]*The terms of trade are one alarm clock for two eggbeaters.*

beaters. The terms of trade must fall between one alarm clock for one eggbeater and one alarm clock for three eggbeaters. Suppose they come to rest at one alarm clock for two eggbeaters.

Through specialization on alarm clocks country A's production possibilities are improved by these terms of trade. Before trade country A could obtain only one eggbeater for each forgone alarm clock. Now, by giving up an alarm clock, two eggbeaters can be obtained. Formerly by giving up 10 alarm clocks only 10 eggbeaters could be produced. Now 10 alarm clocks can be traded for 20 eggbeaters. The "with trade" columns of Table 15-4 and the line ML in Figure 15-1 show the new production possibilities.

We refer to the combinations of goods available to country A through trade with country B as "production" possibilities, although strictly speaking eggbeaters are not produced directly by country A—they are traded for. Yet, it is exactly as though country A had discovered some

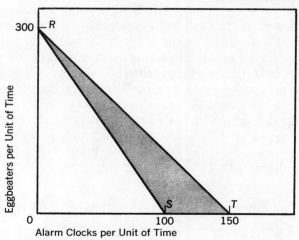

Figure 15-2
Production possibilities of country B before and after trade.

new technique for producing eggbeaters that enabled her resources to turn out a 100 percent larger volume of eggbeaters at a given cost than before. This is precisely what international trade does for a country. Whenever goods can be imported at a cost lower than would be required to produce them at home their importation at the lower cost is analytically identical to the discovery and use of lower-cost technology in producing them at home.

The "with trade" columns of Table 15-5 and the line *RT* in Figure 15-2 show the production possibilities to country *B* available from specialization in the production of eggbeaters and from trading for alarm clocks. Whereas before trade country *B* found it necessary to give up three eggbeaters to obtain an alarm clock, with trade only two eggbeaters need be sacrificed. If all of country *B*'s resources are used in eggbeater production, a total of 300 per unit of time can be produced. By giving up 30 of these 15 alarm clocks can be obtained. Still another 30 eggbeaters can be traded for an additional 15 alarm clocks, making a combination of 30 alarm clocks and 240 eggbeaters available to consumers of the country. Other possible combinations are listed in the table and are plotted in Figure 15-2. Through specialization and trade the efficiency with which alarm clocks can be obtained is increased by 50 percent.

Note that the gains from trade do not in any way depend upon money costs of production being lower in a country than in those with which it trades. Resources in country *A* may be cheap relative to resources in country *B*. Country *A* may be able to produce both alarm clocks *and* eggbeaters at lower *money costs* than country *B*—in fact, in the illustration this is assumed to be the case. Still, both countries can be better off with trade. All that is ncessary in order for both parties to gain is that the *eggbeater cost* or *real cost* of producing alarm clocks be different in country *A* than in country *B* and that, correspondingly, *alarm clock costs* or *real costs* of producing eggbeaters be different in the two countries. (In order to grasp this point firmly, rework the entire set of illustrations, assuming that in Country *A* the *money costs* of producing alarm clocks and eggbeaters are each two dollars instead of four dollars each. What do you think, now, about the commonly expressed idea that as a nation it is to our disadvantage to import goods made with "cheap foreign labour?"

The Bases of Trade

Hopefully, the gains from trade available to countries as a result of specialization in the production of goods and services in which they have a comparative advantage and trade for those in which they have a comparative disadvantage are clearly understood. In this section we probe beneath the surface to determine why it is that comparative advantages crop up for some products while comparative disadvantages appear for others. The reason are not tremendously profound or complex—indeed, they are rather ordinary—but they need to be catalogued.

Differences in Resource Endowments

Comparative advantages or disadvantages in the production of specific foods and services arise among countries partly because of differences in resource endowments. Countries differ in their holdings of both capital resources and labour resources. We shall consider each in turn.

Capital Resources

The so-called natural resources comprise one general class of capital resources that are very unequally distributed among nations. Some countries have an abundance of rich agricultural land while others have arid desert areas and wastelands. There are a limited number of areas especially suited for growing coffee beans; grapes cannot be cultivated in all areas with equal efficiency; some regions favour the growth of forests. Most of us find that the land we own does not contain substantial deposits of gold, oil, diamonds, or uranium—each of these seem to be clustered in relatively small parts of the world. Diversity among countries in available natural resources is characteristic of the world economy.

Countries also differ widely in the quantities and kinds of capital equipment that they have accumulated over time. The Scandinavian countries have accumulated large quantities of ocean-going vessels. Canada has accumulated much equipment for producing electric power, automobiles, and even agricultural products. Some of our less fortunate world neighbours have accumulated relatively small amounts of capital and thus have comparative disadvantages in producing products requiring large ratios of capital equipment to labour.

Labour Resources

Large qualitative differences exist among the labour resources of different countries. General skill levels tend to vary directly with the amount of education available to the labour force, so that countries with better educational facilities for the whole population tend to have relatively more highly skilled workers. Within specific skill levels the types of skills are likely to be very different among different countries. German and Japanese labourers are noted for their skill in producing optical equipment. Labour in Canada is particularly adept at tasks requiring mechanical aptitude. India and Mexico have some of the world's best bronze and silver craftsmen.

In terms of quantities, some economies are comparatively long on labour resources and short on capital resources while others have smaller ratios of labour to capital. In the Far East birth rates are high, per capita incomes are low, and capital accumulation is slow, so that labour is comparatively abundant and inexpensive. Countries in such areas tend to have a comparative advantage in producing products requiring high ratios of labour to capital. In other economies the ratio of labour to capital is much smaller, permitting labour to be more productive and consequently much more expensive relative to capital. Countries like these tend to enjoy a comparative advantage in the production of goods for which low ratios of labour to capital are needed.

Differences in the Resource Mix

The diversity among countries with respect to resource endowments makes it inevitable that there are areas of comparative advantage for some products and of comparative disadvantage for others for any given country *vis-à-vis* the world economy. Certainly we would not expect any two countries to have the identical mix of resources, and therefore it would indeed by surprising to find that the real costs of production of *all* products in one country are the same as they are in another.

Among most countries, differences in the proportions in which resources are available are abundantly evident. With respect to Canada, the United States clearly has a comparative advantage in the production of heavy machinery, and a comparative disadvantage in the production of newsprint. Although Canada could produce large and highly specialized machines, the productive facilities and market conditions of the United States are much better suited for this type of endeavour. On the other hand, our productive forests, which cover nearly one million square miles, and the special skills for paper making that have been developed over time in Canada make it evident that the latter has a comparative advantage in this line of production.

Particularly glaring are the differences that exist in the capital to labour ratios of different countries. By and large the highly developed countries of western Europe, Great Britain, the United States, and Canada have relatively large proportions of capital to labour, while the underdeveloped areas of South America, Africa, and Asia have much lower capital to labour ratios. This means that the highly developed countries tend to have comparative advantages in *capital-intensive* kinds of production, or lines of production requiring high capital to labour ratios. The comparative advantages of the underdeveloped areas tend to lie in more *labour-intensive* lines of endeavour. This state of affairs is not at all to the liking of many underdeveloped countries and, rather than pursuing the gains available from their comparative advantage, they often attempt to develop relatively high-cost lines of industrial production by shutting out competitive industrial imports, a practice that makes industrial goods more costly to them than they would be otherwise.

Differences in Technology

Specific lines of comparative advantage and disadvantage also arise partly because of differences in the technology used in different countries. Among different countries we can identify (1) different general levels of technology and (2) different types of technology. Both are, of course, closely related to the differences in the resources available to the countries.

Different Levels of Technology

We find wide variations in the general levels of technology used as we look at the underdeveloped countries of the world on the one hand and at the advanced countries on the other. In India, for example, agricultural methods are primitive compared with those used in the western world, with water buffalos still widely used for pulling walking plows. In South

American wheat production, grain separators that have not been seen in Canada for 20 years provide a common method of threshing wheat. In most African countries neither the know-how for producing electrical appliances nor the electricity required for operating them is generally available.

Simply to list such examples is to point to why differences in technology come into being. Advanced levels of technology stem from two primary sources: (1) comparatively high levels of educational attainment and (2) adequate stocks of capital equipment on which technical know-how can be put to work. The extent to which these are available differs greatly among countries.

Different Types of Technology

Different countries of the world tend to develop their own special kinds of technological proficiencies, heavily influenced by the kinds of resources available in each. Countries with abundant coal and iron ore deposits are likely to develop an efficient steel-making technology. Maritime economies may develop more sophisticated fishing or ship-building techniques. In view of the vast land areas of Canada, is it any wonder that this country is relatively strong in the production of certain kinds of farm implements and transportation equipment.

Economies of Scale

It is often advantageous to countries, particularly small countries, to specialize in a particular type of production and to trade even if they have almost identical resources and production techniques. This is so because of economies of scale.

Suppose that two countries both produce automobiles and refrigerators before trade. Let country A's resources be such that she can produce and consume 500,000 automobiles and 500,000 refrigerators annually. Country B is in the same position. Suppose that in each country both the output of automobiles and of refrigerators is too small for the firms producing them to utilize optimum scales of plant.

If country A's resources were *all* devoted to automobile production, suppose that the economies of scale realized would permit production of 1,200,000 automobiles. If country B's resources were *all* devoted to refrigerator production, suppose that economies of scale could be realized to the extent that 1,200,000 refrigerators could be produced. Under these circumstances it would be to each country's advantage to specialize and trade. Together they could produce 1,200,000 automobiles and 1,200,000 refrigerators. By trading 600,000 automobiles for 600,000 refrigerators they could each have 600,000 automobiles and 600,000 refrigerators—a net gain of 100,000 of each product for each country over what it could have without trade. Other combinations yielding advantages to both countries are, of course, possible.

A real-life counterpart of this example exists in western Europe. Between World War I and World War II tariff barriers erected by the various small countries of western Europe limited the market in many industries of each country to the country itself. The European Economic Community, usually called the Common Market, established in 1957, is directed toward the elimination of such trade barriers among member countries. It appears that, among other factors, the broadening of the markets available to specific industries in each has contributed to improvements in productive efficiency in the member countries.

Summary

International trade is carried on for the same reason as trade among individuals and among communities and regions within a country; all parties to voluntary exchange expect to gain from it. But because of such factors as nationalism and currency differences, special problems are associated with trade among nations. This chapter examines how and why trade is mutually advantageous to the parties engaging in it.

Patterns of trade for Canada are examined first. The United States is by far our largest export market. The United Kingdom is our second largest market, followed in 1968 by Japan, West Germany, Australia, the Netherlands and mainland China. The dominant source of our imports is the United States. Our second most important supplier of imports in terms of value of goods imported is the United Kingdom. Other important suppliers of imports in 1968 were Japan, Venezuela, West Germany, France and Italy. While the aim of our trade policy since the end of World War II has been multilateralism—trading relationships involving several countries—, the result has been an increasing proportion of trade with the United States. Canada exports a multitude of products, the four most important in 1968 being motor vehicles and parts; copper, nickel and products; newsprint; and grain and cereal preparations. We also import a great many products, automobiles and parts, food goods, ores and primary metals, and fuels and lubricants heading the list.

The mutual benefits possible from international trade are rooted in the principle of comparative advantage. According to this principle, if a country specializes in producing goods and services in which its productive efficiency is greater relative to other goods and services and trades for goods and services in which its productive efficiency is relatively less, its "production possibilities," or the total of all goods and services available to the trading parties, will be greater than they would be in the absence of trade. The alternative costs of trading for goods in which a country has a comparative disadvantage are less to the country than the alternative costs involved in producing such goods itself. Specializing in the production of goods and services in which the country has a comparative advantage and trading for those in which it has a comparative disadvantage yields the same benefits to the country as would the discovery of some cost-reducing technique for producing the latter group.

Every country of the world has a comparative advantage in the production of some goods and a comparative disadvantage in the production of others. This is so because of differences in resource endowments and in levels and kinds of technology among countries. Small countries, whose internal markets for some goods are not large enough to permit taking advantage of possible economies of scale, may find that specialization in some products and trade for others will permit the trading parties to expand outputs of those goods sufficiently to reduce average costs of production. Where this is possible, the trading parties benefit from the higher productive efficiency in each country.

This chapter demonstrates the potential of trade. In the next three chapters we discover the complications that arise in the course of trade and the almost inevitable attempts on the part of some people to restrict its volume.

Exercises and Questions for Discussion

1. Compare the exchange of goods among countries and among individuals. Must one party lose whenever the other party gains? Explain.
2. "If Japan can make transistor radios cheaper than we can make them, we should import radios from Japan." Evaluate this statement.
3. Is the principle of comparative advantage applicable only on an international plane? If not, explain where else it might apply.
4. "The United States as compared with Nigeria has an absolute advantage in all manufacturing lines. It would not, therefore, be mutually advantageous for trade to occur between these countries." Evaluate this statement.
5. "Buy Canadian! The job you save may be your own." Evaluate this statement.
6. Discuss the difference between the real cost of producing a good and the money cost of producing it. Which is relevant for international trade? Elaborate.
7. Is multilateral trade more advantageous economically to the countries involved than bilateral trade? Explain.

Selected Readings

Anderson, R. V., *The Future of Canada's Export Trade*. Ottawa: Queen's Printer, 1957.

Ellsworth, P. T., *The International Economy*. New York: Crowell-Collier, Macmillan, Inc., 1964, Chaps. 4-5.

Kenen, P. B., *International Economics*. Englewood Cliffs, N.J.: Prentice-Hall, Inc., 1964, pp. 7-17.

Kindleberger, C. P., *International Economics*, 3d ed. Homewood, Ill.: Richard D. Irwin, Inc., 1963, Chap. 5.

Reuber, G. L., *The Growth and Changing Composition of Trade Between Canada and the United States*. Montreal: Canadian-American Committee of the Private Planning Association, 1960.

————, *Britain's Export Trade with Canada*. Toronto: University of Toronto Press, 1960.

————, "Western Europe's Demand for Canadian Industrial Materials", *Canadian Journal of Economics and Political Science*. February, 1962, pp. 16-34.

Snider, D. A., *Introduction to International Economics*, 3d ed. Homewood, Ill.: Richard D. Irwin, Inc., 1963, Chap. 3.

16

The Financing of International Trade

Differences in the currencies or monetary units used by countries engaging in international trade lead, unfortunately, to some highly vexing problems. The framework within which international trade is carried on should be such that all mutually beneficial trade can occur with a minimum of effort. Instead, we permit financial arrangements to become so tangled that some trade that would have benefited trading parties is not carried on at all. A major challenge, clearly, is to find and to institute a set of arrangements that will promote a free flow of trade. This chapter sets the stage for understanding the financing of international trade. First, we shall consider the simple mechanics of an international transaction; second, we shall discuss a country's balance of payments, with particular reference to the situation of Canada; third, we shall examine the nature of deficits and surpluses in the balance of payments; and fourth, we shall briefly survey the recent history of the Canadian balance of payments.

International Transactions

In this section we reduce a set of international transactions to its simplest terms. Then, in the remainder of this chapter and in the next we move into the more complex aspects of the financing of international trade. Suppose that a Canadian oil company wants to import crude petroleum into Canada from Venezuela. Suppose also that an enterprise in Venezuela wants to import wheat from Canada. We will first consider each transaction in isolation from the other and then we will view them as a part of regular, continuing trade between the two countries.

Isolated Transactions

If the only transaction possible between a business in Venezuela and one in Canada is the export of wheat from the latter to the former, in all probability no transaction at all will take place. If no other transactions of any kind have occurred and if none is contemplated between Venezuela and Canada, the Venezuelan business firm will have no Canadian dollars and will be able to make payments in bolivars only. But the potential seller of the wheat wants Canadian dollars, since this is the medium of exchange in which he makes his sales, meets his costs, and computes his profits. He will not want bolivars if no other trade with Venezuela is to occur, since he would be unable to use them.

The same stalemate will exist if the only possible transaction is the export of crude petroleum from Venezuela to Canada. The seller of petroleum operates his business in terms of bolivars. He has no use for Canadian dollars if no other transactions are or will be possible.

Continuing Trade

The situation is quite different if the prospective parties to an international sale or purchase of a good or service are confident that the contemplated exchange is only one of many that will occur over time. A Canadian seller of wheat will gladly accept 41,000 bolivars for 5000 bushels of wheat if he knows that there are parties in Canada who import goods from Venezuela. He can sell the bolivars to the oil company, say, for $10,000,[1] thus obtaining the kind of money that he wants and needs to carry on his business. With the 41,000 bolivars the oil company can buy crude oil from a Venezuelan producer. Both transactions are complete and both sellers are paid in the monetary units that they desire.

The transactions could have been accomplished the other way around. The Canadian oil company could buy $10,000 worth of crude oil from a Venezuelan producer, paying the producer in Canadian dollars. The Venezuelan wheat importer could then buy with bolivars the $10,000 from the crude oil producer and use the dollars to import 5000 bushels of wheat from Canada. Again both sellers would have what they desire, payment in their own money for the goods that they have sold.

---

[1] *A Canadian dollar does, in fact, currently exchange for 4.1 bolivars. We shall see in the next chapter how exchange rates are determined.*

Foreign Exchange Markets

The financial aspects of international trade can be readily generalized. Transactions need not be paired. Import and export activities carried on over time by a great many different businesses and persons have caused markets to be established for foreign currencies. These are called *foreign exchange markets*, with the term "exchange" meaning "money", and they are usually operated by commercial banks as a part of their regular business. Anyone in Canada desiring to import from another country can buy with dollars the appropriate foreign money in the foreign exchange market; that is, at his chartered bank. Anyone in Canada who sells abroad can sell for the money of the country to which he exports, and the foreign money or foreign exchange can then be sold for Canadian dollars in the foreign exchange market.

With organized foreign exchange markets in operation it is not even necessary that the exporters and importers of a country trade with the same foreign country. Payments on a *multilateral* basis are possible. Suppose, for example, that Canada exports wheat to Venezuela and imports wine from France. Suppose, further, that France imports coffee from Venezuela. The bolivars earned from the sale of wheat to Venezuela may be used to buy French wine and, in turn, used by French importers to buy Venezuelan coffee.

The Balance of Payments

Most countries keep records of those international economic activities that give rise to what they owe, or to their demands for foreign exchange, and to what is owed them or to the supplies of foreign exchange that are placed on the market; or in the absence of complete records, they attempt to estimate the demand and supply magnitudes involved. A statement of its international accounts is called a country's *balance of payments*. That for Canada for 1968 is given in Table 16-1. Balance of payments transactions are usually classified into two main categories: the current account, and the capital account. The current account includes the purchases and sales of goods and services as well as current receipts and payments of income on investments. The capital account represents transactions in financial assets such as bonds, equities, loans, bank accounts, transactions in fixed plant and equipment, and the acquisition or disposal of non-financial assets, known as direct investments. In addition, there is usually a final item that shows the change in the government's holdings of gold and foreign exchange, and in its net position with the International Mone-

TABLE 16-1
Canadian Balance of Payments, 1968
(Millions of Dollars)

	We Owe (Debits—)	Owed Us (Credits+)
Current Account		
Exports		17,120
Merchandise, adjusted		13,538
Nonmerchandise receipts		3,582
Gold production available for export		120
Travel		992
Interest and dividends		331
Freight and shipping		894
Inheritance and immigrants' funds		370
All other current receipts		875
Imports	17,231	
Merchandise imports, adjusted	12,162	
Nonmerchandise payments	5,069	
Travel	1,015	
Interest and dividends	1,290	
Freight and shipping	937	
Inheritance and emigrants' funds	209	
Official contributions	133	
All other current payments	1,485	
Capital Account		
"Exports"		2,909
Direct investment		610
Portfolio investment		2,133
Government loans repaid		5
Other capital movements (mainly short term)		161
"Imports"	2,798	
Direct investment	135	
Portfolio investment	945	
Government loans	78	
Other capital movements (mainly short term)	1,287	
Changes in official reserves and IMF position	353	
Totals	20,029	20,029
Overall net balance of international payments		

Source: Bank of Canada, Statistical Summary. February 1970, pp. 161-163.

tary Fund.[2] These two major classifications in the balance of international payments are discussed below.

The Current Account

The current account generally covers international exchanges of goods and services. The sales of goods and services, or exports, to other countries generate amounts owed us, and as these amounts are paid *supplies*

[2] *See pp. 395-398 for a discussion of the International Monetary Fund.*

of foreign exchange are placed in the foreign exchange markets from the viewpoint of the selling country or "our" country. These are referred to as *foreign exchange credits* for the selling country. On the other side of the fence we owe for purchases of goods and services or imports from other countries. What we owe creates *demands* for foreign exchange, or foreign exchange *debits*, on our international accounts.

Credits or Receipts

The current account is divided into two main parts: the *merchandise account* section and the *nonmerchandise account* section. The former is made up of the tangible items listed in **Table 15-2** —metals and minerals, motor vehicles and parts, farm and fish products, and a large number of other goods. The latter includes commercial services, investment earnings from abroad, and the funds that immigrants send back home. We sell transportation services to other countries. We carry their freight and passengers and they pay for these in their own currencies, creating supplies of their currencies in foreign exchange markets. When foreigners travel in Canada foreign exchange supplies are also generated. They must give up their money for Canadian dollars to pay for their travels in their own money. In a very real sense we are "exporting" vacations or travel services to them. Interest and dividend payments to Canadian residents result from the use of Canadian capital invested abroad. In essence, we are selling foreigners the continuing services of our investments in their plant and equipment. When we are paid what they owe us for these, the payments— in foreign currencies—generate foreign exchange supplies. The same is true of receipts resulting from transfers into Canada of immigrants' funds and legacies. Gold for export, while not, strictly speaking, a service transaction, gives rise to external claims, and consequently is included as a special item of receipts. All other current receipts, the "catch-all", consists of expenditures by foreign governments for maintaining diplomatic and military establishments in Canada, personal and institutional remittances for charitable and other noncommercial purposes, miscellaneous income including transfers of income and profits by Canadian companies from branch operations abroad not listed separately elsewhere and income from business expenditures for a wide variety of technical, research, management, insurance and advertising services as well as for royalties and patents.

Debits or Payments

Our purchases abroad are direct counterparts of our sales to foreigners, and these transactions create demands for foreign exchange. We purchase *merchandise* items of the kinds listed in Table 15-3. In the *non-merchandise* classification, we purchase travel, transportation, and other services from foreign firms. We also demand foreign currencies in exchange markets to pay interest and dividends on the very large investments that foreigners have made at past dates in Canadian businesses. They desire these payments in their own monetary units. When emmigrants transfer their inheritances and funds abroad, foreign currency demand is likewise generated. Official contributions refer to government remittances for consular and diplomatic representation and military expenditures abroad and membership fees and quotas for the United Nations, International Monetary Fund, World Bank, disaster relief overseas, etc. All other payments from nonmerchandise trade include miscellaneous investment income (other than those covered in the interest and dividends account), and business and personal services and other transactions including payments by Canadian subsidiaries or branches to parent companies abroad.

Historical Record

The current account makes up the largest part of the balance of payments. In fact, when most people think of international trade, goods and services are the items that they have in mind. However, as we shall see, other international transactions are important too. As might be expected, the difference in the value of merchandise imports and exports is known as the trade balance—an excess of merchandise exports over merchandise imports is referred to as a trade surplus. Canada's overall merchandise trade position with all countries has shown a surplus each year since 1961. Conversely, except for 1948, Canada has had an overall deficit position on nonmerchandise account in every year since World War II. In this connection, it should be emphasized that more than half of this nonmerchandise deficit is the result of a net outflow of interest and dividends, mainly to the United States, which holds an overwhelming proportion of total foreign investment in Canada.

The current account balance is the difference between payments and receipts resulting from transactions in goods and services. An excess of receipts over payments is known as a current account surplus. Looking at Canadian data, we find that this country has run a deficit balance on current account for most years since the end of the Second World War.[3] It is perhaps worth noting that this deficit reached very large dimensions of more than a billion dollars annually in the interval between 1956 and

[3]*Current account surpluses appeared in 1946-1947-1948-1949 and 1952. The years since 1952 have been characterized by current deficits.*

1960. The current deficit decreased sharply during the next four years but rose markedly in 1965 and 1966 when it again exceeded one billion dollars annually. Analysis also shows that the 1968 current deficit was the lowest, in the postwar period.

The Capital Account

The capital account reflects transactions in financial assets and liabilities between residents and nonresidents. Within this account there are three important distinctions: long-term capital movements, short-term capital movements, and changes in the government's holdings of gold and foreign exchange, and in its net position in the International Monetary Fund (this refers to IMF holdings of Canadian dollars). "Long-term" is taken arbitrarily to mean a period exceeding one year. When Canadian-owned assets in other countries are increasing or when foreign-owned assets in Canada are decreasing, *a movement of capital* out of Canada is said to be occurring. The opposite of this, a decrease in Canadian owned assets in other countries or an increase in foreign-owned assets in Canada, is called a *movement of capital into Canada* from abroad.[4] Variations in official liquid reserves are the response of the monetary authorities, acting for the Canadian government, to the rest of the balance of payments; that is to say that official reserves are used primarily as a compensating item in a sense to be explained later in the chapter.

Long-term Capital Movements

Direct investment is one of the two major categories of long-term capital movements. Strictly speaking, direct investment involves an international transfer of purchasing power aimed at the acquisition of physical assets such as land, buildings, or machinery and equipment. In practice, it

[4]*Another way to view capital movements is to remember that a long-term capital import gives rise to acquisition of title to Canadian stocks and bonds by foreigners. In other words, an inflow of capital is the result of Canadian exports of stocks and bonds. When foreigners make direct investments in Canada by building plants in this country, we are importing capital but exporting the titles to these plants to foreign countries. Since we are exporting securities, capital imports are classified as credit or receipt items in our capital account. Likewise a short-term capital import into Canada is a credit item since we are exporting our promises to pay (I.O.U.'s). Conversely capital exports are debit or payment items. When private parties, individuals, and businesses invest abroad on long term, they are importing securities (hence a debit item). Short-term capital exports are debit items since we are importing foreign promises to pay. When foreigners return Canadian securities to this country, the transaction is a capital outflow because we are importing our own securities and have to pay for them. Accordingly, capital transactions can be treated like ordinary exports (credits) and imports (debits).*

includes changes in the investment of business firms in their foreign branches or in business firms in which they have a controlling interest. Accordingly, direct investment may take the form of transfer of funds to the subsidiary for working capital or to acquire physical assets and the shipment of physical assets to the subsidiary. It is worth noting here that the repatriation of direct investment capital, resulting from the sale to foreigners of assets held abroad, is entered in the capital account, while the repatriation of profits is entered in the current account.

Another major category of long-term capital flows is *portfolio investment* in new and outstanding securities of governments and corporations. Transactions involving national governments consist of intergovernmental loans and repayments and Canada's subscription to international agencies. Other long-term capital movements include such items as long-term bank loans, mortgage loans, and transfers of funds by insurance companies.

When foreigners increase the quantities of long-term assets that they own in Canada, or are investing in Canadian stocks and bonds, supplies of foreign exchange are placed on the market. In this connection, it should be noted that over the years long-term capital inflows from the United States have been the greatest source of foreign investment for Canada. On the other side of the fence Canadian investments abroad create demands for foreign exchange, or represent capital movements out of Canada.

Short-term Capital Movements

The main categories of short-term capital transactions are resident holdings of foreign bank balances and other short-term funds such as those connected with the Eurodollar market,[5] and nonresident holdings of Canadian dollar deposits, finance company paper, treasury bills, commercial paper and Government of Canada demand liabilities, mainly in the form of interest-free demand notes issued to international agencies. Other short-term capital movements reflect the changes in loans and accounts receivable and payable as well as a balancing item or "plug figure" (a figure which is adjusted to make the balance of payments balance) representing errors and omissions resulting from differences between direct measurements of current and capital accounts.

When foreigners increase their balances with Canadian banks, this transaction is a short-term capital import into Canada; supplies of foreign exchange are generated just as though goods and services were exported. By the same token, decreases in Canadian bank balances abroad, decreases in our holdings of foreign commercial obligations, or foreign short-

[5]*Eurodollars are U.S. dollars deposited mainly with banks in European countries.*

term government securities or decreases in open-book accounts owed to Canadian exporters, are all short-term capital imports into Canada, and thus foreign exchange supplies are also engendered. On the other hand, short-term capital exports, which include increases in our bank deposits abroad, etc., create demands for foreign currencies.

International Reserves

Canada's official international reserves are defined by the Department of Finance as the government's holdings of gold, convertible currencies, and its net reserve position in the International Monetary Fund. Gold has long been popular as a form of international reserves. Under present international monetary arrangements, gold represents generalized claims over the monies of almost all nations, since the monetary authorities of these countries stand ready to buy it at a fixed price and in unlimited quantities by giving their money in exchange. Convertible currencies are those that can be converted into U.S. dollars or other currencies in foreign exchange markets without restriction of any kind. The net reserve position of Canada in the International Monetary Fund represents rights of Canada to draw foreign currencies from that agency almost automatically up to its full amount. Its amount is determined by Canadian gold subscriptions to the International Monetary Fund less the Fund's holdings of Canadian dollars. All of these official monetary reserve assets are readily available for settling Canadian international accounts.

The Structure of International Accounts, Deficits, and Surpluses

The balance of payments, as we shall see, always balances. Quite obviously, therefore, the term balance of payments deficit, along with its reciprocal, balance of payments surplus, must have a special meaning; it cannot refer to the entire balance of payments position since the accounts are so designed as to make equality inevitable. We shall look first at the structure of the international accounts and then at deficits and surpluses in the balance of payments.

Balance of Payments Statement

Balance of payments accounting uses a double-entry system of recording accounts with the rest of the world. From the point of view of residents of Canada, all transactions which give rise to foreigners' claims on Canada are labeled payments or debits (—). All transactions which give rise to money claims of Canadians on foreigners are called receipts or credits (+). Since the balance of payments is drawn up in terms of debits and credits, if the entries are made correctly, the debits may equal the credits. Thus, the net balance on all transactions is exactly zero, as can be seen in Table 16-1.

To put the same point another way, the double-entry format of the balance of payments entails two entries for each transaction. One indicates values of the goods, services, and securities that are imported or exported; a second entry shows how this transaction was financed. Because of the underlying double-entry structure, "payments" to foreigners by Canadian residents must be equal to the value of goods, services and securities purchased from foreigners, while "receipts" from foreigners must be equal to the value of Canadian-produced goods, services, and securities sold to foreigners. This fact accounts for the truism that the balance of payments always balances.

In this context some additional observations may be made. Because, in the Canadian balance of payments statement, capital account entries include unilateral government transfers and an adjustment for errors and omissions under "other short-term capital movements", it follows that the current account balance in Table 16-1 must be equal to the capital account balance but opposite in sign. The current account deficit is equal to the capital account surplus and vice versa. Stated in another way, when all transactions, current dealings (both merchandise and nonmerchandise items), and capital movements (including the net changes in official reserves) are taken into consideration, a nation's international accounts must always balance.

Deficits and Surpluses

Since the balance of payments always balances, what is called a balance of payments deficit or a balance of payments surplus is a matter of definition.

It suits the policies of some countries to regard the difference between payments and receipts resulting from current transactions in goods or services as a surplus or deficit in the international accounts. However, most analysts would admit that this concept of a surplus or deficit balance is significant only in a limited sense: current transactions cannot universally be expected to be in balance over the long run since some countries are exporters or importers of capital.

The concept of *basic balance or basic deficit* is popular with some countries. According to this concept, if a current-account deficit is being matched by a long-term capital inflow, a country is said to have a "basic" balance of payments. Under this concept, Canada's balance has usually been a surplus.

Another balance frequently referred to is the so-called *overall balance*. It includes the net balance on current account, long-term capital movements and short-term capital flows. Overall balance is said to exist if there is no net change in the holdings of official monetary reserves over an extended period of time, say, the whole of a business cycle. Table 16-2 shows the changes in Canada's international reserves from 1946 to 1968.

TABLE 16-2
Changes in Canada's International Reserves, 1946-1968

Year	Millions of Dollars	Year	Millions of Dollars
1946	−267	1958	109
1947	−742	1959	−11
1948	492	1960	−39
1949	128	1961	290
1950	722	1962	155
1951	56	1963	146
1952	37	1964	363
1953	−38	1965	157
1954	124	1966	−359
1955	−44	1967	18
1956	48	1968	353
1957	−105		

Source: Bank of Canada, Statistical Summary, Financial Supplement *1954;* Statistical Summary *various issues.*

The details of the 1968 increase in Canada's official reserves are shown in Table 16-3. The deficit arising from current transactions in goods and services was $111 million, but capital movements in all forms, both long and short term, resulted in a net inflow of $464 million. The difference —$363 million—was used to improve our international monetary position: $604 million was added to our official holdings of gold and foreign exchange; our net creditor position with the International Monetary Fund declined by $249 million. At the end of 1968, Canada's reserves were U.S. $2,848 million. It may be useful to add that Canada's reserves are large relative to the probable current-account deficit.

The Canadian Case

As already indicated, Canada has for many years incurred a deficit balance in current transactions with other countries. But this imbalance has not yet proved troublesome. Large sums of capital have been attracted to Canada, particularly from the United States, and have provided the foreign exchange necessary to finance the deficits on current account.

TABLE 16-3

Capital and Official Monetary Movements, 1968
(Millions of Dollars)

Total capital movements in long term forms	1,590
Total capital movements in short term forms	−1,126
Net capital movements (excluding changes in official reserves)	464
Current account balance	−111
Changes in official reserves	353
Official holdings of gold and foreign exchange	604
Net position in IMF	−249

Source: Bank of Canada, Statistical Summary. February 1970, p. 163.

Movements in official monetary reserves have been nominal and seldom has the external value of the Canadian dollar been under heavy downward pressure.

Not surprisingly, heavy reliance on foreign capital in the post-war era has led to a marked rise in Canadian indebtedness abroad. As a consequence, we are frequently in the position nowadays of being *obliged* to import capital. Needless to say, the obligation to borrow abroad, heavily and regularly, exposes Canada to considerable hazards. The recent measures taken by the United States to improve the over-all performance in that country's balance of payments clearly illustrates this danger.[6] As the Governor of the Bank of Canada put it," . . . it would be unwise to take a detached view of the problems that arise from our dependence on continuing large imports of foreign capital. A situation in which Canada needs to import a great deal of capital from a country which is trying to restrict the export of capital is inherently unsatisfactory, and there is no easy or satisfactory way of dealing with it."[7]

One general remark should be made in concluding this chapter. The

[6]*In mid-1963, the United States proposed an "Interest Equalization Tax" designed to discourage foreign longer-term borrowing in the United States by adding approximately one percent per year to the total cost of the borrower. Under the prevailing circumstances, the proposed tax "raised the imminent prospect of either a dramatic rise in the whole structure of interest rates in Canada, or another foreign exchange crisis, or both" (Bank of Canada,* Annual Report, *1963, p. 4). Fortunately, Canada was able to persuade the United States to exempt all* new *issues of Canadian securities from the tax. More important, U.S. nonbank financial intermediaries were asked by the U.S. Administration to limit their purchases of foreign securities during 1966 and other large corporations were requested to moderate the amount of direct investment they carried out abroad. As a result of negotiations which took place, however, the United States agreed to exempt Canada from the first "guideline", but not from the second. For its part, Canada agreed to reduce its "official reserves target" figure from U.S. $2,700 million set in 1963 to U.S. $2,600 million. The ceiling on Canada's exchange reserves (by now U.S. $2,550 million) was removed in late December, 1968.*

[7]*Bank of Canada,* Annual Report, *1965, p. 10.*

gains from foreign investment, like the gains from foreign trade, are reciprocal: they confer benefits upon the borrower as well as upon the lender. Nevertheless, considerable controversy has been aroused by the size and persistency of the current deficits in the Canadian balance of international payments. All the same, Canada is a developing country and foreign capital will doubtless play an important part in future growth. Even so, the question of whether Canada has been "living beyond her means" is likely to continue as a lively topic of debate in the years ahead.

Summary

This chapter introduces the financing of international transactions. Different countries use different currency systems and, since sellers of goods ordinarily desire payment in their own currency, some system for making international payments must be arranged if trade is to be carried on. The present system consists of foreign exchange markets in which those who receive payments from other countries may sell any foreign currencies that they obtain and in which those who make payments to other countries may purchase the necessary foreign currencies with their own currency.

The international economic transactions of a country that create either supplies of or demands for foreign exchange are summed up in its balance of payments. Items making up the balance of payments can be classified into two major groups: (1) the current account, showing payments and receipts in connection with trade in goods and services; and (2) the capital account, showing the flow of financial resources in both long-term and short-term forms.

Exports of goods and services by a country increase the supplies of foreign currencies available to the country while imports of goods and services draw them down. Capital movements out of a country, or investments in foreign assets, decrease a country's stock of foreign exchange. Capital movements in, or foreign investments in the country, generate increases in foreign exchange holdings of the country. Since trade in goods and services, and capital transactions may not result in equal inflows and outflows, the difference is made up by an increase or decrease in a country's official reserves. In Canada official reserves are taken to mean gold plus foreign currencies owned by or available to the government, including drawing rights on the International Monetary Fund.

When all of a country's economic transactions with the rest of the world for a given period are recorded, the debits are offset by the credits. Put in another way the balance of payments as a whole must necessarily balance.

The use of words such a "deficit" and "surplus" in relation to the balance of payments can be confusing since, on the face of it, it seems to be a contradiction in terms to speak about a balance being somehow out of balance. Clearly, the terms do not represent the balance of all items in the balance of payments statement, but only the balance of a certain selection of transactions. Thus what is called surplus or deficit is not a definite, objective historical fact. Most countries regard changes in their official reserves position as the symptoms of instability. In other words, if a country loses official reserves, it has a deficit in its balance of payments. If it improves its international monetary position, it has a surplus in its balance of payments. Since the figure reported for a country's deficit or surplus is a matter of definition, one should beware of taking it too seriously and being mislead by its meaning.

Since Canada has for many years incurred a deficit on current account, with the difference covered by an inflow of capital, attention in this country has tended to be focused on the current account deficit and its effects on Canada's international indebtedness. For a country such as the United States, for example, whose currency is widely held by other countries as official reserves, attention is centred on changes in gold reserves and short-term liabilities to foreigners which constitute a potential claim on gold.

Exercises and Questions for Discussion

1. "A country can import more goods than it exports and still have balance of payments equilibrium." Evaluate this statement.
2. What, if any, are the limits to the size of the deficit a country can run in its balance of payments? Explain
3. If gold were not used as a means of making international payments, could world trade continue? If so, how?
4. Is a surplus in the current account "favourable"? Discuss.
5. "A country like Canada, which borrows heavily from abroad, is heading for economic ruination." Evaluate this statement.

Selected Readings

Boreham, Gordon F., *et al.*, *Money and Banking: Analysis and Policy in a Canadian Context*. Toronto: Holt, Rinehart and Winston of Canada, 1969, Chap. 23.

Ingram, James C., *International Economic Problems*. New York: John Wiley and Sons, Inc., 1966, Chaps. 2 and 5.

Kenen, Peter B., *International Economics*. Englewood Cliffs, N.J.: Prentice-Hall, Inc., 1964, pp. 51-58.

Slater, David W., *Canada's Balance of Payments – When is a Deficit a Problem?* Montreal: Canadian Trade Committee, 1964.

———, "Canada's International Trade and Payments: An Examination of Recent Trends", *The Canadian Banker*. Autumn, 1963, pp. 5-25.

17

Exchange Rates and International Payments

If you take a trip to Europe this summer, one of the first facts of life that will confront you is that you must have the currency of the country you are visiting in order to pay the porter at the airport, the taxi driver who takes you to your hotel, and for any other goods or services that you may require while abroad. You could have used dollars to purchase the needed foreign currencies before leaving Canada, but more likely you will exchange dollars for the appropriate currency in each country that you visit. In Great Britain you will pay about $2.58 for each pound sterling that you buy; in France a franc will cost you approximately 20 cents; and a West German mark will cost about 29 cents.

What determines the rate at which the money of one country can be converted into that of another? In this chapter we shall examine the mechanism by which *exchange rates* are determined in uncontrolled or free markets and the means by which the rates may be "pegged" or fixed artificially in controlled markets. We shall consider the relations between exchange rates and balance of payments disequilibria, how countries seek to control their balance of payments deficits, and the issue of flexible versus controlled exchange rates. Finally, we shall summarize international financial developments of the present century.

Free Market Exchange Rates

How would the exchange rate betwen the currencies of two countries be established in an ordinary competitive market situation? Several hints were advanced in the preceding chapter. The fact that the people who receive payments from abroad like to be paid ultimately in the currency of their own country leads to the establishment of foreign exchange markets. The operation of foreign exchange markets is ordinarily but not necessarily conducted by banks. In any given country, supplies of foreign currencies come into such a market from the export of goods and services, and from capital movements into the country. Demands for foreign currencies arise from import activities, and from capital movements out of the country. These provide the basis for the determination of exchange rates, or for the establishment of the prices of the various foreign currencies in terms of the monetary units of the home country.

Demand for a Foreign Currency

To establish the home country demand schedule or demand curve for a foreign currency, we should think of the currency as though it were a commodity. The demanders are those who want to make payments to parties in the other country. Suppose, for example, that Canada is the home country and Great Britain the foreign country. The demand schedule or demand curve would show the quantities of pounds sterling per unit of time that people in Canada would be willing to buy at alternative dollar prices of the pound, other things being equal.

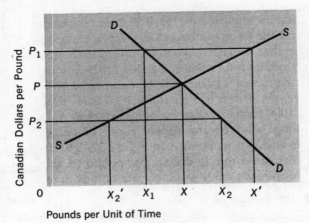

Figure 17-1
Exchange-rate determination.

The demand curve for pounds sterling would be expected to slope downward to the right, as does *DD* in Figure 17-1; that is, the lower the dollar price, the greater the quantity of pounds per year (or whatever the appropriate time unit is) that people in Canada would be expected to want. Why is this so? The lower the dollar exchange rate on the pound, the less expensive are British goods in terms of dollar prices. Consider, for example, a British product priced at one pound sterling per unit. If the exchange rate were three dollars to one pound, the price to the Canadian buyer would be three dollars (ignoring transportation costs). But, if the exchange rate decreased to two dollars per pound sterling, each unit of the product will cost two dollars instead of three. This means that British goods and services become cheaper relative to goods and services produced in Canada, and residents of Canada are induced to substitute some of the British goods for some of those produced at home. Of course, the larger the quantities of British goods that are purchased, given their prices in pounds sterling, the larger the quantities of pounds sterling demanded.

Supply of a Foreign Currency

The supply schedule or supply curve of a foreign currency, say British pounds sterling to Canada, can be established in a similar way. Suppliers of pounds are the British who purchase goods and services from Canada. The supply curve can be defined as showing the quantities of pounds that would be placed on the market at alternative dollar prices of the pound, other things being equal.

The supply curve of pounds is illustrated by *SS* in Figure 17-1, and usually it will slope upward to the right, as do most supply curves. The determining factor in whether it does or does not slope upward to the right is the elasticity of British demand for Canadian goods when the demand curves are expressed in terms of pound sterling prices. Consider Figure 17-2(a), in which some sort of composite units—basketfuls—of Canadian goods and services imported by the British are measured along the horizontal axis and the price per basket in pounds sterling along the vertical axis. Suppose that initially a pound sterling exchanges for two dollars and that Canadian sellers sell baskets of goods for two dollars each. Thus the pound sterling price of a basket will be one pound and, according to our demand curve, the British will purchase 1000 baskets of goods, providing a supply of £1000 on the foreign exchange market.

The resulting point on the supply curve of pounds sterling to Canada is shown as point *A* in Figure 17-2(b). In this diagram we measure the exchange rate in dollars per pound on the vertical axis and the quantity of pounds made available per unit of time on the horizontal axis, just as

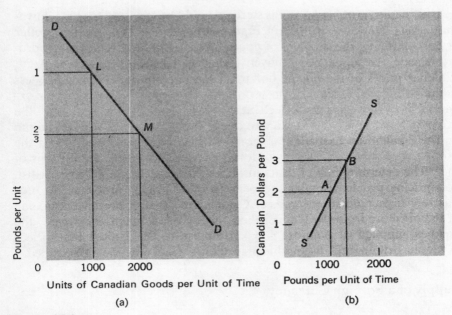

Figure 17-2
Supply of a foreign currency.

in Figure 17-1. Point *A* shows that at an exchange rate of \$2 = £1, a quantity of £1000 will be forthcoming.

Now suppose that the dollar price of the pound, or the dollar exchange rate on the pound, rises to \$3 = £1. With reference to Figure 17-2(a), a basketful of Canadian goods, imported by the British and still priced in Canada at \$2 per basket, now costs only two thirds of a pound per basket. At this lower pound sterling price the demand curve *DD* shows that the British are willing to purchase 2000 baskets per time period. The total expenditures of the British on the imports are £1333⅓. Transferring this data to Figure 17-2(b), we plot point B, showing that at \$3 = £1, the quantity supplied will be £133⅓. Points *A* and *B*, along with other points similarly determined, trace out the pound sterling supply curve *SS*.

A brief review of the basic relations between the elasticity of demand and the total expenditures made on a product, together with another look at the *DD* curve in Figure 17-2(a), should suffice to complete the supply picture. If the British demand curve for imports from Canada is *elastic* for pound sterling price decreases,[1] as we have assumed it is for the move-

_____
[1]*Keep in mind that we assume these are brought about by* increases *in the dollar price of the pound.*

ment from L to M, the British pound sterling expenditure for Canadian goods and therefore the quantity supplied of pounds sterling in the foreign exchange market will increase. This will make the supply curve of pounds sterling of Figures 17-1 and 17-2(b) slope upward to the right. We would expect that by and large this would be the usual case—the British demand for Canadian goods would tend to be elastic, since Canadian sellers must compete with sellers from other countries for British markets. However, if the British demand curve for Canadian goods is of unitary elasticity, the supply curve of pounds sterling will be vertical. If it is inelastic, the supply curve of pounds will be backward sloping for higher dollar prices of the pound. (Can you explain why these two statements are so?)

The Equilibrium Exchange Rate

The determination of the *equilibrium exchange rate* in a free market is a pricing problem similar in nature to other pricing problems. At relatively higher dollar prices of the pound the British are encouraged to import more from Canada, giving rise to relatively larger quantities supplied of pounds sterling. Exports to Canada from Great Britain are discouraged, curtailing relatively the quantities demanded of pounds sterling. At relatively lower dollar prices of the pound the opposite occurs. Quantities demanded of pounds sterling will be relatively larger and quantities supplied will be relatively smaller.

Equilibrium exchange rate determination is illustrated in Figure 17-1. At an exchange rate of P_1 dollars per pound sterling, quantity X_1 will be demanded and quantity X_1' will be supplied. Surpluses of pounds sterling are accumulating in the foreign exchange market. This induces sellers of foreign exchange to undercut each other, thus lowering the dollar exchange rate on the pound. When the exchange rate has been reduced from P_1 dollars to P dollars, the quantity demanded and the quantity supplied of pounds sterling will be the same and equilibrium will exist.

At an exchange rate of P_2 dollars per pound, those wishing to make payments to Great Britain will want X_2 pounds per unit of time. But transactions giving rise to supplies of pounds are discouraged by the low exchange rate and only X_2 pounds are made available. The shortage induces demanders to bid the price up to the equilibrium level P.

Pegged Exchange Rates

The major trading countries of the world have not been willing to let free market exchange rates among their currencies prevail throughout most of the present century. Rather, they have preferred to fix, or *peg*, their exchange rates at specific levels. Historically, two methods of pegging have been used. Prior to the 1920's an *international gold standard* was widely used. In more recent years countries have moved to what might be called a *major currency exchange standard*. We shall examine the main characteristics of each.

The International Gold Standard

Countries participating in an *international gold standard* system each define their monetary units in terms of gold content, or what amounts to the same thing, they each set a fixed price in terms of their own currency on an ounce of gold. Suppose Canada has fixed the price of gold at $35 per ounce and that Great Britain has established a fixed price at £13.6 per ounce. If one ounce of gold is worth $35 in Canada or £13.6 in Great Britain, and if both countries stand ready either to buy or sell gold at these prices, the exchange rate between the two currencies cannot fluctuate far from $2.58 = £1.[2]

If the demand for and the supply of pounds sterling from the point of view of Canada were *DD* and *SS*, respectively, in Figure 17-3(a), then $2.58 = £1 would be an equilibrium exchange rate. At that exchange

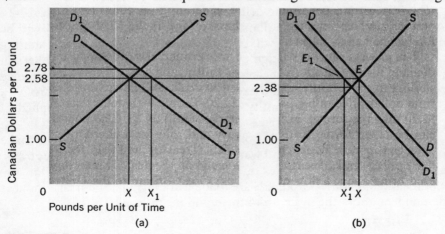

Figure 17-3

Exchange rates under an international gold standard.

[2]*Since $35 = 1 ounce of gold and £13.6 = 1 ounce of gold, then £13.6 = $35 and £1 = $2.58.*

rate the total payments that the British want to make to Canada are X pounds sterling. This is exactly the quantity of pounds sterling needed by people in Canada to make all the payments to the British that they want to make at that exchange rate.

What would be the effect of an increase in Canadian demand for British goods? First, the demand for pounds sterling would increase, shifting the demand curve to the right to some such position as D_1D_1. The shortage of pounds at the original equilibrium price would be XX_1 and would cause the price of the pound to rise. If it were to rise to $2.78 $= £1$—that is, to the new equilibrium level—forces would be set in motion to return it to the $2.58 level. Anyone with a pound sterling to invest can go into the foreign exchange market and buy dollars—$2.78 with each such pound. He can put 20 cents in his pocket, use the remaining $2.58 to buy a chunk of gold from the Canadian Treasury, and sell the gold to the British Treasury for one pound sterling. He can then repeat the process again and again. But note what is happening. *Additional* pounds sterling are coming into the foreign exchange market and an equivalent pound sterling value of gold is flowing from the Canadian Treasury into the British Treasury. As long as the dollar price of pounds sterling is above the $2.58 level, it pays those with pounds to buy dollars, purchase gold, and sell the gold to the British Treasury. This in turn places enough extra pounds sterling on the market to bring the dollar price of the pound back to the $2.58 level. In Figure 17-3(a) XX_1 pounds sterling worth of gold will be shipped to Great Britain per unit of time, generating an equivalent amount of pounds sterling—enough to fill the shortage at the $2.58 price—for the foreign exchange market.

The process can work the other way around as well. Suppose that Canadian demand for British goods decreases, shifting the demand curve for pounds sterling to the left in Figure 17-3(b) to D_1D_1 and decreasing the equilibrium dollar price of the pound to $2.38. People with dollars can now take $2.38 into the foreign exchange market and buy £1. The pound sterling can be taken to the British Treasury and sold for a chunk of gold. The gold can in turn be taken to the Canadian Treasury and sold for $2.58—its fixed price—and 20 cents has been made on the deal. Transactions of this kind bring about a flow of gold from Great Britain to Canada. The increased dollar demand for pounds sterling to buy gold raises the exchange rate back to its original level of $2.58. In effect, the British Treasury by selling gold at £13.6 per ounce generates a dollar demand for pounds sufficient to support the price of the pound at $2.58. For the decrease in the market demand for pounds to D_1D_1 an amount of gold valued at X_1X pounds must be shipped, creating an equivalent extra demand for pounds.

Actually, because of shipping and insurance charges for gold movements, the exchange rate could fluctuate slightly above or slightly below $2.58 = £1. Suppose that on a $2.58 chunk of gold these costs are one cent. The exchange rate must go above $2.59 = £1 to set in motion a gold movement out of Canada. It must fall below $2.57 = £1 in order to cause a gold movement in.

A Major-Currency Standard

An alternative method has been used by some countries to peg their exchange rates. Instead of defining their respective monetary units in terms of gold, they define them in terms of the currency of one of the major trading countries of the world—say, the pound sterling of Great Britain or the dollar of the United States. If the major currency so selected by a country is in turn defined in terms of gold, the country is said to be on a *gold-exchange* standard. To keep the price of the major currency constant in units of the home currency, the home country must stand ready to buy or sell the (foreign) major currency at the established pegged price.[3]

Suppose, for example, that West Germany defines the mark as one fourth of a U.S. dollar; that is, it sets the price of the U.S. dollar at four marks. Suppose in Figure 17-4(a) that price P, the equilibrium price, is at this level. There is neither a shortage nor a surplus of U.S. dollars.

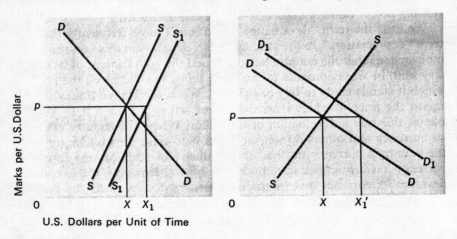

Figure 17-4
Exchange rates under a major-currency standard.

[3] *Alternatively, it may put exchange controls into effect or take other actions to control its foreign trade directly. These alternatives will be considered later.*

Suppose now that U.S. demand for West German goods increases, moving the supply curve of U.S. dollars to West Germany to the right to S_1S_1. A surplus of U.S. dollars comes on the market and tends to drive the mark price of the dollar down. The West German government in this case engages in price-support operations by going into the market and buying the excess of XX_1 U.S. dollars per unit of time. The West German government will be accumulating foreign exchange.

Suppose now that in Figure 17-4(b) the initial equilibrium price of the U.S. dollar is again P marks but that an increase in West German demand for U.S. goods occurs. The demand curve for U.S. dollars will shift to the right to D_1D_1 and a shortage of U.S. dollars occurs at the designated exchange rate. Now, in order to prevent the exchange rate on the U.S. dollar from rising, the West German government must supply dollars in the amount of XX_1 per unit of time.

Countries on major-currency exchange standards historically have established *exchange stabilization funds* to engage in the buying and selling operations just described.[4] Since 1945 the operations of their exchange stabilization funds have been supplemented by, and in some cases supplanted by, foreign exchange drawing rights on the International Monetary Fund (IMF).[5]

Depreciation and Devaluation

Whenever the price of a foreign currency in terms of a given country's monetary units goes up, the currency of the given country is said to have *depreciated* with respect to that of the foreign country. Or, to put it directly in terms of exchange rates, a country's currency is said to have depreciated with respect to a foreign currency whenever its exchange rate on the foreign currency rises. Thus, if in Chile the escudo price of the Canadian dollar rises from nine escudos equals one dollar to ten escudos equals one dollar, the escudo has been depreciated relative to the dollar. Its purchasing power in Canada has been decreased.[6]

We hear the term "devaluation" used much more frequently than the term "depreciation." In the strictest sense, *devaluation* of a country's currency means that the country has decreased the gold content of its mone-

---

[4]*Exchange stabilization funds were set up during the 1930's by Britain (1932), the United States (1934), Canada (1935), France (1936) and Switzerland, Czechoslovakia, Rumania, Colombia, Argentina, Belgium, Latvia and the Netherlands.*

[5]*See pp. 395-398.*

[6]*If the exchange rates between the Canadian dollar and other countries with which Chile trades do not change, the escudo will also have depreciated with respect to the other countries' currencies. The international purchasing power of the escudo will be less.*

tary unit, or what amounts to the same thing, has increased the price at which it stands ready to buy or sell gold. When the United States in 1933 raised the price at which it would buy or sell gold from $21 to $35 per ounce, this was a devaluation of the U.S. dollar. When one country devalues its currency and others do not, the effect is to raise the exchange rate of the country's currency on that of the others. In addition, the country's currency has *depreciated* in terms of the others. However, if one country devalues its currency and its trading partners devalue theirs by proportionate amounts, there will be no changes in exchange rates and, hence, no depreciation of the currency.

Devaluation has come to be used in a broader sense to mean any increase in the pegged exchange rate of one country's currency for others. Thus the 1962 increase in the Canadian dollar exchange rate for other currencies was termed a devaluation of the Canadian dollar. From the point of view of the United Kingdom, the pound sterling price of the Canadian dollar was decreased from approximately £0.35 to £0.33 per dollar. From the Canadian point of view, the dollar price of the pound sterling was increased from approximately $2.90 to $3.01.

Balance of Payments Disequilibria

Though a balance of payments statement always balances, nations are not always in equilibrium in achieving that balance. The situations of the preceding section in which Canada experiences either a gold outflow or a gold inflow, or in which West Germany either accumulates or uses up convertible currencies are obviously examples of balance of payments disequilibria. A country accumulates gold and foreign exchange and may add to its net position in the IMF when it has a balance of payments surplus and it loses gold and foreign exchange and may have to draw on its IMF reserve position when it has a balance of payments deficit. In general, surpluses cause countries little concern—their international purchasing power is increasing. But deficits are a different story. A country facing a shortage of the means of making international payments will exhibit great concern—witness that of Britain and the United States through the decade of the 1960's. It is with deficits that we shall be concerned here.

Most countries cannot meet a prolonged balance of payments deficit without imposing controls or restrictions of some kind on the availability of foreign exchange, on imports, and on other payments abroad or without taking some kind of corrective action to eliminate the causes of the deficit. An outflow of gold or the using up of its stocks of foreign exchange to keep the home-country price of foreign exchange from rising must be short-run expedients for a country. The long-run solutions lie elsewhere.

Causes of Deficits and Surpluses

Balance of payments deficits and surpluses arise as a result of changes in a country's conditions of supply of or demand for foreign exchange when its exchange rate is pegged at a level that is initially in equilibrium. Another way of looking at the same thing is to view exchange rates as being pegged above or below the equilibrium levels that would prevail under differing sets of demand and supply conditions. To get at the fundamental causes of deficits and surpluses, then, we must look to the causes of the demand and supply changes.

Components of Demand and Supply

The major components of the demand for foreign exchange are readily apparent from the balance of payments classification of the items entering into international transactions. For Canada the major part of demand is for the import of goods and services items, including the "importation" of trips abroad. Less important, are capital movements out—new loans and investments made abroad by both the government and private businesses.

The sources of supply of foreign exchange are the same set of items moving in the opposite direction. For Canada the major source consists of exports of goods and services. Capital movements in—investments and loans made in Canada by other countries—are second in importance.

Monetary and Income Causes

One set of causes of changes in a country's demand for and supply of foreign exchange has *monetary and income* origins. A country may find itself in a situation in which its price level is rising relatively faster than the price levels in the countries with which it trades. Or it may find that its national income level is rising relatively faster than those of the countries with which it trades, even though no relative price-level changes are evident. These two forces frequently work in the same direction; however, one may be operative without the other, and in some instances they may work in opposite directions.

To illustrate the effects of relative price changes, suppose in Figure 17-5 that Canadian demand curve for and the supply curve of pounds sterling are *DD* and *SS*, respectively. The equilibrium exchange rate is *P* Canadian dollars per pound. Suppose that the exchange is pegged at this level.

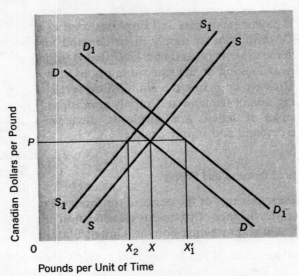

Figure 17-5
Balance of payments disequilibrium from relative price-level changes.

What would be the effects of rising prices in Canada relative to those in Great Britain? As British prices decrease relative to Canadian prices, Canadian buyers shift their purchases toward British goods and import activity is increased, causing an increase in demand for pounds sterling from DD in Figure 17-5 to D_1D_1. At the same time, Canadian exporters find that the rising price level in Canada increases their costs of production, shifting their product supply curves to the left and increasing the prices that the British must pay for those products. Canadian exports and British imports decrease, shifting the supply curve of pounds sterling to the left to S_1S_1. At the pegged exchange rate P there will be a shortage of foreign exchange or a balance of payments deficit of X_2X_1.

The effects of an income increase in Canada relative to that in Great Britain is illustrated in Figure 17-6. Again we suppose that P is initially the equilibrium exchange rate and that it is then pegged at that level. As income in Canada increases, that is, as Canadian purchasing power grows, the demand for import goods and services from Great Britain also increases. Rising affluence in Canada will also increase the desire to lend and to invest abroad. All of these factors serve to shift the demand curve for pounds to the right, toward some position such as D_1D_1. But in this case, since no change is assumed in Canadian costs of production or in British purchasing power, there will be no change in the British desire to import from Canada or in the supply curve of pounds. The Canadian balance of payments deficit will be XX_1 in terms of pounds sterling.

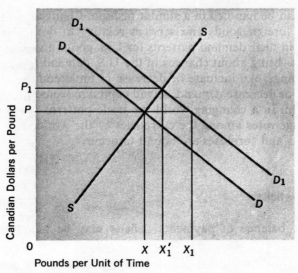

Figure 17-6
Balance of payments disequilibrium from relative income-level changes.

Structural Causes

The other principal causes of changes in the demand for and the supply of foreign exchange are *structural* in nature. They result from changes in the structure of demands for goods and services or from changes in the desire to lend and invest abroad when these changes are not induced by relative price-level and/or income-level changes. In addition, they may result from changes in the supply curves of goods and services—from changes in the quantities and qualities of resources available or from changes in technology in different countries.

For purposes of illustration, suppose that technology in British industries, including export industries, advances rapidly, substantially lowering production costs and shifting British product supply curves to the right. The resulting lower prices of British goods to Canada will induce people in Canada to make larger expenditures for imports from Great Britain, provided the Canadian demand for those goods is elastic, as it is very likely to be. Consequently, Canadian demand for pounds sterling will shift to the right, as illustrated again by the movement from DD to D_1D_1 in Figure 17-6, creating a balance of payments deficit of XX_1 pounds at an exchange of P dollars per pound.

The effects of other structural changes in trade patterns and trade relationships can be handled in a similar fashion. Changes in Canadian demand patterns for foreign goods and services relative to domestic goods and services—or in their demand patterns for Canadian goods and services relative to their own—bring about changes in the Canadian demand for and supply of foreign exchange. An increase or decrease in capital movements out or capital movements in will increase or decrease demand. In a changing world, the trade patterns change, and with fixed exchange rates among the currencies of the world, balance of payments deficits and surpluses are bound to occur.

Control of Deficits

Short-run balance of payments deficits may be met in most cases through the depletion of the deficit country's stock of gold and/or its other international reserves. But what can a country do to correct a chronic or long-term balance of payments deficit? The major possibilities are (1) to bring about a relative contraction of national income and/or a relative decrease in the price level, (2) government control or rationing of foreign exchange, (3) other measures to restrict imports and payments abroad, and (4) depreciation of the currency.

Income and Price-Level Adjustments

In the nineteenth century the classic method of adjustment to a balance of payments deficit was a relative contraction in the deficit country's national income. The major trading countries were on gold standards and the adjustment mechanism worked automatically. A country developing a deficit lost gold to the country (or countries) with a surplus. Since the money supply of each country was tied to the quantity of gold that it had, the money supply of the deficit country contracted while that of the surplus country increased.[7] The decrease in the money supply of the deficit country reduced aggregate demand or total spending, including demand for imports. The expansion of the money supply increased aggregate demand, including the demand for imports, in the surplus countries. Thus the demand for foreign exchange was decreased and the supply of foreign exchange was increased for the deficit country, thereby reducing and eventually eliminating the deficit. If the income contraction in the deficit country was accompanied by falling prices and if the income expansion in the surplus countries was accompanied by rising prices, so much the better. Foreign goods became more expensive to the deficit country, encouraging still less importation from abroad. Deficit country products

[7]*Think of gold as constituting the currency and the reserves of a country's banking system. A loss in gold thus decreases both the currency component and the deposit component of the country's money supply. An increase in gold has the opposite effect.*

became less expensive to the surplus countries, encouraging them to purchase more from the deficit countries.

In terms of national income analysis a balance of payments surplus has the effect on national income as net investment—in fact, it means net investment in the deficit countries by the surplus countries. So the development of a surplus leads to an expansion of national income and an increase in the country's imports. The development of a deficit for the deficit country amounts to a decrease in net investment; in and of itself the deficit represents negative net investment. This leads to income contraction in the deficit country and a consequent reduction in its demand for imports.

In the twentieth century, as countries have gone off the gold standard and have learned more and more about using monetary and fiscal techniques to stabilize and stimulate their own economies, income adjustments are no longer permitted to exercise their corrective influences. What country would be willing to deliberately undergo recession and court depression in order to correct a balance of payments deficit? Certainly not Canada in the 1960s! Still, some lip service is paid to the income method of adjustment. Countries with deficits are encouraged to subject themselves to "balance of payments discipline," but this is usually intended to mean that they should control any inflationary tendencies that they might have rather than that they should actually contract income and the employment level.

Exchange Controls

Exchange controls provide an alternative means of controlling a chronic balance of payments deficit. They require government operation of the deficit country's foreign exchange market. In the typical situation all receivers of foreign exchange must sell what they receive to the government at the official or pegged rate. Then any party desiring to import, invest abroad, or otherwise make payments abroad must go to the government to obtain the necessary foreign exchange.

The economics of exchange control are not new to us. The problem is essentially one of rationing. The balance of payments deficit, or the shortage of foreign exchange, indicates that its price is fixed below the equilibrium level. If price or the exchange rate is not used to ration available supplies of foreign exchange, then some other rationing mechanism must be employed. An exchange control system provides such a mechanism.

Black markets in foreign exchange frequently arise where exchange controls are in effect. Those who want foreign exchange are willing to pay a price higher than that fixed by the government for the quantity that is available, and there are usually persons around who are willing and able to accommodate them—illegally, of course. If the black market were permitted to develop, no transactions would occur at the official exchange rate. Those with foreign exchange to sell would sell it in the black market rather than to the government. The black market rate, which would be the equilibrium rate in such a case, would prevail and the exchange rate at which transactions occur would no longer be pegged.

To prevent black markets from developing, countries resorting to exchange controls use various methods to insure that all foreign exchange supplies will be turned over to the government. *Export licensing* is one such device. This means that a permit must be obtained from the government before exports can be shipped out, thus a record of the transaction and the foreign exchange to be received are in the government's possession from the outset. Additionally, laws or decrees are put into effect, making it illegal for anyone to dispose of any foreign exchange except to the appropriate government agency.

The government of a country employing exchange controls is put in the position of determining what kinds of payments to other countries are to be permitted and the quantities in which those payments can be made. Those desiring to make payments abroad are required to make applications for the necessary foreign exchange and ordinarily must specify the purposes of the payments. The pattern of imports can be determined by the government through the control of the allocations of foreign exchange. Frequently, imports that compete with home-produced goods are restricted. Capital movements out are generally curtailed.

Before leaving this measure, it should be pointed out that Canada utilized exchange controls from October 1, 1939 until mid-December, 1951.

Other Control Measures

A deficit country may resort to still other means of restricting the amounts that can be spent abroad. One of the most venerable methods is the tariff, and its use raises such important issues that most of the next chapter will be devoted to it. Another effective method of limiting the importation of goods is through the use of import quotas. Still others are direct limitations on amounts that can be invested abroad, curtailment of dividend and interest payments abroad, and taxes or direct limitations on foreign travel. Most economists can readily extend the list.

Depreciation of the Currency

A country with a prolonged balance of payments deficit may find it necessary to raise the exchange rate of its currency on other currencies or to depreciate its currency. Great Britain took this step in 1949 and again in 1967. Deficits occur when a country's exchange rate is pegged below the equilibrium level. We would expect, then, that an increase in the price of foreign currencies could eliminate the deficit.

The basic mechanism can be demonstrated with the aid of Figure 17-6. Suppose there is an increase in the demand for pounds from DD to D_1D_1. At the pegged exchange rate P a deficit of XX_1 per time period comes into existence for Canada. Suppose now that the currency of Canada is depreciated by an increase in the pegged exchange rate level P to P_1. At the higher dollar price of the pound, it becomes more expensive to Canada to make payments abroad for whatever reason, cutting down on the quantity of pounds demanded. At the same time, it becomes less expensive to the British to make payments to Canada for imports, for investment purposes, and for any other reason. The higher price of the pound brings forth a larger quantity supplied and induces demanders to ration themselves to that which is made available. Both quantity demanded and quantity supplied will be X_1 at the new exchange rate P_1.

The next corrective step beyond adjustments in the pegged level of exchange rates is simply not to have them pegged at all. Rate that are free to move in response to changes in supply and demand, both monetary and structural, are generally referred to as *flexible exchange rates*. A growing group of economists has been advocating a system of flexible exchange rates instead of the currently used system of pegged exchange rates in order to eliminate both balance of payments problems and problems of shortages (of deficit countries) of international reserves.

Pegged versus Flexible Exchange Rates

Most countries of the world today adhere to pegged exchange rates, and those experiencing balance of payments deficits exercise restrictions over payments abroad rather than permitting exchange rates to rise to equilibrium levels. Why is this so? The answers are not clear-cut. Economists are not agreed on whether pegged exchange rates with restrictions on payments abroad are best for deficit countries or whether it would be best to avoid deficits altogether by means of flexible exchange rates.

Arguments for Pegged Exchange Rates

A principal argument made in favour of pegged exchange rates is that major currency countries such as the United States have an obligation to protect the many holders of their currencies from fluctuations in their international values. Many countries, for example, hold U.S. dollars in their central banks as central bank reserves. It is considered "unfair" to let the dollar depreciate, since this would reduce the international purchasing power of the dollars they hold. It is also thought by many to be unfair to such countries for the United States to let the value of the dollar rise—that is, to let the dollar prices of the currencies of such countries fall—when the United States has a balance of payments surplus and the latter countries have deficits. Appreciation of the dollar means depreciation of the international purchasing powers of their currencies.[8]

Another major argument in favour of pegged exchange rates is that speculation of a destabilizing nature would occur if exchange rates were free to fluctuate. There is a large amount of money in currencies of different countries, so the argument runs, in the hands of persons who would rush this money from country to country in the pursuit of differences in short-term earnings opportunities on it. Suppose, for example, that short-term speculators believe that the dollar price of the pound sterling is going to rise above its present level. They will sell their dollars on foreign exchange markets and demand pounds sterling. The effect, of course, will be to drive up the dollar price of pounds sterling. In a very short time the entire movement could be reversed, driving the dollar price of the pound down again (or, what amounts to the same thing, driving up the pound price of the dollar). This *hot money* may rush from country to country, causing rapid and extensive changes in exchange rates. These, in turn, would have adverse effects on international trade because of the uncertainties they may generate regarding their course over time.

A third reason why deficit countries often prefer pegged exchange rates is that the pegged rate permits them to import at lower prices in terms of their own currencies than would be the case if the price of foreign currencies were permitted to rise. The deficit country's currency is *overhauled* in terms of foreign currencies, and this means better *terms of trade* for the deficit country. Suppose that India has a deficit with respect to its trade with Canada and that the exchange rate is pegged at 7 rupees to one dollar. Ignoring transportation costs, an import from Canada priced at five Canadian dollars will cost Indians 35 rupees at the pegged rate. Now, if the market price of the Canadian dollar were permitted to rise to 9 rupees, the same item would cost Indian 45 rupees. Thus an over-valued rupee permits importation of Canadian goods on more favourable terms.[9]

---

[8]*The important question that arises here is that of what constitutes a "fair" exchange rate. What makes the current pegged exchange rates the "fair" or "correct" ones?*

[9]*Export industries of the deficit country are subjected to adverse discrimination. The artificially low rupee price of the dollar means lower rupee receipts for exporters than they would receive if the rupee price of the dollar were permitted to rise. The country's supply of dollars will be smaller because of the lower volume of exports.*

Still other arguments are brought to bear by those who favour fixed exchange rates. An important factor in the maintenance of pegs, although not an argument usually brought forward by proponents, is that a decrease in the value of a country's currency in terms of that of other countries has come to be regarded as an international loss of face. Such a decrease in the value of the currency is considered an admission of financial irresponsibility on the part of the country concerned. Witness the dialogue over the 1967 British devaluation of the pound and the expressed determination of authorities in the United States to "protect" the U.S. dollar.

Arguments for Flexible Exchange Rates

A principal argument for flexible exchange rates has been advanced already. A system of flexible exchange rates would avoid balance of payments disequilibria and consequent problems of international reserve shortages. Restrictions on payments abroad would be unnecessary. There would be no need for exchange controls, import restrictions, controls on foreign investment, or travel abroad to alleviate balance of payments problems.

Another point often made is that flexible exchange rates would place the values of foreign goods in proper relation to those of domestic goods. If Canadian demand for French goods and services expands relative to that for domestic goods, it should be expected that the dollar price of the franc will rise to reflect the relatively higher value placed by Canadian residents on those goods and services. Exchange rate changes would thus properly reflect the structural changes occurring among the trading countries of the world.

A third argument in favour of flexible exchange rates is that they permit individual countries to pursue independent monetary and fiscal policies with minimum effects on the economies of other countries. Suppose, for example, that the United States experiences rapid inflation while Canada does not. With fixed exchange rates, U.S. goods become more expensive to Canadians, thus cutting down on the amounts that Canada can import. At the same time, the export industries of Canada are stimulated by rising U.S. demand for the now relatively cheaper Canadian goods. The combination of these two effects means that in real terms Canadians have smaller amounts of goods and services to consume. The U.S. inflation is thus harmful to Canada.

Suppose now that in the face of relatively more inflation in the United States than in Canada exchange rates are flexible. Rising U.S. prices cut down on the quantities demanded of U.S. goods by Canada, thus decreasing the supply of Canadian dollars made available to the United States. Rising U.S. demand for Canadian goods increases the demand for

Canadian dollars in the United States. As Canadian dollars become short in the United States, the U.S. dollar price of the Canadian dollar rises until the shortage is alleviated. The rising U.S. dollar price of the Canadian dollar, or the falling Canadian dollar price of the U.S. dollar, thus again makes Canadian importation from the United States attractive, tending to offset the adverse effects of the U.S. inflation. Similarly, the rising U.S. dollar price of the Canadian dollar makes Canadian goods look less attractive to U.S. buyers, thus tending to offset the stimulating effects of the U.S. inflation on Canadian export industries. In summary, the disrupting effects of inflation in one country on its trade with other countries tends to be offset by exchange rate adjustments under a system of flexible exchange rates. This counter-mechanism is missing where exchange rates are pegged.

Proponents of free market exchange rates question whether hot money movements would lead to highly unstable exchange rates. They argue that speculation and forward markets[10] may well serve to stabilize exchange rates in the same way that they stabilize commodity markets in the very short run. They expect speculators to be trying consistently to purchase relatively cheap currencies, thus driving their prices up at times when their values tend to be low. They expect that when currencies become relatively expensive they will be sold, thus driving their prices below what they would be otherwise. These activities are expected to prevent extreme fluctuations from occurring.

Foreign Exchange Policy—The Canadian Experience

Canada has had considerable experience with both fixed and flexible exchange rates. From 1853 to August 1914, Canada followed the gold standard policy of fixed exchange rates. With the outbreak of World War I, the gold convertibility of Dominion of Canada notes was suspended and Canada only resumed gold payments again for a short time from July 1926 to January 1929. During the rest of the period until World War II, Canada had a fluctuating exchange rate.

During World War II Canada pegged its currency to the American dollar at a rate of one Canadian dollar equals 90.9 U.S. cents, and all free foreign exchange in the possession, ownership or control of residents was stringently regulated by the newly created Foreign Exchange Control Board. In July 1946, the Canadian dollar was restored to parity with the

[10]*Forward exchange markets, as distinct from (though directly connected with) normal exchange markets which operate in current (or "spot") transactions, deal in current commitments to buy and sell currencies for delivery and payment at some prescribed time in the future.*

U.S. dollar in an attempt to check the contagion of American price inflation.

The next alteration in the exchange rate was in September, 1949, in association with a general round of devaluation following the 30.5 percent devaluation of the pound sterling. To protect Canada's competitive position and balance of payments, the Canadian dollar was devalued once more to 90.9 U.S. cents but devaluation soon proved a mistake. A growing opinion that the Canadian dollar was undervalued at its new rate led Americans to buy Canadian securities heavily, while Canadians cut their holdings of American securities. By 1950, the inflow of capital had become a flood, and the monetary authorities were faced with a dilemma. The speculative inflow of capital, if unchecked, would increase the reserves of the chartered banks and make the existing inflationary situation intolerable. Yet, to neutralize these reserves required an enormous expansion in the government debt, as new issues were sold to the chartered banks to offset the reserves arising from this influx. To stem the tide, the Government abandoned its policy of maintaining the Canadian dollar at a fixed level and established a flexible rate system on September 30, 1950. As noted earlier, foreign exchange restrictions were gradually relaxed and were completely abolished in the middle of December, 1951.

Immediately after the authorities removed the pegged rate, the Canadian dollar appreciated sharply. It reached parity with the American dollar on January 22, 1952 and, apart from dipping briefly back to parity late in 1955, remained at a premium until mid-1961. Over this period, the Canadian dollar fluctuated in a range of fractionally more than 13 U.S. cents.

In June 1961, amidst signs that the premium on the Canadian dollar was unduly encouraging imports and discouraging exports, thereby worsening the unemployment situation in Canada, the Finance Minister announced the government's intention to manipulate the exchange rate in a downward direction. The immediate effect of this statement was a sharp depreciation of the exchange rate to just below 97 U.S. cents or a drop of about 3 cents overnight. A combination of forces held the Canadian dollar quite steady, at about a 3 percent discount with the American dollar, until the end of October when confidence in Canada's currency began to wane.

By early 1962, far from manipulating the exchange rate downward, the authorities were selling foreign exchange to slow its descent, trying to stabilize it at 95 U.S. cents. When the speculative outflow of funds continued, the Canadian government, in consultation with I.M.F. devalued its currency by 2.9 percent from the prevailing market rate to a new fixed parity of 92.5 U.S. cents (the reciprocal of this official par value is $1.081 Canadian for $1.00 American). This meant that Canada was now obliged to maintain the spot exchange rate of its currency within the official IMF trading limits of 91.575 U.S. cents and 93.425 U.S. cents. In a word, Canada's bold experiment had ended.

There was no pressing need to reconsider the exchange rate adopted in 1962 until the second quarter of 1970 when the domestic cash balances of the Canadian government began to fall rapidly. This implied that large amounts of Canadian dollars were being used to acquire foreign funds and to keep the rate on the Canadian dollar from rising above the upper limit of its fixed range. While there was little long-run justification on economic grounds for a higher exchange value for the Canadian dollar, Canada's remarkably strong trade performance (in the first five months of the year Canada had a record trade surplus just in excess of $1 billion) and its official anti-inflationary policies, which stood out in contrast not only to the United States but also to most major overseas countries, combined through the early months of 1970 to put strong upward pressure on the Canadian dollar at the expense of the government's cash balances. On May 11, the government announced an unusual combination of measures to build up its supply of domestic cash and to check the foreign exchange inflow. The first measure was the borrowing of $250 million through a special issue of treasury bills to the chartered banks. At the same time, in order to prevent this transaction becoming an unwanted source of monetary expansion, the Bank of Canada raised the secondary reserve requirements of the chartered banks from 8 percent to 9 percent, effective in July. The Bank rate was simultaneously reduced from 8 percent to 7½ percent to indicate that the increase in secondary reserves was not to be interpreted as a domestic tightening action but was aimed at external capital movements. Despite these steps the inward flood of foreign exchange continued and over the weekend of May 30-31, the government decided to let the dollar float free again in exchange markets. It immediately bounded up to 97.09 cents, before receding gradually to a low of 95.55 cents on June 16. Since then, the Canadian dollar has traded in a normal range of 96 to 97 cents.

Evaluating the Canadian exchange policy choices since World War II is an extremely complicated problem. Nevertheless numerous scholars agree with Professor Johnson that "the Canadian return to a fixed exchange rate (in 1962) involved a failure of governmental competence, not of the floating rate system. . . . "[11] They cite the inappropriate monetary

---

[11]Harry G. Johnson, *"The International Competitive Position of the United States and the Balance of Payments Prospects for 1968,"* Review of Economics and Statistics, *February 1964, p. 28.*

policy and faulty debt management of the late fifties which kept the exchange rate at a premium relative to the U.S. dollar. They also argue that the exchange emergency of 1962, which led to the fixing of the rate, was really caused by official statements and that nothing "real" had produced it. On the other hand, Professor McLeod contends that "the fluctuating rate policy failed to protect the Canadian economy from externally originating distortions and produced other distortions of its own; that the fluctuating-rate policy left the market leaderless, and vulnerable to self-reinforcing swings in response to hopes and fears rather than economic facts; . . . that a significant overvaluation of the Canadian dollar did occur and persist under the fluctuating-rate policy."[12] The debate concerning that decision still goes on.

Most economists agree that the recent decision to refloat the dollar was the best choice among a number of unattractive alternatives. However, unpegging the dollar has won Canada no friends in the international monetary community. The IMF has recently reminded Canada of its commitment to resume an effective par value "as soon as circumstances permit." In fact the IMF has made it clear that Canada's floating rate policy must be nothing more than a short-term transitional arrangement. However, the continuing strength of the Canadian dollar on exchange markets has put the government in an awkward position. It recognizes Canada's interest in cooperating under the rules of the international monetary system. But at the same time, it is conscious of continuing elements of uncertainty in Canada's balance-of-payments position. To choose a fixed rate before these uncertainties in the balance of payments are allowed to work themselves out of the system would run the risk of once again encouraging unmanageable pressures in the exchange market with consequent disruption to domestic monetary policies. Accordingly many analysts believe that the government is not prepared to repeg the Canadian dollar at the present level (96 to 97 cents) and is ready to wait until the dollar falls to a lower level in six months or so. Canadian officials are hopeful that IMF members will not press Canada to repeg the dollar before then. If they do, the confrontation could become bitter. It should be added that some economists predict that Canada will try to keep the floating exchange rate indefinitely. It is thus by no means clear where or when the Canadian dollar will be repegged.

[12]*A. N. McLeod,* A Critique of the Fluctuating Exchange Rate Policy in Canada. *New York: C. J. Devine Institute of Finance, 1965, Bulletins 34-35, p. 48.*

Twentieth-Century World Financial Developments

Pre-World War I

International trade in the nineteenth century became rather highly developed, with most countries of the world pursuing production and trade largely along comparative-advantage lines. Restrictions to multilateral trade were minimal. Differences in the rate of technological development among countries and the discovery of new resource supplies in some but not in others brought about changing production patterns among different countries. Although rather severe adjustments were necessary at times, these were made without prolonged balance of payments difficulties.

Many economists attribute the successful adjustments of the period to the gold standards that formed the basis of the monetary systems of most countries. Countries that developed excesses of imports over exports, or rather whose payments exceeded their foreign exchange receipts, lost gold. The effect was a contraction of their money supply and a relative deflation. Deflation curtailed their payments abroad and augmented their receipts from abroad, thereby tending to correct the difficulty. The correction was furthered, too, by some degree of inflation in the gold-receiving countries, since their exports were discouraged and their imports were stimulated.

World War I through World War II

During World War I the "old" international payments system experienced severe dislocations. The Great Depression of the 1930's, followed by World War II, administered the *coup de grace*. Disruptions in trade patterns and gold losses by some countries induced them to abandon gold standards. Pegged exchange rates, balance of payments problems, and trade restrictions became the order of the day. The gold standards of the interwar years of countries professing to be on gold standards were different creatures from those of the old days. Governments were beginning to assume the responsibility for the control of their own money supplies. They were beginning to use monetary and fiscal policies both to offset the deflationary forces of gold drains and the inflationary forces of gold receipts that had characterized the "old" gold standards. With individual nations pursuing independent national monetary and fiscal objectives, relative changes in price levels and national incomes could no longer perform balance of payments equilibrating functions as they had under the "old" gold standards with pegged exchange rates. Under the "new" gold standards, gold was used only to define the monetary unit and to make international payments. It no longer served as an effective control agent over national money supplies.[13]

By defining their monetary units in terms of given amounts of gold, the "new" gold standard countries automatically established pegged exchange rates among their currencies. In this respect the "new" gold standards were no different from the "old." But the pursuit of independent monetary and fiscal policies by the different countries made it impossible for some of them to maintain gold reserves at the fixed exchange rates. Great Britain went off the gold standard in 1931 and several other countries followed suit. As already indicated, Canada found it necessary at the beginning of 1929 to revoke the unrestricted convertibility of Dominion notes and to impose an unofficial embargo on the export of gold. In October 1931 these measures were officially sanctioned by an Order-in-Council. This order decreed that the export of gold would be permitted only under licences issued by the Department of Finance and that Canadian mines would dispose of their gold through the Canadian Mint according to definite conditions of purchase.[14] The gold standard was formally abandoned on April 10, 1933, when gold redemption of Dominion notes was suspended. By the late 1930's only five countries— the United States, France, Belgium, the Netherlands, and Switzerland— still claimed to maintain gold standards.

Post World War II

The chaotic state of international trade and exchange rates—partly controlled and partly uncontrolled—in the 1930's and through World War II brought home the idea that international understanding and co-operation would be desirable. The United States invited 50 nations to participate in an international financial conference at Bretton Woods, New Hampshire, in 1944. Out of this conference came the International Monetary Fund (IMF) and the International Bank of Reconstruction and Development (the World Bank). Only the former will occupy our attention at this juncture; we will consider the World Bank in Chapter 19.

The IMF commenced operations in 1947 with four major objectives. One was to provide a forum for consultation on problems of international

[13]*This discussion is not intended to imply that the old gold standard was superior to present-day independent monetary standards. Most economists argue that the classic gold standard is inferior—that changes in national income in gold-losing and gold-receiving countries represent a hard and inefficient way of adjusting to balance of payments disequilibria.*

[14]*The stringent restrictions imposed on gold dealings in 1931 were subsequently eased, and on March 22, 1955, the Canadian government eliminated all remaining obstacles to private gold transactions. In short, it is now possible in Canada to buy, sell or store gold, or trade it internationally without hindrance.*

payments among nations of the world. A second was to promote stability of exchange rates and a means of making orderly adjustments when these seemed to be in order. A third was to assist particular countries in the removal of direct controls over foreign exchange. A fourth purpose was to provide financial aid to countries experiencing *temporary* shortages of foreign exchange.

Toward these ends each member nation, as a condition of membership, must fulfill a quota subscription to the IMF of gold and of its own currency, with the size of the quota depending upon the country's national income and share of international trade. Of its total quota, 25 percent must be paid in gold (called the gold *tranche*) and the remainder may be paid in the country's own currency.

Member countries define their currencies in terms of either gold or U.S. dollars and these are submitted to IMF officials for approval. Once they are approved, exchange rates are, of course, determined. Canada's floating exchange rate from 1950 to 1962 was tolerated as a special exception. Member nations experiencing fundamental balance of payments deficits may devalue or depreciate their currencies by as much as 10 percent, but a greater devaluation or depreciation may be allowed to correct persistent deficits. This was the case in the British devaluation of 1967. However, it is expected—but not always accomplished in fact— that international consultation through the medium of the IMF will precede devaluation or depreciation.

From quota subscriptions the IMF has at its disposal a large assortment of foreign exchange which member nations may borrow to meet temporary balance of payments deficits. In any one year a member may borrow —that is, purchase with its own currency—foreign currencies amounting to 25 percent of the value of its own quota. When the total amount of foreign currencies purchased reaches a point such that the IMF holds 200 percent of the particular country's quota in the currency of the country, its purchasing rights are used up and the IMF will assist the country in correcting what has developed into a fundamental disequilibrium.

The IMF can supplement its financial resources by borrowing. Under the General Arrangement to Borrow, effective October 1962, 10 industrial countries voluntarily agreed to provide the Fund with standby credits up to U.S. $6 billion in addition to their subscriptions to the Fund. Canada's loan commitment is $200 million.

At their 1967 annual meeting, the governors of the IMF approved the creation of a new facility to meet the need for a supplement to existing reserve assets—gold, official foreign exchange holdings, and access to the IMF. The following two years were occupied with arduous technical discussions and negotiations to give form to the proposal which was ratified by a sufficient number of countries during the summer of 1969.

The new reserve asset takes the form of special drawing rights (SDR's) in a separate IMF account. These drawing rights, denominated in units of account equivalent to the gold value of one U.S. dollar, are distributed to IMF members in proportion to the Fund quotas. Unlike the existing rights available in the general account of the IMF, which are subordinate to various conditions, the use of SDR's are not subject to consultation or prior challenge nor contingent on the adoption of prescribed measures designed to restore balance-of-payments equilibrium. The amounts to be allocated over the first basic period of three years beginning January 1, 1970, are approximately $3.5 billion for 1970, $3 billion for 1971, and $3 billion for 1972. The SDR's are created as bookkeeping entries, since recipients do not have to exchange national currencies for them. The IMF will direct nations in need of convertible currencies to nations, willing to swap them for SDR's. The SDR's that are transferred to the creditor countries will earn a moderate rate of return while the debtor countries will pay a comparable rate of interest on the amounts which they employ. Clearly the SDR's add to the liquidity of an individual country, since they provide it with an addition to its international reserves.

The extent of IMF success in smoothing out international monetary arrangements is difficult to measure. Certainly it has provided an important forum for discussion of international financial problems. Although intended by its founders to provide short run stability to exchange rates while permitting long run flexibility (through devaluation of deficit country currencies), it has in fact brought about a large measure of inflexibility in exchange rates, a situation that has created serious problems for some countries which have not been satisfactorily resolved. On the other hand, the recent establishment and activation of the special drawing rights facility is generally believed to constitute a momentous innovation in the international monetary system. Whether the SDR scheme lives up to its promise remains to be seen.

Several general remarks should be made in concluding this chapter. In its early years the IMF was confronted by serious balance of payments deficits in Great Britain and Western Europe. World War II had played havoc with the domestic productive capacities of these countries, restricting the production of goods and services for export as well as for domestic consumption. The United States, on the other hand, emerged from the war with greater productive capacity than before. Sales of these countries to the United States were small and their purchases from the United States were large. Additionally, their overseas investments, together with their merchant marines, were reduced materially during the war, curtailing foreign exchange earnings from these sources. The deficit countries were not willing to let exchange rates of their currencies on U.S. dollars rise to what would have appeared at the time to be fantastic levels in order to achieve balance of payments equilibrium. Great Britain at last depreciated the pound by some 30 percent in 1949, and France depreciated the franc in both 1957 and 1958.

Since 1950 the shoe has been on the other foot. The United States has been running persistent balance of payments deficits since that time, with the exception of 1957, and has given up large quantities of gold to European countries as a result. By early 1968 the dwindling gold stock of the United States had created sufficient concern both in the United States and in the major countries of Western Europe to induce them to agree to restrict their gold purchases and sales to official transactions among themselves. Greater restrictions on payments abroad have been put into effect and more severe measures are being considered. The official U.S. position is that devaluation and depreciation of the dollar are out of the question. But intensive study of the alternatives facing that country is in order. Which would be the least costly to them and to the world in the long run: (1) restrictive monetary and fiscal policies leading to relative income- and price-level adjustments; (2) exchange controls and restrictions on other transactions, leading to payments abroad, or (3) depreciation of the U.S. dollar?

Summary

The exchange rate between any two currencies is simply the price of one in terms of the other. In a competitive market, the equilibrium exchange rate would be determined by the forces of demand and supply in the same way that any competitive price is determined. Alternatively, exchange rates may be pegged or fixed at given levels. Countries may peg their exchange rates by defining their monetary units in terms of gold. The resulting system is called an international gold standard. Pegging can also be accomplished among different countries by means of their defining par values for their currencies in terms of the currency of some major trading country such as the United States or Great Britain. This system is referred to as a major currency standard.

When countries peg their exchange rates, balance of payments problems may be created by monetary and income factors and by structural factors. These bring about long-run changes in demand for and supply of foreign exchange for any given country. Balance of payments deficits (surpluses) arise when the pegged exchange rate is below (above) an equilibrium level.

Countries employ a number of measures to control long run deficits.

Under the old gold standards of the nineteenth century national income and price changes occasioned by gold flows from country to country provided the equilibrating machinery. In the world today countries are not willing to let their national incomes or their prices rise or fall in accordance with balance of payments needs. Rather, they attempt to pursue monetary and fiscal policies geared to full employment, stability, and economic growth. Exchange controls and other restrictions on payments abroad, designed to conserve the limited supplies of foreign exchange available, are used instead. Countries sometimes depreciate their currency to eliminate the cause of the deficit.

Although it is widely agreed that flexible exchange rates would avoid balance of payments disequilibrium, countries—and many economists—prefer pegged exchange rates. They argue that stability and fairness in the international monetary system depend upon exchange-rate stability. They maintain, further, that speculation in exchange markets would render free market exchange rates highly unstable. In addition, deficit countries like the terms of trade provided them by exchange rates that overvalue their currencies. In general, countries believe that any deterioration in the exchange rate of their currencies for others would mean an international loss of face.

Proponents of free market exchange rates argue that such a system would eliminate balance of payments problems and would place the import prices of foreign goods in proper relation to prices of domestic goods. They would insulate countries from the effects of irresponsible monetary and fiscal policies used by others. They argue that speculation in exchange markets would more likely be stabilizing than destabilizing.

In 1944 the major trading countries of the world agreed to establish a mechanism to assist in international payments problems. Subsequently the International Monetary Fund commenced operation in 1947. It promotes stability in exchange rates by making foreign exchange available on a loan basis to countries experiencing temporary balance of payments deficits. On a long run basis it is supposed to provide the mechanism for alleviating deficits through adjustments in exchange rates. However, it appears in practice to have made exchange-rate adjustments by deficit countries more difficult than they were prior to its existence.

Exercises and Questions for Discussion

1. A recent article states, "The international gold standard is like the Bible. It is the best kind of guide available, but we do not have to use it." Comment on this statement.
2. If, by allowing its currency to depreciate, a country can improve its balance of

payments position, why are most countries hesitant to permit depreciation of their currencies? Explain in detail.

3. Distinguish between devaluation and depreciation. Can a country's currency be devalued and yet not depreciated? If so, how? What domestic or international factors might dictate the devaluation of a country's currency?

4. In principle, a flexible–exchange–rate country needs neither foreign exchange reserves nor foreign exchange authorities. Assess.

5. What caused the Canadian currency crisis of 1962? Did the depreciation solve the crisis? Why was 92.5 U.S. cents chosen as the exchange rate?

Selected Readings

Boreham, G. F., *et al.*, *Money and Banking: Analysis and Policy in a Canadian Context*. Toronto: Holt, Rinehart and Winston of Canada, 1969, Chaps. 22, 24, and 25.

Crouch, R. L., "The Canadian Experience with Flexible Exchange Rates: An Alternative Hypothesis". *The Canadian Journal of Economics,* November, 1968, pp. 815-819.

Ingram, James C., *International Economic Problems*. New York: John Wiley & Sons, Inc., 1966, Chaps. 4 and 7.

Kenen, Peter B., *International Economics*. Englewood Cliffs, N.J.: Prentice-Hall, Inc., 1964, Chap. 5.

18

Tariffs and Trade Organizations

Why does an Irish linen tablecloth cost less in Panama than in Canadian shops, or why is a Japanese camera less expensive in Hong Kong than in Canada? A practical answer, of course, is that Canada places a special tax called a tariff on Irish linen and cameras imported into Canada. These are examples of a long list of items on which Canada levies import duties —and Canadian tariffs are not as extensive as those of most countries. Panama and Hong Kong at the other extreme provide well-known examples of free trade areas.

In this chapter we shall examine the reasons why tariffs are levied and what implications they have for economic efficiency. The tariff issue has served so well as a focal point for political campaigns that it has become difficult for people to separate fact from fiction and logic from emotion. We shall attempt to pull these apart. In the latter part of the chapter recent international efforts to reduce tariffs are summarized.

The Rationale of Tariffs

"The free traders win the arguments but the protectionists win the votes," so the saying goes. In Chapter 15 the principle of comparative advantage that underlies all voluntary trading relations was examined in detail. We learned there that trade along comparative-advantage lines can operate for a country in exactly the same way as any technological development that increases the outputs attainable from given quantities of resources. Yet for centuries governments have persisted in throwing obstacles into the way of international trade. Among the restrictive devices used, tariffs—duties or taxes on imports—loom large.[1] Why have governments insisted on placing tariff barriers in the way of importation of goods and services? Some of the reasons have been discussed already and will be treated in a summary fashion. Others will require more elaboration.

For Revenue Purposes

Tariffs have been used for several centuries to provide revenue to governments. For example, custom duties comprised 60 percent of the revenue of the Province of Canada in 1860 and 66 percent in 1866, and about 75 percent of the total revenue of the Dominion government between 1867 and 1914. Among the large, economically advanced countries, other revenue sources have been developed, and the contribution of tariffs to total government receipts are relatively small today; in Canada about 9 percent of federal revenue comes from tariffs. But among many of the less economically advanced nations tariff collections still constitute a significant part of government revenue.

Tariffs or import duties, like the sales taxes that they are, may be levied either as specific or as *ad valorem* duties. Specific duties are based on such physical measures of product quantity as volume or weight, while *ad valorem* duties are levied as a percentage of a product's price.

A tariff levied for revenue purposes should never be high enough to shut off the importation of the product to which it is applied. Elasticity principles determine the tariff level at which revenue from the tariff will be maximized. Given the demand for importation of the product, the quantity imported will vary inversely with the level of the tariff. If the elasticity of the quantity imported with respect to the level of the tariff is greater than 1, total tariff collections can be increased by lowering the tariff. If the elasticity is less than 1, an increase in the tariff will increase revenue collections from it. Tariff collections are maximum at the tariff level at which the elasticity of the quantity imported with respect to the tariff is 1.

The tariff for revenue cannot be faulted completely—no more so than can a sales tax. But one can ask whether there are alternative ways of raising revenue that may be superior. Tariffs for revenue share the faults—and virtues—of sales and excise taxes, for the latter are essentially what

---

[1]*Other devices to protect the home producer against foreign competition include import quotas, foreign exchange control, anti-dumping duties, sanitary regulations, and the judgment of customs officials (the so-called "invisible tariff of administrative discretion").*

they are. They make the goods on which they are levied more costly relative to goods that escape them, thus inducing buyers to discriminate against the covered goods in favour of those that are not covered. It is frequently argued that the burden of the tariff is on the foreign seller, but its incidence, like that of any excise tax, is usually split in some way between the seller and the buyer, the split depending upon the elasticities of demand and of supply.

For Balance of Payments Purposes

Balance of payments deficits have provided an important stimulus to countries to increase their tariffs. Underdeveloped countries experiencing rapid inflation have used them extensively for this purpose. But major countries, too, when confronted by shortages of foreign currencies have resorted to import duties in an attempt to reduce the size of the deficit.

The anticipated effects of the tariff for this purpose are simple enough. The tariff is expected to increase the prices that importers must pay for their imports, thereby reducing the quantities demanded. Since the duties themselves are paid in the currency of the country that imposes them, the smaller volume of imports requires smaller quantities of foreign ex-

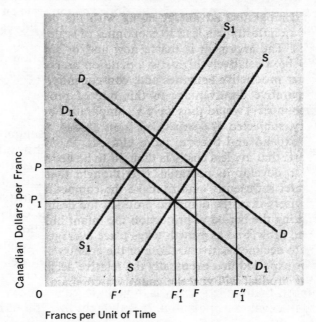

Figure 18-1
The effects of retaliatory tariffs.

change to pay to foreigners. The reduction in the demand for foreign exchange is expected to reduce the shortage.

Unfortunately for the deficit country, other countries do not always sit still when it enacts tariffs on the goods that it imports from them. Suppose, for example, that in Figure 18-1 the demand for and the supply of French francs are DD and SS, while the Canadian dollar price of francs is P_1. At that price Canada has a franc deficit of $F_1'F_1''$. Now suppose that Canada raises tariffs on imports from France, cutting back demand for francs to D_1D_1 in order to eliminate the franc deficit. France is quite likely to retaliate, raising its tariffs on goods imported from Canada. This countermove on the part of France cuts down on the goods purchased from Canada and moves the supply curve of francs to the left. If France suceeds in cutting its value of imports from Canada by as much as Canadian imports from France were cut, the new supply curve for francs will be S_1S_1. The deficit $F'F_1'$ will be as large as it was before and both countries will be denying themselves the advantages of international specialization and exchange.

For Promotion of Economic Development

Tariffs have been widely used by underdeveloped countries in an attempt to promote economic development. At least two overlapping sub-categories of tariff objectives within the general category can be distinguished: (1) the protection of infant industries and (2) the promotion of industrialization.

Infant Industries

The *infant-industry* argument for a tariff relies for its support on the principle of comparative advantage along with the possibility that the expansion of an industry can lead to economies of scale and long-run decreasing costs. The argument is that a new and/or small industry of a country may be a relatively high-cost operation as compared with the country's other productive activities and, consequently, the country may have a comparative disadvantage in this line of production. Another country (or countries) would thus have a comparative advantage and the given industry, subjected to competition from abroad, would never have a chance to expand and become more efficient. Protection from competitive imports that are less costly is thought to be necessary in order for the industry to develop its potential. It is thought that if a tariff is imposed with rates sufficiently high to make the competitive imports more expensive to users than the domestic product, the desired results can be obtained. During the period of protection the infant industry is expected to prosper and grow, and as growth takes place average production costs are expected to decline relative to those of the country's other productive activities. It is expected that eventually the relative decline in the costs of producing the product will give the country a comparative advantage in its production. If so desired, the tariff can then be eliminated.

On the face of it the argument appears to be logical enough. One possible trouble spot is that when a country has a comparative advantage in the production of some items it must necessarily have a comparative disadvantage in the production of others. As the infant industry grows and, as we assume it does, develops a position of comparative advantage, the country must at the same time be developing a comparative disadvantage in some product or products in which it previously had a comparative advantage. A position of comparative advantage in all products is not possible. The switch in the products in which a comparative advantage is held is not necessarily adverse, although under some circumstances it may be. Once the new industry is in a comparative-advantage position it may contribute more to the country's economic growth than the ones it displaces. Then again, it may not.

The infant industry argument is usually challenged on grounds of practice and experience with tariffs levied to protect the infants. In the first place, many question whether government officials or legislators—or economists for that matter—have the information and the analytical tools necessary to determine what infant industries of a country show the greater promise of developing a comparative advantage at some future date. Secondly, they argue that infant industries that are really promising will not need protection to grow up but will develop on their own. Thirdly, they point out that high-cost infant industries usually become high-cost adult industries and continue to require tariff protection for their existence. The babies never really grow up.

In Canada, a long list of industries have had tariffs for 70 years or more and still show little evidence of being able to survive without effective protection. As a matter of fact, the agricultural implements industry appears to be the only important Canadian example of an infant which has grown up.

Industrialization

Some countries, especially the less developed ones of Asia, Africa, and South America, use tariffs partly in the hope of spurring their economic development. They hope and expect that the tariffs will help them *industrialize*, or develop manufacturing industries, and industrialization is thought to be an essential ingredient in economic development. Through the selective use of tariffs it is thought that the composition of the country's imports can be controlled in such a way that growth in the industrial sector will be accelerated.

The typical tariff pattern of a country following this course of action favours the importation of industrial raw and semifinished materials while it discriminates against any manufactured products that are likely in any way to compete with home products. High tariffs are placed on the importation of expensive goods deemed to be luxury goods. Automobiles, for example, are frequently subjected to extremely high tariffs, if their importation is permitted at all. On the other hand, capital goods such as industrial machinery will carry low tariff rates or be admitted duty free. So, too, will industrial chemicals and fuels not produced domestically. Sometimes the country chooses specific industries to be promoted—for example, the steel industry or the fish-meal industry—and provides favourable treatment for imports that are needed for the industry's operation while imposing tariffs on imports of a competitive nature.

The shadowy point in this line of reasoning is whether industrialization is really a prime mover of economic development. Many people believe that it is, but there are some cogent economic arguments that will deny it. Economic development depends upon improvements in techniques of production and accumulation of *capital in general*—in agriculture, mining, services, and *all* lines of endeavour—not just in the area of manufacturing. Capital accumulation within a country requires that some part of *NNP* be saved to add to the country's stock of capital. The higher the country's *NNP*, the greater the possibilities for saving and for capital accumulation.

Tariffs used for any purpose, including the promotion of manufacturing of industrialization, limit the size of the country's *NNP* by denying the country the additional product that it can obtain through specialization and exchange along the lines of its comparative advantage. When they are used to favour manufacturing industries, these industries are promoted at the expense of the other sectors of the economy, including the export sectors. It is precisely the development of products for export that will make it possible for a country with small internal markets to grow and develop. Although there may be some correlation between economic development and industrialization, it is possible that industrialization follows or results from rather than precedes and causes eonomic development.

For Purposes of Protection

Another reason for the existence of tariffs is simply that of protecting certain domestic producers from foreign competition. This is the international trade manifestation of the almost universal desire to monopolize, to exclude as much competition as possible from the markets in which domestic producers sell.

Particular Interests versus the General Interest

Although we have demonstrated that countries can gain through international trade based on comparative advantages, not everyone within a specific country loses when trade is inhibited by the imposition of tariffs on the import of particular products. Producers of products sheltered from foreign competition and those who furnish resources to those producers ordinarily gain. The imposition of the import duties makes it relatively more expensive to purchase those products from abroad. Consumers shift away from consumption of the imported items toward consumption of the domestic substitutes. The increase in demand for the domestically produced products generates the same sort of gains for those furnishing resources to the industry as does an increase in demand from any other source.

The advancement in the economic well-being of those associated with the protected industry cannot be generalized to the entire economy. In fact, the principle of comparative advantage leads us to the conclusion that the opposite occurs. The tariff simply increases the cost of importing goods in which the country has a comparative disadvantage, thus reducing the total amount of product available to the country through trade below what it could be in the absence of the tariff. From a slightly different point of view, the tariff that increased demand for the protected products makes the latter more costly to consumers. The general price level is raised somewhat and the real income of consumers in general declines correspondingly. The direct economic effects of the tariff are, then, that it serves the particular interests of those engaged in producing the protected item, but it is contrary to the interests of consumers in general.

Cheap Foreign Labour

One common argument made for protective tariffs in Canada is that they protect us from the competition of products made by "cheap foreign labour." Thus Parliament is urged to enact tariffs on the importation of Japanese toys, transistor radios, and other products. The fear seems to be that Canadian producers will be undersold across the board by the cheaper foreign-made goods and that unemployment of Canadian labour along with lower living standards will be the end result.

At the outset it may be noted that cheap labour does not always enable foreign firms to produce at a lower money cost than Canadian firms that use more expensive labour. At existing exchange rates between the rupee and the Canadian dollar, can India, for example, using large amounts of inexpensive labour, build an aeroplane comparable to a Beaver or Otter at as low a dollar cost as Canadair? Probably not. The point is that comparative dollar costs per unit of producing a given kind of product do not necessarily depend upon comparative hourly costs of the labour used in producing the product. Comparative costs of *all* resources used, together with comparative technologies, determine comparative dollar costs of production.

More important, differences in the absolute money-cost levels of producing given products among countries are not the determinants of the gains to be obtained from engaging in trade. If Canada and the United States consume products A and B, with Canada holding a comparative advantage in the production of A while the United States does likewise with B, trade will permit gains for both countries even if costs of producing both products are higher in Canada. If Canada by giving up production of a unit of B can increase production of a unit of A by more than can the United States, and if the United States by giving up production of a unit of A can increase production of B by more than can Canada, then if Canada concentrates on the production of A, trading for B, while the United States concentrates on the production of B, trading for A, both countries can obtain larger amounts of A and B regardless of the money cost of labour or other resources in one country or the other.[2]

It should be reiterated that even though the interests of the consumers of a country are best served by the absence of a tariff seeking to exclude products made with cheaper foreign resources, some particular producing groups in the country will be better off with such a tariff. These are the groups who would produce domestically the products that the tariff would exclude. If they were engaged in producing the product prior to the time the threat of competition from abroad became a reality, the foreign competition would indeed hurt them. But the case does not differ in principle from any other dislocation of resource owners coming from dynamic changes in the economy. Temporary dislocations of certain groups of resource owners are the price we pay for economic progress and a growing national income.

For National Self-Sufficiency

Sometimes tariffs are levied in an effort to make a country less dependent on other countries for certain goods and services. Reasons for self-sufficiency policies vary. Nationalistic zeal coupled with a "we don't need anyone else" attitude may provide the motivating force. Another may

[2]*See pp. 343-350.*

be that a country is desirous of strengthening certain industries that it believes to be vital to its national security. These include the merchant marine, aircraft manufacturing, steel, oil, rubber, and others providing products and services that if not available in time of war would lead to disaster. In both cases the country is willing to sacrifice immediate economic well-being for the attainment of other goals.

Some countries may pursue self-sufficiency policies because they fear having their own economic destiny tied to that of countries with which they trade. Prior to the Great Depression of the 1930's Chile depended heavily on foreign trade. Its chief exports were nitrate up to 1920 and copper through the decade of the 1920's. Import restrictions were relatively mild and a wide range of goods were imported. Between 1929 and 1933 the world market for copper collapsed, severely curtailing the quantities of foreign exchange that the country could earn and its ability to import goods and services. There was a precipitous drop in living standards. Experiences of this kind are not easily forgotten and lead to import duties in order that "import-substitute" industries may be developed at home—albeit at production costs above the costs of importing the goods during more stable times.

Toward Tariff Reductions

Not quite all the votes are won by the pro-tariff interests. Countries have been somewhat ambivalent in their expressed attitudes toward trade. At times they have pressed toward formidable restrictions and at other times they have sought to reduce them. Sometimes, in the 1960's, for example, they have tried to work both sides of the street at the same time. Over the last 100 years we find an ebb and flow of trade restrictions by Canada and the other trading countries of the world. At the time of writing, uncertainty over trade policies exists. While lip service is paid to further reductions in trade barriers among nations, balance of payments disequilibria seem to be forcing deficit countries toward greater trade restrictions.

Canadian Tariff Policies

In the interval between 1846 and 1878, Canada used the tariff chiefly to raise revenue for the government; the protective element in the tariff was mostly incidental. In 1879, however, Canada adopted a tariff policy then in vogue in most trading countries other than Britain. The so-called *National Policy* of higher tariffs aimed at fostering manufacturing in Canada by customs rates of from 25 to 35 percent. Throughout the 1880's the general trend of the minor revisions made in the tariff was still upwards, but in the 1890's a downward tendency became manifest.

Around the turn of the century, Canada unilaterally provided preferential duties favouring imports from Britain. The Customs Tariff Act was revised in 1907, providing for three levels of duty—Preferential, Intermediate, and General. In 1911, in response to a United States initiative, a reciprocal trade agreement was negotiated. A wide list of natural products was to be admitted by both countries free of duty and lower tariffs were to apply to certain other articles including various manufactured goods. But Canada, which had formerly sought reciprocity with the United States, now turned it down; the defeat of the party in power in the 1911 federal election was interpreted as a defeat of the reciprocity agreement which was never implemented.

There was little change in the general level of the tariff (except for the wartime additions of 7½ and 5 percent) until 1930 when it was sharply increased. The intent behind this increase was to reduce domestic depression and unemployment but in addition was a retaliation against the infamous Hawley-Smoot Tariff of 1930 which raised U.S. tariffs to their historically all-time high level. The high U.S. tariff, together with retaliatory tariffs levelled by other countries besides Canada, undoubtedly contributed toward the breakdown of world trade during the Great Depression of the 1930's.

In 1932 Canada began a long, slow process of liberalizing its import restrictions. In that year Britain, Canada and other Commonwealth countries adopted a systematic, widespread system of tariff preferences. After prolonged negotiations a trade agreement was concluded with the United States in 1935. The concessions granted to Canada were not of a far-reaching character, but the agreement included a most-favoured-nation clause—both countries agreed to extend to each other any tariff concessions or benefits that they might offer to other countries without the necessity of concessions in return. In 1937-38, in return for U.S. tariff reductions, Britain and Canada reduced tariffs and tariff preferences. Another significant change was the removal in 1944 of the tariff on agricultural implements and agricultural machinery. Canada strongly supported the General Agreement on Tariffs and Trade (or GATT) which came into force in 1948. The Canada-United States Agreement on Automotive Products was signed in 1965. It provides for the removal of tariffs and other impediments to trade between the two countries in motor vehicles and original equipment parts. The basic objective of the agreement is to provide access to expanded markets for Canadian motor vehicle and component producers.

In summary, Canada has played a leading part since the mid-1930's in tariff reductions, in international efforts to bring about a general reduction in tariffs and other trade restrictions, and in promoting a greater degree of freedom of trade on a multilateral basis.

ITO and GATT

Following World War II representatives from the major trading countries of the world drew up a charter for a proposed International Tade Organization (ITO). The ITO was intended (1) to promote the reduction of tariffs, of other barriers to trade, and of discriminating trade treatment of some countries by others; (2) to promote the economic development of underdeveloped areas; and (3) to provide a forum for the discussion and solution of problems relating to international trade. The U.S. Congress refused to ratify the charter and thus effectively scuttled the ITO. In its place, a much weaker General Agreement on Tariffs and Trade, generally referred to as GATT, was signed by Canada, the United States, and 21 other nations on October 30, 1947, at Geneva, and came into force on January 1, 1948.

The Agreement provides for scheduled tariff concessions and the exchange of most-favoured-nation treatment among the signatory countries, and lays down rules and regulations to govern the conduct of international trade. In 1970, there were 77 full members in the GATT.

So far there have been six rounds of multilateral trade negotiations held under GATT arrangements. The first, at Geneva in 1947, constituted a major step in the reduction of tariffs on a world-wide basis.[3] This was followed by four further tariff conferences of more modest scope—in 1949 at Annecy, in 1951 at Torquay, in 1956 at Geneva and in 1960-62 the "Dillon Round" at Geneva. About 60,000 tariff concessions were involved in the first five rounds of tariff negotiations conducted under the aegis of the GATT. The sixth round of negotiations (the so-called Kennedy Round) began in May 1964. Many difficulties were encountered but essential elements were finally negotiated by May 15, 1967. After full implementation of the Kennedy Round agreement (a five-year transition period was involved), the average level of duties in the United States, Britain and the European Economic Community will be in the range of 6½ to 8½ percent compared with 12 to 18 percent prior to the agreement. No Canadian rate should be much above 20 percent by January 1, 1972. Further, the agreement includes tariff concessions covering about $45

[3]*Under the first agreement, in 1947, Canada reduced the tariff to other GATT members on 590 items and undertook not to increase rates on another 460 items. Other countries made similar concessions. The list was extended in later agreements.*

billion of world trade in 1966 terms. Even so, the tariff reductions do not cover all products and are relatively small for some. Thus "the Kennedy Round has not ushered the world economy on to the threshold of a millennium of completely free trade."[4]

Although the total results have fallen far short of the hopes of the founders, it is probable that, without the GATT, tariff and other trade barriers would have been higher than they are now.

Regional Economic Integration

The reduction of tariff barriers and other restrictions to international trade tends to be more easily accomplished with one's neighbours than with countries that are geographically and ideologically more remote. Thus in recent years there have been several moves among the countries of specific regions of the world to band together in groups for purposes of freeing themselves from at least some of the restraints on the trade among them. These groups are said to be seeking *regional economic integration,* that is, to move toward integration of their productive capacities along comparative-advantage lines.

Regional organizations of countries for trade purposes are frequently classified as common markets, customs unions, or free trade associations. A *common market* in its pure form is an association in which no restrictions are placed on sales of goods and services or movements of resources among the participating countries. The economies of the countries are truly integrated. The closest approximation to a pure common market occurs among the provinces of Canada. A *customs union* imposes much less interdependence on the participating countries. The usual objective of a customs union is to eliminate the tariff barriers against goods moving among the countries that comprise it, but for the group as a whole to confront outside countries with a common set of tariffs. The *free trade association* is even less demanding on its members. The ultimate objective is free trade among member countries, but each one is left to make whatever trade arrangements it desires with outside countries. Suppose we look at the major examples of organizations of these types.

The European Economic Community, 1957

The European Economic Community, or EEC, created by the Treaty of Rome in 1957, has common market characteristics. It evolved from the Organization for European Economic Cooperation that was established by the United States and the western European countries following World

[4]*Dominion Bureau of Statistics,* Canada Year Book, 1968. *Ottawa: Queen's Printer, p. 949. See also pp. 946-954 and pp. 990-991.*

War II for the allocation of funds sent to that area under the Marshall Plan to aid in the reconstruction of war-torn Europe. Originally it was hoped in official circles in the United States that all of the countries of western Europe would join in setting up the European Economic Community. But several countries, Great Britain in particular, were fearful of tying their economies as closely to those of other countries as the objectives of the common market would require. Consequently the EEC included only France, Germany, Italy, Belgium, Luxembourg, and the Netherlands. Since 1961 Great Britain has made belated attempts to join the group; however, every attempt thus far has been vetoed by France. Had Great Britain been admitted, it is likely that the northern European countries would have followed suit and the EEC would have embraced almost the whole of western Europe.

The avowed purpose of EEC is to remove restrictions on economic transactions among member countries. Toward this end the Treaty of Rome calls for (1) the gradual removal of tariffs, import quotas, and other kinds of trade restrictions among the member countries; (2) a uniform tariff among the member countries on goods imported from outside the group to any one of them; (3) the free movement of both labour and capital resources among member countries; (4) the coordination of monetary and fiscal policies of the members; and (5) the establishment of common policies with respect to agriculture, business, labour, and social security. These objectives are to be accomplished over a 12–15 year period.

What economic benefits may be expected to be derived from an arrangement of this kind? A first and most obvious set includes those that arise from specialization and exchange in accordance with the principle of comparative advantage—the ordinary gains that always arise from voluntary exchange. Second, it can expand the markets available to specific industries of given countries. Third, it may increase the amount of competition that exists among the sellers of products in the member countries. The first point has been discussed in detail previously. Some elaboration of the second and third points is in order.

With respect to the benefits to be derived from market expansion, we should keep in mind that a great many countries of the world are small and that the internal markets available to the industries of such countries are limited in size. Consequently, it may not be possible for a firm selling only to the internal market to produce a large enough volume of a product to take advantage of economies of scale. Suppose that such a country has only 300,000 automobiles operating within its borders. How large a market will exist for automobile jacks? A free trade arrangement with other countries may expand the markets available to such a firm, permitting larger output rates, economies of scale, and lower costs of production.

Increasing competition among sellers of products in a region where trade barriers are reduced will ordinarily be expected to benefit consumers of the region. Domestic sellers in a small country may well be monopolists in the sale of their products. The small size of the internal market, together with tariffs against competing imports, may make it so. If tariffs among countries of the region are reduced, the producers in the country may not only find their markets larger but may at the same time find themselves subjected to competition from abroad. This erosion of their monopoly positions tends to bring about improvements in the quality of the products, larger quantities of the products, and lower prices for consumers.

The precise impact of the EEC on the member countries is hard to measure, but it appears that it has been positive. There have been large increases in GNP, employment, and productivity in the region since its inception. Large increases in trade among the member countries and in the trade of the group with the rest of the world have occurred. But it is difficult to say how much of this would have taken place if the EEC had not existed.

European Free Trade Association, 1960

In 1960 Great Britain, Norway, Sweden, Denmark, Austria, Switzerland, and Portugal signed a treaty creating the European Free Trade Association, or EFTA. The Association was formed as a countergroup to the EEC. Great Britain had not been willing to go all the way with the common market characteristics of the EEC, and when it became apparent that the EEC would be formed anyway, the British countered with a proposal for a free trade area including all of the countries now members of the two groups. The Treaty of Rome, giving birth to the EEC, was signed while the British proposal was under discussion eliminating the six EEC countries from possible membership and leaving the others to establish the Association.

Some measure of success has been achieved by EFTA in reducing tariffs among the member countries. In fact, reductions have been similar to those accomplished by EEC. However, there has been no intent on the part of the group to establish a customs union or a common market. The tariff policy of each member country toward countries outside the group is considered to be its own affair. Comparison between the economic performance of EFTA countries and the EEC countries may or may not be meaningful because of differences in the economic circumstances in which member countries of the two organizations find themselves. However, for whatever it is worth, trade among EFTA countries and between

EFTA countries and outsiders appears to have increased about on a par with that of EEC countries.

The Central American Common Market, 1958

In 1958 the countries of Costa Rica, El Salvador, Guatemala, Honduras, and Nicaragua set up the Central American Common Market. According to the generally accepted definition of a common market, this is somewhat of a misnomer. The first objective of the organization is to establish a free trade association, lowering trade restrictions among the member countries so that after 10 years trade would be free. The free trade association is then expected to evolve into a customs union, with common tariffs on imports into member countries.

Again, measurement of the degree of success is not an easy task. Tariffs have been reduced and many goods now flow across the borders of member countries duty free. Trade has increased greatly both internally and externally over the last few years, but the extent to which the organization has made this so has not yet been determined. In any case it has introduced the idea that reductions in trade barriers are beneficial where not so long ago the pressures were exerted in the other direction.

The Latin American Free Trade Association, 1960

The major countries of South America, plus Mexico and with the exception of Venezuela, formed the Latin American Free Trade Association (LAFTA) with the signing of the Treaty of Montevideo in 1960. The objectives, according to the framers of the treaty are: (1) to expand the South American markets of member countries, (2) to expand the trade among member countries relative to that with the rest of the world, and (3) to achieve greater economic integration and complementarity among the industries of the participating countries. These statements recognize the importance of increasing the size of the market for the industries of a member country beyond the country itself. However, they avoid giving the impression that competition among the industries of the participating countries will be permitted to increase. Many Latin Americans are distrustful of competition. The treaty leaves the impression that planned *industrial complementarity* will be sought among the countries of the association—that is, that specific major industries will be assigned to certain countries and will not be permitted to develop in others.

The treaty provides for a 12-year program of tariff reductions. Annual negotiations are to reduce average tariff barriers against each country's imports from the others by 8 percent per year. By the end of 12 years trade among the countries is supposed to be free. The first year's round of negotiated reductions came off well, with most of the reductions being made where special interest groups were hurt the least. But in succeeding rounds, seeking to remove the protection afforded larger important industries, negotiations became progressively more difficult. Free trade appears to be a remote goal. Again it is difficult to draw any conclusions as to the impact of the association on trade among the countries. However, the member countries at least have the reduction of tariff barriers under discussion.

Summary

The economic impact of tariffs has been a subject of debate since the birth of economics as an area of systematic study. Although it can be demonstrated by means of the principle of comparative advantage that in most cases the national income of trading countries will be greater without tariffs than with them, countries have persisted in building up tariff walls against imports. One reason is that tariffs can provide revenue for the central government. Another, and a more important one today, is that they can be used to restrict imports into countries with balance of payments deficits. A third reason is the belief that tariffs can hasten industrialization and thus the economic development of underdeveloped countries. A fourth is to provide protection of home producers from competition from abroad, a simple monopolization motive in which the protected producing interests gain at the expense of the rest of the economy. A fifth reason for tariffs is to promote self-sufficiency on the part of individual countries.

Historically tariff policies of the world's trading countries have evidenced periods of increasing tariffs and periods of decreasing tariffs. Canadian tariffs moved generally upward from 1873 to 1890, downward until the mid-1920's, and upward again to 1932. Since 1932, under the system of Commonwealth preferences, reciprocal agreements with the United States, and the General Agreements on Tariffs and Trade, they have moved downward. At the present time Canada appears to be slowly moving in the general direction of a low-tariff nation.

A number of agreements have been signed and organizations have been formed among the countries of the world to reduce trade barriers. On a multicountry basis, the General Agreement on Trade and Tariffs established in 1947 has provided a forum within which negotiations can be conducted for tariff reductions. Additionally several organizations to promote liberalization of trade barriers among member countries are in operation. These include the European Economic Community, the

European Free Trade Association, the Central American Common Market, and the Latin American Free Trade Association. The economic success of these organizations is difficult to assess, but they represent substantial steps in the direction of unrestricted trade.

Exercises and Questions for Discussion

1. "Canada must sooner or later join a common market or free trade association. Otherwise its position in international trade will be weakened." Discuss.
2. Can the infant-industry argument be justified with respect to the principle of comparative advantage? Explain.
3. Canadian beef producers argue that the elimination of tariffs on Argentine beef would drive down the price of beef in Canada to a level at which small producers could not continue in business. Is this sufficient reason to warrant the continuance of a protective tariff? Elaborate.
4. "German labour works for much less money than Canadian labour. This is why Volkswagens are less expensive than Canadian cars. If tariffs were removed from these automobiles thousands of Canadian workers and their families would be affected." Are these statements valid? Expand.
5. Make a list of several goods that now carry import tariffs. What would be the likely effect on the Canadian industries involved if these tariffs were lifted? on the Canadian economy?
6. Can you think of any industries today that clearly should have protective tariffs? If so, why should they be allowed such protection?

Selected Readings

Belarssa, Bela, *Trade Liberalization Among Industrial Countries: Objectives and Alternatives*. New York: McGraw-Hill Book Company, Inc., 1967.

Economic Council of Canada, *Fifth Annual Review*. Ottawa: Queen's Printer, 1968, pp. 154-156 (National Tariff Policy).

Ingram, James C., *International Economic Problems*. New York: John Wiley & Sons, Inc., 1966, Chaps. 3 and 6.

Johnson, H. G., "The Case for Tariff Reform," *The Business Quarterly*, Spring, 1961, pp. 25-33.

Wonnacott, Paul and Ronald J., *U.S.-Canadian Free Trade: The Potential Impact on the Canadian Economy*. Montreal: Private Planning Association of Canada, 1968.

Young, J. H., *Canadian Commercial Policy*. A study for the Royal Commission on Canada's Economic Prospects, Ottawa: Queen's Printer, 1957.

19

Underdeveloped Economies

A large part of the world's population lives under adverse economic circumstances. Some two thirds of all mankind live in countries producing not more than one third of the world's income. The large concentrations of poverty-ridden people are in Asia, Africa, and Latin America. Most of those that we call poor in Australia, New Zealand, Europe, and North America are relatively much better off. No analysis of the world economy would be complete without a discussion of the economically under-developed countries and their problems, nor can we find a better capstone for an introduction to economic theory. The underdeveloped economies present one of the major challenges facing the world today.

Meaning and Measurement of Underdevelopment

Underdeveloped countries are those in which a large proportion of the population is very poor. A number of means have been used to measure the level of well-being of different countries—daily per capita calorie intakes, infant mortality rates, life expectancies, literacy rates, and others —but all of these add up to low income levels. The almost universally used measures of comparative levels of development are per capita income figures.

Although per capita income data have certain shortcomings for purposes of comparing countries on the basis of level of development, they provide one of the best measures available. One shortcoming is that income distribution is left out of account. The poor of a country can be very poor indeed, yet there may be enough extremely wealthy people in the economy to pull per capita income figures up to a level tending to mask the poverty that exists. We should also keep in mind that such data do not provide a fine measure of the comparative economic well-being of persons in different countries. The typical bundle of consumer goods in one country is not the same as in another. Further, if one country's currency is pegged in foreign exchange markets so that it is substantially overvalued, its per capita income will appear unduly high relative to that of a country whose currency is undervalued. But despite factors such as these that reduce the accuracy of per capita income comparisons, the differences among countries are so large that the general validity of the comparisons is not seriously affected.

Table 19-1 gives some idea of the relative levels of development of a representative group of countries. It is apparent that a vast difference exists between the highest and the lowest countries, the former being almost 62 times the latter. The countries usually considered to be relatively advanced economically are clustered in the $1000 and above range. Where income levels are below $1000 we can guess that a rather large proportion of the population lives in acute poverty. Casual observation tends to confirm that in many of the countries in the $500–$1000 range there are substantial disparities in income distribution. In Venezuela, for example,

TABLE 19-1
Per Capita Gross National Product
Estimates for Selected Countries, 1968.
(Constant 1967 Prices)

Country	Exchange Rate per Dollar		U.S. Dollars	Country	Exchange Rate per Dollars		U.S. Dollars
United States			4,120	Greece	30	drachmas	849
Sweden	5.17	kronor	3,130	Argentina	350	pesos	668
Canada	1,081	C. $	2,877	South Africa	0.714	rands	633
Switzerland	4.35	S francs	2,702	Chile	5.79	escudos	610
France	4.937	F francs	2,399	Mexico	12.5	pesos	546
Australia	0.893	A $	2,190	Guatemala	1	quetzal	436
Germany	4	D. M.	2,154	Brazil	2.0	cruz.	359
New Zealand	0.719	N. Z. $	2,078	Peru	38.7	soles	318
United Kingdom	0.357	pounds	2,071	Taiwan	40	N.T. $	282
Netherlands	3.62	guilders	1,877	Ghana	1.02	cedis	215
Israel	3	I pounds	1,678	Bolivia	12	pesos	171
Austria	26	schillings	1,499	Thailand	20.8	baht	157
Italy	625	lira	1,358	Pakistan	4.76	rupees	116
Japan	360	yen	1,283	Uganda	7.14	shillings	93
Venezuela	4.5	bolivars	928	India	7.50	rupees	86
Spain	60	pesetas	866	Ethiopia	2.5	E. $	68

Source: Agency for International Development. Gross National Product, Growth Rates and Trend Data, *April 25, 1969.*

the lower classes are as poor as in most other Latin America countries, but per capita income is higher because there is a proportionally larger number of wealthy people. The economic circumstances of the large majority of the population in countries with per capita incomes under $500 per year are self-evident. In this context, it should be pointed out that of the 115 countries having populations of one million or more, 77 have annual per capita incomes of less than $500. And the average per capita income in these countries as a whole is about $145 a year. Twenty-nine, in fact, have per capita incomes of $100 or less—some as low as $40.[1] From the standpoint of the gap between the rich and the poor countries, however, an even more significant datum is this: in the past two years alone, the average per capita income of Canadians has *increased* by more than $180.

Recent Concern with an Old Problem

Although poverty is as old as mankind itself, the urgency for economic development that is making itself felt throughout the world today is of comparatively recent origin. World War II and the ensuing Cold War seem to have been the catalytic agents. Prominent among the factors contributing to such world-wide concern have been: (1) the travel and social interchange that took place during and following World War II, (2) the Cold War struggle for power between the Communist countries and those of the Western world, (3) expansion in the distribution and use of mass communications media, and (4) the decline in colonialism and the emergence of nationalism in the underdeveloped areas of the world.

Travel and Social Interchange

Never in the history of the world were so many people transported to so many different countries and exposed to so many different cultures as was the case during World War II. Military personnel from the advanced countries stationed in the Mediterranean lands, Asia and the Pacific islands saw firsthand and for the first time the grinding poverty in which the majority of the world's population lives. At the same time, soldiers from the underdeveloped areas found themselves in countries where living standards were almost beyond their wildest dreams. Too, the civilian populations in the underdeveloped areas became acquainted with what to them appeared to be high income levels and lavish spending habits of North American, Australian and European troops. Out of the exchange

[1]*Canadian International Development Agency*, Annual Review, *1969, p. 5.*

came an awareness on both sides of what economic conditions in the rest of the world are like.

Travel abroad has become commonplace, albeit on a smaller scale than during World War II; growing investments abroad by Western firms have induced a flow of technical personnel and their families to the countries where the investments are made; international loans and aid to underdeveloped countries by the governments of advanced countries have done the same thing; student and teacher exchanges are on the increase; tourism has flourished. All of these exchanges have been beneficiaries of the transportation revolution brought about by the advent of jet aircraft.

The Cold War

The ideological competition between the Communist world and the West for the allegiance and support of the smaller, and in many cases underdeveloped, countries has undoubtedly contributed to a greater awareness of and concern for the underdeveloped countries. The European Recovery Program first proposed by George C. Marshall, United States Secretary of State, to provide U.S. financial aid in the reconstruction of war-torn Europe, demonstrated the possibilities arising from massive loans and grants to other countries to help them build up their productive capacities.[2] This program was followed by U.S. aid to underdeveloped countries, first through the Point Four Program (so named because it was the fourth point in President Harry S. Truman's inaugural address of January, 1949) and later through the Agency for International Development (AID). Our foreign assistance program began in 1950 when Canada became one of the founding members of the Colombo Plan for the development of the newly independent Commonwealth nations of south and southeast Asia. The Soviet Union entered the field of aid to underdeveloped countries in the mid-1950's.

The fear on the part of the Western nations that the less advanced countries would turn to communism as a route to development has played an important role in recent concern for the underdevelopment areas of the world. By the same token, the Soviet Union and Communist China have worked the other side of the street. Rivalry between the two blocs has been strong in Africa, Asia, and in Latin America.

[2]*Over the 1948-1951 period of operation of the European Recovery Program, the United States extended $11.4 billion of aid to Western European nations, almost 90 percent of which was in the form of outright grants. The major recipient countries were the United Kingdom (24 percent), France (20 percent), the Federal Republic of Germany (11 percent) and Italy (10 percent). In consequence, industrial production in Western Europe in 1951 was about 40 percent greater than in 1938.*

Mass Communications Media

Technological developments in communications media since World War II have brought people in all parts of the world in closer touch. Developments in radio—particularly the transistor—enable people to hear, even if they cannot read, of events and conditions outside their own areas. In most underdeveloped areas a transistor radio is a much sought after and highly prized possession. Widespread distribution of motion pictures has had an impact, and some countries that were formerly rather isolated now have limited access to television.

Nationalism

The growth of nationalism and the dismantling of colonial empires have played important roles in the recent interest in economic development. Newly independent nations have sought to establish the superiority of home rule over rule by an outside power in the development of their economies. Pakistan and India provide major examples. Over 30 small independent nations have come into being in Africa. World-wide interest has been generated in the successes and failures that these countries have experienced as they attempt, among other things, to improve their economic performance.

Requisites of Economic Development

How does economic development of a country come about? The economic requisites for growth in per capita income are easily stated, but the cultural, social, psychological, and political underpinnings necessary to bring them about pose formidable problems. Growth in national income results from the accumulation of more and better resources and from increases in the efficiency with which they are used. But population growth also means more mouths to feed. Per capita income can grow only if national income is increasing at a greater rate than is population. Suppose we examine the forces at work.

Capital Accumulation

Capital accumulation is, of course, a basic ingredient in economic development. If national income is to grow, the economy must accumulate capital, and if per capita income is to grow, capital per worker must be increasing, assuming that the labour force increases at least as fast as does the population. We should keep in mind that an economy's capital is made up of all of its nonhuman resources—communications and transportation facilities; educational facilities; tools, machines, and factories for producing industrial goods; mining equipment; agricultural land and tools; ore deposits and other "natural" resources; and so on. All of these contribute to the total output of the economy.

If an economy is to accumulate capital without outside help, it must refrain from consuming its entire net output. Some part of its output must be in the form of new capital goods, over and above the amounts used to keep the economy's capital resources intact or to take care of depreciation. Thus the size of the economic machine and its capacity to produce will grow over time. The rate of growth in the productive capacity of its capital resources depends upon the willingness of the populace to forgo consumption in order that resources that would otherwise be employed to produce consumer goods can be used to produce capital goods.

Capital accumulation is not confined to increases in the quantities of the capital resources available; it can also take the form of improvements in the qualities of resources. Soil fertility can be increased; through careful selection of seed stocks crop yields can be expanded; river channels can be widened and deepened; better educational facilities can be made available; dams built to control erosion and to store up water supplies for irrigation can also frequently be made to yield electrical energy.

Technological Development

Through technological development not only can the quality of resources be improved but better and more efficient ways of using resources of given qualities are devised. Technological advancements go hand in hand with capital accumulation and with advancing educational levels. Education provides the foundations underlying technological development. But in order for ideas to bear fruit—or even to survive—the means of testing them and putting them into practice must be available. Capital resources provide the laboratory for this purpose. High levels of technology are rarely developed in capital-poor countries.

In the world today underdeveloped economies seldom find it necessary to come up with entirely new technological developments on their own. They can borrow from the more advanced countries. They can send students abroad to be trained as engineers and as scientists and to bring home technical knowledge in a wide range of fields. They can also import complete sets of techniques, as the Japanese have done with great success since World War II. They can bring in from the advanced countries the ways and means of producing electrical and other kinds of energy. They can copy—and perhaps improve upon—manufacturing techniques of many kinds. And, as in the case of Japan, these can give them a strong boost along the way to higher per capita incomes without subtracting from the incomes of those from whom the techniques are borrowed.

Qualitative Improvements in Human Resources

Higher literacy rates, higher average levels of educational attainment, and training and development in specific skills constitute essential ingredients in the economic growth of any economy. As Galbraith has aptly put it, "Literate people will see the need for getting machines. It is not so clear that machines will see the need for getting literate people."[3]

In order to increase its per capita income a poor economy must educate its population so that a climate is provided in which capital accumulation and technological development can thrive. Through primary and secondary education of a general nature, as well as through higher education in the liberal arts, a spirit of inquiry can be encouraged and initiative for the improvement of one's lot can be instilled. The correlation between average levels of general education and per capita incomes is high and positive within Canada. From the data available, it appears to be equally strong throughout the world.

In addition to raising its literacy rate and advancing its general level of education, a developing country must increase the technical competence and skill levels of its work force. We expect technical training to increase the capacities of workers to contribute directly to the economy's output of goods and services. We also know that without it technological advancements are not likely to occur. The accumulation of capital by a developing economy must necessarily be accompanied by the acquisition of skills on the part of a larger and larger proportion of its labour force. Trade schools, technical schools, adult education classes, and on-the-job training all contribute toward this end.

Improved Employment and Allocation of Resources

National income and per capita income of an economy can be increased through improvements in the employment and allocation of whatever resources it has. Underdeveloped economies typically have rather high unemployment rates; or, in the event that obvious unemployment does not occur, labour may be *underemployed*, that is, more man hours are used to perform specific tasks than are really necessary.

Capital too can be underemployed. For example, land tenure systems may be such that most of the agricultural land is held in very large farms owned by the aristocratic wealthy class of society. The owners may take

[3]*John K. Galbraith,* Economic Development. *Cambridge, Mass.: Harvard University Press, 1964, p. 42.*

little interest in the actual operation of the farms. Traditional methods rather than the best ones available, used by peasants who have little interest in efficiency, may hold productivity far below what it could be. Mineral deposits and forest areas may not be contributing as much as they are capable of contributing to national income.

In underdeveloped economies there is usually a large possibility of increasing national income through a more efficient allocation of resources among alternative employment opportunities. Whenever resources are pulled out of less productive uses and placed in more productive ones, the gains more than offset the losses and national income rises.[4] Suppose, for example, that land is being utilized to grow lentils but that most people do not think much of lentils as a form of nourishment. They value the yearly product of an acre of land used in producing lentils at $100. Suppose that the public values the amount of beans that the same acre could grow each year at $150. Clearly, national income would rise if land were reallocated from the production of lentils to the production of beans. Similarly, reallocations of labour from less productive to more productive employments will cause national income to rise.

Internal Obstacles to Economic Development

The economic forces that contribute to growth in national income are easy to list, yet it is difficult for underdeveloped countries to bring them into being under their own steam. Many obstacles stand in the way of capital accumulation, technological advancement, improvements in labour force quality, and more efficient use and allocation of resources. Among these are the country's initial state of poverty, its social structure, inflation, its rudimentary financial system, political instability, and population growth. Others could be listed but these seem to be among the most important.

Initial State of Poverty

In countries with low per capita incomes the forces leading to growth are extremely difficult to set in motion. How can a country that produces barely enough food to keep its population alive divert resources from the production of consumer goods to the production of capital goods in large enough quantities for significant capital accumulation to take place? How can it shift resources away from production of the bare essentials of living toward provision of the education necessary for technological

[4]*See Vol. I p. 341.*

advancement and for upgrading the quality of the labour force? Those countries most in need of rapid economic development are precisely the ones that find it most difficult to generate development. The relatively rich countries find it much easier to forgo a large measure of current consumption and to use the resources thus released to expand the productive capacity of the economy.[5]

The internal means of generating growth for many underdeveloped countries may be limited to the new capital they can produce or the additional education they can achieve through increasing the efficiency with which existing resources are used. If unemployment and under-employment can be reduced, gains in national income are possible. Some further gains may be obtainable through reallocation of resources from less to more productive uses. Any additions to net national product thus obtained conceivably can be used for capital accumulation and education purposes. However, if living standards are initially at very low levels, there is no certainty that gains of this sort will not be consumed. As a matter of fact, not much optimism is warranted for the possibilities of increasing the efficiency of resource use. Apathy on the part of the general public and gross administrative ineptness on the part of governments are the rule rather than the exception in low income countries.

Social Structure

In many underdeveloped countries social and economic class lines are rather strongly drawn and the resulting class structure is not conducive to economic growth. In India, for example, the caste system, even though abolished by law, still exists in fact and tends to prevent workers from moving out of hereditary caste employments such as sweeping, personal service, cooking, laundering, and so on, into occupations that may be more productive and more remunerative. In Latin America the aristocracy tends to be an aloof, exclusive group that the present working classes can never hope to join. The aristocrats are wealthy; the working classes are poor. The latter work for the former in their family businesses and on their farms, and there is no burning desire on the part of the aristocacy to see the economic and social order change—it serves their ends well.

There is some evidence that class structures are cracking. In many low-income countries the poorer classes are obtaining representation in government and are pressing for measures that will change the status quo. In many such countries there is a growing middle class of businessmen, entrepreneurs, and professionals. The step from the working class

---

[5]*See pp. 299-301.*

to the middle class is much smaller than that to the aristocracy and as time passes it can be taken by working-class people. As the middle class grows it accumulates capital and generates employment opportunities. Too, the aims of the poor and the middle class may be furthered by their growing political strength.

Inflation

Many underdeveloped countries have experienced rates of inflation high enough to be detrimental to economic development. Inflation in most underdeveloped countries is generated by large-scale deficit financing of government expenditures. Governments are reluctant to collect sufficient taxes to cover their expenditures for fear that they will be replaced if taxes appear onerous. Welfare-minded governments establish expenditure levels too high for the tax-collecting merchanism to support. Special interest groups generate fiscal policies with inflationary biases by pressing for public expenditures to further their particular ends. There is pressure at the same time from such groups to obtain relief from tax loads. In almost all underdeveloped countries these forces create large government deficits and large increases in the money supply. Increases in total spending outstrip increases in output and price levels rise.

The argument is frequently made that inflation is conductive to economic development. It is said that a constantly expanding monetary demand for goods and services will provide profit incentive to use production facilities at capacity. Also, through deficit spending, it is said that the government can bid resources away from the production of consumer goods and services and use them to produce capital goods.

To be sure, an excess of expenditures over tax collections can be used by a government to accumulate capital. Government demand for goods and services, effected through increases in government expenditures, increases relative to private demand. The government than *can* bid resources away from the private production of consumer goods and *can* put them to work building dams, roads, schools, steel mills, and so on. The decrease in consumer goods available for the general public to buy, coupled with constant consumer purchasing power, causes prices to rise and the real income of the general public to fall. Inflation of this sort has the same general effect as a tax—real purchasing power is transferred from the public to the government.

There is, however, little evidence to support the theory that inflation has in fact stimulated the real growth of underdeveloped economies. More often it seems to have repressed growth, both by discouraging direct investment in new plant and equipment and by inducing government units to enact control measures that inhibit growth.

On the first point, the inflation of most underdeveloped countries is highly erratic. It is not deliberately planned to stimulate the economy. Rather, it occurs because the governments concerned are unable or unwilling to take the necessary steps to prevent it. In one year price levels may rise by 20 percent. The next year the increase may be 80 percent. The following year it may be 30 percent. The effect is to create a high degree of uncertainty on the part of would-be investors concerning the real rate of return on investment. Consequently, only those investments offering an extraordinarily high rate of return are likely to be undertaken.

In addition, inflation tends to cause investment to be channelled into already existing items that are known to increase in price at a rate at least as high as that of the general price level. Real estate and objects of art are outstanding examples. But investment in these creates no additional jobs and no increases in productive capacity; it simply causes their prices to rise to higher levels.

On the second point, the government is likely to take steps to suppress inflation. Price ceilings are often set on a select list of the most important consumer goods. Suppose, for example, that a ceiling price is put on fluid milk but not on manufactured dairy products such as butter and cheese. The latter become relatively more profitable to produce and dairying resources are shifted from the production of milk to the production of butter and cheese. This situation, however, represents a worse rather than a better allocation of resources, since resources move from uses where they are valued more highly (but where the price ceiling prevents that value from being expressed in the market place) to uses in which they are not so highly valued. The principle can be generalized. A system of partial price controls will cause resources to be shifted out of the production of the products where controlled prices are effective and into the production of those where prices are free to move. The former are the goods most valuable to consumers as a whole while the latter are the ones least valuable.

Price controls may also be established on certain resources deemed to be important, strategic, or critical to the economy. If the controls are effective, shortages will occur and government agencies will be assigned the task of allocating these materials or resources to the producing units or business firms that use them. Under the best of circumstances the administrative machinery is cumbersome. Delays in allocations occur; manpower and machines lie idle while firms wait. Further, administrative techniques in underdeveloped countries are usually far from perfect and their shortcomings add to the built-in problems of allowing scarce resources to be allocated by government agencies rather than by prices.

Underdeveloped economies generally develop balance of payments problems as a result of inflation and thus they are prevented from obtaining full measure from international trade based on comparative-advantage principles. Underdeveloped countries typically have a rate of inflation higher than that of the advanced countries with which they trade. Their desire to import is stimulated and the incentives for export are dampened, creating either foreign exchange shortages or rising prices of foreign currencies. Like most of the rest of the world, these countries attempt to peg their exchange rates, but the pegged rate tends to be below equilibrium levels because of inflation and foreign exchange shortages result. In order to live with this situation a variety of trade restrictions are put into effect. These include exchange controls, import quotas, tariffs, restrictions on investment abroad, and others. The countries are placed in a situation in which they are unable to import what they desire of the capital goods they so urgently need from the advanced countries. At the same time, they penalize through overvaluation of their currencies the export of primary goods in which they have a comparative advantage and which provide their sources of foreign exchange.

Financial System

The significance of financial institutions in the process of economic development lies in their making available the means to utilize savings. As economist Edward Nevin has commented:

"However poor an economy may be there will be a need for institutions which allow such savings as are currently forthcoming to be invested conveniently and safely, and which ensure that they are channelled into the most useful purposes. The poorer a country is, in fact, the greater is the need for agencies to collect and invest the savings of the broad mass of persons and institutions within its borders. Such agencies will not only permit small amounts of savings to be handled and invested conveniently but will allow the owners of savings to retain liquidity individually but finance long-term investment collectively."[6]

To an increasing extent the individual in advanced countries has turned his savings over to financial intermediaries such as commercial banks, life insurance companies, trust companies, pension funds and the like, instead of investing or lending directly. These institutions, in turn, transfer the pooled funds to those undertaking capital formation. But in underdeveloped countries savings and investment are far more personal

[6]*Edward Nevin*, Capital Funds in Underdeveloped Countries. *London: Macmillan and Co., 1961, p. 75.*

transactions. In these countries, to a considerable degree still, there is a great reluctance to entrust funds to some manager who has no family ties with the investor to protect him from dishonest manipulating or outright absconding. Yet, it is hard to imagine how any country can develop economically without a rather large volume of indirect investment.

In advanced countries the use of money as a medium of exchange is universally practised. But in underdeveloped countries a significant part of the economy is still outside the orbit of monetary transaction (i.e. the rural subsistence sector). Moreover, of the two broad kinds of money, currency notes and coin is much more important than chequable deposits at commercial banks. These facts have important implications for economic growth. For one thing, commercial banks will charge higher interest rates in countries where the public prefers cash to bank balances because less credit will be extended by banks when currency drains are severe. For another, the scope for the traditional functions of central banks in underdeveloped countries is very limited by the existence of extensive nonmonetised sectors of the economy, and by the narrow range of bank credit and lack of other financial institutions.

Most of the advance of commercial banks in underdeveloped countries are primarily for short-term purposes. However, in such economies, capital for medium and long-term purposes is even more scarce than for short-term. Some countries have attempted to fill this gap in the capital market through the establishment of specialized credit agencies but for a variety of reasons their operations have not expanded on the required scale.

Most of the advances of the banks are fully secured, either by pledge or hypothecation of goods and certificates. In addition, the amount of the loans are generally not more than 50 or 60 percent of the value of such collateral. Clearly these are very conservative lending provisions.

A comparatively small part of the commercial banks' volume of business goes to such vital and considerable sectors as agriculture and small-scale rural areas. These basic sectors depend for their credit requirements largely on the unorganized credit markets where the rates of interest charged on funds by local moneylenders, grain merchants, and indigenous bankers may often be relatively high.

As a rule, commercial banks in underdeveloped countries do not make personal loans for the purchase of consumer goods or to cover personal debts and services. In these countries the village moneylenders as a class still remain the biggest credit agency for the finance of consumption. This system with its high rates of interest and other charges and its obvious gross abuses, badly serves the minimum needs of consumers.

Commercial banks in underdeveloped countries do not finance house construction or the purchase of residential land. Here again, some countries have established specialized credit agencies in both of these areas but these institutions have done little to meet the effective demand for housing loans.

Enough has already been said to indicate that in the underdeveloped countries generally, financial institutions have not fully responded to the changing needs of borrowers and lenders either through structural or functional adaptation. The question raised by this conclusion is: what can be done to make financial markets and financial intermediaries more effective instruments in the process of development? An obvious and negative way is to make the control of inflation an object of government policy. Government can also encourage private saving for private indirect investment in other more positive ways: (1) by enacting and enforcing measures that will protect shareholders from management and so increase their confidence in this kind of indirect investment; (2) through the establishment of stock and bond exchanges, so that the demand and supply for corporate securities can be focussed upon one another; (3) by making payments for its material purchases into a bank account owned by its trade creditors, thereby compelling persons doing business with government to maintain bank accounts; (4) by insuring and guaranteeing bank deposits up to some maximum value per depositor; (5) by excluding the return on bank deposits from the tax base; (6) by paying a small subsidy to banks for each account they carry; (7) by making savings accounts immune from liens; and (8) by making certain categories of corporate securities always acceptable as collateral against bank loans.[7]

If the banking habit of the community is to be effectively promoted, the commercial banks, which are the most important of the financial intermediaries in underdeveloped countries, must be encouraged to broaden and deepen the scope of their operations both in geographical and functional terms.

They must be induced to make more loans on the basis of the character and integrity of the borrower, his earning power and repayment capacity rather than mere security. More important, efforts must be made to meet the sound credit requirements, whether short-, medium- or long-term, of agriculturists, small traders and industries, and prospective home owners. If the longer-term resources of the banks need to be augmented (in many underdeveloped countries, the banks are in a position to obtain long-term funds through the sale of shares or debentures in the domestic capital market or by borrowing from abroad), the banks could be provided with rediscounting facilities of their medium and long-term port-

[7]*See, Stephen Enke*, Economics for Development. *Englewood Cliffs, N.J.: Prentice-Hall Inc., 1963, pp. 217-220 and Chapter 14.*

folios on reasonable terms. Additionally, an arrangement that would guarantee such loans in greater or smaller part might overcome the hesitancy of banks in underdeveloped countries to lend more freely to these sectors. In short, by providing all types of services, promptly and with a minimum of formality, the banks will promote their obligations as a highly desirable form of savings. This, in turn, should result in an increase in the total volume of both savings and investment.

Specialized development institutions have been established in most underdeveloped countries in order to fill serious gaps in medium and long-term industrial credit facilities. These institutions provide not only funds but also technical appraisal (i.e. whether the proposal is technically sound, feasible and practicable), technical knowledge and expert managerial advice and assistance. While many national development institutions have played and continue to play an important role in the process of economic development, others are desperately short of resources, many lack the proper managerial and organizing talent, many are performing marginal roles and all of them have large "overhead" expenses. In addition, some have become dispensers of political patronage while others have become indirect instruments of nationalization.

These observations imply that there is a plethora of such institutions. As a result there is a misallocation of scarce resources. Hence, what is needed is a reduction in the number of such institutions, particularly among those which specialize according to the time-period of their assistance (i.e. short-, medium-, long-term) and which serve the same industries. It follows that the surviving institutions should be given enlarged roles. It is equally important, however, that the activities of all these institutions be co-ordinated. These steps would serve to overcome the diseconomies of scale and also ameliorate the dearth of qualified personnel. In addition, many institutions need to strengthen their own capital base and improve their operating procedures.

Concerning other measures for improving financial performance, central banks, by assuring the solvency of the banking system (through a thorough, but not rigid, system of inspection); encouraging and extension of banking services, especially in the rural areas; and promoting broader and more efficient money and capital markets, can do much to reduce the problem of a large nonmonetary and unorganized subsistence sector of the economy, thereby increasing the direct influence of monetary policy in the less developed countries. Central banks can also, by opting in favour of a sound tax system, do much to protect savers and investors from large-scale deficit financing of government expenditures.

In sum, the existence of a well developed financial infrastructure will aid in the collection and distribution of investible funds. Indeed, as W. W. Rostow, a prominent U.S. economist noted:

". . . Virtually without exception (the transitions from a traditional to a modern society) have been marked by the extension of banking institutions which expanded the supply of working capital: and in most cases also by an expansion in the range of long-term financing done by a central, formally organized, capital market."[8]

Thus, until financial institutions in the underdeveloped countries refashion their procedures, perspective and functions, private savings will not flow readily into investments, and economic development will be restricted accordingly.

Political Instability

Political instability exercises a significant retarding influence on economic growth in underdeveloped countries. The mortality rates of governments in Latin America and in the new countries of Africa have been high. Even in countries such as India, where political processes have been more orderly than in most, the number of different political groups and the diversity among them have made the promulgation of policies conducive to growth difficult. Economic development is not likely to occur in the absence of political stability. At the same time, political stability in and of itself will not assure growth.

The causes of government instability and inefficiency in underdeveloped countries are not hard to find. They are rooted in poverty. In countries where most of the population lives in poverty and is largely uneducated there is a dearth of qualified persons to serve in government positions. Many of those selected, whether by democratic processes or otherwise, are inept under the best of circumstances and corrupt under the worst. Even governments that are doing their best to establish and administer policies to promote growth will find themselves severely criticized. Growth may not come fast enough or be tangible enough to convince the public that the government is doing all it can, with the result that pressure mounts to have the group in power replaced.

Political instability has several adverse effects on economic growth. Capital accumulation may be handicapped if there is uncertainty concerning the attitude of the government toward private property, since there is little incentive to accumulate when the possibility of confiscation is present. Another deterrent is the inflation that almost inevitably accompanies political instability. Additionally, inconsistent policies and rapid changes in policies over time may place restraints on already meager productive efforts.

[8]*W. W. Rostow,* The Stages of Economic Growth. *Cambridge, Mass.: Cambridge University Press, 1960, p. 48.*

Population Growth

In some underdeveloped countries population growth seems to be an important obstacle to economic growth or to rising per capita income. Table 19-2 indicates that Ghana, India, Brazil, and Venezuela all have relatively high rates of population growth and relatively low rates of increase in per capita income. Other countries, such as Taiwan and Thailand, have high rates of population growth *and* high rates of growth in per capita income. But from Table 19-1 we see that the per capita incomes of all of these countries are still very low. A large proportion of the underdeveloped countries have high rates of population growth, and even those

TABLE 19-2
Gross National Product Per Capita and Population, Average Annual Growth Rates (Percent)

Country	G.N.P. Per Capita 1960-1968	1968[1]	Population 1968[1]
Japan	9.3	10.8	1.0
Taiwan	6.9	7.3	2.8
Greece	6.5	5.2	0.8
Spain	6.2	3.3	0.8
Israel	5.0	11.9	2.3
Italy	4.8	4.2	0.8
France	4.1	3.2	1.0
Thailand	3.8	5.0	3.3
South Africa	3.7	2.6	2.4
Sweden	3.6	2.9	0.9
Austria	3.3	3.2	0.5
Netherlands	3.3	4.1	1.3
United States	3.3	3.9	1.2
West Germany	3.3	6.6	0.9
Canada	3.2	2.6	2.0
Pakistan	3.2	3.2	2.7
Ethopia[2]	3.1	2.6	1.8
Mexico	2.8	3.5	3.5
Bolivia	2.7	4.2	2.4
Australia	2.6	1.8	1.9
Switzerland	2.6	2.3	1.1
Peru	2.5	−1.0	3.1
United Kingdom	2.3	2.8	0.6
Chile	2.1	0.9	2.3
New Zealand	1.8	1.1	1.8
Brazil	1.6	3.3	3.0
Guatemala	1.5	1.6	2.5
India	1.5	1.8	3.2
Argentina	1.3	2.9	1.6
Uganda	1.3	0.4	2.5
Venezuela	1.2	2.0	3,5
Ghana	0.0	1.1	2.6

[1]*1968 average over 1967 average.*
[2]*1961-1968 only.*
Source: Agency for International Development, Gross National Product, Growth Rates and Trend Data. April 25, 1969.

with high rates of increase in per capita income could undoubtedly do better if their populations were increasing more slowly.

In the latter part of the eighteenth century an English economist by the name of David Ricardo, influenced by Thomas Robert Malthus,[9] handed down what has become known as the "iron law." Wages, said Ricardo, can never be much above the bare subsistence level because temporary departures therefrom on the up side will be compensated for by an increase in births, which will force the wage down again, while short run reductions below the subsistence level will have the obvious effect of eliminating the surplus people, thereby bringing the population and the means of subsistence once more into equilibrium. Although the so-called "iron law of wages" appears to have little or no relevance in the advanced countries, it may have a glimmer of truth with respect to the underdeveloped areas.

Economic growth of underdeveloped areas brings with it forces tending to reduce the death rate, which is initially high in most of them. With economic growth come improvements in nutrition and better systems of sanitation. Health measures are effected that combat communicable diseases, decrease deaths from infection, reduce infant mortality, and increase longevity.

The birth rate, which is also typically high, does not respond correspondingly to economic growth. Folkways and mores concerning reproduction and birth are not as amenable to change as are the forces governing the death rate. As a consequence, even if a country can bring about a respectable rate of growth in GNP—say 4 or 5 percent per year—it may find that the gain is wiped out, wholly or in part, by population increases. Thus, as Paul Hoffman, director of the United Nations Special Fund, has

---

[9]*Malthus was an English economist and clergyman who published, in 1798, a long pamphlet called "An Essay on the Principle of Population as It Affects the Future Improvement of Society." In essence, Malthus maintained that the world's population tends to increase faster than its means of subsistence. Man, he contended, is impelled by a natural urge to reproduce. Therefore, in the absence of preventive checks (continence and late marriage) population will increase rapidly and without limit. Moreover, it tends to increase by geometrical progression (for example, 1, 2, 4, 8, 16, 32, etc.). Malthus claimed, however, that the means of subsistence, especially the food supply, could be increased only by arithmetic progression (for example, 1, 2, 3, 4, 5, 6, etc.). Hence population would always tend to increase until the food supply became inadequate to support more people. After that, any further increases in population would be prevented by such positive checks as pestilence, famine and wars. The great majority of the people of the world were doomed, according to Malthus, to a perpetual state of poverty and distress. Although Malthus' prediction has not come to pass in the industrial nations of the world, many Asian, African and Latin-American countries still have difficulty in expanding agricultural production as fast as their population grows.*

succinctly said, "Many countries are having to run hard just to stand still."[10]

From an estimated 250 million people about the time of Christ, the world's population has grown more than 14 times in the last 20 centuries to its present size of 3.63 billion people. For the first 1650 years A.D. the average time needed for a one percent rise in population was 20 years, and for the next 200 years, just 2½ years. For the period 1850 to 1930, a one percent increase in the population took only 14 months to achieve, from 1930 to 1960 about 8 months, and currently about 6 months. From the standpoint of economic development, however, an even more significant datum is that by the beginning of the 21st century, the 4.68 billion people (it is estimated that world population will be about 6.13 billion by the year 2000) expected to be living in underdeveloped countries will comprise 76.3 percent of the world population, compared with 65 percent in 1967. It would appear that these facts speak for themselves.

The population problem has been widely recognized and 27 underdeveloped countries have officially adopted family limitation as a matter of national policy and are actively engaged in the dissemination of knowledge concerning methods of birth control. The Indian government, for example, has established a system of small payments to those who undergo sterilization operations. But population control measures are touchy subjects, particularly where religious beliefs oppose them. The discipline of economics has little to say on this matter—it can only point out the consequences of population growth for economic development.

External Aids to Economic Development

Since World War II the economically advanced countries have provided economic assistance to most of the underdeveloped countries. One reason for aid of this type is undoubtedly a humanitarian one, with those in more fortunate circumstances helping those in less fortunate circumstances. But this is not the only reason. Rivalry in giving aid has developed between the Communist countries and those of the Western world. Each bloc uses its assistance program for ideological purposes—but not always with overpowering success.

Aid is supplied jointly and individually by the advanced countries. An important part of the joint effort on an international level is made through the International Bank for Reconstruction and Development (the World Bank), together with its affiliate organizations, the International Develop-

---

[10]*Paul Hoffman,* World Without Want. *New York: Harper and Row, 1962, p. 63.*

ment Association and the International Finance Corporation. Their activities are discussed in the next section. Other international organizations operating in this area include the Organization for Economic Cooperation and Development, the United Nations Development Program, the International American Development Bank, the European Development Fund and the European Development Bank, the African and Asian development banks, and others. In addition, individual countries have their own aid programs, the United States Agency for International Development (AID) and the Canadian International Development Agency (CIDA) being good examples. In 1968 total Free World governmental and private aid to underdeveloped countries amounted to some U.S. $12,753 million. Roughly 80 percent of the total official and private aid originates from the four largest donors—the United States, France, West Germany and the United Kingdom. Some data on comparative aid-giving performance of 16 individual countries in 1968 are provided in Table 19-3. These countries supply more than 95 percent of the total aid to the underdeveloped countries of the world. Canada, despite ranking third in gross national product per capita, at 0.49 percent of the GNP for foreign aid, was at the bottom of the list.

Canadian Assistance

Government Aid

Historically, the Canadian external aid program commenced in 1950 when Canada became one of the six founding members of the Colombo Plan for Co-operative Economic Development in South and Southeast Asia. Originally envisaged for a six-year period, the Plan has been renewed three times (the latest extension is for the 5-year period from 1971 to 1976) and has been expanded to include 24 countries. Since its inception, about $1.1 billion of Canada's development assistance has been channelled through the Colombo Plan.

In 1958, a program of Canadian assistance to the Commonwealth Caribbean area was introduced and over the past ten years about $81.5 million have been allocated for that program. It may be useful to add that these countries received more Canadian aid per capita than any other area of the world.

Canadian assistance to Africa began in 1960 after a meeting of Commonwealth Prime Ministers. Canada joined a Special Commonwealth African Assistance Plan (SCAAP) to provide help on a continuing basis to dependent as well as independent Commonwealth African countries. A year later a program of aid was launched for the French speaking nations of Africa giving expression in the Canadian program to Canada's bilingual

TABLE 19-3
Comparative Aid-Giving Performance in 1968

Countries Ranked in order or Per Capita Gross National Product	Gross National Product per Capita $	Rank	Foreign Aid as a Percentage of GNP %	Rank
United States	4,360	1	0.65	12
Sweden	3,230	2	0.50	15
Canada	3,000	3	0.49	16
Switzerland	2,760	4	1.42	1
Denmark	2,750	5	0.55	14
France	2,500	6	1.17	3
Australia	2,330	7	0.67	10
Norway*	2,330	8	0.65	12
Belgium	2,190	9	1.15	4
West Germany	2,180	10	1,26	2
Netherlands	1,970	11	1.10	5
Britain	1,840	12	0.75	8
Austria	1,530	13	0.66	11
Japan	1,410	14	0.74	9
Italy	1,360	15	0.76	7
Portugal	540	16	0.94	6

Same as United States.
Source: Organization for Economic Co-operation and Development (OECD) Development Assistance Committee (DAC).

and bicultural heritage. By the end of March 1969, the total allocation for Commonwealth Africa amounted to $95.1 million; the total in Francophone Africa amounted to nearly $57 million.

The Canadian development assistance program was extended to include Latin America in 1964, when an agreement was signed with the Inter-American Development Bank setting out the arrangements under which the Bank would act on behalf of Canada as administrator of the newly created development loan fund. Since then, $51.5 million in loans have been made available to the area.

Until 1960, Canadian external aid programs were administered through a division of the Department of Trade and Commerce and were considered an integral part of Canada's commercial and foreign policy. In November 1960, the External Aid Office was created as a separate entity and was charged with the administrative responsibility for all of Canada's development assistance programs. In 1968 the External Aid Office was reconstituted as the Canadian International Development Agency. The Agency, which has quasi-departmental status, reports directly to the Secretary of State for External Affairs. Its policies are co-ordinated by a Board composed of the Under-Secretary of State for External Affairs, the Deputy Ministers of Finance, and Industry, Trade and Commerce, the Governor of the Bank of Canada, and the President of CIDA, who is also Chairman of the Board.

Approximately four-fifths of the assistance provided underdeveloped countries by the Canadian government is channelled through bilateral programs. Developing countries negotiate directly with the Canadian government for development loans, capital grants, technical assistance, food aid, and emergency relief. Canada also supports the multilateral agencies concerned with international development and makes contributions to the World Bank Group, the United Nations Development Program, the Asian Development Bank, the Caribbean Development Bank, and many other specialized agencies.[11] Although recorded as a transfer of financial resources to underdeveloped countries, the funds provided through the Export Development Corporation (former Export Credits Insurance Corporation) to finance Canadian exports are not regarded as part of Canada's official development assistance because their primary purpose is the promotion of the flow of Canadian exports and they are not designed to be concessional for development purposes. Table 19-4 shows the volume and the principal categories of the flow of official Canadian financial resources to developing countries and multilateral agencies in the years 1967, 1968 and 1969.

TABLE 19-4
Flow of Official Canadian Financial
Resources to Developing Countries
and Multilateral Agencies
(Net Disbursements)
for 1967, 1968 and 1969

	Millions of U.S. Dollars		
	1967[2]	1968[2]	1969[2]
Official Development Assistance			
Bilateral			
Capital Grants	34.59	18.38	22.65
Technical assistance	22.66	26.10	30.64
Food aid	74.08	53.18	51.80
Emergency relief	0.23	0.14	0.13
Development loans	20.17	44.26	54.97
Multilateral			
Grants	26.38	24.53	27.49
Advances (from Dept. of Finance)	19.75	8.10	57.48
Other Official Flows			
Export credits	15.09	29.35	25.25
Purchase of IBRD bonds	——	10.00	25.00
TOTAL	212.95	214.04	295.41

[1]*Figures in $U.S. exchange rate 1.081.*
[2]*Calendar year.*
Source: Canadian International Development Agency.

[11]*The Inter-American Development Bank, organized in 1960 to foster the economic development of its member countries in Latin America, administers approximately $10 million per annum of Canada's bilateral funds. IDB membership consists of the United States and 19 Latin-American countries.*

Capital grants and development loans are made for a host of purposes. They are used to help underdeveloped countries accumulate capital—to build industrial facilities such as power plants, steel mills, and cement plants; to build communications and transportation facilities; and to develop agricultural facilities. They are also used to enable recipients to import Canadian goods and services, presumably essential to development, which they cannot afford from their own supplies of foreign exchange or cannot finance from regular commercial sources. (Why do you suppose foreign exchange for these purposes is not available?) Among such items are fertilizers, base metals such as copper, nickel, zinc and aluminum, industrial equipment, and spare parts.

It is worth noting there that two types of development loans are provided: (1) noninterest bearing, up to 50-years maturity, with 10 years of grace for initiation of repayment of principal; (2) 3 percent interest, up to 30 years maturity, with 7 years of grace for capital repayment. Also deserving of mention is the fact that most Canadian aid is tied, i.e., is made available subject to two joint conditions: (1) that the proceeds of the grant or loan be spent in Canada, and (2) that the project supported by Canadian aid have a Canadian value-added content of 66⅔ percent.[12] Under certain circumstances, however, up to 25 percent of Canada's contribute to a project may be used to cover local costs. In this connection, it should be mentioned that Canadian multilateral aid is provided on an untied basis except for multilateral food aid and for Canada's contribution to the Special Funds of the Asian Development Bank which is tied to the procurement of goods and services in Canada only on the first round of disbursements.

Technical assistance is intended to accomplish two objectives: (1) to help develop special skills and technical competence where there seem to be critical manpower needs and (2) to help provide the framework and the facilities within which such trained personnel can function effectively. CIDA turns much of its technical assistance effort toward increasing agricultural productivity, improving educational levels, and raising public health standards. Grants are made to build educational and health facilities. Technical personnel from Canada are sent to develop demonstration farms, to assist and advise in plant and animal genetics, and to provide instruction in how to increase agricultural productivity. Education specialists consult and advise on matters of educational curricula and teacher training. Tax experts help devise more effective tax laws and more efficient collection procedures. Additionally, persons from underdeveloped countries are sent to Canada to acquire new areas of competence or to

---

[12]*It is estimated that aid-tying reduces the real value of the aid to recipients by anywhere between 15 and 30 percent.*

improve on what they have. Universities in Canada have been heavily involved in the technical assistance programs, both in supplying specialists to underdeveloped countries and in training persons sent to Canada from those countries.

Direct food aid is an important aspect of CIDA's program. Although it can never be a satisfactory long-term solution to the problem of hunger in the underdeveloped countries, food aid can and does relieve immediate needs caused by crop failure and natural disasters. Its provision can also contribute to long-term development of freeing scarce foreign exchange so that the recipient country can use its resources for developmental purposes. The so-called "green revolution" caused by high-yielding grain seeds, has largely overcome the threat of immediate mass starvation, but food aid will likely remain as a significant though diminishing element of Canada's development cooperation program.

In addition to supplying development assistance through bilateral and multilateral channels, Canada takes part in several international forums that discuss and analyze the need for development assistance and the performance of donor and recipient countries. These include: the consortia for India, Pakistan, Turkey and Greece, and the consultative groups for Colombia, Ecuador, Korea, Malaysia, Peru, Thailand, Nigeria, Tunisia, Morocco, and East Africa; the Development Assistance Committee (DAC) of the Organization for Economic Cooperation and Development (OECD); the United Nations Conference on Trade and Development (UNCTAD); the United Nations General Assembly, the United Nations Development Program (UNDP), the United Nations Organization for Industrial Development (UNOID) and the specialized agencies.

Before leaving official aid, it should be noted that Parliament has recently established the *International Development Research Centre*. The Centre will be funded from development assistance allocations—it will have a minimum budget of $30 million over the first five years—and its Board of Governors will be international in character. The purpose of the Centre will be to initiate, encourage, support and undertake research into the problems involved in the economic development of the poorer regions of the world. The main emphasis will be on technical and scientific matters that bear on development. The Centre will involve active cooperation with Canadian universities and other Canadian and international institutions, and will enable Canada to play a special role in this important aspect of the development process.

Participation of the Private Sector

Canadian business firms as well as individuals make private investments in underdeveloped countries where the prospective rates of return are attractive, or higher than they are at home. These investments, of course, contribute to capital formation or capital accumulation in the recipient countries. Much of the investment from these sources is direct, involving the setting up of branch plants or new firms. The Bata Shoe organization sets up a factory in India. Another avenue of private investment in underdeveloped countries is the purchase by private parties in Canada of securities of firms established and operated by the nationals of those countries. The Caribbean and Latin American regions have been the major areas of Canadian private investment. Recent DBS estimates indicate that total Canadian private direct investment in underdeveloped countries in 1969 was about U.S. $71 million, including a net capital outflow of about U.S. $51 million and reinvested earnings of about U.S. $21 million. Total private flows (including private long-term capital and private monetary institutions but excluding contributions of voluntary agencies) is estimated by DBS to have been about U.S. $69 million in 1969. In previous years Canadian private investment in developing countries averaged about U.S. $40 million but with substantial year-to-year variations.

Private investment in such countries by Canadian businesses or individuals sometimes tends to be looked upon with a jaundiced eye by the recipient countries. Nationalism rears its head in such cases, with Canada or other foreign companies being looked upon as exploiters of the local economy.[13] An economy should be run by its own citizens, the argument runs.

A small and underrated source of private aid to underdeveloped countries is that of eleemosynary institutions such as church mission groups, the Y.M./Y.W.C.A. World Service Committee and the Salvation Army. The work of these organizations has seldom been of a spectacular nature, since they do not build dams or steel mills. But they have done much in the way of providing educational and medical facilities. They have provided orphanages and foster-home care for homeless children. They have often been able to develop a sense of community pride and community responsibility where none existed before. These efforts are, of course, supported by private contributions. CIDA has estimated that the total value of such assistance is about $35 million annually, primarily in the fields of education, health and welfare.

Recognizing the potential for even more varied activity on the part of voluntary agencies in the international cooperation field, the government last year (1969) set aside $6.5 million of CIDA's budget to assist Canadian non-governmental organizations in broadening their aid efforts. Furthermore, the government has indicated that it intends to increase its

---

[13]*Does the principle of mutual gain from voluntary exchanges provide any enlightenment on this issue?*

support for these non-profit organizations over the next five years. Assistance to any private project or program is based on a "matching" principle; as a rule, the voluntary organization supplies one half to two thirds of the funds required in each instance, with CIDA contributing the balance. The largest CIDA grant in 1968 went to Canadian University Services Overseas (CUSO), a private body which recruits graduates of university, technical and other post-secondary school institutions and has nearly 1,000 volunteers abroad on two-year contracts in 40 countries. Another CIDA grant to non-governmental agencies during the past year included one to the Canadian Executive Service Overseas (CESO), a non-profit organization designed to make available the service of top-ranking Canadian business and professional people on short-term assignments in developing countries.[14]

The World Bank Group

The International Bank for Reconstruction and Development, commonly called the World Bank, along with the International Monetary Fund, grew out of the Bretton Woods Conference of 1944. It was established originally to make long-term loans for reconstruction following World War II and for economic development purposes. Today, with its affiliate organizations, the International Development Association and the International Finance Corporation, most of its activities are in the latter area.

The Bank makes loans for development projects to any one of the over 100 countries that comprise its membership. Loans are made to private enterprises as well as to governments. Loan applications are carefully screened by the Bank's management and loans are made only for projects that appear to be financially sound and that show every promise of paying off both interest and principle. The Bank has been extremely successful in this respect and has been subjected to much criticism as a result. It is often argued that if the Bank's loan standards were lowered, loan activities and aid could be expanded far beyond that which has actually been accomplished.

Funds for loans come from two major sources. Member countries each fulfil a basic capital subscription to the Bank. Additionally, the Bank can sell its own bonds and notes in member countries to obtain appropriate foreign exchange for loans. Its hard-nosed reputation has made it

---

[14]*The principal sources for this section were: (1) Canadian International Development Agency, Annual Review, 1969; (2) booklets and memos prepared and written by the Information Division of CIDA; (3) various speeches delivered by Mr. Maurice F. Strong, President, CIDA, in different locales.*

possible for the Bank to resell the financial paper representing loans or parts of loans that it has made to private financial institutions such as banks, insurance companies, and the like in member countries.

The International Development Association (I.D.A.) was organized in 1960 to provide loans under more liberal conditions than the World Bank. Its loans are for a term of 50 years, with repayment commencing only after a 10-year grace period. Thereafter, one percent of the principal is repaid annually for 10 years and three percent annually for the remaining 30 years. Although no interest is paid, a service charge of three-quarters of one percent per annum is charged to meet administrative costs. The I.D.A. loans money for a wider range of purposes than the World Bank does, including, for instance, educational purposes. It derives its funds mainly from 19 high-income countries,[15] aggregating $3 billion in 1970. It is expected that these funds will have been committed by June 30, 1971.

The International Finance Corporation (I.F.C.) was established in 1956 and provides risk capital for the private enterprise sector in the less developed world. The I.F.C. lends to or invests in private companies usually by supporting joint ventures. Such ventures bring together foreign and local capital and know-how. At the outset of 1970, I.F.C. had 92 members, which have subscribed approximately $107 million capital. In addition, it had a reserve against losses of $54 million derived from accumulated earnings, and some $428 million that it may borrow from the World Bank for use in its lending operations.

The total loans and credits extended by the World Bank and the I.D.A. during the fiscal year 1969, amounted to $1,784 million, compared with $953.5 million in 1968, an increase of 87 percent. In addition, financing by the I.F.C. totalled $93 million, compared with $51 million in 1968.

Regional Development Institutions

Other international sources of funds for development and mutual economic assistance include the Arab Financial Institution for Economic Development which was established in 1959, the Inter-American Development Bank set up in 1960, the African Development Bank launched in 1964, the Asian Development Bank organized in 1966, and the Caribbean Development Bank formed in 1968. In addition to these regional development institutions the six European Common Market countries have established the European Investment Bank. All of these regional banks lend

[15]*These are, Australia, Austria, Belgium, Canada, Denmark, Finland, France, Germany, Italy, Japan, Kuwait, Luxembourg, the Netherlands, Norway, South Africa, Sweden, Switzerland, the United Kingdom, and the United States.*

funds, promote investment of public and private capital and provide technical assistance to developing member nations, and generally foster economic development and cooperation in their respective areas. Consequently, such institutions are a useful instrument of economic progress.

Report of Commission on International Development

The Commission on International Development was established by the World Bank in 1968. The members of the Commission were the Rt. Hon. Lester B. Pearson (Canada), Sir Edward Boyle (United Kingdom), Mr. Roberto Campos (Brazil), Mr. Douglas Dillon (United States), Dr. Wilfried Guth (Germany), Professor Sir W. Arthur Lewis (Jamaica), Dr. Robert Marjolin (France), and Dr. Saburo Okita (Japan). The Commission's report, entitled "Partners in Development", was made public on October 1, 1969. It is one of the most comprehensive analyses of international development assistance that has ever been made. The report concludes with several major recommendations. These are:

1. Economic growth: Every effort should be made to help the underdeveloped countries increase their average annual growth of GNP during the 1970's from 5 percent to 6 percent.

2. Volume of aid: Total public and private development assistance should reach the U.N. and DAC goal of one percent of GNP of developed countries by 1975. Public or official aid in the form of grants or long-term loans with interest rates of no more than 2 percent (plus the terms to maturity and grace periods, etc.) should make up 0.7 percent of GNP by 1975 and in no case later than 1980.

3. External debts: Liberal provisions for rescheduling of debts and debt servicing charges could be written into aid agreements. Debt relief should be recognized as a legitimate form of assistance.

4. Multilateral aid: The proportion of official aid flows through multilateral agencies should be increased from 10 percent to 20 percent by 1975. In addition, donor countries should be encouraged to see that more of their bilateral assistance is programmed in a multilateral setting.

5. Tied aid: Steps should be taken to untie aid which has been tied to purchases in aid-giving countries. Donor nations should allow aid funds to be used by recipients for purchases in other underdeveloped countries. More emphasis should be given to aid which is not project-oriented.

6. Trade: Quantitative restrictions on manufactured imports from underdeveloped countries should be abolished during the 1970's. Developed nations should eliminate import duties and excessive excise tax on primary commodities produced only by the less developed countries. Financing should be available to create buffer stocks in support of commodity agreements.

7. Investment: Less developed countries should eliminate impediments to foreign investment and assure stability and improved procedures affecting foreign firms.

8. Population control: Competent family planning help should be available to all. Both donors and recipients, when planning aid programs, should stress control of population growth.

9. Direction and coherence of existing agencies: The World Bank should call a conference in 1970 to "consider the creation of machinery essential to the efficiency and coordination of the international aid system."

In Canada's case, the Commissions recommendations require the following:

1. The level of official development assistance allocation must be increased by $461 million from the level of $364 million in the fiscal year 1970-71 if the Commission's target of 0.7 percent of GNP is to be achieved by 1975.

2. Removing the general requirement to buy in Canada subject to prescribed Canadian content provisions.

3. Eliminating quantitative restrictions on the import of manufactured goods from underdeveloped countries.

In this connection, it should be emphasized that the Canadian government:

> " . . . intends to increase the amount of funds allocated to international development assistance over the coming years to move towards the internationally-accepted targets; to confirm as the primary objective of the programme the economic and social development of the developing countries; to maintain the concessional financial terms of Canadian development assistance and to make a significant move towards untying it as to procurement; to increase the proportion of Canadian assistance allocated to multilateral programmes to about 25 percent of total assistance; to continue to allocate most bilateral assistance to countries of concentration, but to provide some 20 percent of bilateral assistance to other developing countries; and to increase support of the private sector's participation in the development programme."[16]

One can hope that these decisions will advance the day when the poor countries can realize their aspirations with regard to economic progress without relying on foreign assistance. As the Rt. Hon. Lester B. Pearson has outlined the stark alternatives:

---

[16]*White Paper on Foreign Policy,* International Development. *Ottawa: Queen's Printer, June, 1970.*

"The question is not whether development will happen. It will. Rather, the choice is between slow, halting growth in an environment of desperation with declining levels of assistance and embittered international relations, or growth as part of a positive concerted campaign to accelerate and smooth the absorption of the technological revolution in the poorer countries, with a reasonable chance that the spirit of shared concern and effort will reduce the frictions and the dangers, and facilitate and expedite positive results."[17]

Summary

Underdeveloped economies are those with relatively low per capita incomes. Although not a perfect measure of a country's state of development relative to other countries, per capita income provides the best that is currently available. A large part of the world's population lives in countries in which per capita income amounts to less than $500 per year.

The present world-wide concern with economic development dates largely from World War II and was brought about by several factors. First, during and since the war there has been an increasing amount of travel and social interchange between the citizens of the advanced and the underdeveloped countries. Another contributing factor has been the ideological struggle between the Communist countries and the West. A further factor has been the advances made in communications media and the distribution of the latter throughout the world. The rise in nationalism and the decline of colonialism that has been occurring in recent years has also helped focus attention on the underdeveloped countries.

The factors necessary to bring about economic growth are easily identified from the nature of economic activity. Economic growth, or rising per capita income, comes partly from the accumulation of capital resources by an economy. Capital accumulation is aided and abetted by technological advancement. Qualitative improvements in the labour force constitute another essential ingredient. Growth can be further enhanced by putting unemployed resources to work and by reallocating employed resources from less to more productive employments.

A number of obstacles stand in the way of self-development of underdeveloped countries. Among the most important is the initial state of poverty of country, a situation that almost precludes capital accumulation. Social and economic class lines make it difficult for an economy to use its

[17]*From Mr. Pearson's address to the World Bank Board of Governors, Washington, October, 1969.*

resources in a more efficient way. Among other things, they tend to stifle entrepreneurship. Inflation is another deterrent to economic development, and so too is political instability. Similarly, the financial infrastructure may not be geared to the special requirements of economic development and therefore need substantial overhauling. Additionally, population growth may be spurred by increases in GNP to the detriment of a more even distribution of income on a per capita basis.

External aid is provided to most underdeveloped areas by the advanced countries. The Government of Canada through the Canadian International Development Agency makes loans and grants to underdeveloped countries for a wide range of projects. Private investment and lending have also made substantial contributions, mostly in mining and smelting activities and utilities Eleemosynary institutions have provided a considerable amount of unheralded aid. On an international basis the International Bank for Reconstruction and Development and its affiliates, the International Development Association and the International Finance Corporation, and regional development banks, through long-term loans, has provided the major avenue for joint or international efforts to help underdeveloped countries.

Exercises and Questions for Discussion

1. In 1968 annual per capita GNP in Sweden was $3,130 while in Pakistan it was $116. How do you account for the difference?
2. Per capita GNP in Canada increased at a rate of 3.2 percent per year from 1960 to 1968. In the same period the rate of increase in Ethiopia was almost the same (3.1 percent). What conclusions can you draw from this comparison?
3. From 1960 to 1968 the growth rate of per capita income in India was 1.5 percent. What forces seem to have been responsible for a rate as low as this?
4. Do you think that loans and grants made by the Canadian International Development Agency should be made with no strings attached or that they should be made for specific, approved projects, with their expenditure by the recipient government or private institution carefully supervised by Canadian experts? Explain your answer carefully.
5. "In terms of sacrifice, Canada's economic aid to the underdeveloped countries is relatively insignificant." Do you agree? Why or why not?

Selected Readings

Baldwin, R. E., *Economic Growth and Development*. New York: John Wiley and Sons, Inc., 1966.

Boreham, G. F., "1—Banking Problems with Special Reference to Developing

Countries, 2—The Basic Preconditions for Economic Development," *Fiftieth Anniversary Commemoration Lectures*. National Bank of Egypt, Cairo, 1967.

Galbraith, J. K., *Economic Development*. Cambridge, Mass.: Harvard University Press, 1964.

Johnson, H. G., *Economic Policies toward Less Developed Countries*. New York: Fredrick A. Praeger, 1967, Chaps. I and II.

Kindleburger, C. P., *Economic Development*, rev. ed. New York: McGraw-Hill Book Company, Inc., 1965, Chaps. 1, 15, and 20.

McCord, William, *The Springtime of Freedom: the evolution of developing societies*. New York: Oxford University Press, 1965.

Meier, G. M., *Leading Issues in Development Economics*. New York: Oxford University Press, 1964.

Myrdal, Gunnar, *Asian Drama: An Inquiry Into the Poverty of Nations*. Volumes I, II, III. New York: Pantheon, 1968.

Organization for Economic Cooperation and Development (OECD), *Development Assistance Efforts and Policies of the Members of the Development Assistance Committee*. Paris, 1970.

Report of the Commission on International Development, *Partners in Development*. New York: Praeger Publishers, 1969.

Reuber, G. L., "Canada's Economic Policies toward the Less Developed Countries," *The Canadian Journal of Economics*, November, 1968, pp. 670-698.

Sanger, Clyde, *Half a Loaf: Canada's Semi-Role Among the Developing Countries*. Toronto: Ryerson Press, 1969.

Index